AF691224

A Contemporary Look at Organizational Justice

Multiplying Insult Times Injury

ORGANIZATION AND MANAGEMENT SERIES

Series Editors

Arthur P. Brief
University of Utah

Kimberly D. Elsbach
University of California, Davis

Michael Frese
University of Giessen/London School of Business

Ashforth (Au.): *Role Transitions in Organizational Life: An Identity-Based Perspective.*
Bartel/Blader/Wrzesniewski (Eds.): *Identity and the Modern Organization.*
Bartunek (Au): *Organizational and Educational Change: The Life and Role of a Change Agent Group.*
Beach (Ed.): *Image Theory: Theoretical and Empirical Foundations.*
Brett/Drasgow (Eds.): *The Psychology of Work: Theoretically Based Empirical Research.*
Brockner (Au): *A Contemporary Look at Organizational Justice: Multiplying Insult Times Injury.*
Chhokar/Brodbeck/House (Eds.): *Culture and Leadership Across the World: The GLOBE Book of In-Depth Studies of 25 Societies.*
Darley/Messick/Tyler (Eds.): *Social Influences on Ethical Behavior in Organizations.*
Denison (Ed.): *Managing Organizational Change in Transition Economies.*
Dutton/Ragins (Eds.): *Exploring Positive Relationships at Work: Building a Theoretical and Research Foundation.*
Elsbach (Au): *Organizational Perception Management.*
Earley/Gibson (Aus.): *Multinational Work Teams: A New Perspective.*
Garud/Karnoe (Eds.): *Path Dependence and Creation.*
Harris (Ed.): *Handbook of Research in International Human Resource Management.*
Jacoby (Au.): *Employing Bureaucracy: Managers, Unions, and the Transformation of Work in the 20th Century, Revised Edition.*
Kossek/Lambert (Eds.): *Work and Life Integration: Organizational, Cultural and Individual Perspectives.*
Kramer/Tenbrunsel/Bazerman (Eds): *Social Decision Making: Social Dilemmas, Social Values and Ethical Judgments.*
Lampel/Shamsie/Lant (Eds.): *The Business of Culture: Strategic Perspectives on Entertainment and Media.*
Lant/Shapira (Eds.): *Organizational Cognition: Computation and Interpretation.*
Lord/Brown (Aus.): *Leadership Processes and Follower Self-Identity.*

Margolis/Walsh (Aus.): *People and Profits? The Search Between a Company's Social and Financial Performance.*

Miceli/Dworkin/Near (Aus): *Whistle-blowing in Organizations.*

Messick/Kramer (Eds.): *The Psychology of Leadership: Some New Approaches.*

Pearce (Au.): *Organization and Management in the Embrace of the Government.*

Peterson/Mannix (Eds.): *Leading and Managing People in the Dynamic Organization.*

Rafaeli/Pratt (Eds.): *Artifacts and Organizations: Beyond Mere Symbolism.*

Riggio/Murphy/Pirozzolo (Eds.): *Multiple Intelligences and Leadership.*

Roberts/ Dutton (Eds): *Exploring Positive Identities and Organizations: Building a Theoretical and Research Foundation.*

Schneider/Smith (Eds.): *Personality and Organizations.*

Smith (Ed.): *The People Make The Place: Dynamic Linkages Between Individuals and Organizations.*

Thompson/Choi (Eds.): *Creativity and Innovation in Organizational Teams.*

Thompson/Levine/Messick (Eds.): *Shared Cognition in Organizations: The Management of Knowledge.*

A Contemporary Look at Organizational Justice

Multiplying Insult Times Injury

Joel Brockner

Routledge
Taylor & Francis Group
New York London

Routledge
Taylor & Francis Group
711 Third Avenue
New York, NY 10017

Routledge
Taylor & Francis Group
27 Church Road
Hove, East Sussex BN3 2FA

First issued in paperback 2014

Routledge is an imprint of the Taylor and Francis Group, an informa business

© 2010 by Taylor and Francis Group, LLC

International Standard Book Number-13: 978-1-84872-832-5 (Hardcover)
International Standard Book Number-13: 978-0-415-65056-4 (pbk)

For permission to photocopy or use material electronically from this work, please access www.copyright.com (http://www.copyright.com/) or contact the Copyright Clearance Center, Inc. (CCC), 222 Rosewood Drive, Danvers, MA 01923, 978-750-8400. CCC is a not-for-profit organization that provides licenses and registration for a variety of users. For organizations that have been granted a photocopy license by the CCC, a separate system of payment has been arranged.

Trademark Notice: Product or corporate names may be trademarks or registered trademarks, and are used only for identification and explanation without intent to infringe.

Library of Congress Cataloging-in-Publication Data

Brockner, Joel.
A contemporary look at organizational justice : multiplying insult times injury / Joel Brockner.
p. cm. -- (Organization and management series)
Includes bibliographical references and index.
ISBN 978-1-84872-832-5
1. Organizational justice. I. Title.

HD6971.3.B76 2010
658.3'14--dc22 2009030997

Visit the Taylor & Francis Web site at
http://www.taylorandfrancis.com

and the Psychology Press Web site at
http://www.psypress.com

To our three sons, Lucas, Dustin, and Eliot, and to my dear wife, Audrey, who make the whole process worthwhile

Contents

List of Figures

List of Tables

Series Foreword

Joel Brockner has written an important book. Justice scholars will find it so for it breaks new theoretical ground in the tradition of Thibaut and Walker's 1975 *Procedural Justice: A Psychological Analysis* and Lind and Tyler's 1988 *The Social Psychology of Procedural Justice*. In a nutshell, Joel details a contingency perspective by arguing that process fairness is more or less consequential depending on peoples' outcomes. He goes on to place process-by-outcome interactions in a much broader conceptual space, thereby appealing to scholars beyond the justice community. While the book clearly is scholarly in nature, Joel devotes a chapter to implications for practice. We know you will enjoy this one, and we could not be prouder to have it in our series.

Arthur Brief
University of Utah

James Walsh
University of Michigan

Preface

Conventional wisdom posits that our reactions to events and decisions depend on the outcomes we receive, or *what* happens, and the processes associated with those outcomes, or *how* things happen. As implied by the expression, "It's not only what you say, but also how you say it," we generally react positively when our outcomes are favorable and when the process accompanying the outcome is fair. In this book, I suggest that conventional wisdom underplays the complexity of how we are affected by what happens and how things happen. More often than not, the effects of outcomes and processes cannot be considered in isolation of one another; the effects of what you say *depend on* how you say it.

This book examines how the favorability of outcomes interacts with the fairness of the process to influence what people think, feel, and do. Among the questions considered are why such interaction effects are theoretically and practically important, when they are more versus less likely to happen, why they happen, and how they happen. To be sure, this is hardly the first scholarly treatment of the interactive relationship between outcome favorability and process fairness. Initial research was conducted by Robert Folger and his colleagues (e.g., Folger, Rosenfield, & Robinson, 1983), and Brockner and Wiesenfeld (1996) reviewed many studies that showed evidence of an interactive relationship between outcome favorability and process fairness. One way to describe the interaction effect is that people's tendencies to respond better when their outcomes are more favorable is reduced when process fairness is high rather than low.

Research conducted and theory developed since 1996 have taught us a great deal about the "process–outcome" interaction. For one thing, it has been shown to take different forms. Many studies continue to find that high process fairness reduces the effect of outcome favorability on employees' attitudes and behaviors relative to when process fairness is low. However, other studies have found that high process fairness *heightens* the effect of outcome favorability relative to when process fairness is low. This book takes the Brockner and Wiesenfeld (1996) review article as its point of departure and essentially asks the following questions: What have we learned since then about the interactive relationships between outcomes and processes? Just as important, why should organizational scholars and practitioners care? Not only does the book provide a contemporary look at the burgeoning area of organizational justice, but also it forges numerous connections between organizational justice and other prominent literatures in organizational and social psychology, such as trust, social identity, attribution theory, regulatory focus theory, and cross-cultural differences in people's beliefs and behaviors, to name a few.

Whereas there is a host of excellent books on organizational justice, relatively few provide a unifying, research-based lens through which to view a great deal of recent work in the area. Two of the seminal scholarly books on procedural justice were those of Thibaut and Walker (1975) and Lind and Tyler (1988). In both instances, the authors took a hard-nosed, research-based approach; this book does likewise. I try to demonstrate that much of the interesting work in the justice arena may be organized around the interactive relationships between outcome favorability and process fairness. Whereas Thibaut and Walker (1975) and Lind and Tyler (1988) argued for the importance of process fairness over and above the effects of outcome favorability, my thesis is not that process fairness influences people "over and above" outcomes, but rather that process fairness needs to be considered *in conjunction with* outcome favorability; that is, process fairness may be more versus less consequential, depending on people's outcomes.

My intended audience consists of scholars and sophisticated laypeople with an interest in theory and research in the broad arena of microorganizational behavior, with particular emphasis on organizational justice as well as related literatures in social psychology. The book describes a great deal of empirical research but tries to do so in a reader-friendly way. For instance, little mathematical sophistication is required to understand the research evidence presented.

CHAPTER DESCRIPTIONS

The first chapter locates the interactive relationship between outcome favorability and process fairness within the broader literature in organizational justice and offers a host of reasons why the interactive relationship is theoretically and practically important. As suggested, the process–outcome interaction takes two rather different empirical forms. High process fairness may reduce the impact of outcome favorability on people's beliefs and behaviors, relative to when process fairness is low, *or* it may heighten the effect of outcome favorability. Chapters 2 and 3 describe many noteworthy empirical and conceptual advances pertaining to the former interactive relationship, whereas Chapter 4 does so for the latter. Chapter 5 is designed to integrate the two interactive relationships by delineating when and why one rather than the other is more likely to emerge.

Chapter 6 locates both interaction effects in broader conceptual spaces. As well replicated as the effects are, they are part of a broader constellation of factors that drive people's beliefs and behaviors. By connecting the interaction effects to the "bigger picture," I hope to broaden their reach and to shed light on matters of conceptual importance outside the confines of the organizational justice literature. Finally, whereas I suggest early on that the process–outcome interactions have applied significance, and allude to this point throughout, Chapter 7 explicitly considers the practical implications of the interactive relationships between outcome favorability and process fairness.

As much as we have learned about the process–outcome interactions and their implications, there is still much more that we need to know. Accordingly, I have sprinkled recommendations for further research throughout all of the chapters. I hope that at least some of my specific suggestions are pursued. More generally, I hope that this book inspires justice scholars to embark on their own programs of research and find them to be as enjoyable as this one has been, and continues to be, for me.

ACKNOWLEDGMENTS

I would like to take this opportunity to thank many wonderful colleagues who have helped me in various ways to write this book. I am particularly grateful to four people, who, first as doctoral students and for many years thereafter, have worked long and hard with me on the ideas central to this book: Ya-Ru Chen, Ariel Fishman, Phyllis Siegel, and, of course, Batia Wiesenfeld, who coauthored the 1996 article that serves as this book's point of departure and who has engaged me since then in many fruitful discussions about the contents of this book. My current doctoral student, Emily Bianchi, also has contributed mightily to the ongoing enterprise. Whereas it is hard to quantify the positive influences that Batia, Ya-Ru, Ariel, Phyllis, and Emily have had, suffice it to say that the book either would have taken a lot longer to write or would not have been nearly as well developed were it not for their keen insights and tireless efforts.

I also benefitted greatly from the feedback of the many gifted scholars who offered insightful comments on previous drafts of the manuscript: Corinne Bendersky, Ramona Bobocel, Steve Blader, Art Brief, Jared Curhan, Adam Grant, Larry Heuer, Rebecca Levine, Roy Lewicki, Joshua Margolis, Andy Molinsky, Michael Morris, Jochen Reb, Deborah Rupp, Kelly See, and Kees Van den Bos. To all of you, a heartfelt thanks.

About the Author

Professor Joel Brockner earned a BA in psychology from SUNY–Stony Brook in 1972 and a PhD in social/personality psychology from Tufts University in 1977. Since that time, he taught at Middlebury College, SUNY College at Brockport, Tufts University, and the University of Arizona prior to joining the faculty at Columbia Business School, where he is currently the Phillip Hettleman Professor of Business.

Professor Brockner is a leading authority on a variety of psychological issues in the workplace, including change management (e.g., the effects of layoffs on the productivity and morale of survivors), leadership, decision making, the role of the self, and cross-cultural differences in work behavior. He has published two books (one on decision making in "sunk cost" situations and the other on the causes and consequences of employees' self-esteem). In addition, he has published more than 100 articles and book chapters in a variety of prestigious outlets, including *Administrative Science Quarterly*, the *Harvard Business Review*, and the *Journal of Personality and Social Psychology*, to name a few.

He has served (or is currently serving) on the editorial board of numerous journals in the fields of management and psychology, including the *Academy of Management Journal*, the *Academy of Management Review*, *Organizational Behavior and Human Decision Processes*, and the *Journal of Personality and Social Psychology*. He also is frequently called on to review for the National Science Foundation. Professor Brockner is a Fellow of the Academy of Management; he is also a Fellow of the American Psychological Association (Division of Industrial and Organizational Psychology).

Professor Brockner is the chair of the Management Division at Columbia Business School and is the faculty director of the highly regarded executive education program (High Impact Leadership) at Columbia Business School. In addition, he has served as an expert witness, and he has consulted to a variety of organizations (including Citigroup,

ConocoPhillips, Eastman Kodak, IXIS Capital Markets, MBNA, Pfizer, State Farm Insurance, Southern New England Telephone, and Stratus Technologies) about the planning and implementation of significant organizational change, leadership development, decision making, and negotiation behavior.

CHAPTER

1

Introduction

> "It's not only whether you win or lose, but also how you play the game."
>
> "It's not only what you do, but also how you do it."
>
> "It is not only about the results, but also about the journey."

These expressions remind us of an important lesson: Our reactions to life experiences depend on the outcomes we receive, or *what* happens, and the processes associated with those outcomes, or *how* things happen. We generally react better to events and decisions when our outcomes are more favorable or fair and when the procedures associated with those outcomes are implemented more fairly. It all sounds simple and straightforward. Indeed, consider yet another everyday life expression that people sometimes use to describe instances in which they have been treated especially badly by another party: "To *add* insult to injury ..." (my emphasis added), which essentially amounts to the perception of having received an unfavorable outcome (injury) accompanied by an unfair process (insult).

But, things are rarely as simple as they seem, and so it is with the joint effects of outcomes and processes. In fact, the effects produced by outcomes and processes often are not merely *additive*. A more intriguing possibility is that our reactions to outcomes and processes cannot be considered in isolation of one another; rather, the nature and magnitude of the effects of one depend on the other. In statistical parlance, outcomes and processes often *interact* with each other to influence our perceptions, feelings, attitudes, and behaviors. This book is about the interactive effects produced by outcomes (outcome favorability or outcome fairness) and processes (process fairness). Among the questions considered are why such interaction effects are theoretically and practically important, when they are more versus less likely to happen, why they happen, and how they happen.

It is only relatively recently that organizational and social psychologists have even concerned themselves with the interactive effects of outcomes and processes. Initially, researchers tended to focus on the effects attributable to either outcomes *or* processes. For example, early exchange theorists examined the effects of outcome favorability (Blau, 1964; Homans, 1961). According to these viewpoints, the more that people benefit—economically, socially, or psychologically—from their interactions and relationships with other people, the more attracted they feel toward those others. Equity theory (Adams, 1965) was another early outcome-oriented theory of social relations, concerned with people's perceptions of distributive fairness. According to Adams, people experience fairness when the ratio of their benefits to contributions is commensurate with the benefits-to-contributions ratio of appropriate targets of comparison, such as coworkers. Perceptions of inequity lead to feelings of distress (anger or guilt, depending on whether the inequity is negative or positive, respectively), which motivate people to take action or to restructure their thinking to engender a greater sense of fairness. For example, employees experiencing negative inequity may withhold effort as a way of evening the score, whereas those feeling positive inequity may inflate their perceived contributions to make their high outcomes seem more deserved and hence fair. Deutsch (1975) further suggested that outcome fairness takes forms other than equity, such as equality or need, depending on the goals of the collective.

Procedural theorists recognized the incompleteness of outcome-oriented perspectives. That is, what people feel, think, and do are determined not only by the outcomes associated with decisions but also by the process through which decisions are planned and implemented. To date, the process dimension that has received the greatest attention is fairness. In their seminal work, Thibaut and Walker (1975) conceptualized process fairness as voice, which is whether people were allowed to have input into a decision process (process control) or whether people were allowed to have any say in the actual making of the decision (decision control). Thanks to subsequent theory and research (e.g., Bies, 1987; Colquitt, 2001; Leventhal, Karuza, & Fry, 1980), we now know that many other elements besides voice shape people's judgments of process fairness.

Whereas early outcome-oriented research largely ignored process considerations, initial research on process fairness did not entirely ignore the effects of outcomes (e.g., Lind & Tyler, 1988; Thibaut & Walker, 1975). An important goal of process-oriented theorists was to show that how decisions are planned and implemented could explain people's justice judgments and related attitudes and behaviors apart from that which was attributable to outcomes. Consequently, process-oriented theorists tended to treat outcome factors (favorability or fairness) as control variables. Indeed, studies showed that how things were done accounted for additional variance beyond that attributable to outcomes (and that sometimes process factors were even more important than were the outcomes; Colquitt, 2001; McFarlin & Sweeney, 1992). Note, however, that whether process fairness accounts for additional variance beyond that attributable to outcomes or whether process fairness is more versus less consequential than outcome factors are fundamentally different empirical questions from the ones that are the focus of this book: why, when, and how process fairness *interacts* with outcomes to influence what people think, feel, and do.

Robert Folger was the first to examine the interactive effect produced by outcome and process (e.g., Folger & Martin, 1986; Folger, Rosenfield, & Robinson, 1983). Subsequent to Folger's initial studies, many researchers examined the process–outcome interaction in a variety of contexts, using multiple conceptions and operationalizations of independent and dependent variables (see Brockner & Wiesenfeld, 1996, for a review). Like Folger, some researchers examined the interaction effect under controlled laboratory conditions (e.g., Greenberg, 1987a). Others did so in the field. Some field studies examined how ordinary citizens respond to their encounters with legal authorities, such as the police or the courts (Lind & Tyler, 1988). Other studies investigated how employees respond to an assortment of workplace events. Some of these events, including layoffs, pay freezes, and changes in human resource policies such as smoking bans and drug-testing procedures, affected many employees simultaneously. Other events were more targeted to the individuals studied, such as how expatriates respond to their overseas assignments or how employees react to their negotiations with one another.

Whereas there were many contextual and operational differences between studies, at a deeper conceptual level they shared the same basic design. Independent variables included people's perceptions of (1) their outcomes and (2) the fairness of the processes that accompanied their outcomes. Outcome perceptions typically took one of two forms. Some studies examined the effects of outcome *fairness*, that is, how much people believed that the outcomes they received were deserved. An even larger number of studies looked at the effects of outcome *favorability*, that is, how much people believed that the outcomes benefitted them in tangible or in intangible ways.

Whereas outcome fairness and outcome favorability are conceptually distinct, they tend to be highly correlated with one another (in the neighborhood of .70; e.g., Brockner et al., 2003). In the appendix to this chapter, I consider some of the ways in which outcome fairness and outcome favorability are meaningfully different from one another. However, for the purposes of this book it is more appropriate to focus on what outcome fairness and outcome favorability have in common rather than on how they differ. I say this because research shows that outcome fairness and outcome favorability generally behave similarly in interacting with process fairness, both across studies (Brockner & Wiesenfeld, 1996) and within studies (Brockner et al., 2003).

From this point, in referring to outcomes I use the term *outcome favorability* in a more general sense, which refers to the extent to which the outcome is one that people want or prefer. People may want or prefer an outcome because it satisfies their desire for fairness, or they may want or prefer an outcome because it satisfies their need to be better off, either tangibly or intangibly. Whereas it is certainly possible for outcomes to be perceived as both unfair and favorable (e.g., those that produce positive inequity) or for them to be perceived as both fair and unfavorable (e.g., which may arise when people do not receive much and believe that they have not contributed much), people often perceive these two forms of preference similarly rather than differently; we tend to see favorable outcomes as fair (and vice versa), and unfavorable outcomes as unfair (and vice versa). In summary, and to foreshadow the discussion of this matter in the Appendix, whether people's outcomes make them better or worse off (favorability) is not identical to whether their outcomes are deserved according to the prevailing resource allocation rule (fairness). However, the two judgments overlap to a considerable extent, and the research suggests that it is what they have in common (hereafter referred to as a more generic notion of *outcome favorability*) that interacts with process fairness to influence people's beliefs and behaviors.

Process fairness also has been examined in a variety of ways. In many studies, process fairness has been operationalized on the basis of voice, that is, whether people were allowed to have input into the decision process. Other researchers implemented process fairness using one or more of the criteria set forth by Leventhal et al. (1980), such as whether the decisions were implemented (1) on the basis of accurate information, (2) consistently, and (3) neutrally or free from bias, to name a few. Process fairness also has taken the form of "interactional justice" (Bies, 1987), based on the recognition that people's fairness perceptions also depend on the interpersonal treatment shown by those responsible for planning and implementing decisions. Interactional justice in turn is comprised of two elements: (1) informational justice, which largely refers to whether the parties responsible for decisions provide an adequate explanation of why the decisions were made, and (2) interpersonal justice, which refers to whether the decisions are implemented in dignified and respectful ways, for example, whether the responsible parties express caring and concern toward those who may be adversely affected by the decisions (Colquitt, 2001).

Whereas the outcome variable in previous research has taken the form of fairness or favorability, the same cannot be said for the process dimension. Process *favorability* refers to the extent to which the methods accompanying resource allocation yield outcomes that favor a given target. I know of few studies that have examined the interactive relationship between outcome favorability and process "favorability." My hunch is that the positive relationship between process fairness and process favorability (if one were to be found) may be less pronounced than is the sizable positive relationship that exists between outcome fairness and outcome favorability. In fact, one study has illustrated how process fairness even could be inversely related to process favorability. Lind and Lissak (1985) operationalized process fairness on the basis of neutrality, that is, whether a friendly relationship existed between a judge and one of the lawyers involved in a legal case. Whereas the presence of a friendly relationship between the judge and the lawyer violated the process fairness element of neutrality, such an arrangement clearly reflects high process favorability, at least from the vantage point of the lawyer and the lawyer's client, in that it predisposed the judge to rule in their favor. In short, the outcome variables considered throughout the book refer to fairness or to favorability, whereas the process factor refers to fairness.

An assortment of dependent variables also has been assessed, such as people's psychological strain as well as various attitudinal and behavioral indicators of their willingness to support (1) the decision that was reached, (2) the parties responsible for making or implementing the decision, and (3) the institution in which the decision was made. Across more than 40 independent samples included in the Brockner and Wiesenfeld (1996) review, and in numerous subsequent studies (e.g., Garonzik, Brockner, & Siegel, 2000; Greenberg, 2006; Kickul, Lester, & Finkl, 2002; Tepper, 2001), a consistent interactive relationship between outcome favorability and process fairness emerged. Of course, to say that the interaction effect often has occurred is not to say that it *always* occurs; Brockner and Wiesenfeld reported a handful of studies that failed to provide evidence of an interactive relationship (e.g., Walker, LaTour, Lind, & Thibaut, 1974). In the course of accounting for the interaction effect between outcome favorability and process fairness in the ensuing chapters, I also provide several analyses of when the effect may be unlikely to emerge.

So, what is the nature of the interaction effect? As shown in Figure 1.1, the effect may be described in three different ways, depending on the theoretical lens through which it is being viewed. First, it is appropriate to say that one combination of conditions stands out from all others: The joint presence of an unfavorable outcome and an unfair process elicits particularly negative reactions. For example, Folger's referent cognitions theory (e.g., Folger, Rosenfield, & Robinson, 1983) and his more recent fairness theory (e.g., Folger & Cropanzano, 2001) portray the interactive relationship as one in which people's reactions are much more negative when they receive an unfavorable outcome with an unfair process relative to when their outcomes are favorable, the process is fair, or both.

Second, outcome favorability has a moderating influence on process fairness. Throughout the book I make reference to the *fair process effect*, a term originally coined by Folger, Rosenfield, Grove, and Corkran (1979), which refers to the well-established finding for people to respond better (i.e., with less psychological strain or with greater support for decisions, decision makers, and organizations) when they judge a decision-making

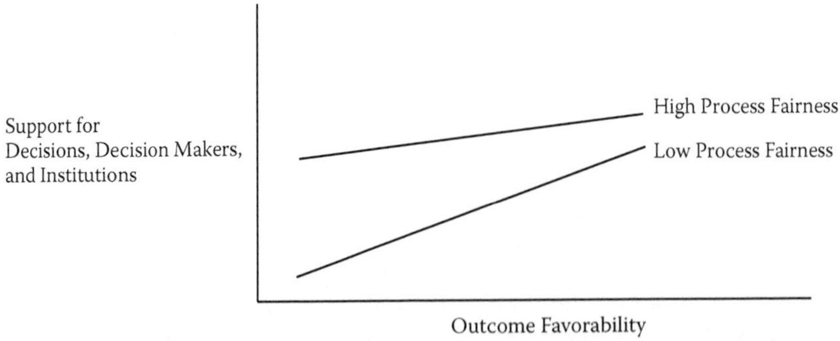

Figure 1.1 Interactive effect of outcome favorability and process fairness on people's support for decisions, decision makers, and institutions (Brockner & Wiesenfeld, 1996).

process as more fair. The process–outcome interaction effect shows, however, that the fair process effect is considerably reduced when people see their outcomes as relatively favorable; that is, "the ends justify the means." Said differently, the fair process effect is more likely to emerge when people's outcomes are relatively unfavorable.

Third, process fairness has a moderating influence on outcome favorability, or the "means justify the ends." More specifically, high process fairness reduces the influence of outcome favorability on people's psychological strain or on their willingness to support decisions, decision makers, and organizations relative to when process fairness is low. In other words, as long as the process is done fairly, people are much more willing to accept whatever outcome comes their way (that is, outcome favorability is less consequential) relative to when process fairness is low.

Throughout the book, I move back and forth between these various ways of describing the interactive relationship between outcome favorability and process fairness. The depiction used most frequently is the one that treats process fairness as having a moderating influence on outcome favorability, in which high process fairness reduces the effect of outcome favorability relative to when process fairness is low. Describing the interaction effect this way makes it easier to compare it with another process–outcome interaction effect that has gained traction subsequent to the Brockner and Wiesenfeld (1996) review, namely, that high process fairness also may *heighten* the influence of outcome favorability on people's beliefs and behaviors relative to when process fairness is low. In other words, process fairness has been shown to have two different types of moderating influences on outcome favorability; high process fairness may reduce *or* may heighten the influence of outcome favorability on people's beliefs and behaviors relative to when process fairness is low (Brockner, 2002).

WHY THE INTERACTIVE RELATIONSHIP BETWEEN PROCESS FAIRNESS AND OUTCOME FAVORABILITY IS IMPORTANT

More Than Common Sense

The ubiquity of the interaction effect shown in Figure 1.1 is not the only basis of its conceptual significance. Another reason is that the effect is at least somewhat nonintuitive. We social scientists often have been taken to task for spending too much time proving the obvious. In a now-classic article, McGuire (1973; see also McGuire, 1997) challenged social psychologists to generate more intriguing empirical questions and offered a number of idea-generating heuristics designed to help them do so. One of his suggestions was for investigators to take some well-established finding as their point of departure and then to identify factors that may make the finding more versus less pronounced or possibly even reversed (see also Davis, 1971).

The statistical main effects produced by outcome favorability and process fairness exemplify such well-established findings. It comes as little surprise that people generally react more positively when they perceive their outcomes to be more favorable or decision-making processes to be fairer. Considerably less obvious, however, are the moderating influences of each of outcome favorability and process fairness on the other. At the least, such findings give pause to the notions that favorable outcomes or fair processes invariably have positive consequences.

Whether empirical findings are mundane also may be reflected by whether they are reflected in "commonsense," everyday life expressions. For example, let's return to the phrase mentioned that describes the state of affairs in which decision makers dole out an unfavorable outcome with an unfair process: "*adding* insult to injury." Studies that examined the interactive relationship between outcome favorability and process fairness suggested that the recipients of the decisions see things somewhat differently. When people believe that they have received an unfavorable outcome (injury) via an unfair process (insult), their experience may be more accurately described as "*multiplying* insult times injury." Because the product of two numbers is typically greater than the sum of those same two numbers, the expression "adding insult to injury" actually *underestimates* how negatively people are likely to feel and respond when they receive an unfavorable outcome that is accompanied by an unfair process. In short, the interactive relationship between outcome favorability and process fairness is important because it helps to refine conventional wisdom.

In addition to being robust and at least somewhat nonintuitive, the interactive relationship between outcome favorability and process fairness has a variety of noteworthy conceptual and practical implications. These implications, considered next, are perhaps the most important reasons for us to pay heed to the interactive relationships between process and outcome.

When Informs Why

As theorists, we seek to explain relationships between variables. For example, the tendency for process fairness to be positively related to people's attitudes and behaviors has been well established. The more challenging and unresolved question is why. One way to gain insight into the why question is by asking when a given relationship between variables is more versus less pronounced. That is, what does the fact that the fair process effect may be stronger when outcomes are less favorable tell us about why the fair process effect emerges in the first place? One possibility is that because unfavorable outcomes are more threatening, people may engage in greater sense-making to understand how and why the outcomes emerged (Shaver, 1985; Walster, 1966). One way to make sense of outcomes is to pay attention to the process through which they came about or to the process that accompanied them, which would have the effect of heightening the impact of process fairness information. If this reasoning is correct, then factors other than unfavorable outcomes that elicit sense-making also should heighten the influence of process fairness information. For example, uncertainty (e.g., not being sure of one's status in an organization) also instantiates sense-making, and therefore may be expected to heighten people's tendencies to respond more positively to higher levels of process fairness. Indeed, this is precisely what Van den Bos and Lind (2002) found in numerous empirical tests of their uncertainty management model of fairness.

The same logic of "when informs why" suggests that the interaction effect also may help to shed light on the well-established tendency for people to respond more positively when their outcomes are more favorable. That is, what does the fact that outcome favorability often is less impactful when the process is fairer tell us about why the outcome favorability effect emerges in the first place? One possibility is that people are "realistic" outcome maximizers. That is, they would like to get as much for themselves as possible in both the short term and the long term, but they also are reasonable enough to know that, as Mick Jagger once put it, "You can't always get what you want." As a result, they may be willing to trade off short-term outcomes provided that they believe that they will receive their share of desired outcomes over the longer haul.

People may use process fairness information in turn to make judgments about their longer-term outcomes. Like personality traits, processes are perceived to be stable. People are likely to think that how things are done today is revealing of how they will be done in the future. For example, if a manager shows process fairness by seriously considering his or her employees' input into a particular decision, employees are more likely to support the manager's decision, even if their current outcomes are relatively unfavorable. Moreover, if employees expect a voice-giving manager to consider seriously their input into future decisions, it is reasonable for them to believe that they will receive more favorable outcomes over the longer term. Alternatively, if the process fairness accompanying a decision is low, people are likely to feel far less reassured that they will receive their share of desired outcomes over time.

If this reasoning is correct, then other factors that influence how reassured people feel about their longer-term outcomes (besides process fairness) also may moderate the impact of the favorability of their current outcomes. For example, people are likely to differ dispositionally in their tendencies to maintain optimistic beliefs about their future outcomes (Scheier & Carver, 1985; Seligman, 1991). Perhaps those who are dispositionally less optimistic about their future outcomes may assign greater importance to, and hence may be more affected by, the favorability of their current outcomes, much like people who have been treated with lower process fairness.

In summary, the interactive relationship between outcome favorability and process fairness is important because it may provide insight into the mechanisms through which each of these two rather broad categories of factors affect people's beliefs and behaviors. This is not to suggest that sense-making is the only basis through which process fairness exerts influence or that people's trade-offs between short- and long-term outcomes is the only way in which outcome favorability exerts influence. They may, however, be among the mechanisms responsible for the separate (main) effects of process fairness and outcome favorability, brought to light by studying the interactive relationship between the two.

New Theoretical and Empirical Developments

In the years since the Brockner and Wiesenfeld (1996) review, there have been a number of theoretical and empirical extensions of the interactive relationship between outcome favorability and process fairness (Brockner & Wiesenfeld, 1996). Some of the explanations set forth in the previous review have been updated (e.g., Folger's 1986 referent cognitions theory has been supplanted by fairness theory; Folger & Cropanzano, 1998, 2001). Some new explanations in the justice literature have emerged, such as Van den Bos and Lind's (2002) uncertainty management model, that have implications for the process/outcome interaction effect. Furthermore, theoretical frameworks not considered in the prior review have been invoked to account for the interaction effect. For example, Tepper (2001) suggested and empirically confirmed that stress and coping theory (Lazarus & Folkman, 1984) may help to explain the interactive relationship between outcome favorability and process fairness.

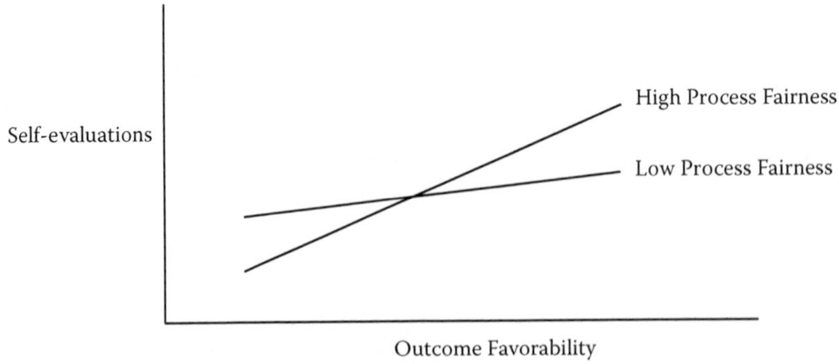

Figure 1.2 Interactive effect of outcome favorability and process fairness on people's self-evaluations.

Perhaps the most notable empirical development subsequent to Brockner and Wiesenfeld's (1996) review is that the interactive relationship between outcome favorability and process fairness has been shown to take a different form from the one exhibited in Figure 1.1. Whereas Figure 1.1 shows that high process fairness reduces the influence of outcome favorability relative to when process fairness is low, more recent studies have shown that high process fairness may heighten rather than reduce the impact of outcome favorability relative to when process fairness is low. To be sure, this finding was reported in the 1996 review, but at that time it was confined to a relatively small number of studies (e.g., Gilliland, 1994), in which the dependent variable consisted of people's self-evaluations; Figure 1.2 provides a graphical representation.

Many studies have since replicated this finding (e.g., Brockner et al., 2003; De Cremer & van Knippenberg, 2003; Schroth & Shah, 2000) and showed that it is not limited to measures of self-evaluations (Chen, Brockner, & Greenberg, 2003; Van den Bos, Bruins, Wilke, & Dronkert, 1999). In sum, the "original" interactive relationship between outcome favorability and process fairness (shown in Figure 1.1) is noteworthy because it has since given rise to a number of important conceptual and empirical developments. Now would be an opportune time to consider these developments along with their implications for justice theory as well as for other frameworks in organizational and social psychology.

Practical Implications

People with decision-making authority have tough jobs. On the one hand, their decisions often have meaningful consequences for many people. On the other hand, they usually operate with limited resources. For example, baseball umpires cannot call a runner safe and out. Managers in work organizations cannot give big raises, promotions, and tickets to the fast track to all or even to many of their employees. To maintain social order, decisions must be made to elicit the greatest support from as many of the affected parties as possible. When decision makers' concern is to garner support for themselves, for their decisions, or for the organization as a whole, the interaction effect shown in Figure 1.1 suggests that they may be able to do so provided that they offer either favorable outcomes or fair processes (or both). More often than not, however, it is more economically feasible to implement decisions affecting many people with fair processes than with favorable outcomes. For example, in work settings it usually does not cost a lot of money to allow employees to provide input into how resources should be allocated. It does not cost much money to express concern for people who lose their jobs as a result of a layoff or to explain the reasons for a pay cut. Moreover, implementing decisions with high process fairness often attenuates the influence of tangibly costly resources (outcomes) on employees' support for decisions, decision makers, and institutions.

This is not to suggest that decision makers should emphasize process fairness to the exclusion of or instead of outcome favorability. For people to support decisions and decision makers, especially over the long haul, their outcomes need to be at least moderately favorable. People may be willing to tolerate unfavorable outcomes on a short-term basis, provided that process fairness is relatively high. However, they may be much less tolerant of outcomes that are consistently unfavorable, even if process fairness is high. Once people's ongoing outcomes are at least moderately favorable, however, it may be more cost effective for managers to ensure that they enact decisions with high levels of process fairness than it would be for them to try to increase the outcomes to be even more favorable.

Furthermore, whereas implementing decisions with high process fairness may be financially inexpensive, I am not suggesting that doing so is cost free, which may help to explain an apparent paradox of process fairness: On the one hand, high process fairness is cost-effective. The behaviors comprising high process fairness often are not financially costly in their own right, and the interactive relationship between process fairness and outcome favorability set forth in Figure 1.1 suggests that high process fairness may minimize the impact of (the often economically costly) factors that comprise outcome favorability. On the other hand, we know that decisions often are not implemented with high process fairness. In the final chapter of the book, I discuss the (mainly social and psychological) barriers that prevent decision makers from practicing process fairness and what can be done on an organizational or on an individual level to overcome such barriers. For now, however, suffice it to say that the interactive relationship between outcome favorability and process fairness is important because of its practical implications. In particular, it may help managers make more informed judgments about how to plan and implement decisions.

Forging Connections

Janus, the Roman god of doorways and gateways, represents an apt metaphor for some of my purposes in writing this book. Referring to Janus, Quinion (2004) said: "As doors can be passed in either direction, he came to represent both the past and the future. Because of that, his image was of a man with two faces, looking both forwards and backwards" (p. 1). In describing the intricacies of the interactive relationships between outcome favorability and process fairness, I also look back at what theory and research already have told us and look forward, pointing out potentially fruitful avenues for further research.

Prior research on the interactive relationship between outcome favorability and process fairness also illustrated the conceptual gains that may be accrued when researchers conjointly examine variables embedded in different theoretical traditions. Factors comprising outcome favorability (e.g., being selected for a job or not, surviving an organizational downsizing or not, and suffering a pay cut or pay freeze or not) tend to be conceptualized in economic or tangible terms (Adams, 1965; Gouldner, 1960; Homans, 1961). In contrast, the variables comprising process fairness (e.g., giving people input into decisions or not, providing adequate explanations of the reasons for decisions or not, and treating people with dignity and respect or not) are related to more psychological considerations (e.g., Folger & Cropanzano, 2001; Tyler & Lind, 1992). More generally, the interactive relationships between outcome favorability and process fairness may provide economically and psychologically minded scholars with a useful way to think about variables and theories from the "other side of the conceptual fence." As the interaction effects illustrate, the impact of psychological factors depends on the economic context in which they are examined, and the impact of economic factors depends on the psychological context in which they are examined.

This way of thinking entails more than researchers treating factors from the "other side" as control variables. Rather, the interaction effects represent a potential avenue for healthy cross-disciplinary or at least cross-literature exchanges. A cardinal principle of creativity is that novel insights are more likely to emerge when people approach problems from different perspectives (e.g., McLeod, Lobel, & Cox, 1996). For example, theory and research on human judgment and decision making have received a great deal of attention from a heterogeneous group of scholars. Those with more of an economics orientation work in areas known as "behavioral economics" or "behavioral finance." Psychologically minded types call the topic "behavioral decision making." Regardless of the label that is applied, my hunch is that progress has been more forthcoming in this area because of the diverse group of scholars who have been attracted to it relative to what may have occurred if those studying the topic were more homogeneous in their orientations. Thus, the interactive relationship between outcome favorability and process fairness is important because it may provide an arena in which connections may be forged between diverse scholars who have much to say to, and learn from, one another, thereby sowing the seeds for additional creative insights.

OVERVIEW OF THE BOOK

Taking prior theory and research as its point of departure (see Brockner & Wiesenfeld, 1996), this book considers what we have since learned about the interactive relationships between outcome favorability and process fairness, why organizational scholars and practitioners should care about what we have learned, and what we still need to learn. Of the two forms of interaction effects (illustrated in Figures 1.1 and 1.2), there has been much more research on why, when, and how high process fairness reduces the influence of outcome favorability relative to when process fairness is low. Indeed, I devote two chapters (Chapters 2 and 3) to describing noteworthy conceptual and empirical extensions of the finding illustrated in Figure 1.1 that high process fairness reduces the effect of outcome favorability on people's thoughts, feelings, and behaviors. Chapter 2 describes research that broadens the external validity of this particular interaction effect by showing how it may emerge in new contexts and on an important new category of dependent variable relative to the studies that were included in the 1996 review. Moreover, in the course of enhancing the external validity of the interaction effect, the new findings shape how we conceptualize the interaction effect (e.g., its underlying mechanisms and its theoretical implications). Chapter 3 provides recent theory and research on why this particular form of interaction effect occurs and, relatedly, delineates when this effect may be more versus less likely to occur. Chapter 4 presents theory and research pertinent to the other form of interactive relationship between outcome favorability and process fairness (illustrated in Figure 1.2), in which high process fairness heightens the impact of outcome favorability relative to when process fairness is low.

The material presented in Chapter 5 adheres to another of McGuire's (1973) prescriptions for generating interesting research ideas. McGuire suggested that social science would benefit enormously if scholars did more to reconcile seemingly conflicting research findings. Given that Chapters 2–4 show that process fairness may interact with outcome favorability in different ways, we need to explain why this is so, for example, by delineating when the interaction effect may take one form rather than another. Thus, informed by our understanding of the reasons underlying the different forms of interaction effects, Chapter 5 discusses when we may expect to find one form of interaction effect or the other or perhaps even no interaction effect at all. Chapter 6 casts the interaction effects in broader conceptual spaces. As well replicated and as important as the effects appear to be, they may actually be exemplars of more general social and psychological processes extending well beyond the confines of justice theory. Indeed, throughout the book I attempt to show how studying the interactive relationships between outcome favorability and process fairness may inform related literatures in organizational and social psychology. Chapter 7 focuses on practical implications. I consider what managers and organizations have to gain by understanding and making use of the interactive relationships between process fairness and outcome favorability, and I discuss the kind of additional research scholars need to do that ultimately may help managers do their jobs more effectively.

CHAPTER

2

High Process Fairness Reduces the Effect of Outcome Favorability (Part A)

INTRODUCTION

Brockner and Wiesenfeld (1996) reviewed studies examining the interactive relationship between outcome favorability and process fairness, with many showing that high process fairness reduced the effect of outcome favorability on people's willingness to support decisions, decision makers, and institutions relative to when process fairness was low. Subsequently, there have been many notable extensions of these findings. Some have increased the generalizability of the previous findings, for example, by extending the interaction effect to other contexts. Moreover, whereas the interaction effect previously was exhibited on various attitudinal and behavioral indicators of people's willingness to support decisions, decision makers, and institutions, more recently it has been found on a different and important type of dependent variable: psychological strain.

Furthermore, in previous studies the independent variables of outcome favorability and process fairness typically referred to the same event or decision. For example, a manager in a work organization may have taken some action that had implications for his or her direct reports. Outcome favorability referred to the direct reports' perceptions of the consequences of the manager's action, for example, whether the manager's decision made the direct reports better off or worse off. Process fairness was in reference to how the manager went about planning or implementing the decision. More recent research has shown, however, that the interactive relationship between outcome favorability and process fairness is not limited to those instances in which the two constructs refer to the same event.

These new findings are meaningful because they do more than simply enhance the external validity of the interaction effect. Research methodologists have suggested that results extending the external validity of an effect also may have implications for how we understand the effect (e.g., Cook & Campbell, 1979). As I will discuss, the fact that the previous findings have been extended to new contexts, to other dependent variables, and to instances in which the outcome and process factors do not refer to the same event provide insight into the mechanisms underlying the interaction effect as well into its theoretical implications.

CHAPTER OVERVIEW

Two chapters are needed to capture the many meaningful extensions of the process–outcome interaction effect, in which high process fairness reduces the effect of outcome favorability relative to when process fairness is low. The present chapter, the first of the two, consists of five sections. First, I describe research that has extended the interaction effect to two new contexts with literatures of their own: how expatriates react to their overseas assignments and how employees respond to work–life conflict. Second, I analyze recent research that shows that the interactive relationship also emerges on measures of psychological strain. Also included in these first two sections are findings that show that the interaction effect is not limited to instances in which outcome favorability and process fairness refer to the same event. Taken together, the first two sections broaden the generality of the interaction effect, induce us to think differently about the interaction effect, and may provide some fresh insights for scholars working in the areas of expatriation, work–life conflict, and psychological strain.

The third section of the chapter brings together a prominent model of psychological strain (Lazarus & Folkman, 1984) and the process–outcome interaction. Just as the Lazarus–Folkman framework offers a somewhat different way to conceptualize the interaction effect, the interaction effect may provide an extension to the Lazarus–Folkman conceptualization. Furthermore, the Lazarus and Folkman model makes predictions about the magnitude of people's negative emotional experiences as a function of outcome favorability and procedural fairness. As might be expected, people are most likely to experience negative emotion when they receive an unfavorable outcome that is accompanied by an unfair process relative to all other combinations of conditions. However, as I explain in the fourth section of the chapter, theory and research suggest that people also may experience qualitatively different emotions (both negative and positive) as a function of outcome favorability and process fairness.

The interactive relationship between outcome favorability and process fairness is rather general, in the sense that many different forms of outcome favorability have been shown to interact with many different elements of process fairness to influence an (expanding) array of dependent variables. In contrast, the fifth section of the chapter summarizes research that examines the interaction effect with greater granularity. More specifically, I discuss evidence that suggests that certain forms of outcome favorability may be especially likely to interact with certain forms of process fairness to influence certain forms of dependent variables.

Chapter 3 extends what we have learned since 1996 about the mediators and moderators of the interactive relationship process fairness and outcome favorability. Put differently, the focal questions examined in Chapter 3 are (1) Why does the interaction effect occur? and (2) When is the interaction effect more versus less likely to occur? Chapters 2 and 3 also consider how the new findings deepen our understanding of not only the justice literature but also others in organizational and social psychology. Moreover, suggestions for future research are sprinkled throughout both chapters.

EXTENDING THE INTERACTION EFFECT TO NEW CONTEXTS

Whereas the earlier review of studies (Brockner & Wiesenfeld, 1996) showed that the interactive relationship between outcome favorability and process fairness emerged in many organizational and social contexts, subsequent research has extended the effect to entirely new settings, thereby broadening its reach. Hence, the external generalizability of the previous findings, not low initially, has been heightened. Two such extensions into new contexts are considered: expatriates' adjustment to their overseas assignments and employees' reactions to work–life conflict. Whereas these are not the only new arenas to which the process–outcome interaction has been extended, they were selected for two reasons: (1) They reflect important topics in their own right, having attracted the attention of many scholars, including those not grounded in organizational justice theory; and (2) on the face of things, the two areas seem relatively disconnected. However, viewing them through the lens of the interactive relationship between process fairness and outcome favorability may help to forge connections between heretofore disparate literatures.

Expatriates' Adjustment

As business has become highly globalized, it has become especially important to better understand a long-standing human resource (HR) management practice: tendencies of companies to send employees to work in foreign countries for lengthy periods of times (often 3 to 5 years). And, make no mistake about it: There is a lot at stake in these expatriate assignments, for employers and employees alike. Expatriates' work productivity may have important consequences for their firm's performance and for their longer-term career prospects either within their current organizations or outside them. Another way to conceptualize the stakes associated with expatriates' assignments is by considering their costs. Black and Gregersen (1999) reported that a fully loaded expatriate package (including benefits and cost-of-living adjustments) costs anywhere from $300,000 to $1 million annually, which is probably the single largest expenditure most companies make on any employees other than their chief executive officer (CEO).

Given the high stakes associated with expatriation, it is important to understand the factors that affect expatriates' adjustment to their new environments. One indicator of expatriates' adjustment is whether they complete their assignments or depart prematurely. Black, Gregersen, and Mendenhall (1992) identified a host of variables that influence expatriates' tendencies to depart prematurely. One rather broad category of factors refers to the nonwork aspect of expatriates' lives, such as their living conditions, health care, and the adjustment of their family members. As might be expected, when the nonwork outcomes of expatriates' lives are relatively unfavorable, they are more likely to give serious consideration to departing prematurely from their assignments (Shaffer & Harrison, 1998).

Garonzik et al. (2000) evaluated the interactive effect of outcome favorability and process fairness on how much expatriates gave serious consideration to departing prematurely from their overseas assignments. More specifically, Garonzik et al. evaluated whether high process fairness reduced the relationship between nonwork outcome favorability and how much expatriates gave serious consideration to departing prematurely relative to when process fairness was low. Two different samples of expatriates completed a survey that included measures of the independent variables of nonwork outcome favorability and process fairness. The measure of outcome favorability consisted of how well expatriates and their family members had adjusted to various nonwork aspects of their lives, such as their housing conditions and health care arrangements.

Unlike the measure of outcome favorability, process fairness referred to expatriates' perceptions of how decisions generally were made in the organization rather than to expatriation per se. The dependent variable consisted of the extent to which expatriates thought seriously about departing prematurely. In both samples, Garonzik et al. (2000) discovered an interaction effect between outcome favorability and process fairness, such that high process fairness reduced (indeed, eliminated) the inverse relationship between expatriates' perceptions of outcome favorability and their tendency to think seriously about departing prematurely from their overseas assignments. Put differently, it was only among those who felt that the organization was generally low in process fairness that outcome favorability bore a significant (inverse) relationship with their tendency to think seriously about departing prematurely.

One noteworthy shortcoming of the Garonzik et al. (2000) studies is that the dependent variable consisted of how much expatriates thought seriously about departing prematurely from their assignments rather than their actual turnover behavior. Whereas withdrawal-related cognitions (e.g., turnover intentions) have been shown to be substantially related to actual turnover behavior (e.g., Steel & Ovalle, 1984), further research is needed to evaluate whether the interactive relationship between outcome favorability and process fairness manifests itself on expatriates' actual turnover behavior. In a nonexpat study, Jones and Skarlicki (2003) found evidence of a process–outcome interaction effect on actual turnover behavior, such that outcome favorability was more strongly (inversely) related to turnover when interactional justice was low rather than high. Nevertheless, it still remains to be seen whether outcome favorability and process fairness will interact to influence the actual turnover behavior of expatriates. Moreover, whereas Garonzik et al. (2000) found a significant process–outcome interaction effect even though process fairness did not refer specifically to expatriation, it would be worth examining in future research whether the interaction effect would be even more pronounced if process fairness was in reference to participants' expatriation experience.

Chen, Choi, and Chi (2002) provided yet another way to examine the process–outcome interaction effect in the expatriate context. Expatriates often are compensated much more handsomely than their local counterparts working in the same organization. Chen et al. examined whether process fairness would have a moderating influence on locals' perceptions of the relative favorability of their outcomes. More specifically, locals indicated the relative disparity between their compensation and that of expatriates. Process fairness referred to the extent to which the locals believed that the expatriates treated them with interpersonal sensitivity. The dependent variable was the perceived fairness of their compensation. An interaction effect emerged in which the (inverse) relationship between locals' perceptions of their compensation disparity vis-à-vis the expatriates and the fairness of their compensation was significantly less pronounced when the locals believed that the expats treated them with greater interpersonal sensitivity.

It is interesting to note that in the Chen et al. (2002) study process fairness was in reference to the target of comparison (the expats), in contrast to the studies by Garonzik et al. (2000), in which process fairness was in reference to the behavior of organizational authorities. An important question for future research is whether the process fairness exhibited by decision-making authorities would have even more of a moderating influence on compensation disparity than the process fairness exhibited by the expatriates. After all, it is organizational authorities who are ultimately responsible for the compensation disparities between locals and expatriates rather than the expatriates themselves. Therefore, it may be that the palliative effect of high process fairness (in reducing the negative impact of an unfavorable outcome) may be stronger when the process fairness emanates from the party who is more responsible for the unfavorable outcome. High process fairness exhibited by the party whom the focal actors deem to be responsible for their unfavorable outcomes may do more to "right the wrong" than high process fairness expressed by a third party who was the beneficiary of the distribution of outcomes. In any event, the Chen et al. findings suggest that high process fairness exhibited by the target of comparison is sufficient to reduce the adverse influence of compensation disparity on locals' perceptions of the fairness of their compensation.

These findings are all the more noteworthy when we consider that the locals' perceptions of the fairness of their compensation were related to their turnover intentions; as might be expected, the more that locals deemed their compensation to be unfair, the stronger were their intentions to turnover. Indeed, although it is not reported in the published version of the article, one of the authors of the Chen et al. (2002) study reported that there was a significant interactive effect of compensation disparity and the expatriates' process fairness on the locals' turnover intentions, such that high process fairness on the part of the expatriates reduced the relationship between the locals' perceptions of compensation disparity and their turnover intentions relative to when the expatriates exhibited lower process fairness (J. Choi, personal communication, January 9, 2007).

Whereas the Chen et al. (2002) findings were drawn from the expatriate context, they may have implications for a growing trend in employer–employee relationships that extend well beyond the confines of expatriation. Rousseau (2005) reported that nearly a third of all employees have negotiated special workplace arrangements, known as *idiosyncratic deals*, or "i-deals." I-deals can come in a variety of forms, such as reduced or flexible working hours, telecommuting, limits on required travel, child care assistance, and opportunities for career development. Whereas the organizational tendency to grant i-deals may grow out of employers' well-intentioned desire to be flexible and responsive to employees' needs, it runs the risk of violating one of the cardinal principles of organizational justice: consistency in the allocation of benefits and burdens and consistency in the methods used to make such allocation decisions (Leventhal et al., 1980). The Chen et al. findings suggest that one factor that may reduce how much inconsistent allocations will be seen as unfair by underbenefitted parties is the extent to which the overbenefitted party exhibits interactional fairness.

Future research also would do well to evaluate whether the Chen et al. (2002) findings are affected by the locals' attributions of responsibility for expatriates' highly favorable compensation packages. Presumably, the fact that expatriates receive more than locals is due to organizational policies. However, what would happen if locals believed that their relatively unfavorable outcomes were due to the fact that expatriates had negotiated sweet i-deals for themselves? If the expatriates were to exhibit high process fairness while being seen as more personally responsible for the i-deals that made locals feel underbenefitted by comparison, it may not have the same positive effect on locals' perceptions of the fairness of their compensation as that found by Chen et al.

Work–Life Conflict

Work–life conflict refers to competing role pressures brought on by the multiple demands people face, such that fulfilling one's work responsibilities makes it difficult to attend to activities outside the work domain and vice versa. For a variety of reasons, work–life conflict is probably at an all-time high, at least within the United States. Moreover, work–life conflict produces negative consequences for both organizations and employees alike. On the organization front, work–life conflict has been associated with absenteeism, turnover, reduced performance, and lower organizational commitment (Bond, Galinsky, & Swanberg, 1998; Thompson, Beauvais, & Lyness, 1999). For employees, work–life conflict has been shown to lead to emotional exhaustion, depression, cardiovascular illness, alcoholism, and reduced life satisfaction (Bacharach, Bamberger, & Conley, 1991; Frone, Russell, & Cooper, 1997).

Given the huge downsides of high work–life conflict, a question of considerable theoretical and practical significance is whether such negative effects are inevitable. Perhaps certain factors may serve to buffer people and organizations against the negative effects of high work–life conflict. A series of studies by Siegel, Post, Brockner, Fishman, and Garden (2005) tested the hypothesis that high process fairness may be one such buffer. In these studies, work–life conflict was conceptualized as a proxy for outcome favorability, such that higher levels of work–life conflict reflect less-favorable outcomes. Siegel et al. evaluated whether process fairness would have a moderating influence on the negative effects attributable to high work–life conflict.

Indeed, Siegel et al. (2005) found an interaction effect between work–life conflict and process fairness in three separate studies (two field surveys and a vignette-based experiment). Specifically, high process fairness reduced the effect of work–life conflict on employees' organizational commitment relative to what was observed when process fairness was low. In fact, when process fairness was relatively high the relationship between work–life conflict and organizational commitment never even approached significance. Thus, it may not be inevitable for high work–life conflict to elicit negative effects on employees' attitudes or behaviors. As Siegel et al. found, as long as process fairness was relatively high, high work–life conflict did not lead to a reduction in employees' organizational commitment.

Analogous findings were also reported by Carr, Gregory, Ensley, and Tepper (2005), who examined the interactive relationship between procedural fairness and work–status congruence (WSC), a likely proxy for work–life conflict. WSC refers to the extent to which employees' work schedules (e.g., when they work, how often they work) match their preferences (Holtom, Lee, & Tidd, 2002). The greater the WSC, the less likely are employees to experience work–life conflict.

Not surprisingly, Holtom et al. (2002) found that WSC was positively associated with employees' work attitudes and behaviors, such as organizational commitment. Of greater importance, Carr et al. (2005) found that the relationship between WSC (a form of outcome favorability) and organizational commitment was moderated by process fairness. As found in the studies of work–life conflict, whereas WSC was positively related to organizational commitment when process fairness was low, WSC and organizational commitment were unrelated to one another when process fairness was high.

Synthesis

At first blush, the tasks of minimizing premature expatriate departures and reducing the negative effects of high work–life conflict appear to be distinct HR management challenges. On closer analysis, however, they may be quite similar. Both reflect situations in which organizations often attempt to meet the HR challenge at hand by allocating tangible resources. Thus, to reduce premature expatriate departures companies often go to considerable expense to ensure that expatriates and their families have adjusted to their living environments. To reduce the harmful effects of work–life conflict, organizations build day care centers, offer concierge services, provide dependent and elder care allowances, and construct gymnasiums, to name a few.

There are two possible downsides, however, with trying to meet these HR challenges via resource allocation, also known as "throwing money at the problem." First, studies evaluating the effects of resource allocations have produced mixed results. For example, whereas some researchers have found that work–life conflict initiatives of these firms had positive effects on productivity (Konrad & Mangel, 2000), organizational citizenship behavior (Lambert, 2000), and retention (Grover & Crooker, 1995), others have found that such interventions either had no effects on employees' attitudes or behaviors (Dalton & Mesch, 1990) or actually *increased* employees' experience of work–life conflict (Dunham, Pierce, & Casteneda, 1987). Second, even when the work–life conflict initiatives were effective in producing their hoped-for results, they may not have been *cost-effective*. Many resource-based initiatives may be quite costly, especially when they are rolled out on a large-scale basis.

There may be an alternative, however: treating employees with high process fairness. High process fairness reduced the effect of outcomes likely tied to economic expenditures (i.e., how well expatriates and their significant others had adjusted to their living arrangements) on expatriates' tendencies to think seriously about departing prematurely (Garonzik et al., 2000). Furthermore, high process fairness eliminated the harmful effect of high work–life conflict on employees' organizational commitment (Siegel et al., 2005). An important feature of high process fairness (e.g., routinely treating employees with dignity and respect) is that it may not be financially expensive to enact. Ironically, whereas high process fairness may be cost-effective, executives in many industries and countries practice process fairness far less often than might be expected, or at least far less often than they think they do. In Chapter 7, some of the reasons why managers do not practice process fairness, in spite of its cost effectiveness, are considered, as is what organizations can do to make it more likely that their managers will practice process fairness.

EXTENDING THE INTERACTION EFFECT TO A NEW CATEGORY OF DEPENDENT VARIABLE

Whereas the interactive relationship between outcome favorability and process fairness previously was shown to emerge on a variety of measures of support for decisions, decision makers, and institutions (Brockner & Wiesenfeld, 1996), studies have extended the interaction effect to another noteworthy dependent variable: psychological strain. *Psychological strain* refers to the reactions people exhibit when they perceive stress, which refers to the felt discrepancy between the demands of a situation and their biological, psychological, or social resources to cope with the demands (e.g., Quick, Cooper, Nelson, & Gavin, 2003). Psychological strain is worthy of attention for many reasons, not the least of which is that its effects may be manifested on dimensions of importance to both organizations (e.g., organizational commitment, work motivation) and employees (e.g., their emotional and physical well-being). Moreover, the effects of psychological strain are generally (although not always) negative. Hence, further insight into the determinants of psychological strain may lead to the development of strategies that will help to alleviate their typically harmful consequences.

A spate of studies has provided evidence that outcome favorability and process fairness interact to influence psychological strain. Tepper (2001) conducted two studies with the use of a two-wave research design in which employees completed measures of outcome favorability and process fairness at Time 1 and a measure of their psychological strain at Time 2, assessed up to 6 months later. Measures of psychological strain included depression, emotional exhaustion, and anxiety. The interaction effect that emerged in both of Tepper's studies showed that the inverse relationship between outcome favorability and psychological strain was much less pronounced when process fairness was high rather than low.

Greenberg (2006) provided evidence of an analogous interaction effect using different ways of operationalizing the independent and dependent variables. Outcome favorability varied on the basis of whether employees had experienced a change in the way that they were paid. For one group, the change in compensation had the effect of lowering their pay for the same amount of work that they had performed prior to the change (unfavorable outcome condition). The other group experienced no such change in compensation (control condition). Process fairness was operationalized on the basis of whether the employees' supervisors had taken part in a training program designed to improve the interactional justice they exhibited toward their direct reports. In fact, employees whose supervisors were trained rated them as showing greater process fairness than did the employees whose supervisors did not take part in the training, confirming that the training had its desired effect.

The dependent measure of psychological strain consisted of employees' self-reported levels of insomnia in both the short term (1 week after the process fairness manipulation) and the longer term (6 months after the process fairness induction) (Greenberg, 2006). The results were dramatic and provided further evidence that outcome favorability and process fairness interact to influence psychological strain. When their supervisors had not completed the training, employees who experienced a reduction in pay reported greater insomnia in both the short and long term relative to those who did not experience any change in their compensation. However, among employees whose supervisors had completed the training, there was much less of a tendency for the pay cut to lead to higher levels of insomnia in both the short and long term. In other words, high process fairness reduced the effect of outcome (un)favorability on psychological strain relative to when process fairness was low.

In a rather impressive sample, consisting of more than 25,000 Finnish employees from many different towns, industries, and organizations, Elovainio et al. (2007) examined whether process fairness moderated the effects of a significant negative life event on a behavioral measure of strain. Participants completed measures of the procedural and interactional fairness that they experienced in their workplaces. At the same time, they provided information on outcome favorability, namely, whether they had experienced the death or onset of severe illness of their spouse or close member of the family within the past year. The dependent measure consisted of the number of participants' days of sickness-related absences from work over the next 30 months. Results yielded an interaction effect between outcome favorability (i.e., the presence or absence of the negative life event) and process fairness. Whereas participants had more days of sickness-related absence for the next 30 months if they had rather than had not experienced the major life event, the magnitude of this effect was significantly lower when process fairness in the workplace was high rather than low. In other words, high process fairness significantly reduced the number of sickness-related absences associated with a major life event months and even years later, relative to when process fairness was low.

These findings extend the types of outcomes on which process fairness may have a moderating effect. In the earlier review of studies examining the interactive effects of outcome favorability and process fairness (Brockner & Wiesenfeld, 1996), the two constructs typically were associated with the same event. For example, Magner, Welker, and Johnson (1996) studied how a performance appraisal influenced employees' intent to remain with their employers as a function of how positively they were appraised (outcome favorability) and whether they were allowed to have any input into their performance appraisals (process fairness).

The Elovainio et al. (2007) findings suggest that process fairness may interact with outcome favorability even when the two constructs are not associated with the same event. Process fairness referred to the general level of procedural and interactional justice with which organizational authorities planned and implemented decisions, whereas outcome favorability referred to whether employees experienced a significant negative life event outside the workplace (i.e., the onset of a severe illness of a close family member). The results of these and other studies (Garonzik et al., 2000; Siegel et al., 2005) show that the effects of process fairness in the workplace may spill over to affect people's reactions (e.g., their psychological strain) to events transpiring outside the workplace.

The facts that the interactive relationship between process fairness and outcome favorability emerges: (1) on a new dependent variable (strain) and (2) when the process and outcome do not refer to the same event, do more than heighten the external validity of the interaction effect. Such findings also may lead to a new way to conceptualize the interaction effect. One way to interpret the effect is that higher process fairness is more reassuring to people about the favorability of their future outcomes, which is important for both economic (Thibaut & Walker, 1975) and psychological reasons (e.g., Lind & Tyler, 1988). If people feel relatively assured about their future outcomes, then they may assign less importance to, and hence be less affected by, the favorability of their current outcomes. Put differently, low process fairness does little to reassure people about the favorability of their future outcomes, in which case their willingness to support decisions, decision makers, and organizations is much more likely to depend on the favorability of their current outcomes.

However, if the process and outcome do not refer to the same event and yet still interact with each other to influence people's psychological strain, then we may need to rethink the underlying mechanism. For example, when a family member suffers a serious illness, high process fairness in the workplace is unlikely to reassure people about the favorability of the family member's health over time (Elovainio et al., 2007). Yet, high process fairness at work makes it less likely for people whose family member has suffered a serious illness to be absent from work on account of sickness. Relatedly, when family members of expatriates do not adjust well to their nonwork environments, the process fairness with which expatriates are treated by organizational authorities is unlikely to influence how reassured the expatriate feels about how well his or her family members are likely to adjust over time. Nevertheless, high process fairness reduces the relationship between family members' adjustment to their living conditions and the extent to which expatriates think seriously about departing prematurely from their overseas assignments (Garonzik et al., 2000).

Whereas being treated with high process fairness by organizational authorities may do little to counteract the specific event occurring in another arena in people's lives, it may have implications for the psychological state elicited by that event. Events that people experience as threatening to their well-being (e.g., the severe illness of a family member) may heighten their desire to perceive a sense of control or to experience a boost to their self-esteem. High process fairness may make the world seem more predictable (and hence controllable) than low process fairness. Moreover, the relational model of fairness has suggested that people feel better about themselves when they are treated with higher process fairness (Tyler & Lind, 1992). In sum, high process fairness may not counteract the event per se but rather may serve as an antidote for the negative feelings that are elicited by the event and in so doing reduce psychological strain. Research has shown that the act of engaging in self-affirmation in a domain unrelated to the one in which people experience a threat to their self-integrity may be sufficient to counteract the threat (Steele, 1988). Perhaps being treated with high process fairness is self-affirming to people, which may reduce the sting of threatened self-integrity that they experienced in another domain of their lives.

Vermunt and Steensma (2003) showed that the interaction between outcome favorability and process fairness even manifests itself on a physiological measure of strain. In a laboratory experiment, college students were asked to perform a rather difficult task. Beforehand, they were told that how well they did on the task was a good predictor of their academic success, thereby motivating them to want to perform well. In the high outcome favorability condition, participants were given enough time to complete the task, whereas in the low outcome favorability condition they were not. The manipulation of process fairness took place subsequent to their task performance. Those in the high process fairness condition were allowed to explain why they had performed the way that they did, whereas those in the low process fairness condition were given no such opportunity for voice. The measure of strain consisted of heart action.

Once again, an interaction effect between outcome favorability and process fairness emerged: In the low process fairness condition, participants exhibited much more of a physiological strain reaction when outcome favorability was low rather than high. When participants were given the opportunity to explain why they performed the way that they did, however, they were no more physiologically strained in the low outcome favorability condition than in the high outcome favorability condition. In summary, across different contexts, types of studies, and types of dependent measures (self-reports, behavioral, and physiological), outcome favorability and process fairness interact to influence psychological strain, such that high process fairness reduces the (inverse) relationship between outcome favorability and psychological strain relative to when process fairness is low.

In addition to interacting with one another to influence people's felt strain, outcome favorability and process fairness recently were shown to interact in the course of moderating the relationship between other factors and strain. More specifically, Janssen (2004) evaluated the relationship between how much employees engaged in innovative behavior and the extent to which they experienced strain. Whereas innovation generally is thought of as a good thing for employees and employers, the process of making it happen may be stressful. As Janssen suggested:

> Innovative behavior is ... change-oriented. Others ... in the work environment may ... resist those changes because of the insecurity and uncertainty they may bring. Moreover, habits and preferences for familiar practices ... are "hard to break" because people have a built-in tendency to return to their original behaviors. Hence, innovative employees are likely to be confronted with workers ... who want to prevent change. Convincing resistant workers of the benefits of innovation can be emotionally taxing ... that may give rise to stress reactions. (p. 202)

Across several different measures of strain (anxiety and burnout), Janssen found a three-way interaction effect among innovation, outcome favorability, and process fairness. Innovation was positively related to strain only when outcome favorability and process fairness were both low. In the next section, I consider how to explain these findings as well as the aforementioned results of other studies that examined the two-way interaction effect of outcome favorability and process fairness on psychological strain.

CONNECTING THE PROCESS–OUTCOME INTERACTION TO A PROMINENT FORMULATION OF STRESS AND STRAIN

Given that outcome favorability and process fairness interact to influence psychological strain, it may be possible to link the interaction effect to extant theory and research on psychological strain. Lazarus and his colleagues (e.g., Lazarus & Folkman, 1984; Lazarus & Launier, 1978) have suggested that the extent to which people experience strain depends on two types of judgments: a *primary appraisal,* which refers to how much people perceive events in their environments to be threatening to their well-being (perceived threat), and a *secondary appraisal,* which refers to people's beliefs about how much they can muster the resources to deal with the potential sources of threat in their environment (perceived control). According to this viewpoint, people experience strain most intensely when perceived threat is high and perceived control is low.

What has received far less attention in the Lazarus conceptualization is the notion that the experience of strain is likely to be an *interactive* function of perceived threat and perceived control. That is, when perceived threat is relatively low, people's control perceptions are likely to be less consequential and therefore less likely to influence their level of felt strain. In contrast, when perceived threat is relatively high, perceived control is likely to be far more meaningful and therefore much more likely to be (inversely) related to people's level of felt strain. To state differently the interaction between perceived threat and perceived control, perceived threat is much more likely to be (positively) related to felt strain when perceived control is low rather than high.

Within the context of the Lazarus framework, outcome favorability may be a proxy for the primary appraisal of perceived threat, whereas process fairness may be a proxy for the secondary appraisal of perceived control. By definition, unfavorable outcomes are likely to be experienced as more of a threat to people's well-being than are favorable outcomes. Moreover, people's control perceptions (i.e., the belief that they will be able to deal with the potential source of threat) may depend on process fairness. For one thing, certain *specific* elements of process fairness may shape people's perceptions of control. For example, whether people are allowed to have voice in a decision process may influence the extent to which they believe that they will be able to deal with the threat; indeed, Thibaut and Walker (1975) originally conceived of voice as process *control* and decision *control.* Moreover, when people believe that they have been treated with interactional justice (such as when others express genuine caring and concern for their well-being), they may experience social support, which in turn may make them feel more empowered to deal with the threat in their environment.

People's control perceptions also depend on the extent to which they believe that outcomes, especially unfavorable outcomes, are predictable (e.g., Affleck, Tennen, Pfeiffer, & Fifield, 1987). Fair processes *in general* are more likely to engender greater outcome predictability than are unfair processes, especially over the longer haul. As Greenberg (2005) put it, "An authority figure who plays by the rules surely is more predictable than a loose cannon. The resulting sense of control such predictability brings is likely to buffer reactions to stressful situations" (p. 363). In short, to the extent that outcome favorability acts as a proxy for the primary appraisal of threat and process fairness acts as a proxy for the secondary appraisal of perceived control, and to the extent that primary appraisal and secondary appraisal interact with each other to influence felt strain, the appraisal theory of Lazarus and colleagues may explain the interactive effect of outcome favorability and process fairness on psychological strain.

Moreover, the appraisal theory of strain may help to account for Janssen's (2004) three-way interaction between engaging in innovation, outcome favorability, and process fairness. One interpretation of the finding that innovation was positively related to strain only when outcome favorability and process fairness were both low is that employees may have experienced particularly high levels of threat to their well-being when they engaged in innovative behavior and outcome favorability was low. No one likes to be played as a sucker, and yet the combination of being innovative and receiving relatively unfavorable outcomes may have led participants to believe that they were being treated particularly unfairly (more so than, for example, when the same level of high innovation was associated with favorable outcomes). The high level of threat (emanating from the primary appraisal, which in turn was shaped by the disconnect between high innovation and low outcome favorability) combined with a low level of control (emanating from the secondary appraisal, which in turn may have been driven by low process fairness) may have engendered particularly high levels of strain, as manifested in the three-way interaction Janssen found among innovation, outcome favorability, and process fairness.

Note, moreover, that Lazarus' appraisal theory of strain also may account for the interaction effect even when people use process fairness information as a basis for the primary appraisal of threat rather than for the secondary appraisal of control (Greenberg, 2005). For example, people sometimes receive process fairness information before they learn of their outcomes. When process fairness information comes first and when people believe that the process is unfair (e.g., that decisions are not being made on the basis of accurate information or that certain parties have been denied legitimate input into the decision-making process), they may experience threat. The subsequent receipt of outcome information in turn is likely to further affect their level of felt threat. An unfavorable outcome may confirm or further heighten the threat initially felt in response to low process fairness. A favorable outcome, however, is likely to reduce felt threat. In contrast, when people first learn that the process is fair, concerns about threat are less likely to be aroused, in which case people may assign less importance to outcome information and in so doing reduce its impact on perceived threat. Hence, process fairness and outcome favorability information—when received in that order—also may interact with each other to influence the threat component of felt strain.

As this reasoning suggests, the primary appraisal leading to perceived threat may be instigated by the receipt of an unfavorable outcome or by an unfair process. Regardless of whether it is outcome or process information that instantiates the primary appraisal process, people may draw on the other source of information to make sense of what is going on, which in turn may influence their level of psychological strain. Van den Bos, Vermunt, and Wilke (1997) conducted several studies in which they varied the order of presentation of outcome favorability and process fairness information and found that whichever came first had more of an impact on a variety of dependent variables (e.g., intention to protest the decision that gave rise to their outcomes). Van den Bos and his colleagues emphasized the finding that whichever fairness information came first was more consequential, as reflected in the title of the article, "Procedural and Distributive Justice: What Is Fair Depends More on What Comes First Than on What Comes Next." However, these studies also showed that regardless of the order in which outcome favorability and process fairness information was presented, the two produced the typical interaction effect: High process fairness reduced the influence of outcome favorability relative to when procedural fairness was low.

In summary, the Lazarus appraisal model may account for the interactive relationship between outcome favorability and process fairness, particularly on dependent measures that reflect or are affected by psychological strain. Unfavorable outcomes (which are presumably associated with high perceived threat) lead to greater strain when process fairness is low (i.e., perceived control is low) than when process fairness is high (i.e., perceived control is high). In contrast, the effect of favorable outcomes (which are associated with less threat) on felt strain is not as affected by the level of process fairness. Furthermore, the primary appraisal of perceived threat also may be an interactive function of process fairness and outcome favorability, for example, when people receive the former information prior to the latter. Conceiving of the interaction effect as a determinant of strain reactions also suggests some new ways of thinking about how people combine outcome favorability and process fairness information, as suggested next.

Three-Way Interaction Effects

Numerous elements make up the broader construct of process fairness, including procedural justice and interactional justice (Colquitt, 2001). Theory (e.g., Lazarus & Folkman, 1984) and research (e.g., Elovainio et al., 2007) suggest that each of procedural justice and interactional justice interact with outcome favorability to influence people's experience of strain. The Lazarus–Folkman framework also raises the possibility of a three-way interaction effect among outcome favorability, procedural justice, and interactional justice. Outcome favorability is likely to influence the salience of future outcomes, such that people are more likely to wonder and perhaps worry about their future outcomes when their current outcomes are relatively unfavorable. In response to unfavorable current outcomes, people may use procedural justice information to make inferences about their future outcomes. When procedures are fair, people may be more likely to believe that they will receive their share of desired outcomes over the longer haul or at least more so than when they believe that procedures are not fair. If the process of making inferences about future outcomes is elicited more strongly when (current) outcome favorability is relatively low, then the primary appraisal of perceived threat may be an interactive function of outcome favorability and procedural justice. One way to describe this interaction effect is that people will feel most threatened when current outcomes are unfavorable and when procedural justice is low relative to all other combinations.

Interactional justice in turn may influence the secondary appraisal of perceived control, that is, how much people feel that they will be able to counteract the perceived threat. Interactional justice is comprised of both informational justice and interpersonal justice. The former "focuses on the explanations provided to people that convey information about why procedures were used in a certain way or why outcomes were distributed in a certain fashion," whereas the latter reflects "the degree to which people are treated with politeness, dignity, and respect by authorities or third parties involved in executing procedures or determining outcomes" (Colquitt, Conlon, Wesson, Porter, & Ng, 2001, p. 427). The information provided in an explanation may help people to feel a greater sense of control over a certain threat. For example, if people learn why they received an unfavorable outcome, they may be able to do things to increase their chances of receiving a favorable outcome in the future, thereby enhancing their sense of control. Moreover, interpersonal justice may enhance people's sense of control. For example, when people receive emotional support from others in the face of unfavorable outcomes, such as the death of a loved one or the loss of a job, they may feel less alone and therefore see themselves as better able to counteract or manage the threat.

This reasoning gives rise to the prediction of a three-way interactive effect of outcome favorability, procedural justice, and interactional justice on people's level of felt strain, such that the aforementioned two-way interaction between outcome favorability and procedural justice will be more strongly pronounced when interactional justice is relatively low. To state the three-way interaction effect differently, people should react most negatively when outcome favorability, procedural justice, and interactional justice are low, relative to all other combinations of circumstances. In fact, the results of three independent studies support this assertion (Cropanzano, Slaughter, & Bachiochi, 2005; Goldman, 2003; Skarlicki & Folger, 1997).

Cropanzano et al. (2005) had a sample of black engineers indicate how attracted they would feel to a hypothetical organization as a function of the distributive (outcome), procedural, and interactional justice of the organization's affirmative action policies. Goldman examined whether terminated workers filed a discrimination legal claim as a function of the distributive, procedural, and interactional justice of their termination. Skarlicki and Folger looked at the effects of distributive, procedural, and interactional justice on employees' tendencies to engage in retaliatory behaviors toward the organization, such as taking supplies home without permission. In spite of these contextual differences between studies, all of them yielded a three-way interaction between distributive justice, procedural justice, and interactional justice, such that participants responded most negatively when all three forms of justice were relatively low.

Strain as a Mediator

The dependent variable in many studies in the review of process–outcome interaction effects consisted of people's willingness to support decisions, decision makers, or institutions (Brockner & Wiesenfeld, 1996). Another possibility suggested by Lazarus's conceptualization is that felt strain may mediate the interactive effects of outcome favorability and process fairness on people's willingness to support decisions, decision makers, or institutions. That is, outcome favorability and process fairness interact to influence felt strain. Moreover, strain may be (inversely) related to people's willingness to support decisions, decision makers, and institutions for several reasons. First, when the basis of the strain consists of feelings of anger or resentment toward the other party for meting out unfavorable outcomes with an unfair process, people are unlikely to be supportive. If anything, they may take active steps to indicate their lack of support, perhaps in the form of retaliation. Second, to the extent that the basis of the strain is a more undifferentiated form of emotional exhaustion (e.g., Tepper, 2001), people may not have the energy needed to behave supportively.

I know of no research that has examined whether psychological strain mediates the two-way interaction effect of outcome favorability and process fairness on people's support for decisions, decision makers, and institutions; therein lies an important opportunity for future research. However, one of the studies testing for the three-way interaction among distributive, procedural, and interactional justice suggested that strain may well play a mediating role. In the Goldman (2003) study, which examined terminated employees' propensity to file suit, the author also measured state anger. Not only did the three-way interaction effect emerge on state anger (similar in nature to the three-way interaction found on the measure of propensity to file suit), but also a mediation analysis showed that the three-way interaction on propensity to file suit was partially attributable to felt anger.

DIFFERENTIATING BETWEEN STRAIN REACTIONS: AN APPRAISAL THEORY OF EMOTIONAL EXPERIENCES

To this point, the discussion of cognitive appraisal theory (e.g., Lazarus & Folkman, 1984) helps to illustrate how *the degree of* psychological strain may be jointly influenced by outcome favorability and process fairness, such that strain is greatest when outcomes are relatively unfavorable and the process is relatively unfair (and multiplicatively rather than additively so) relative to all other combinations of conditions. One indicator of degree of psychological strain is negative emotion, with studies showing that people experience a number of different negative emotions most intensely (e.g., depression, anxiety, and "emotional exhaustion") when their outcomes are relatively unfavorable and the process is relatively unfair (Tepper, 2001).

In the face of the primary appraisal of threat to well-being, however, people's perceptions of control (that is, how much they believe that they will be able to counteract the threat) may not be the only type of secondary appraisal they make. To interpret the meaning of the threat more fully, they also may make the related judgments of deservingness and causality, such as how much to attribute outcomes to themselves or to other entities external to themselves. Depending on the type and level of these other secondary appraisals, people may have *qualitatively* different emotional experiences. For example, unfavorable outcomes that are seen as undeserved may elicit resentment, anger, or outrage, whereas unfavorable outcomes that are seen as deserved may give rise to more self-relevant negative emotions, such as shame, guilt, or sadness.

It is important for two reasons to consider the qualitatively different emotions that people may experience. First, whereas certain attitudes or behaviors (e.g., creativity, helping) may be predicted by whether people's emotions are *generally* negative or *generally* positive (e.g., Amabile, 1996; Isen & Baron, 1991), others may be differentially predictable depending on the specific nature of the emotion. Consider, for example, the negative emotions of anger and guilt. As Weiss, Suckow, and Cropanzano (1999) suggested:

> Anger has been shown to relate to aggression … and coronary heart disease … while guilt has not. Guilt, on the other hand, can induce feelings of helpfulness in people … in a way that anger does not. Consequently, ignoring discrete emotions in favor of general positive or negative affective states can reduce the ability to predict specific behaviors. (p. 787)

Second, just as process fairness and outcome favorability may influence the secondary appraisal of perceived control and thereby influence *how much* negative emotion people experience, so may process fairness and outcome influence these other types of secondary appraisals, such as judgments of deservingness. In other words, process fairness and outcome favorability may interact to influence the *qualitative* nature of people's emotional experiences.

Note that the last assertion may not be obvious from a simple extrapolation of results of previous studies in which the dependent variable consisted of support for decisions, decision makers, and organizations. In many of these studies, people responded most negatively when their outcome was unfavorable and the process was unfair relative to all other combinations of conditions (Brockner & Wiesenfeld, 1996). Moreover, the results in the other three circumstances (unfair process/favorable outcome, fair process/favorable outcome, and fair process/unfavorable outcome) tended to be quite similar to one another. As such, it is tempting to predict that people's emotional experiences will follow suit, that is (1) they will show the highest degree of negative emotion of all sorts when they receive an unfavorable outcome that is accompanied by an unfair process, and (2) they will have relatively similar experiences of negative emotion in all conditions other than the one in which an unfavorable outcome is accompanied by an unfair process.

Recent theory and research suggest, however, that the different conditions created by the various combinations of outcome favorability and process fairness elicit qualitatively different emotional experiences. Again, cognitive appraisal theory may provide a useful framework in which the primary appraisal refers to the extent to which people judge the event or situation as threatening to their well-being, and the secondary appraisal refers to judgments of causality or deservingness. Moreover, outcome favorability or process fairness information are quite fluid in the sense that both may influence people's primary appraisals or their secondary appraisals.

Consider, for example, the emotions people may experience when outcome favorability acts as a proxy for primary appraisal. The more that outcomes are unfavorable (i.e., the greater the perceived threat), the more likely are people to engage in a secondary appraisal in which they seek to understand the cause of their outcomes (Wong & Weiner, 1981). For example, when employees do not receive the pay raise that they wanted or when they fail to land a coveted assignment, they are likely to try to figure out why, which directs their attention to process fairness information. Unfavorable outcomes accompanied by an unfair process are more likely to be attributed to the parties who made or implemented the decision (Barclay, Skarlicki, & Pugh, 2005; Brockner et al., 2007; Folger & Cropanzano, 2001), giving rise to feelings of anger or resentment toward those parties. In contrast, when people believe that unfavorable outcomes are accompanied by fair processes, they may be less likely to externalize the reasons for their outcomes and instead may make more self-attributions, which in turn may engender the kinds of negative emotions associated with self-blame (shame, guilt, sadness, or depression).

The perceived fairness of the decision process also may be used in the primary appraisal stage, in which people evaluate possible threats to their well-being. Unfair decision-making processes may be seen as whimsical and capricious, thereby threatening people's sense of predictability and control. For example, one important predictability judgment pertains to people's beliefs about whether the outcomes that they and others receive are deserved. The more unfair the process, the less likely are people to believe that they and others will receive the outcomes that they deserve. Moreover, there are two different ways in which processes may be unfair and thereby bring about undeserved outcomes. Sometimes, the unfair decision process may be perceived to be biased *toward* people receiving the outcomes they want. In other instances, and probably more typically, the unfair decision process may be perceived to be biased *against* people receiving the outcomes that they want.

In both of these instances of unfair process, the precise nature of people's emotional experience is likely to be determined by the favorability of their outcomes. When the unfair decision process is judged to be biased toward them and their outcomes are favorable, people are likely to feel guilty. According to equity theory, people may feel guilty when they experience positive inequity, that is, when their ratio of outcomes to inputs or contributions is greater than that of an appropriate target of comparison, such as a coworker (Adams, 1965). The present analysis suggests that people may feel that their outcomes were undeserved (and, as a result may feel guilty) when they received a favorable outcome due to the decision-making process being unfairly biased toward the individual. Indeed, an unfair decision process that is biased toward giving people favorable outcomes may be one of the routes through which people's ratio of outcomes to inputs exceed that of the target of comparison.

When an unfair decision process is biased toward people but their outcomes are unfavorable nonetheless, they may feel shame or embarrassment; after all, they failed to succeed even though the deck was stacked in their favor, suggesting that it was something about themselves that brought about the unfavorable outcome. In contrast, when the unfair decision process is biased against them and their outcomes are favorable, they may feel particularly high levels of pride or happiness over having "beaten the odds." Finally, when the unfair decision process is biased against them and their outcomes are unfavorable, they may feel resentment and anger toward the agent of the decision (Lind & Lissak, 1985)

Tests of Predictions Based on the Appraisal Theory of Emotional Experiences

The above reasoning suggests that the appraisal theory of qualitatively different emotions maps onto six different cells created by a 3 × 2 matrix crossing three different process fairness conditions (fair, unfair/biased toward, and unfair/biased against) with two levels of outcome favorability (favorable vs. unfavorable) (see Table 2.1).

The only cell that has not been considered thus far is the favorable outcome/fair process condition. There, it may be expected that people will feel a sense of happiness and pride to the extent that the fair process leads them to make more self-attributions for their favorable outcomes (Weiner, 1985). However, in the absence of perceived threat (that is, when outcomes are favorable and the process is fair), the appraisal process may not be instantiated to the same degree as in

TABLE 2.1 Predicted Emotional Experiences as a Function of Process Fairness and Outcome Favorability

	Outcome Favorability	
Process Fairness	**High**	**Low**
High	Muted pride	Dejection "I blame myself"
Low (biased toward)	Guilt "I'm not worthy"	Shame "I must have really messed up"
Low (biased against)	Strong pride "I beat the odds"	Anger "The nerve of them"

the other five conditions, in which at least one source of threat is present. As a result, the emotional experience in the favorable outcome/fair process condition, while certainly positive in tone (e.g., pride), also may be somewhat more muted than in one or more of the other five conditions.

The results of several studies are consistent with some of the predictions set forth in Table 2.1. For example, Barclay et al. (2005) examined the emotional reactions of people who experienced an unfavorable outcome: the loss of their jobs due to organizational layoffs. Whereas participants generally were likely to view being laid off as an unfavorable outcome, some probably experienced it as more unfavorable than did others. Among those who experienced their outcomes as more unfavorable, process fairness was (1) positively related to their experience of shame and guilt and (2) inversely related to their experience of anger. In other words, high process fairness accompanying relatively unfavorable outcomes elicited shame and guilt, whereas low process fairness accompanying those same outcomes engendered anger. Moreover, this was true regardless of whether the process dimension referred to procedural fairness (e.g., "The procedures used by the company to conduct the layoffs were fair") or interactional fairness (e.g., "My supervisor listened to my personal concerns").

In several experimental studies (Krehbiel & Cropanzano, 2000; Weiss et al., 1999), anger was shown to be most pronounced in the unfavorable outcome/biased against condition, and guilt was found to be highest in the favorable outcome/biased toward condition. However, whereas pride and related positive emotions such as happiness and joy were high in the favorable outcome/biased against condition, they were no higher than they were in the other two favorable outcome conditions (although obviously higher than they were in the unfavorable outcome conditions).

The various conditions in the 3 × 2 matrix in Table 2.1 also may differ with respect to the *number* of different emotions that they elicit. For example, in the cell in which guilt was highest (the favorable outcome/

biased toward condition), Krehbiel and Cropanzano (2000) found that participants also reported feeling the highest level of anxiety. Perhaps this resulted from an additional secondary appraisal process in which people seek to establish whether their current outcomes are likely to continue. Favorable outcomes resulting from an unfair process may not only be seen as undeserved, thereby engendering guilt, but also as fleeting. After all, if people believe that they were lucky to be the beneficiaries of an unfair process, they also may believe that they will not be as lucky in the future. The perception of the possibility of future "downward mobility" may elicit anxiety.

On the Episodic Nature of Emotional Experiences

Multiple emotions also may be experienced in certain conditions on an episodic basis, in which people's reactions to their initial emotion set the stage for subsequent emotions. For example, both Krehbiel and Cropanzano (2000) and Weiss et al. (1999) found that in the favorable outcome/biased toward condition, people not only felt the most guilty (as predicted), but also felt just as much pride as they did in the other favorable outcome conditions, which was not predicted. Perhaps people in the favorable outcome/biased toward condition may have initially felt that they did not deserve the favorable outcome, eliciting feelings of guilt, but subsequently convinced themselves that they deserved to receive favorable outcomes. For example, those with higher levels of self-esteem may have decided that they were worthy of favorable outcomes (Brockner, Davy, & Carter, 1985). Or, regardless of their self-esteem, they may have believed that outcomes "even out" over the long haul, and that this was their turn to be lucky. Early tests of equity theory, which examined people's reactions to being paid more than they deserved, showed that people attempted to redress positive inequity in different ways over time (Lawler, 1968). Initially, they tried to redress the inequity behaviorally by working harder. Later, however, motivational boosts were not observed. Rather, people came to convince themselves that they were actually deserving of their overpayment. In other words, whereas people initially redressed positive inequity behaviorally, they subsequently did so psychologically by heightening their perceived contributions. In like fashion, people who are the beneficiaries of an unfair process may feel guilt at first but may subsequently believe that their favorable outcomes were deserved, leading to feelings of pride.

Other combinations of process fairness and outcome favorability conditions may elicit different types of emotional episodes. For example, when people receive unfavorable outcomes as a result of an unfair process that is biased against them, they are likely to feel angry and resentful (Folger et al., 1983; Krehbiel & Cropanzano, 2000; Weiss et al., 1999). However, numerous factors may affect the extent to which employees believe that the expression (or even the experience) of anger is admissible in the workplace. For example, when interacting with customers, employees are expected to adhere to certain norms, such as expressing positive emotions or hiding negative emotions. How might employees respond, however, if customers meted out unfavorable outcomes (e.g., chose not to buy the product or service that the employees were trying to sell) and did so with low process fairness (e.g., showed a lack of courtesy or respect toward employees)? The tension between what employees are likely to experience (anger and resentment) and how they are expected to behave toward customers (with civility and concern) may make it more difficult for employees to engage in successful emotional labor, manifesting itself in emotional expression that is inauthentic or inappropriate (Rupp & Spencer, 2006).

In addition to situational factors such as workplace norms, dispositional factors may influence the ease with which people experience or express negative emotions. For example, certain people may have difficulty acknowledging their angry feelings, perhaps having been taught early in life that the expression or experience of anger is not appropriate. Angry feelings may ultimately be transformed into anxiety, particularly when people believe that their angry feelings are not admissible. If nothing else, people may feel anxious about whether they will be able to control or manage their "unacceptable" feelings.

Or, when people receive unfavorable outcomes as a result of fair process, they may see themselves as responsible for their outcomes. Blaming themselves (often accompanied by feelings of anger or frustration), they may redouble their efforts to bring about more favorable outcomes. For example, when people fail to perform at a certain level even though their superiors used fair processes, they may contemplate the possibility that they are personally responsible for their unfavorable outcomes. In response, they may try to channel the energy associated with their resulting feelings of personal frustration into performing more capably. If, however, they continue to perform poorly they may be even more convinced that they have no one to blame but themselves. At this point, they may start to show signs of sadness or dejection (Wortman & Brehm, 1975).

The study of how outcome favorability and process fairness interact to influence the magnitude, nature, number, and sequencing of people's emotional experience is a ripe area for future research. Future research on the sequencing of emotion requires the use of longitudinal designs, in which people's emotional experience is gauged at multiple points in time. Future research on emotional sequencing also would do well to assess the appraisal processes that facilitate people's transition from one emotion to the next.

Additional Future Research Opportunities

Toward Purifying the Measures of Discrete Emotions

In testing for the effects of outcome favorability and process fairness on discrete emotions, moreover, researchers may need to control for the effects of other discrete emotions or at least those that carry the same affective tone. Several reanalyses of data from published studies showed that different conclusions may be reached when researchers do versus do not control for other discrete emotions when testing for the interactive relationship between outcome favorability and process fairness. For example, Tepper (2001) asked employees to rate the outcome fairness and process fairness that they experienced in their work organization. Six months later, participants rated their level of anxiety and depression. In the published version of the study, Tepper reported significant interactions between outcome fairness and process fairness on the measures of anxiety and depression, showing that participants exhibited both forms of psychological strain to the greatest extent when outcome fairness and process fairness were low relative to all other combinations of conditions.

At first blush, these findings may be interpreted as suggesting that outcome and process fairness interact to influence the *magnitude* of strain and not necessarily the *nature of* the strain. Further reinforcing this perception is that anxiety and depression were themselves highly correlated with each other (.79). However, subsequent reanalyses of the Tepper data (graciously undertaken by Professor Tepper) suggested a somewhat different picture. In one reanalysis, the interactive effect of outcome fairness and process fairness on anxiety was tested, controlling for depression. In another, the interactive effect of outcome fairness and process fairness on depression was examined, controlling for anxiety. By controlling for one type of strain reaction while testing for the interaction effect on the other, we were able to purify the measures of anxiety and depression. Interestingly, the interaction between outcome fairness and process fairness on depression was completely eliminated when anxiety was controlled. In contrast, the interaction between outcome fairness and process fairness on anxiety was hardly affected when depression was treated as a control. Thus, the interactive effect of outcome fairness and process fairness did not merely influence the magnitude of people's negative emotions. Being much more likely to emerge on the agitation-related negative emotion of anxiety than it was on the dejection-related negative emotion of depression, the interactive relationship between outcome and process fairness also affected *the nature of* their emotional experience.

The fact that the interaction effect emerged on the measure of anxiety also is consistent with my speculation about the episodic nature of emotion that people may experience in response to the combination of an unfavorable outcome and an unfair process. Whereas theory and research suggest that people experience high levels of anger and resentment toward the other party under such conditions (Folger & Cropanzano, 2001), I suggested that anger and resentment also may lead to the experience of anxiety, which is precisely what Tepper found in both the original analyses and in the reanalyses of the data.

Evidence about the need to differentiate between negative emotions also stems from reanalyses of findings presented by Barclay et al. (2005), who examined the interactive effect of outcome favorability and process fairness on both inward-focused negative emotions (shame, guilt) and outward-focused negative emotions (anger, hostility). As might be expected, outcome favorability was inversely related to both of these negative emotions. Of greater importance, Barclay et al. reported that process fairness had a moderating effect on the relationship between outcome favorability and both types of negative emotions, such that the inverse relationship between outcome favorability and negative emotions was more pronounced when process fairness was high rather than low. Whereas it may be expected that high process fairness would intensify the inverse relationship between outcome favorability and the inward-focused emotions, it is far less clear why these findings would emerge on the measure of *outward*-focused emotions. Folger and his colleagues (Cropanzano & Folger, 1989; Folger et al., 1983) have repeatedly shown that high process fairness *reduces* the impact of outcome favorability on anger and resentment relative to when process fairness is low.

In testing for the interactive effect of outcome favorability and process fairness on each of these two types of negative emotion, Barclay et al. (2005) did not control for the other type of negative emotion. In fact, the two types of negative emotion were modestly positively correlated with each other ($r = .28$, $p < .01$). Reanalyses in which the other negative emotion was included as a control variable showed that the interaction effect remained significant on the measure of inward-focused negative emotions but was no longer significant on the measure of outward-focused negative emotions. (My thanks go to Professor Barclay for her willingness to conduct these reanalyses.) Thus, when outward-focused negative emotions were controlled, high process fairness continued to heighten the magnitude of the inverse relationship between outcome favorability and the negative inward-focused emotions of shame and guilt relative to when process fairness was low. However, when the inward-focused negative emotions were controlled, process fairness no longer had a moderating effect on the relationship between outcome favorability and the negative outward-focused emotions of anger and hostility.

Examining the Consequences of Discrete Emotions

Future research also should examine the consequences of the discrete emotions that people experience as a function of outcome favorability and process fairness. In some instances, it may be the mere fact that people are emotionally aroused that affects their subsequent attitudes and behaviors. Emotions often produce rumination, in which people think about their emotional state. Howard Weiss and his colleagues found that arousing people into negative and positive emotional states had similarly debilitating effects on their subsequent task performance

(H. Weiss, personal communication, November 23, 2005). That is, both positive and negative emotional states elicited rumination, which detracted from people's ability to concentrate on the task at hand. In other cases, it may be the overall affective tone of the emotion—that is, whether it is negative or positive—that is consequential. For example, the relationship between anxiety and job satisfaction may be comparable to the relationship between anger and job satisfaction. In this case, what is consequential is that people are experiencing *some* negative emotion that is detracting from their job satisfaction, but the nature of the negative emotion may be less important.

However, in other instances the nature of the emotional states may make a difference. For example, when working on a relatively simple task, people are likely to be more productive when they are feeling angry or anxious than when they are feeling sad or depressed. The greater levels of arousal associated with anger and anxiety than with sadness and dejection may enable people to devote more energy to the task. Provided that the task does not require complex thinking, in which all of these negative emotions may serve as sources of distraction, people may be likely to perform better when their negative emotions are more rather than less arousing. Given these various possible patterns of emotional effects on people's attitudes and behaviors, future research needs to identify the factors that make each pattern more versus less likely to emerge.

PURIFYING THE INTERACTION EFFECT

The initial sections of this chapter suggest that the interactive relationship between outcome favorability and process fairness is even more generalizable than that implied by the review of previous studies (Brockner & Wiesenfeld, 1996). We now see that the interaction effect has emerged in new contexts and on a rather broad new category of dependent variable. The generality of the interaction effect is further underscored by the fact that both outcome favorability and process fairness have been operationalized in a variety of ways. Across many contexts, it has been shown that various forms of outcome favorability interact with many different forms of process fairness to influence an assortment of dependent variables.

Greenberg (1990b) suggested that our understanding of organizational justice may be enhanced through attempts to integrate various findings as well as through attempts to differentiate between findings. Hence, yet another way to gain insight into the process–outcome interaction is by looking at it in a more fine-grained rather than in a more general manner. Said differently, and in the form of a question, are *all* forms of outcome favorability *equally* likely to interact with *all* forms of process fairness to influence *all* forms of people's willingness to support decisions, decision makers, and institutions? Or, are *certain* forms of outcomes especially likely to interact with *certain* forms of process fairness to influence *particular* forms of reactions? Next, I describe various research findings that suggest that the answer to the latter question is affirmative.

Level of Outcome Favorability × Level of Process Fairness

The process–outcome interaction shows that high process fairness reduces the effect of outcome favorability on people's support for decisions, decision makers, or institutions relative to when process fairness is low. In other words, people may not react particularly badly to unfavorable outcomes provided that process fairness is relatively high. Within this rather broad claim, however, the interaction effect may be even more pronounced when the degree or level of high process fairness is appropriately matched to the degree or level of low outcome favorability. Simply put, the more unfavorable outcomes inflict pain on people, the more necessary it may be for them to experience high process fairness for them to be at least reasonably supportive of decisions, decision makers, or institutions. If their unfavorable outcomes are less severe, then smaller doses of high process fairness may be all that are needed.

A study by Ohbuchi, Kameda, and Agarie (1989) yielded results consistent with this last line of reasoning. Participants were asked to imagine that they were walking along the street with a friend when they experienced an unfavorable outcome: They were knocked to the ground by two men who had dashed out of an alley. The harm inflicted was either more severe or less severe. Moreover, in half of the cases the harmdoers exhibited high process fairness by spontaneously offering an apology, whereas in the other half they did not. An interactive effect between the severity of the harm and process fairness emerged on several measures of how angry participants were at the harmdoers, such that being treated with high process fairness was much more likely to reduce participants' anger when their unfavorable outcome was less severe rather than more severe.

Although the following idea was not tested in the Ohbuchi et al. (1989) study, it is possible that participants who had experienced the more severe unfavorable outcome would have responded better (that is, their anger would have been reduced to a greater extent) if they had been treated with even greater process fairness than that shown by the harmdoers in the "high" process fairness condition. In a work setting, for example, the more employees are harmed by a certain resource allocation decision, the more they may need to be convinced that process fairness is high. Prior to the decision, they may need to believe that their views were seriously considered, and that the Leventhal et al. (1980) criteria of high process fairness (e.g., accuracy, consistency, bias suppression, etc.) were satisfied. Moreover, as the decision is implemented the affected parties may need to believe that they were treated with high interactional fairness. The greater the unfavorability of the outcome, the more likely are people to experience threat to their economic or psychological well-being, and hence the more likely they are to be in need of the economic or psychological support associated with being treated with high process fairness. Said differently, and to invoke key concepts from the Lazarus and Folkman (1984) appraisal theory of stress, the more that outcomes threaten people's well-being (i.e., the more that outcomes are unfavorable), the more people may need to perceive control (the more they may need to be treated with higher levels of process fairness).

This is not to suggest that moderately high process fairness will be more likely than very high process fairness to reduce the negative effect of moderately unfavorable outcomes. Thus, in suggesting that the magnitude of the process–outcome interaction depends on the congruence between the level of unfavorable outcomes and the level of high process fairness, I am considering the minimal degree of high process fairness that may be needed to counteract the threat posed by an unfavorable outcome. Moderately high process fairness may be sufficient to offset the effects of moderately unfavorable outcomes but may not be sufficient to counteract the effects of very unfavorable outcomes. Very high process fairness may offset the effects of both moderately unfavorable outcomes and very unfavorable outcomes, but it may not be *necessary* for process fairness to be very high to counteract the effects of moderately unfavorable outcomes; moderately high process fairness may be sufficient to do the trick. These conjectures need to be tested in future research.

Type of Outcome Favorability × Type of Process Fairness

The preceding discussion suggests that the magnitude of the process–outcome interaction may depend on the relationship between the *levels* of (low) outcome favorability and (high) process fairness. The more that lower levels of outcome favorability are met with higher process fairness (or that moderately unfavorable outcomes are met with moderately high process fairness), the stronger the interactive relationship may be. Here, I consider the possibility that certain *types* of outcomes may be more likely to interact with certain *types* of process fairness dimensions to influence employees' attitudes and behaviors. Results consistent with this conjecture were provided in a study by Kickul et al. (2002). Participants came from organizations that had undergone a radical organizational change within the past year, such as a merger or an acquisition. They were asked about the favorability of two types of outcomes: extrinsic and intrinsic. Extrinsic outcomes referred to competitive salaries, rewards, and flexibility in scheduling, whereas intrinsic outcomes consisted of employee freedom, participation in decision making, and increased responsibilities. Employees indicated the favorability of both types of outcomes by indicating the extent to which the organization made good on its promises to deliver them. Furthermore, participants rated two different forms of process fairness: the formal procedures used by organizational authorities to plan and implement decisions, as captured by the Leventhal et al. (1980) dimensions of consistency, accuracy, and the like, and interactional fairness, which referred to the interpersonal behavior exhibited by authorities, such as the extent to which they treated the affected parties with kindness and consideration and how much they provided sensible explanations of the reasons for their decisions. Dependent variables included job satisfaction, intentions to leave the organization, in-role job performance, and organizational citizenship behavior directed toward the organization (OCBO) and organizational citizenship behavior directed toward their supervisor (OCBI).

Across all five dependent variables, extrinsic outcome favorability interacted with procedural fairness in its typical fashion, such that high procedural fairness reduced the relationship between extrinsic outcome favorability and the various dependent variables relative to when procedural fairness was low. For example, extrinsic outcome favorability was less positively related to job satisfaction when procedural fairness was high rather than low. Extrinsic outcome favorability did not interact with interactional fairness, however, to influence any of the dependent variables.

This is not to say that interactional fairness did not interact with outcome favorability. Rather, interactional fairness interacted with *intrinsic* outcome favorability to influence four of the five dependent variables (the lone exception being OCBO). Again, this interaction effect took the same form as that found in previous research (e.g., Greenberg, 1993), such that high interactional fairness reduced the relationship between intrinsic outcome favorability and the dependent variables relative to when interactional fairness was low. Furthermore, the interaction effect between procedural fairness and intrinsic outcome favorability generally was not found; a significant effect only emerged on the measure of in-role job performance.

How might we account for these more fine-grained sets of interaction effects? At least two related possibilities come to mind. First, assuming that employees tried to determine the reasons for their outcomes, they may have found one type of process fairness information more useful for causal attributional purposes than the other. People generally are more motivated to understand the reasons for outcomes that are unfavorable rather than favorable (e.g., Shaver, 1985; Wong & Weiner, 1981). Hence, in response to unfavorable extrinsic outcomes, participants may have felt that procedural fairness information (that is, the structural aspects of the decision process) would better help them answer the "why" question than would interactional fairness information (that is, the interpersonal behavior shown by authorities when implementing decisions). With their attention drawn to procedural fairness information, it stands to reason that they would react more positively on the various dependent measures when procedural fairness was high rather than low. Moreover, this causal attribution process was probably less apt to be instantiated when extrinsic outcomes were favorable, giving rise to an interactive relationship between extrinsic outcome favorability and procedural fairness.

An attributionally similar but substantively distinct set of questions may have arisen among participants who received unfavorable intrinsic outcomes. These participants may have been asking themselves something like the following: Why did I receive these "psychologically unfavorable" outcomes? Was it because of psychological insensitivity on the part of the authorities? To answer these questions, employees may be well served by attending to the interactional fairness exhibited by authorities. If authorities' interactional fairness is high, employees will understandably respond much more positively than if interactional fairness is low. Moreover, people may have been less likely to ask this particular "why" question if their intrinsic outcomes are favorable, thereby sowing the seeds for an interactive relationship between intrinsic outcome favorability and interactional fairness.

Second, and related to this reasoning, the receipt of unfavorable extrinsic outcomes and unfavorable intrinsic outcomes may raise somewhat different concerns. Let us assume that people are concerned with both their short-term outcomes and their long-term outcomes. In response to unfavorable outcomes in the short term, it is understandable that people may wonder (and perhaps worry) about what their longer-term outcomes are likely to be. Thus, if they receive unfavorable extrinsic outcomes in the short term, they may feel the need to reduce uncertainty about their longer-term extrinsic outcomes. Similarly, if they receive unfavorable intrinsic outcomes in the short term, they may need to make inferences about their longer-term intrinsic outcomes. One possible interpretation of the Kickul et al. (2002) results is that people find procedural fairness and interactional fairness information useful for making somewhat different types of judgments about their longer-term outcomes. People may believe that procedural fairness information is more informative about their longer-term economic outcomes than is the interpersonal behavior exhibited by authorities in the course of implementing decisions. Conversely, they may judge interactional fairness information to be more revealing of their longer-term psychological outcomes (that is, the extent to which they will be treated as valued organizational members) than is procedural fairness information.

The outcome variable in the vast majority of studies previously reviewed (Brockner & Wiesenfeld, 1996) tended to be extrinsic. How do we understand, then, that both procedural and interactional fairness interacted with this form of outcome favorability across the various studies included in the prior review, whereas Kickul et al. (2002) found more fine-grained sets of interaction effects? When people have interactional fairness information, they may or may not have procedural fairness information. Research inspired by fairness heuristic theory (Lind, 2001) has shown that when people lack one form of fairness information they use the information that they do have to "fill in the blanks" (e.g., Van den Bos, 1999; Van den Bos, Lind, Vermunt, & Wilke, 1997).

Hence, if they did not have procedural fairness information, they may have used interactional fairness as a basis for judging procedural fairness, which in turn may have interacted with extrinsic outcome favorability to influence their beliefs and behaviors.

Alternatively, people often do have information about both interactional and procedural fairness. Moreover, the two tend to be substantially related to one another; for example, the correlation was .67 in the Kickul et al. (2002) study. In previous studies showing a significant interactive relationship between extrinsic outcome favorability and interactional fairness (when procedural fairness information also was likely to be available), researchers tended to test for interaction effects between extrinsic outcome favorability with each of procedural fairness and interactional fairness in *separate* regression equations (e.g., Brockner, 1990; Cropanzano & Konovsky, 1995). Thus, it may not have been interactional fairness per se that interacted with extrinsic outcome favorability. Rather, it may have been the procedural fairness *associated with* interactional fairness that was responsible for the interactive relationship between interactional fairness and extrinsic outcome favorability.

In the published version of the Kickul et al. (2002) article, the interaction effect between extrinsic outcome favorability and interactional fairness was entered into the regression equation *after* the authors had entered the interaction effect between extrinsic outcome favorability and procedural fairness. In other words, when both interaction effects were *simultaneously* entered into the regression equation the interaction effect between extrinsic outcome favorability and procedural fairness was significant on all dependent variables, whereas the interaction effect between extrinsic outcome favorability and interactional fairness was not significant on any of the dependent variables.

This pattern of findings is consistent with the notion that it is not interactional fairness per se but rather the procedural fairness associated with interactional fairness that may elicit the interaction effect found in previous studies (Brockner & Wiesenfeld, 1996) between interactional fairness and extrinsic outcome favorability. What we need to know to evaluate this possibility further in the Kickul et al. (2002) study is whether the interaction effect between extrinsic outcome favorability and interactional fairness would have been significant if it had been examined in a regression analysis *in the absence of* the interaction effect between extrinsic outcome favorability and procedural fairness. If the interaction effect between extrinsic outcome favorability and interactional fairness had been found to be significant in such an analysis, it would provide additional support for the notion that interactional fairness per se does not interact with extrinsic outcome favorability, but rather interactional fairness, through its association with procedural fairness, interacts with outcome favorability to influence people's support for decisions, decision makers, and organizations.

Target Similarity Effects

The Kickul et al. (2002) findings suggest that there is something about the relationship between outcome favorability and process fairness that makes certain types of outcome favorability more versus less likely to interact with certain types of process fairness to influence employees' support for decisions, decision makers, and institutions. Next, I consider the possibility that the magnitude of the interactive relationship between outcome favorability and process fairness also may depend on the similarity between the targets of people's judgments of process fairness and outcome favorability (that is, the independent variables) and the targets of their work attitudes and behaviors (that is, the dependent variables).

An intriguing problem that has long plagued social psychologists is that people's attitudes often have been found to be weakly or not at all predictive of behaviors, even when the two constructs appear to be conceptually related to one another (Wicker, 1969). In response to this disappointing empirical yield, attitude researchers have posited that the strength of the relationship between attitudes and behaviors depends on the extent to which the two constructs are similar in their scope. In many of the studies that yielded little or no relationship between attitudes and behaviors, the two constructs had different scopes; researchers tried to predict *specific* behaviors on the basis of *general* attitudes. Subsequent studies showed that general attitudes do much better in predicting how people behave across times and situations relevant to the attitude object rather than by measuring their behavior at a given time and place. For example, Weigel and Newman (1976) measured people's general attitudes toward protecting the environment and measured their attitude-related behaviors on 12 different occasions. Whereas the average correlation between the general attitude and each of the 12 different behavioral measures was a mere .29, the correlation between the general attitude and an index based on a composite of the 12 behaviors was a considerably more robust .62.

Just as general attitudes predict general behaviors, specific attitudes predict specific behaviors (Weigel, Vernon, & Tognacci, 1974). One basis of specificity is the target toward which the attitude and behavior are directed. People's attitudes toward a specific target (e.g., the Sierra Club) are more likely than are their general attitudes (e.g., concern for the environment) to be related to their behaviors directed toward the target (e.g., willingness to donate to the Sierra Club). Furthermore, their attitudes toward the specific target are more predictive of their behaviors toward the target than they are of behaviors toward more general targets in that same attitudinal category (e.g., willingness to donate to the many different groups concerned with protecting the environment). In sum, attitude research has provided evidence of a "target similarity effect," in which attitudes are stronger predictors of behaviors when the two refer to the same target than when they refer to different targets.

There is growing evidence across different literatures in organizational behavior (organizational justice, trust, identification, commitment, and organizational citizenship behavior) that employees maintain meaningfully distinct beliefs about multiple targets in the workplace, such as the organization as a whole, their supervisor, and fellow workgroup members. One way in which employees' "multifoci" perspective manifests itself is via target similarity effects among the aforementioned constructs (Lavelle, Rupp, & Brockner, 2007). For example, Aryee, Budhwar, and Chen (2002) found that the organization's procedural justice was related to trust in the organization (but was not related to trust in the supervisor), whereas the supervisor's interactional justice bore more of a relationship with employees' trust in the supervisor than with their trust in the organization. Moreover, a meta-analytic review found employees' beliefs about the organization's procedural fairness to be more strongly related to the citizenship behaviors that they direct toward the organization than to the citizenship behaviors that they direct toward their supervisors (Cohen-Charash & Spector, 2001).

It is worth noting that previous demonstrations of target similarity effects involving process fairness consisted of "main effects." I am not aware of any studies that have tested for a target similarity effect in the context of an interactive relationship between process fairness and outcome favorability; hence, future research needs to evaluate this possibility. However, in light of the considerable main effect evidence of target similarity, it stands to reason that it would manifest itself in the form of an interaction effect as well. That is, we already know that unfavorable outcomes heighten the positive relationship between process fairness and people's willingness to support decision makers and organizations relative to when outcomes are favorable. The target similarity effect would predict, for example, that particularly in the face of unfavorable outcomes, process fairness perceived to emanate from the organization (i.e., its policies, rules, and norms) would be strongly predictive of attitudes and behaviors (commitment, citizenship behavior) directed toward the organization, whereas process fairness emanating from the supervisor would be strongly related to those same attitudes and behaviors directed toward the supervisor.

Thus far, research inspired by the multifoci perspective has examined the relationship between process fairness and various dependent variables (e.g., commitment and citizenship behavior), finding that relationships are stronger when the targets are matched (or similar) than when they are not matched. Just as people maintain meaningfully distinct beliefs about the process fairness shown by different entities, they also may do so for judgments of their outcomes. For example, they may perceive the outcomes they receive from the organization to be differentially fair or favorable than the outcomes they receive from their supervisors. Accordingly, there should be stronger main effects of outcome favorability on employees' attitudes and behaviors when the source of the outcome and the target to which the attitude or behavior is directed are similar rather than different.

Furthermore, and more pertinent to the interactive relationship between process fairness and outcome favorability, the moderating effect of process fairness on the relationship between outcome favorability and employees' attitudes or behaviors should be more pronounced to the extent that the source of the process fairness and outcome favorability and the target to which the attitude or behavior is directed are the same rather than different. In other words, the interactive effect of process fairness and outcome favorability on a particular dependent variable (e.g., citizenship behavior) is expected to be more pronounced when the targets for *all three* variables are similar relative to when the targets for any two variables are similar.

In the section of this chapter on extending the interaction effect to a new category of dependent variable, I suggested that outcome favorability and process fairness have been shown to interact with each other even when they do not refer to the same event (Elovainio et al., 2007; Garonzik et al., 2000; Siegel et al., 2005). Part of what constitutes an "event" is the target who serves as the source of outcome favorability and process fairness that people experience. These findings suggest that it is not *necessary* for outcome favorability and process fairness to emanate from the same target for the two to interact with each other to influence people's reactions. For example, in the Elovainio et al. study the process and outcome variables came from distinctly different targets; process fairness was based on how people had been treated by organizational authorities, whereas outcome favorability was in reference to whether a family member had encountered a serious illness within the previous year. At first blush, the fact that Elovainio et al. found that process fairness interacted with outcome favorability (to influence employees' sickness-related absences) may appear to contradict the spirit of the target similarity effect, which posits that effects are likely to be more pronounced when the targets in the independent and the dependent variables are similar rather than different. On closer inspection, however, one finds no true contradiction. It is entirely possible for outcome favorability to interact with process fairness even when the targets of the two constructs are not similar *and* for the interactive relationship to be *stronger* when the targets in the two constructs *are* similar.

CHAPTER SUMMARY

Whereas previous studies showed that process fairness interacts with outcome favorability to influence people's support for decisions, decision makers, and institutions (Brockner & Wiesenfeld, 1996), this chapter described a number of meaningful extensions of the earlier findings. More specifically, the process–outcome interaction effect has emerged in a number of new contexts (e.g., expatriates' reactions to their overseas assignments and employees' reactions to work–life conflict), on an important new dependent variable (psychological strain), and even when outcome favorability and process fairness do not refer to the same event. Taken together, these findings suggest that the interactive relationship is even more robust or generalizable than was suggested by the previous review.

The results of studies featuring psychological strain as the dependent variable also help to forge connections between the process–outcome interaction and (1) Lazarus and Folkman's (1984) influential appraisal theory of stress and (2) theory and research on the qualitative nature of people's emotional experience (e.g., Weiss & Cropanzano, 1996). Outcome favorability and process fairness interact to influence the magnitude of people's emotional experiences, such that they are most likely to experience negative emotion when they receive an unfavorable outcome that is accompanied by an unfair process (Tepper, 2001). Furthermore, outcome favorability and process fairness interact to influence the nature of people's emotional experience, such that they are likely to have qualitatively different emotional experiences in each of the various conditions created by a factorial crossing of the two constructs.

Whereas the beginning sections of the chapter did much to enhance the already high degree of generality of the interaction effect, the final section viewed the effect with greater granularity. More specifically considered were how certain forms of outcome favorability may be especially likely to interact with certain forms of process fairness to influence certain forms of dependent variables, depending on (1) the degree of congruence between the level of (low) outcome favorability and (high) process fairness, (2) the pairing of different types of outcome favorability (extrinsic and intrinsic) with different types of process fairness (procedural and interactional, respectively), and (3) whether the targets alluded to in the independent and dependent variables are similar or not.

CHAPTER

3

High Process Fairness Reduces the Effect of Outcome Favorability (Part B)

INTRODUCTION

In further examining the interactive relationship between process fairness and outcome favorability, this chapter addresses two closely related questions of considerable theoretical significance: (1) Why do outcome favorability and process fairness interact with each other? and (2) When is this interactive relationship more versus less likely to occur? Put differently, what factors mediate the interactive effect of outcome favorability and process fairness on people's reactions, and what factors moderate the interactive relationship between outcome favorability and process fairness? Theory and research generated subsequent to the Brockner and Wiesenfeld (1996) review have addressed both of these important questions, and it is to these matters that attention is now directed.

ACCOUNTING FOR THE INTERACTION EFFECT: PSYCHOLOGICAL MEDIATORS

In their review of research showing an interactive relationship between outcome favorability and process fairness, Brockner and Wiesenfeld

(1996) provided a synopsis of various explanations that could account for the finding that high process fairness reduces the influence of outcome favorability on people's support for decisions, decision makers, and institutions relative to when process fairness is low. Other frameworks, most notably fairness theory (Folger & Cropanzano, 1998, 2001), also have attempted to account for the interaction effect. Fortunately, since 1996 we have witnessed empirical research explicitly designed to account for the interaction effect.

Two factors have been shown to play a mediating role: (1) people's trust in the decision-making authority and (2) the extent to which people see the decision-making authority as responsible for their outcomes, particularly their unfavorable outcomes. Before describing the relevant research, I should mention that the nature of the mediating role of these two factors is somewhat different. In the case of trust, the findings to be presented suggest that process fairness influences trust in the decision-making authority, which in turn interacts with outcome favorability to influence people's support for decisions, decision makers, and institutions. In the case of how much people perceive the decision-making authority as responsible for their outcomes, the findings to be presented suggest that process fairness interacts with outcome favorability to influence the extent to which people see the authority as responsible for their outcomes, such that the inverse relationship between process fairness and how much people see the other as responsible for their outcomes is stronger when outcomes are relatively unfavorable. The extent to which people see the other as responsible for their outcomes in turn determines their willingness to support the decision, the decision maker, and the organization as a whole. For a graphical representation designed to help clarify the subtle distinction between these two mediating pathways, see Figure 3.1.

Trust

One explanation of the interactive relationship between process fairness and outcome favorability is based on the notion that people use process fairness information to make inferences about how much to trust the other party; the greater the process fairness, the higher the trust is (Konovsky & Pugh, 1994; Van den Bos, Wilke, & Lind, 1998). The

(A): (Process Fairness → Trust) × Outcome Favorability → Support for Decisions, Decision Makers, and Organizations

(B): (Process Fairness × Outcome Favorability) → Attributions of Responsibility → Support for Decisions, Decision Makers, and Organizations

Figure 3.1 The mediating role played by (A): Trust in the decision-making authority, and (B) Attributions of responsibility to the decision-making authority, in the interactive relationship between process fairness and outcome favorability.

link between process fairness and trust thus lends itself to an instance of "mediated moderation" (Muller, Judd, & Yzerbyt, 2005); that is, the reason why process fairness has a moderating influence on outcome favorability is because process fairness influences trust in decision-making authorities. The greater the trust (much like the greater the process fairness), the less likely is outcome favorability to influence people's support for decisions, decision makers, and organizations.

Whereas it seems reasonably straightforward that process fairness is positively related to people's trust in decision-making authorities, it still needs to be explained why trust interacts with outcome favorability. The interactive relationship between trust and outcome favorability may come about for at least two reasons. The first is based on the assumption that people seek to maximize their tangible or economic outcomes in both the short and the long term. Given that people cannot always get what they want, they learn to make trade-offs between their short-term and long-term outcomes. In particular, they are more willing to take a hit in the short term when they believe that they will receive their share of favorable outcomes in the long term. In other words, short-term outcome favorability is likely to be less consequential when people are more rather than less reassured about the favorability of their outcomes in the longer term.

People use process fairness information to make inferences about how much to trust a decision-making authority and the institution that the authority represents. In so doing, they develop beliefs about what their outcomes are likely to be over the longer haul. Processes deemed to be fair provide greater reassurance about future outcomes than do processes believed to be unfair. For example, the more employees believe that their manager will seriously consider their input into decisions, the more likely they are to believe that they will be able to influence the outcomes of future decisions, even if their input had no impact on a current decision. Or, the more that people believe that decisions are correctable (that is, give people the right to appeal), the more optimistic they may be about their longer-term outcomes. In contrast, low process fairness (and the low trust that it elicits) is much less reassuring to people about the favorability of their longer-term outcomes. This reasoning suggests that people may assign less importance to, and hence be less affected by, the favorability of their current tangible outcomes when trust in the decision-making authority is high rather than low.

The second reason that trust may interact with outcome favorability is based on the notion that people may assign importance to different kinds of outcomes in their social encounters entailing high versus low levels of trust. In high-trust encounters, people not only care about economic or tangible outcomes but also assign importance to more psychological concerns such as feeling respected by the other party, feeling included by others, and feeling connected with others, to name a few. In less-trusting exchanges, however, people may assign relatively greater importance to the economic or tangible outcomes and relatively less importance to the more psychological concerns (Clark & Mills, 1993; Rousseau & McLean Parks, 1993). Lind (2001) offered a similar line of reasoning, in which he suggested that an elicitor of trust, high process fairness, "leads to a shift from responding to a social situation in terms of immediate self-interest ... to responding to social situations as a member of the larger social entity." In the latter case, "there is far less concern with ... the individual material payoffs associated with any given behavior" (p. 67). Hence, people should be less affected by the favorability of their current tangible outcomes when trust is relatively high.

In summary, process fairness influences people's trust in a decision-making authority, and trust is expected to interact with outcome favorability to influence people's support for decisions, decision makers, and organizations. These hypotheses were tested in three different organizational contexts (Brockner, Siegel, Daly, Tyler, & Martin, 1997). In one study, the dependent variable consisted of employees' support for their supervisors; in a second study, the dependent variable was employees' organizational commitment following a companywide relocation; in a third study, the dependent variable was the organizational commitment of the employees who remained ("survivors") subsequent to an organizational downsizing. Independent variables included people's perceptions of process fairness and outcome favorability, along with measures of trust in organizational authorities.

The results of all three studies were highly consistent with one another, in spite of their many contextual and operational differences. Replicating previous findings, Brockner et al. (1997) found that process fairness and trust were positively related to one another, and that process fairness interacted with outcome favorability, showing that the positive relationship between outcome favorability and people's willingness to support decisions, decision makers, and organizations was significantly less pronounced when process fairness was high rather than low. Extending previous findings, we also found an interaction effect between outcome favorability and trust, showing that the positive relationship between outcome favorability and support was significantly less pronounced when trust was high rather than low. We also conducted a mediation analysis, in which the interaction effects between (1) outcome favorability and process fairness and (2) outcome favorability and trust were entered simultaneously into the regression equation. Whereas both of these interaction effects were significant when entered into separate regression equations, a different result emerged when they were entered simultaneously: In all three studies, the interaction between outcome favorability and trust remained significant, whereas the interaction between outcome favorability and process fairness no longer even approached significance. These findings suggest that the effect of process fairness was mediated by trust; it was not process fairness per se but rather the degree of trust elicited by process fairness that interacted with outcome favorability to influence employees' support for decision makers and their institutions.

Given the conceptual significance of the interactive relationship between trust and outcome favorability, it also may be useful to evaluate the conditions under which the trust–outcome favorability interaction may be more or less likely to occur. For example, suppose that the effect were attributable, at least in part, to the tendency for high trust in the decision-making authority to reassure people about the favorability of their longer-term outcomes, thereby reducing the effect of the favorability of their current outcomes. Note that "reassuring people about the favorability of their longer-term outcomes" may mean two somewhat different things. On the one hand, it could refer to the possibility that people expect their longer-term outcomes to be *good*, that is, to approach positivity. Alternatively, it could mean that they expect their longer-term outcomes to be *not bad*, that is, to avoid negativity.

One way to distinguish between these two possibilities is by examining whether people's regulatory focus orientation (Higgins, 1998) has a moderating influence on the interactive relationship between trust and outcome favorability. According to regulatory focus theory, people engage in self-regulation (the process of trying to bring themselves into alignment with relevant goals and standards) in two different ways: promotion focused or prevention focused. One important difference between being promotion focused or prevention focused is the type of outcome to which people assign significance. When promotion focused, people assign greater psychological significance to favorable outcomes. Hence, relative to those with more of a prevention focus orientation, those who are more promotion focused are more affected positively by perceived gains. When prevention focused, people assign greater psychological significance to unfavorable outcomes. Thus, relative to those with more of a promotion focus orientation, those who are more prevention focused are more affected negatively by perceived losses (e.g., Idson, Liberman, & Higgins, 2000). Prior research has shown that people's regulatory focus orientation may be affected by both situational and dispositional factors (Higgins, 1998). Moreover, promotion and prevention reflect two distinct self-regulatory dimensions rather than lying at opposite ends of a single continuum.

If feeling reassured about the favorability of longer-term outcomes means that people believe that their longer-term outcomes will be good, then the interaction effect between trust and outcome favorability should be shown to a greater extent by those with more of a promotion focus, who assign greater importance to approaching positivity. On the other hand, if it means that people believe that their longer-term outcomes will be not bad, then the interaction effect should be stronger among those with more of a prevention focus, who assign more importance to avoiding negativity. Emily Bianchi and I conducted a study that evaluated these possibilities. Participants were asked to imagine that they had applied for a coveted job in a well-known organization. The manager making the decision was described by highly credible sources as very trustworthy or as not at all trustworthy. Moreover, half of the participants were told that they were going to be hired (favorable outcome), whereas the other half were told that they would not be hired (unfavorable outcome). Participants also completed a survey measuring their dispositional tendencies to be promotion focused and prevention focused (Higgins et al., 2001). The dependent variable consisted of how much participants felt attracted to the organization.

As might be expected, participants reported being much more attracted to the organization when the manager making the decision was trustworthy rather than untrustworthy and when they were offered the job than when they were not. Of greatest importance, there was also a significant three-way interaction among prevention focus, outcome favorability, and trust, such that the tendency for high trust to reduce the positive relationship between outcome favorability and attraction to the organization was exhibited to a greater extent by those with more rather than with less of a prevention focus orientation. Furthermore, there was a significant three-way interaction among promotion focus, outcome favorability, and trust. In this instance, however, the tendency for high trust to reduce the effect of outcome favorability on participants' attraction to the organization was stronger among those who had *less rather than more* of a promotion focus orientation.

These findings suggest that when people cognitively represent their longer-term outcomes on the basis of how much they trust the decision-making authority, they are likely to be thinking about the extent to which their longer-term outcomes will be "not bad" rather than "good." The interactive relationship between process fairness and outcome favorability and the interactive relationship between trust and outcome favorability are based on the premise that it is particularly in response to *unfavorable* outcomes that people engage in sense-making activity, which includes trying to make inferences about the favorability of their outcomes over time. To address this concern about their longer-term outcomes, people attend to and are therefore likely to be influenced by process fairness or other trust-related information. If people are in fact more strongly prompted to engage in sense-making in response to unfavorable outcomes, then it stands to reason that the nature of their sense-making concern is to determine whether they will be able to avoid a recurrence of their current outcomes. That is, what may be on their minds is to determine the extent to which their longer-term outcomes will be not bad, more so than to determine the extent to which their longer-term outcomes will be good. The finding that higher prevention focus (but not higher promotion focus) heightens the interactive relationship between trust and outcome favorability lends further support to this reasoning.

Future Research Opportunities

Whereas the Brockner et al. (1997) findings suggest that it was the trust associated with process fairness (rather than process fairness per se) that had a moderating influence on outcome favorability, we need to learn more about the mechanisms through which process-fairness-elicited trust interacts with outcome favorability to influence people's support for decisions, decision makers, and institutions. Previously, I suggested that higher levels of trust (1) allow people to feel more reassured about their future outcomes and (2) induce people to assign greater significance to more psychological concerns or to assign less significance to economic outcomes. Either or both of these mechanisms could have reduced the effect of outcome favorability on people's support relative to when trust is low. However, none of the studies evaluated whether trust was indeed related to either or both of these mechanisms. Future research needs to do so and, relatedly, to evaluate the relative importance of these two mechanisms in accounting for the interaction effect between trust and outcome favorability.

Evaluating the relative importance of these two mechanisms may not only shed light on the process(es) through which trust had a moderating influence on outcome favorability, but also may speak to broader theoretical concerns in the justice literature. That is, the mechanisms relate to two explanations that have gained traction in the justice literature of why people prefer greater process fairness. One is known as the *instrumental explanation* (Thibaut & Walker, 1975), which posits that people prefer fair decision-making processes because they believe that they are more likely to receive the material or tangible outcomes that they desire when process fairness is high rather than low. The other is known as the *relational explanation* (Lind & Tyler, 1988), which asserts that people prefer high process fairness because it communicates that they are held in high regard by the other party, which in turn enhances their senses of esteem, identity, and belongingness.

If the moderating influence of trust on outcome favorability were due to the tendency for trust to affect their beliefs about their longer-term outcomes, it may support the instrumental explanation. That is, high trust would make people more optimistic about their longer-term outcomes, thereby reducing the importance (and hence impact) of their current outcomes. On the other hand, if the moderating influence of trust on outcome favorability were due to the tendency for trust to influence the extent to which people assign significance to psychological rather than to tangible outcomes, it may support the relational explanation. That is, higher trust would lead people to assign greater importance to psychological concerns, thereby reducing the importance (and hence impact) of the more tangible outcomes. Note that these two possibilities are not mutually exclusive. Lind and Tyler (1988) suggested that process fairness effects are pervasive and robust precisely because they are multiply determined. Nevertheless, it is of considerable theoretical significance to delineate why the trust (elicited by process fairness) interacts with outcome favorability to influence people's support for decisions, decision makers, and organizations.

The conceptual distinction between cognition-based trust and affect-based trust also may provide insight into how and why trust helps to account for the interactive relationship between process fairness and outcome favorability. According to McAllister (1995), cognition-based trust is grounded in people's beliefs about the other party's reliability and dependability, whereas affect-based trust is "grounded in reciprocated interpersonal care and concern" (p. 25), reflecting the emotional bonds between people. In further elaborating the distinction between the two, McAllister suggested that "external factors making the behavior of relationship partners predictable provide foundations for cognition-based trust, [whereas] insights into the motives of relationship partners provide foundations for affect-based trust" (p. 30).

In prior research showing that it was the trust associated with process fairness that interacted with outcome favorability (Brockner et al., 1997), participants were merely asked to indicate the extent to which they "trusted" the other. The extent to which such trust was cognition based or affect based was not examined. Future research that teases these two forms of trust apart may shed additional light on the interactive relationship between process fairness and outcome favorability. Cognition-based trust may be more related (than affect-based trust) to the instrumental explanation of the interactive relationship, whereas affect-based trust may be more closely linked (than cognition-based trust) to the relational basis of the interactive relationship. More specifically, people may use process fairness information to make inferences about the other's reliability and dependability. To the extent that the other uses fair procedures and hence is seen as reliable and dependable, people may be less concerned with and hence less affected by the favorability of their current outcomes; the other's reliability and dependability reassure them about the favorability of their longer-term outcomes.

People also may use process fairness information to make inferences about the other party's motives and, relatedly, how much they are cared for by the other party. To the extent that the other shows high process fairness, and hence is seen as having favorable intentions and truly caring about them, people may assign more importance to the psychological aspects and less importance to the economic aspects of their exchange. After all, the fact that the other is so benevolently oriented toward them suggests that the exchange is not simply about the money. As a result, people may be less affected by the favorability of their current, tangible outcomes. In sum, delineating the relative effects of cognition-based trust and affect-based trust in interacting with outcome favorability may help to elucidate the nature of the mechanism governing the interactive relationship between process fairness and outcome favorability.

Yet another possibility that may be examined in future research is that certain aspects of process fairness influence cognition-based trust, which in turn interacts with outcome favorability, whereas other aspects of process fairness influence affect-based trust, which in turn interacts with outcome favorability. Cognition-based trust may be more affected by the structural aspects of the decision process, such as whether decisions are made consistently, on the basis of accurate information, with opportunities for correction, and so on (Leventhal et al., 1980). This speculation is consistent with McAllister's (1995) suggestion that cognition-based trust is based on external factors (e.g., the structure of decision-making procedures) that make the other party's behavior predictable. Affect-based trust may be more influenced by interactional justice (Bies, 1987), that is, the interpersonal behavior of the parties who plan and implement the decision, such as whether they express caring and concern for those affected by the decision or otherwise treat them with dignity and respect. This reasoning raises the intriguing possibility that phenotypically similar interactive relationships between process fairness and outcome favorability (and, by extension, between trust and outcome favorability) may be driven by genotypically different processes, depending on the aspects of process fairness on which people are focusing their attention.

Attributions of Responsibility

In his earlier theory of referent cognitions, Folger (1986) suggested that how people react to their outcomes depends on counterfactual thinking, that is, their beliefs about how things might have turned out and how the outcomes generated by those beliefs compare with their current outcomes. According to this viewpoint, unfavorable outcomes by themselves need not elicit negative reactions toward the other party, such as feelings of anger and resentment. Rather, it is when people believe that their unfavorable outcomes did not have to be this way, that is, when their outcomes are lower than the referent generated by counterfactual thinking, they are likely to respond with feelings of anger and resentment toward the other.

According to referent cognitions theory, the role of process fairness information is to influence people's judgments of or reactions to their outcomes, as shaped by counterfactual thinking. Thus, when the process is perceived to be unfair people are likely to believe that they could have or should have received a more favorable outcome (i.e., if only a fair process had been used). In contrast, when the process is fair people are far less likely to engage in counterfactual thinking in which they imagine that they could have or should have received more favorable outcomes. With a fair process, they may be more likely to believe that their unfavorable outcomes were inevitable (they could not have turned out differently) and legitimate (they should not have turned out differently). Thus, referent cognitions theory provided one explanation of the interactive effect of outcome favorability and process fairness on feelings of anger and resentment, in which people felt most angry and resentful when they received an unfavorable outcome as a result of an unfair process relative to all other combinations of conditions (Cropanzano & Folger, 1989).

Folger updated referent cognitions theory (Folger, 1993), which then developed into the fairness theory set forth by Folger and Cropanzano

(1998, 2001). Whereas fairness theory continues to place heavy emphasis on the role of counterfactual thinking, unlike referent cognitions theory it assigns pivotal importance to the extent to which people hold the other party as responsible or accountable for their outcomes, especially unfavorable outcomes. The more that people view the other as responsible for their unfavorable outcomes, the more likely they are to experience anger and resentment toward the other and the less likely they are to be supportive of (1) the other's decision that yielded the unfavorable outcomes, (2) the other, and (3) the institution in which the decision was rendered. For instance, studies have shown that people are more likely to behave aggressively toward others when they see the others' aggression toward them as intentional rather than as unintentional (Ferguson & Rule, 1983).

One determinant of how much people hold the other as responsible for their unfavorable outcomes, in turn, is process fairness. As Folger and Cropanzano (1998) suggested, "could" and "should" counterfactuals influence people's judgments of responsibility for their outcomes. Particularly when people's outcomes are unfavorable and the authority exhibits low process fairness, people are likely to conclude that the authority *could* have used a different (i.e., fairer) process, which presumably would have yielded better outcomes. Hence, the perception that the authority could have used a fair process *but did not* leads people to hold the authority responsible for their outcomes.

Fairness theory further posits that people react to unfair procedures by comparing them to the ones that authorities *should* have used, according to prevailing moral and ethical standards. Folger (2001) suggested that justice theorists have excessively assumed that people are motivated by egocentric concerns such as the favorability of their outcomes (Thibaut & Walker, 1975) or their standing in the eyes of the party enacting the process (Lind & Tyler, 1988). What also matters is whether social interactions are seen as affirming or violating fundamental principles of morality. As Cropanzano, Goldman, and Folger (2003) put it:

> When people behave with fairness or react negatively to unfairness, they can have reasons other than the pursuit of psychological control or social esteem. Justice includes treating others as they *should* or *deserve* to be treated by adhering to standards of right and wrong. In other words, justice is in part a judgment of the morality of an outcome, process, or interpersonal interaction. It is concerned with what people view as ethically appropriate, and not merely what serves their economic self-interest or group-based identity. (p. 1019; italics in original)

According to this viewpoint, all of us are obligated to behave in morally correct ways. For example, implicit in the expression, "*common* courtesy" (my emphasis) is the notion that people have a moral responsibility to adhere to the social norm of planning and implementing decisions with high process fairness. Courtesy is akin to high process fairness. Moreover, the fact that such courtesy is common suggests that it is normative. Therefore, when decision makers do not exhibit high process fairness they are likely to be violating social norms based on moral principles. And, as attribution theorists noted long ago, behavior that violates social norms tends to be attributed to something about the actor (Jones & Davis, 1965). Thus, when an organizational authority acts contrary to social norms, those adversely affected by the authority's decisions (i.e., the recipients of unfavorable outcomes) are likely to hold the authority responsible for their outcomes.

In sum, fairness theory suggests that when process fairness is low (i.e., lower than it could have been and should have been), people are more likely to see the authority as responsible for their unfavorable outcomes, which in turn will lead them to react more negatively to decisions, decision makers, and institutions. As Folger and Cropanzano (1998) put it:

> Holding someone else accountable for injustice, and directing responses toward the accountable party, emerges as an overall integrative theme across various models of justice. Thus, we propose that certain basic processes involving accountability are central for understanding the way individuals react to injustice. (p. 174)

My colleagues and I tested the fairness theory proposition that people will be more likely to hold the other party as responsible for their unfavorable outcomes and, as a result, react more negatively toward the other when the other delivers unfavorable outcomes with low process fairness (Brockner et al., 2007). We expected process fairness and outcome favorability to interact to influence how much people judged the other party to be responsible for their outcomes, which in turn was expected to influence their willingness to support the other party's decisions, the other party, or the institution in which the other party made the decision. In other words, attributions of responsibility to the other party were hypothesized to mediate the interactive effect of outcome favorability and process fairness on the various forms of support.

Before the studies are described, it may be useful to articulate why the hypothesized inverse relationship between a decision maker's process fairness and the extent to which people see that party as responsible for their outcomes is moderated by outcome favorability (i.e., why the fairness–responsibility relationship is stronger when outcomes are relatively unfavorable). Folger and Cropanzano (1998) suggested that fairness theory "focuses on accountability for events with negative impact on material or psychological well-being. The theory could also be extended to positive events [favorable outcomes] ... but we have chosen to focus on negative events [unfavorable outcomes] in order to keep the presentation more concise" (p. 173). In addition to possible concerns with keeping the presentation concise, there are at least two conceptual bases to suggest that the inverse relationship between process fairness and people's judgments of an authority's responsibility for their outcomes will be stronger when outcomes are relatively unfavorable.

First, people generally are more likely to initiate a process of sense-making, in which they seek to understand the meaning of their outcomes by assigning causality for them, in response to outcomes that are unfavorable rather than favorable (Lazarus & Folkman, 1984; Pyszcznski & Greenberg, 1981; Shaver, 1985; Walster, 1966; Wong & Weiner, 1981). In other words, the causal attribution process that draws people's attention to process fairness information is more strongly instantiated when outcomes are relatively unfavorable.

Second, self-serving attributional tendencies may play a role. People want to feel good about themselves. They may protect their self-esteem by making external or other attributions for unfavorable outcomes, and they may enhance their self-esteem by making internal or self-attributions for favorable outcomes (Weary Bradley, 1978; Zuckerman, 1979). Whereas attributing unfavorable outcomes to the other is protective of self-esteem, attributing favorable outcomes to the other may reduce people's opportunity for self-enhancement. After all, the more that the other is seen as responsible for favorable outcomes, the less likely they may be to give themselves credit for the outcome. Thus, people are more eager to make external or other-directed attributions of responsibility for their unfavorable outcomes.

In their first study, Brockner et al. (2007) had participants take part in a vignette-based experiment in which they were asked to imagine how they would react to their performance appraisal meeting with their supervisor in which they learned about their pay raise for the upcoming year. Outcome favorability and process fairness were experimentally manipulated. The outcome favorability variable consisted of three levels. In the favorable outcome condition, participants were told that their pay raise "can only be considered to be a great raise." In the moderate outcome condition, they were told that their pay raise "can best be considered to be neither a great raise nor a lousy one." In the unfavorable outcome condition participants were told that their "raise can only be considered to be lousy."

Regarding the process fairness manipulation (Brockner et al., 2007), one group was led to believe that their supervisor exhibited high fairness, making pay raise decisions consistently and on the basis of accurate information. Another group was informed that the procedures used to arrive at their pay raise decision were considerably less fair along the consistency and accuracy dimensions. All participants were then asked to indicate the extent to which they held their supervisor responsible for the size of their pay raise. An interaction between outcome favorability and process fairness emerged. As can be seen in Table 3.1, it was only in the unfavorable outcome condition that process fairness was inversely related to how much participants judged the supervisor as responsible for the size of their pay raise. Process fairness and attributions of responsibility were unrelated in the moderate outcome favorability condition,

TABLE 3.1 Mean Ratings of Supervisor Responsibility as a Function of Process Fairness and Outcome Favorability

	Outcome Favorability		
Process Fairness	Unfavorable	Moderate	Favorable
High	4.27 (0.40)	4.19 (0.41)	5.47 (0.43)
Low	5.64 (0.43)	4.89 (0.41)	3.93 (0.38)

Note: Participants' sex was a covariate. Standard errors are in parentheses. Scores could range from 1 to 7, with higher scores reflecting stronger attributions of responsibility to the supervisor.

and somewhat unexpectedly, the two were positively related to each other in the favorable outcome condition.

A second study was designed to extend these promising results in two important respects (Brockner et al., 2007). First, it is appropriate to question the generalizability of the findings of this vignette-based experiment, in which participants were asked to respond to a hypothetical situation. Would similar results emerge if we measured how much people judged the decision-making authority to be responsible for the outcomes of an event that they actually experienced? Second, it is important to evaluate whether attributions of responsibility influence people's willingness to support decisions, decision makers, or institutions and in particular whether the interactive effect of outcome favorability and process fairness on people's support is mediated by their attributions of responsibility to the decision-making authority.

Accordingly, Brockner et al. (2007) conducted a field survey in which employees of a financial services organization were asked about their reactions to their firm having been acquired by another organization approximately 8 months earlier. The survey included measures of outcome favorability (i.e., employees' perceptions of whether their compensation and overall career prospects had become better, worse, or remained the same relative to before the acquisition) and the fairness of the procedures used by organizational authorities to implement the acquisition (e.g., "I have been able to express my views to management about the implementation of this acquisition"). As in the vignette study, participants judged the extent to which they saw their managers as responsible for their outcomes, and they completed a measure of organizational commitment.

Again, outcome favorability and process fairness interacted to influence how much participants held their managers responsible for their outcomes. As can be seen in Figure 3.2, there was an inverse relationship

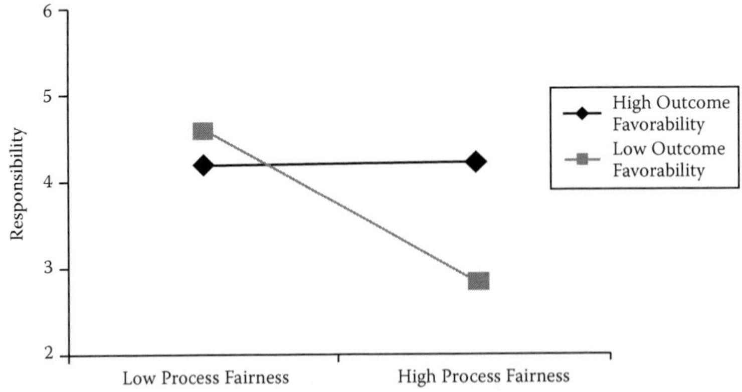

Figure 3.2 The interactive effect of process fairness and outcome favorability on how much participants judged management to be responsible for their outcomes (Brockner et al., 2007, Study 2).

between employees' perceptions of process fairness and judgments of their managers' responsibility for their outcomes when their outcomes were relatively unfavorable, and that process fairness and judgments of responsibility were unrelated when their outcomes were relatively favorable.

An interaction effect also emerged on the measure of participants' organizational commitment. Consistent with the well-replicated pattern established in many previous studies (Brockner & Wiesenfeld, 1996), high process fairness reduced the (positive) relationship between outcome favorability and organizational commitment, relative to when process fairness was low, as illustrated in Figure 3.3.

Furthermore, we conducted several analyses to evaluate whether the interactive relationship between process fairness and outcome favorability on organizational commitment was mediated by how much participants judged the organizational authorities as responsible for their outcomes.

Previously, I reported that process fairness interacted with outcome favorability to influence both the hypothesized mediator (attributions of responsibility in Figure 3.2), and the dependent variable (organizational commitment in Figure 3.3). Furthermore, the hypothesized mediator, attributions of responsibility, was significantly (and inversely) related to the dependent variable, $p < .01$. We then reanalyzed organizational commitment in a regression analysis, in which the hypothesized mediator was included as an additional predictor. Consistent with the notion that attributions of responsibility mediated the interactive effect of process fairness and outcome favorability on organizational commitment, the effect of the hypothesized mediator, attributions of responsibility, remained significant ($p < .01$), but the interaction between process fairness and outcome favorability was no longer significant ($p > .20$).

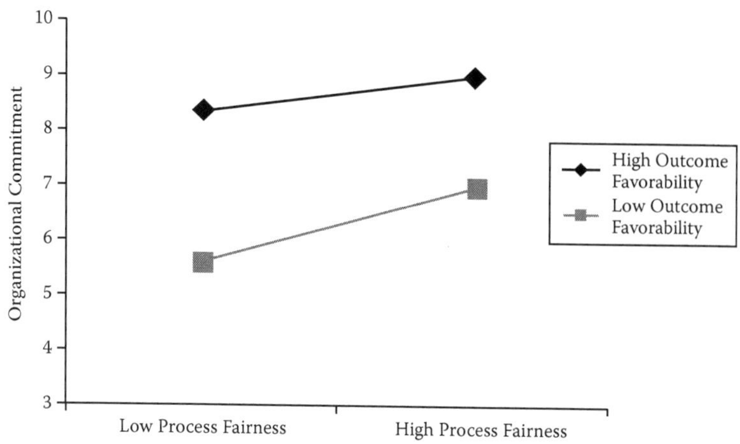

Figure 3.3 The interactive effect of process fairness and outcome favorability on organizational commitment (Brockner et al., 2007, Study 2).

Another way to conceptualize the mediating effect described (and the guiding logic of fairness theory) is that it is particularly when outcomes are unfavorable that how much people see the other party as responsible for their outcomes will mediate the relationship between process fairness and organizational commitment. Accordingly, Brockner et al. (2007) selected those participants in the upper and lower quartiles of outcome favorability. For each group, they evaluated whether attributions of responsibility mediated the relationship between process fairness and organizational commitment. In fact, there was evidence that attributions of responsibility fully mediated the relationship between process fairness and organizational commitment among the low outcome favorability group. However, there was not even a hint of a mediating effect of attributions of responsibility among those in the high outcome favorability group. According to Muller et al. (2005), this is an instance of "moderated mediation." The extent to which attributions of responsibility played a mediating role depended on outcome favorability, such that attributions of responsibility played more of a mediating role when people's outcomes were more unfavorable.

Brockner et al. (2007) reported a third study in which they evaluated the mediating role played by attributions of responsibility to organizational authorities in an entirely different field setting. Participants who had lost their jobs (on account of being laid off, fired, forced to resign, or indefinitely suspended) completed a survey while waiting in line at an unemployment office. Whereas job loss generally entails unfavorable outcomes, the participants in this study were feeling particularly aggrieved in that all of them were thinking of filing a claim against their former employers for wrongful termination. All of them indicated that they had gone through "standard procedures" in the organization for dealing with terminations, such as "specific people to talk to or a grievance procedure of some sort." The measure of process fairness was in reference to their organization's "standard procedures" for dealing with terminations. The survey also included measures of how much they judged their former employers to be responsible for their termination, how angry they felt toward their employers at the time that they lost their job, and how committed they were to file a legal claim against their employers for wrongful termination.

Outcome favorability was not an independent variable. Rather, it was assumed (and independently verified) that participants in this setting generally experienced the outcomes associated with being terminated as unfavorable. Given that participants in this study generally experienced unfavorable outcomes, and given that the results of the previous studies showed that process fairness was especially likely to be inversely related to how much people judged the authority to be responsible for their unfavorable outcomes, which in turn influenced their subsequent reactions, Brockner et al. (2007) predicted the following: (1) process fairness should be inversely related to how much participants' judged their former employers to be responsible for their termination, (2) process fairness should be inversely related to each of participants' anger at their employers for their termination and their commitment to filing a legal claim against their employers for wrongful termination, and (3) how much participants judged their former employers to be responsible for their termination should mediate the relationship between process fairness and each of their anger at their employers and their commitment to their legal claims. The results supported all three predictions.

Taken together, the results of all three of the Brockner et al. (2007) studies showed that when people's outcomes are unfavorable, procedural fairness was inversely related to how much they judged the organizational authority to be responsible for their outcomes. Moreover, two of the studies showed that particularly when outcomes are unfavorable, attributions of responsibility to the authority mediated the relationship between process fairness and employees' subsequent reactions, such as their organizational commitment and their felt anger. In sum, consistent with fairness theory (Folger & Cropanzano, 1998, 2001), how much people judged the decision-making authority as responsible for their outcomes played a significant role in accounting for the interactive relationship between outcome favorability and process fairness.

The vignette study conducted by Brockner et al. (2007) also yielded some other noteworthy results that were not included in the published version of the article. Recall that the study was described as consisting of a 3 × 2 design, in which the outcome factor had three levels and the process fairness manipulation had two levels. In actuality, there was a fourth level of the outcome favorability variable, in which a different type of unfavorable outcome was examined. Whereas in the previously described unfavorable outcome condition participants were told that their pay raise could only be considered to be "lousy," in this additional unfavorable outcome condition participants were told the following: "Not only will you not be getting a pay raise, you actually are being asked to take a small pay cut."

Furthermore, process fairness also was varied in a different way. Previously, I mentioned that the process fairness manipulation consisted of telling half of the participants that the procedures used to determine their pay raises were fair (i.e., consistent and on the basis of accurate information), whereas the other half were informed that the procedures were unfair (i.e., inconsistent and on the basis of inaccurate information). In other words, these participants received *procedural* fairness information. For an entirely different group of participants, we varied the *interactional* fairness with which participants were told about the size of their pay raise. Those treated with greater interactional fairness were asked to imagine that during the performance review their boss treated them with dignity and respect, whereas those treated with lower interactional fairness were asked to imagine exactly the opposite. Thus, those in the high and low interactional fairness conditions were given information about the fairness of the process that *accompanied* their outcomes, but unlike those who had received procedural fairness information, they were told nothing about the fairness of the procedures used to *determine* those outcomes in the first place.

Participants who were given interactional fairness information were not given procedural fairness information. Moreover, participants who were given procedural fairness information were not given interactional fairness information. Thus, the full-blown design actually consisted of three independent variables: outcome favorability (with four levels), type of process fairness information given (procedural or interactional), and the level of process fairness (high or low).

The results on the measure of how much participants judged the authority as responsible for the size of the pay raise yielded several noteworthy findings. First, within the additional unfavorable outcome condition (in which participants were told that they would be taking a small pay cut), level of process fairness was significantly inversely related to how much participants saw their supervisor as responsible for the size of their pay raise. In fact, the means in the high and low process fairness conditions were virtually identical to those reported in the high and low process fairness conditions within the unfavorable outcome condition already reported in Table 3.1.

Second, a 4 × 2 × 2 analysis of variance continued to show a significant interaction between process fairness and outcome favorability, such that it was only in the two unfavorable outcome conditions that process fairness was inversely related to how much the authority was seen as responsible for the pay raise decision. Importantly, there was no trace of a three-way interaction. That is, the interactive pattern shown in Table 3.1 was equally pronounced regardless of whether the process fairness information referred to that which influenced participants' outcomes (procedural fairness) or that which merely accompanied their outcomes (interactional fairness). Whereas it stands to reason that people's judgments of the authority's responsibility for their outcomes may be shaped by procedural fairness information, that is, the methods used by the authority to arrive at their outcomes, it is less intuitively obvious that judgments of the authority's responsibility also may depend on interactional fairness information, that is, how the authority went about delivering the outcomes. I offer a speculation on this matter in the discussion under Implications for Fairness Heuristic Theory.

In summary, the results of additional analyses from Brockner et al.'s (2007) vignette study provided further evidence that process fairness is inversely related to how much people judge an authority to be responsible for their unfavorable outcomes. We found this to hold true for an additional type of unfavorable outcome (that is, in which participants were asked to imagine that they were taking a small pay cut, not merely incurring a lousy pay raise). The finding also held true for an additional type of process fairness information, namely, interactional fairness.

Implications for Fairness Heuristic Theory

In addition to strengthening the generality of the results of the vignette study conducted by Brockner et al. (2007), the findings that did not appear in the published version of the research have implications for fairness heuristic theory. As Van den Bos, Lind, et al. (1997) wrote, fairness heuristic theory

> assumes that, because ceding authority to another person provides an opportunity for exploitation and exclusion, people frequently feel uncertain and uneasy about their relationship with an authority. ... It is further argued that the most common approach to the resolution of this uncertainty is to refer to impressions of fairness. ... Once a person has established a fairness judgment, perceived fairness serves as a heuristic that guides the interpretation of subsequent events. (p. 1035)

The most important source of information is that which is directly relevant to the type of judgment to be made. Thus, procedural fairness information is most relevant for making judgments of procedural fairness, interactional fairness information is most relevant for making judgments of interactional fairness, and outcome information is most relevant for making judgments of distributive fairness. However, an important element of fairness heuristic theory is the notion of *substitutability*, which suggests that "crossover" effects may occur as well. So, for example, people may use procedural fairness information to make inferences about distributive fairness and vice versa (Van den Bos, Lind, et al., 1997). Moreover, substitution is most likely to occur when the most relevant form of information is lacking or ambiguous. For example, when procedural information is missing people will draw on outcome fairness information to form judgments of procedural fairness (Daly & Tripp, 1996; Van den Bos, 1999).

The principle of substitutability suggests that participants who were only told about the interactional fairness with which the authority implemented the pay raise may have used that information to make a judgment about how much to hold the authority responsible for the size of the pay raise itself. That is, it stands to reason that people may use procedural fairness information to make judgments about how much to hold the authority responsible for their outcomes. After all, procedures are determinants of outcomes. Thus, if an authority used procedures to arrive at decisions that were unfair, and if those unfair procedures caused people's unfavorable outcomes, then it is reasonable for people to judge the authority as responsible for their outcomes.

However, when people lack procedural fairness information, they may use the fairness information that they do have at their disposal (in this instance, interactional fairness) to make inferences about procedural fairness. Regardless of whether participants in the vignette study of Brockner et al. (2007) received procedural fairness information or interactional fairness information, all were asked to make ratings of both. Consistent with the notion of substitutability, the correlation between the two was a substantial .72.

It is also worth noting that previous demonstrations of substitutability have examined how people use procedural fairness information as a heuristic to make judgments of their outcome fairness or outcome satisfaction or how they may use outcome fairness information as a heuristic to make judgments of procedural fairness (Daly & Tripp, 1996; Van den Bos, 1999; Van den Bos, Lind et al., 1997). The additional results from the vignette study conducted by Brockner et al. (2007) provide the first evidence of which I am aware that people may use one type of process fairness information (in this case, interactional fairness) as a heuristic to make inferences about another type of process fairness (in this instance, procedural fairness).

Moreover, whereas fairness heuristic theory has suggested that substitutability occurs, it has not considered the possibility that certain substitutions may be more fluid or natural than others. To date, the theory has not considered the possibility that there may be asymmetries in people's tendencies to use one form of fairness information to make inferences about another. To evaluate this possibility, we conducted checks on the manipulations of both procedural and interactional fairness. To check on procedural fairness, participants rated their agreement with the following statement: "I feel that the procedures used to decide on my pay raise were fair." To check on interactional fairness, participants rated their agreement with the following statement: "When I got my pay raise, I feel that I was treated with dignity and respect." Note that these items had been deliberately worded to make it appropriate to have participants respond to both of them, regardless of whether they had been assigned to receive procedural fairness information or interactional fairness information.

Separate analyses of covariance (4 × 2 × 2) were conducted on each of the two measures. Given the aforementioned high correlation between

TABLE 3.2 Perception of Procedural Fairness as a Function of Level × Type of Process Fairness, With Interactional Fairness as a Covariate (Adjusted Means)

	Fairness Type	
	Procedural	**Interactional**
High process fairness	4.15 (0.19)	3.52 (0.19)
Low process fairness	2.64 (0.18)	3.59 (0.18)

Note: Standard errors are in parentheses.

the measures of procedural fairness and interactional fairness (r = .72), each served as a covariate in the analysis of the other. Of greatest relevance to the present discussion, both analyses yielded a significant two-way interaction between the level of process fairness and type of process fairness. The most parsimonious way to describe the interaction effect is that the type of fairness induction that was more closely linked to the item designed to measure it had more effect than did the other type of fairness induction. Thus, as can be seen in Table 3.2, perceptions of procedural fairness were significantly greater in the high procedural fairness condition than in the low procedural fairness condition, whereas perceptions of procedural fairness did not differ in the high interactional fairness condition and in the low interactional fairness condition.

Analogous (although not identical) findings emerged on the item designed to measure interactional fairness. As shown in Table 3.3, perceptions of interactional fairness were considerably greater in the high interactional fairness condition than in the low interactional fairness condition, whereas perceptions of interactional fairness did not differ nearly as much in the high procedural fairness condition and the

TABLE 3.3 Perception of Interactional Fairness as a Function of Level × Type of Process Fairness, With Procedural Fairness as a Covariate (Adjusted Means)

	Fairness Type	
	Procedural	**Interactional**
High process fairness	4.03 (0.19)	4.60 (0.17)
Low process fairness	3.40 (0.18)	2.56 (0.16)

Note: Standard errors are in parentheses.

low procedural fairness condition. It is worth noting, however, that the effect of the procedural fairness manipulation on judgments of interactional fairness was still significant according to the results of a simple effect analysis.

The results on the manipulation check measures of procedural fairness and interactional fairness identify a possible asymmetry in how people use one form of information to make inferences about the other. As can be seen in Table 3.3, the experimental manipulation of procedural fairness influenced perceptions of interactional fairness (even after we controlled for perceptions of procedural fairness); that is, the difference between the means of 4.03 and 3.40 in the high and low procedural fairness conditions, respectively, was statistically significant, $p < .02$. In contrast, and as can be seen in Table 3.2, the experimental manipulation of interactional fairness did not influence perceptions of procedural fairness (after we controlled for perceptions of interactional fairness). The simple effect comparing the means of 3.52 and 3.59 in the high and low interactional fairness conditions, respectively, was trivial.

Further research is needed to explain this possible asymmetry in people's use of procedural fairness and interactional fairness information to make inferences about the other. It could be that people view procedural fairness information as symbolic of how much they are being treated with dignity and respect, which could account for the significant effect of procedural fairness information on judgments of interactional fairness. Alternatively, it could be that interactional fairness in the present study referred to the point in time at which the pay raise decision was *implemented,* which did not necessarily lend itself to participants going back in time psychologically to ponder the procedural fairness with which the decision was *made,* thereby explaining the nonsignificant effect of interactional fairness information on judgments of procedural fairness.

Yet another possibility, more methodological than conceptual in nature, is that the manipulation of procedural fairness may have simply been stronger than the manipulation of interactional fairness. To evaluate this possibility, we examined the magnitude of the relationship between the manipulations of procedural fairness and interactional fairness and participants' perceptions of the corresponding measures. From Table 3.2, it can be seen that participants perceived procedural fairness to be much higher in the high procedural fairness condition than in the low procedural fairness condition (*Ms* = 4.15 vs. 2.64, respectively); the simple effect comparing the difference between these two means was highly significant, $F(1, 205) = 36.53$, $p < .001$. From Table 3.3, it can be seen that participants perceived interactional fairness to be much higher in the high interactional fairness condition than in the low interactional fairness condition (*Ms* = 4.60 vs. 2.56, respectively). Furthermore, the simple effect comparing the difference between these two means was even *more* pronounced, $F(1, 205) = 70.77$, $p < .001$, than was the corresponding simple effect of the procedural fairness manipulation on perceptions of procedural fairness. In short, the asymmetry in which procedural fairness information had more of an effect on interactional fairness judgments than the other way around occurred *in spite of* the fact that interactional fairness appeared to be more strongly manipulated than was procedural fairness.

Further analyses of Brockner et al.'s (2007) Study 2 (also not presented in the published version of the research) provided evidence consistent with the fairness heuristic theory proposition that when people have fairness information that is both directly and indirectly relevant to the judgment that they need to make, the former prevails over the latter. As previously indicated, the measure of process fairness that we included in the published version of the article was based on procedural fairness, that is, the methods used by organizational authorities that likely were perceived by participants to influence the favorability of their outcomes (e.g., "The procedures used to implement the acquisition have been based on accurate information"). We also asked participants in Study 2 to rate the interactional fairness with which the acquisition was handled (e.g., "In implementing this acquisition, management has treated members of this organization with dignity and respect"). We created two subscales of process fairness, dubbed "procedural fairness" and "interactional fairness," respectively.

In separate regression analyses, each of procedural fairness and interactional fairness was found to interact with outcome favorability to influence how much participants judged their supervisor to be responsible for the changes in outcomes that they experienced as a result of their company having been acquired. The interaction between procedural fairness and outcome favorability was shown in Figure 2.2; moreover, its significance level ($p < .001$) was considerably higher than that of the interaction involving interactional fairness ($p < .02$), although the form of the interaction effect was similar in both instances.

We then conducted a "uniqueness analysis," to see which of the two interactions (Procedural fairness × Outcome favorability and Interactional fairness × Outcome favorability) accounted for a significant portion of the variance in how much people saw the other party as responsible for their outcomes. The results showed that the interaction involving procedural fairness remained significant ($p < .02$), whereas the interaction involving interactional fairness became trivial.

Taken together, some hitherto unreported findings from the Brockner et al. (2007) studies lend support to fairness heuristic theory. When people do not have direct evidence on the fairness judgment that they need to make, they will latch on to whatever (indirect) fairness information they do have to make the necessary judgment. In the vignette study, participants provided with interactional fairness but not with procedural fairness information used the former to make a causal judgment: how much to hold the supervisor responsible for their outcome. However, in the field setting, in which participants presumably had information about both procedural fairness and interactional fairness, they relied much more heavily on procedural fairness information.

Future Research Opportunities

Additional empirical questions are generated by the findings that process fairness is inversely related to how much people hold others responsible for their outcomes, particularly when their outcomes are relatively unfavorable. Brockner et al. (2007) provided evidence consistent with the notion that how much people held the authority as responsible for their outcomes mediated the interactive effect of process fairness and outcome favorability on (1) people's willingness to support decisions, decision makers, and institutions and (2) their psychological strain.

First, however, how much people judge the authority as responsible for their outcomes may not be restricted to the role of "mediating variable." For example, it could be that attributions of responsibility to the other party *reflect rather than cause* the dependent variables of support or psychological strain. Perhaps blaming the other party for unfavorable outcomes when process fairness is low is a way of psychologically distancing oneself from the other party; distancing oneself, in turn, may be a manifestation of lack of support. Alternatively, attributions of responsibility to the other party may be the *result rather than the cause* of other reactions. When people experience high levels of psychological strain (e.g., anger) in response to an unfavorable outcome caused by or accompanied by low process fairness, they may seek to understand the cause of their experience of strain. One way to explain their strain experience is to see the other party as responsible for their outcomes. Thus, future research needs to disentangle the various ways in which attributions of responsibility are related to the interactive effect of outcome favorability and process fairness on measures of support and psychological strain.

Second, if attributions of responsibility to the other party play a mediating role, that is, if they account for the interactive effect of outcome favorability and process fairness on support or psychological strain, then it would be worthwhile to delineate how attributions of responsibility may be related to the other mediator discussed in this chapter, namely, trust in the other party (Brockner et al., 1997; Konovsky & Pugh, 1994). One possibility is that attributions of responsibility to the other party mediate the relationship between process fairness and trust, particularly when outcomes are unfavorable, that is, when concerns about evaluating the trustworthiness of the other are likely to be more salient. In other words, when outcomes are unfavorable low process fairness may lead people to hold the other as responsible for their outcomes, which in turn may lead to less trust in the other.

Third, throughout this section we have distinguished between elements of process fairness that cause outcomes (procedural fairness) versus those that accompany outcomes (interactional fairness). Given the potentially important consequences of how much people hold the other party as responsible for their outcomes, further research is needed to evaluate whether the two types of process fairness elements differentially affect people's tendencies to see the other as responsible for their outcomes. Subsequent analyses of the vignette study of Brockner et al. (2007) suggested that people's attributions of responsibility to their supervisor for their pay raise were an interactive function of outcome favorability and process fairness, and that the type of process fairness had no moderating effect. That is, their tendency to see the boss as more responsible when process fairness was low (and especially when outcomes were unfavorable) was equally pronounced regardless of whether the information about the boss pertained to procedural fairness (which truly had an impact on their outcome) or to interactional fairness (which merely accompanied how they were treated when receiving their outcomes).

However, there may be instances when process fairness information that directly bears on the judgment to be made (in this case, how the outcomes were arrived at) elicits different reactions than process fairness information that is less directly relevant to the judgment to be made. On the one hand, fairness heuristic theory suggests that people will use the less-direct information when direct information is lacking but reach the same conclusion nonetheless. On the other hand, there may be different consequences of the perception that is arrived at, depending on whether it was based on direct versus indirect information. Fazio and Zanna (1981) found that attitudes formed on the basis of direct experience have different consequences than attitudes formed on the basis of indirect experience. Attitudes formed on the basis of direct experience are held with greater confidence and certainty and, as a result, are more strongly correlated with future behavior relative to attitudes formed on the basis of indirect experience. Thus, even if people make the same fairness-related judgment regardless of whether it was based on direct information or indirect information, the consequences of those judgments may differ. For example, future research may examine whether outcome fairness judgments based on outcome fairness information have different consequences than when the same outcome fairness judgments were arrived at on the basis of procedural or interactional fairness information.

In summary, people's trust in a decision-making authority and the extent to which they see the authority as responsible for their outcomes play an important role in accounting for the interactive relationship between outcome favorability and process fairness, albeit in somewhat different ways. Process fairness influences perceptions of trust, which in turn interact with outcome favorability to influence people's willingness to support decisions, decision makers, and institutions (Brockner et al., 1997). Process fairness also interacts with outcome favorability to influence how much people judge an authority to be responsible for their outcomes, which in turn influences people's affective reactions toward the authority (i.e., anger) as well as their willingness to support the authority, the authority's decisions, or the institution in which the decision was rendered (Brockner et al., 2007).

MODERATORS OF THE INTERACTION EFFECT

Research on mediators is designed to delineate the mechanisms underlying the interactive relationship between outcome favorability and process fairness. Yet another way to get at the psychological underpinnings of the interaction effect is by examining its moderators, that is, by investigating *when* the effect is more versus less likely to emerge. In the opening chapter, I suggested that the form of the process–outcome interaction effect may be described in different ways depending on the theoretical lens through which the effect is viewed. For example, the interaction effect may be represented as (1) outcome favorability having a moderating influence on process fairness, (2) process fairness having a moderating influence on outcome favorability, and (3) one set of circumstances (an unfavorable outcome combined with an unfair process) eliciting particularly negative reactions relative to all others. Conceptualizing the form of the interaction effect in these different ways helps to organize the various factors that have been shown to moderate the process–outcome interaction.

Brockner and Wiesenfeld (1996) suggested that the interaction effect generally reflects people's attempts to make sense of their encounters and relationships with decision-making authorities. For both economic and psychological reasons, people want to know such things as the kinds of outcomes that they can expect to receive from the other party, the causes of the outcomes of their exchanges with the other party, how they are viewed by the other party, and so on. One analysis of such sense-making processes takes people's receipt of outcomes as its point of departure. Attribution theory suggests that one way in which people make sense of their environments is by making causal attributions for their and others' outcomes (Kelley, 1973). Research on attributional instigation (the study of when people ask why) shows that people are more likely to ask why when outcomes are relatively unfavorable (e.g., Wong & Weiner, 1981). Thus, particularly when their outcomes are relatively unfavorable, people may draw on process fairness information for the sense-making reasons as set forth here, which would explain why the level of process fairness with which they are treated is more influential relative to when their outcomes are more favorable. This conceptualization treats outcome favorability as having a moderating influence on process fairness.

An alternative analysis of sense-making takes people's perceptions of process fairness as its point of departure. Given that decision-making processes precede outcomes, people may have formed judgments about the fairness of the process before learning of their outcomes. For example, process fairness informs people about the nature of their relationship with the other party (Lind, 2001). The higher the process fairness, the more likely they may be to see their relationship with the other as more relational or communal and as less transactional or economically based (Mills & Clark, 1982; Rousseau & McLean Parks, 1993). If so, then it stands to reason that people's beliefs and behaviors toward the other party will be less influenced by the favorability of their outcomes (particularly tangible outcomes) when process fairness is relatively high. This reasoning treats process fairness as having a moderating influence on outcome favorability.

Although the content of the sense-making processes in these two instances differs somewhat, both suggest that the interactive relationship between outcome favorability and process fairness should be stronger when the sense-making processes have been more strongly instantiated. Two broad categories of factors in turn have been shown to influence the intensity with which people engage in sense-making: (1) uncertainty and (2) the importance of the outcomes at stake. The more uncertain people are, or the more important the outcomes, the more likely are people to try to make sense of things. Uncertainty reflects people's ability to make sense of what is happening; the greater the uncertainty, the less *able* are people to make sense of the situation as things currently stand, which in turn prompts them to engage in activity that will allow them to make sense of things. Outcome importance influences people's motivation or desire to engage in sense-making; the greater the outcome importance, the more people *want or need* to figure out what is happening.

This reasoning suggests that the interactive relationship between outcome favorability and process fairness should be moderated by factors that influence or reflect (1) uncertainty (greater uncertainty should magnify the interaction effect) and (2) the degree of importance that people assign to their outcomes (greater outcome importance should magnify the interaction effect). In fact, the results of a host of studies are consistent with these assertions. In some studies (described first), the moderator variables are more closely linked with uncertainty, whereas in others (described second) the moderator variables reflect outcome importance.

Yet another way to conceptualize the process–outcome interaction is that people respond particularly negatively (e.g., they should be especially unlikely to support decisions, decision makers, or institutions) when they receive an unfavorable outcome that is associated with an unfair process. Whereas people experience an unfavorable outcome accompanied by an unfair process to be quite negative in its own right (indeed, akin to "multiplying insult times injury"), this tendency may be even more pronounced when such a negative experience comes as a surprise. In other words, the contrast between what people expected and what they actually experienced may make them especially likely to respond negatively to having experienced an unfavorable outcome accompanied by an unfair process.

Hence, after discussing uncertainty and outcome importance as moderators I consider an additional category of moderators of the process–outcome interaction, which consists of factors likely to affect how much people are (unpleasantly) surprised by the receipt of an unfavorable outcome with an unfair process. For example, imagine two decision-making authorities, one people believe is trustworthy and another seen as less trustworthy. How would people respond to receiving an unfavorable outcome via an unfair process from these two authorities? Whereas they are unlikely to be pleased in either instance, they may be more negatively surprised if they expected the authority to be more rather than less trustworthy. In other words, the interaction effect in which the combination of an unfavorable outcome and unfair process elicits the most negative reactions may be even stronger when the authority was previously believed to be more trustworthy.

Uncertainty

People engage in sense-making when they perceive the situation to be uncertain (and therefore demands sense to be made of it). Thus, the interactive relationship between outcome favorability and process fairness may be more pronounced when uncertainty is higher, when people are less able to make sense of things without further analysis. Particularly in the face of unfavorable outcomes, employees may need to make sense of a variety of matters relevant to their economic and psychological well-being, such as (1) why they received the outcomes that they did; (2) the likelihood that they will be able to receive their share of desired tangible outcomes in both the short run and the long run; (3) the nature of their relationship with the other party, be it an organizational authority or the organization as a whole; (4) how much to trust the organization or its authorities; and (5) how well they are regarded by the organization or its authorities. Process fairness information addresses people's needs to make sense of these matters (again, needs that are felt more acutely in the face of unfavorable outcomes), leading them to respond more positively (e.g., with higher organizational commitment) when process fairness is relatively high.

If process fairness information is responsive to people's sense-making needs, then it stands to reason that process fairness information will be more influential when uncertainty is relatively high. Indeed, the uncertainty management model (Van den Bos & Lind, 2002) has provided compelling evidence that the fair process effect is more pronounced when uncertainty is relatively high. Moreover, various sources of uncertainty have been shown to heighten the fair process effect, including mortality salience (Van den Bos & Miedema, 2000; Van den Bos, Poortvliet, Mass, Miedema, & Van den Ham, 2005), uncertainty about the decision maker's trustworthiness (Van den Bos et al., 1998), and even instructing people to contemplate their reactions to feeling "uncertain about themselves" (Van den Bos, 2001).

Given that research derived from the uncertainty management model has consistently shown a two-way interaction between process fairness and uncertainty (such that high uncertainty magnifies the fair process effect), it also may be possible to predict a three-way interaction among process fairness, outcome favorability, and uncertainty, such that high uncertainty magnifies the process–outcome interaction. Here is how: Particularly in response to unfavorable outcomes, people strive to make sense of their standing as organizational members. In other words, unfavorable outcomes are more psychologically threatening to people, giving them more reason (than do favorable outcomes) to be concerned about their standing as organizational members. One type of information they draw on to make sense of their standing is process fairness. The more they perceive process fairness to be high, the more likely they are to infer that they are in good standing as organization members and to respond with greater support for decisions, decision-making authorities, and institutions.

From an economic point of view, higher process fairness, such as allowing those affected by a decision to have more input into a decision-making process, may lead people to be more optimistic about their chances to receive their share of desired outcomes in the future, even if their current outcomes are unfair or unfavorable. From a psychological vantage point, higher process fairness symbolically communicates to employees that they are held in higher regard relative to how they are likely to feel if they were treated with lower process fairness (De Cremer & Sedikides, 2008; Tyler & Lind, 1992; Van Prooijen, Van den Bos, & Wilke, 2002). Again, these sense-making activities that heighten people's susceptibility to influence by process fairness information are less likely to be instantiated when outcomes are relatively favorable, giving rise to the two-way interaction between process fairness and outcome favorability (Brockner & Wiesenfeld, 1996).

An important implication of the sense-making analysis underlying the two-way interaction between process fairness and outcome favorability is that people should be more likely to engage in sense-making when they are, in fact, more uncertain about their standing as organizational members. Put differently, if this sense-making analysis of the process–outcome interaction is correct, then the interaction effect should be even more pronounced when people are more uncertain about their standing. Van den Bos and Lind (in press) offered a similar prediction: "It may be that it is especially *when* [italics added] negative outcomes salientize feelings of personal uncertainty that the procedure × outcome interaction reported by Brockner and Wiesenfeld (1996)" is most likely to occur.

The word *when* in the Van den Bos and Lind (in press) quotation suggests that employees' uncertainty about their standing as organization members is expected to moderate the interactive relationship between process fairness and outcome favorability. Like Van den Bos and Lind, I believe that unfavorable outcomes may be associated with people's uncertainty about their standing to varying degrees, and that it is precisely when uncertainty is *more* associated with unfavorable outcomes that the process–outcome interaction is more likely to occur. Unlike Van den Bos and Lind, however, I do not believe it is necessary for uncertainty to be caused (or made salient) by the unfavorable outcome. Rather, my reasoning is more general; I posit that when the unfavorable outcome occurs in a context in which people are more uncertain about their standing (that is, when the unfavorable outcome is associated with higher uncertainty, even if the unfavorable outcome is not the cause of the uncertainty), the process–outcome interaction will be stronger. One factor that may induce uncertainty about standing is the receipt of an unfavorable outcome. However, high uncertainty about standing may come about for many other reasons (e.g., if people are relatively new to the organization or if their organization is about to undergo a downsizing and, as a result, they are not sure if they will be able to keep their jobs). Regardless of the basis of people's uncertainty about their standing as organizational members, however, I hypothesize that those who are more uncertain about their standing are more likely to exhibit the process–outcome interaction than are their less-uncertain counterparts.

In short, the two-way interaction between process fairness and outcome favorability may reflect employees' tendencies to make sense of their standing as organization members, which has implications for their economic or psychological well-being. If so, then the sense-making processes underlying the two-way interaction should be more strongly instantiated when employees are more uncertain about their standing as organization members. Said differently, if the two-way interaction between process fairness and outcome favorability reflects employees' tendencies to make sense of their standing as organization members, then the interaction effect should be more pronounced when employees are more uncertain about their standing.

We tested for the predicted three-way interaction effect (Process fairness × Outcome favorability × Uncertainty about standing) in no fewer than six organizational field studies, although only four of the six studies were reported in the article itself (De Cremer, Brockner et al., in press). The dependent variable consisted of various measures of employees' willingness to support their organizations (organizational commitment, customer service, and organizational citizenship behavior). Uncertainty was operationalized in a variety of ways. In several instances, we drew on demographic factors likely to be proxies for uncertainty about standing, such as employees' tenure in the organization in one study and whether they were employed on a part-time or full-time basis in another. We assumed that lower tenure would be associated with greater uncertainty, based on Kramer's (2001) observation that newcomers in organizations seek to reduce uncertainty about their status. We also assumed that employees who worked part time would be more uncertain about their standing as organizational members than would those employed on a full-time basis (Feldman, 1995).

Employees' uncertainty about their standing as organizational members was measured more directly in the other studies. For example, in

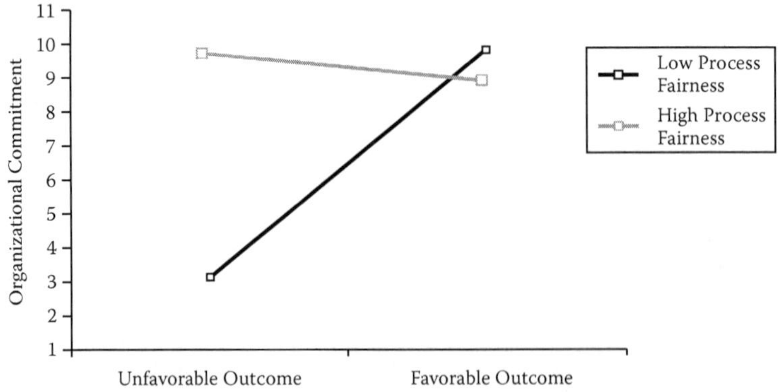

Figure 3.4 Organizational commitment as a function of process fairness and outcome favorability when uncertainty is high (De Cremer, Brockner et al., in press).

one study uncertainty was operationalized in reference to participants' judgments of their organization-based self-esteem (OBSE), which has been defined as "the degree to which organizational members believe that they can satisfy their needs by participating in roles within the context of an organization" (Pierce, Gardner, Cummings, & Dunham, 1989, p. 625). In another study, we measured uncertainty by asking employees to indicate how much they agreed with items such as, "How I feel about my position within the company changes from day to day." The self-report measure of uncertainty in yet another study was adopted from one developed by De Cremer and Sedikides (2005), for example, "I spend a lot of time wondering whether I have a positive standing in my relations with others." Finally, we even conducted a study in which the measure of uncertainty about standing was based on peers' (rather than on self-) reports.

The results of all six studies yielded a similar three-way interaction among process fairness, outcome favorability, and uncertainty. An illustrative pattern of findings from one of the six studies is shown in Figures 3.4 and 3.5. As can be seen, the typical two-way interaction between process fairness and outcome favorability (in which high process fairness reduced the positive relationship between outcome favorability and organizational commitment relative to when process fairness was low) was more pronounced among employees who were more uncertain (see Figure 3.4) than less uncertain (see Figure 3.5) about their standing as organizational members. The consistency in results across all six studies emerged even though we (1) operationalized uncertainty in rather different ways, (2) examined different dependent measures of employees' willingness to support the organization, (3) used different items to measure the independent variables of process fairness and outcome favorability, and (4) conducted the studies in different countries

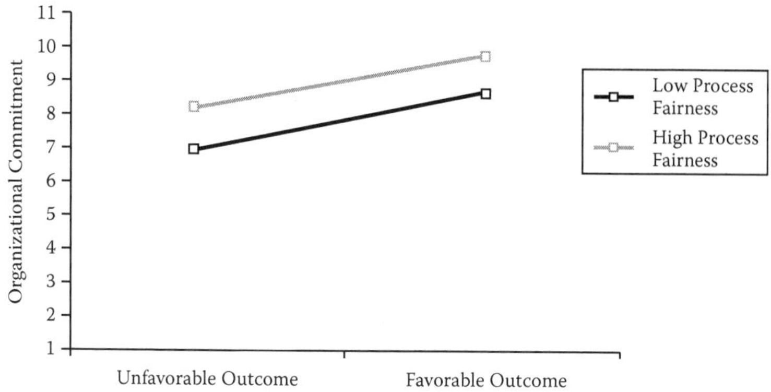

Figure 3.5 Organizational commitment as a function of process fairness and outcome favorability when uncertainty is low (De Cremer, Brockner et al., in press).

(The Netherlands, Germany, and the United States). Thus, the similarity of the findings bodes well for their generality and reliability.

Operationalizing Uncertainty

The fact that De Cremer, Brockner et al. (in press) obtained converging results across multiple studies using different operationalizations of uncertainty is reassuring about the reliability of their findings. However, one shortcoming of several of their studies is that uncertainty took the form of proxies (length of tenure; full-time vs. part-time employment status) rather than direct assessments. Moreover, the direct measure of uncertainty in one of the studies was somewhat unusual. Specifically, participants completed items from Pierce et al.'s (1989) OBSE scale (e.g., "Before the acquisition, I felt good about myself at this company"). Eleven-point rating scales were used for each item, with the endpoints labeled "Strongly agree" (1) and "Strongly disagree" (11). The exact midpoint of the scale was explicitly labeled "neither agree nor disagree" (6).

The moderating impact of participants' responses to the OBSE measure on the interactive relationship between process fairness and outcome favorability was examined in several ways. In one analysis, we took the average of participants' ratings on the various items comprising the OBSE measure, based on the notion that the *level* of people's self-evaluations will be correlated with the *certainty* of those evaluations; the lower the level is, the greater is the uncertainty (Campbell, 1990). However, De Cremer, Brockner et al. (in press) did not find the average level of OBSE to moderate the interactive relationship between process fairness and outcome favorability.

We had better luck, however, when we operationalized uncertainty in a different way. More specifically, there is some evidence that the *extremity of an attitude* (defined as the extent to which the judgment deviates from the midpoint of an evaluative dimension) is strongly related to the certainty of the attitude (Krosnick, Boninger, Chuang, Berent, & Carnot, 1993). Since the midpoint is essentially the lowest extremity rating a person can make, it is reasonable to believe that selecting the midpoint is reflective of an uncertain response. Hence, we calculated the number of OBSE items for which participants chose the exact scale midpoint (or one point on either side of the midpoint) as their answer, the logic being that the more frequently participants made their rating at or near the exact scale midpoint, the greater their uncertainty about their OBSE. Indeed, with uncertainty operationalized in this manner, we obtained a significant three-way interaction among process fairness, outcome favorability, and uncertainty (illustrated in Figures 3.4 and 3.5).

Psychometricians have long wrestled with how to interpret the meaning of people's responses that lie at or near the middle of the dimension in question (the so-called middle-of-the-scale problem). For example, do such responses mean that people have a certain but moderate belief, or that they are uncertain about their beliefs? To evaluate the possibility that choosing at or near the scale midpoint reflects a relatively uncertain response, we asked a separate group of employees whose organization was undergoing change a series of questions about their OBSE (e.g., "I am taken seriously at this company," and "I can make a difference at this company"). Responses to all questions were made along 7-point scales, with endpoints ranging from "strongly disagree" (1) to "strongly agree" (7). After each item measuring OBSE, participants were asked the following: "How certain are you of your answer to the immediately preceding question?" Responses to these questions also were provided along 7-point scales, with endpoints labeled "not certain at all" (1) and "very certain" (7). We then examined the relationship between the frequency with which participants answered at or near the scale midpoint on the various items measuring OBSE and their ratings on the certainty questions that succeeded the items measuring OBSE. As expected, those who selected at or near the scale midpoint more frequently were less certain of their judgments, $r = -.52$, $p < .01$.

Theoretical Implications

Brockner and Wiesenfeld (1996) speculated that the receipt of unfavorable outcomes is especially likely to elicit a sense-making process in which people draw on and hence are influenced by process fairness information. Whereas Brockner and Wiesenfeld implied that the interactive relationship between process fairness and outcome favorability would be stronger when uncertainty is relatively high, they never tested this hypothesis. Moreover, they did not specify the nature of the uncertainty that is likely to have a moderating effect on the interactive relationship.

Fortunately, more recent theory and research have delineated the kinds of uncertainties that process fairness information is particularly well-suited to address, which in turn are precisely the sorts of uncertainties that are likely to moderate the interactive relationship between process fairness and outcome favorability. Whereas early theorizing suggested that people use process fairness information to make inferences about future economic outcomes they may expect to receive from the other party (e.g., Thibaut & Walker, 1975), more recent evidence suggests that people also use process fairness to make a number of related but conceptually distinct social or psychological judgments, such as the nature of their relationship with the other party (e.g., Lind, 2001), the extent to which the other party can be trusted (e.g., Brockner et al., 1997), and the extent to which they are held in high regard by the other party (e.g., De Cremer & Tyler, 2005). Hence, when people are more uncertain about one or more of these matters, as reflected in the various operationalizations of uncertainty examined by De Cremer, Brockner et al. (in press), they are more likely to draw on and hence be affected by process fairness information, particularly in the face of unfavorable outcomes.

The results of the De Cremer, Brockner et al. (in press) studies also speak to the closely related question of when the interactive relationship between process fairness and outcome favorability may be *unlikely* to emerge. Whereas the process–outcome interaction has been found on many occasions, it does not always appear (Brockner & Wiesenfeld, 1996). De Cremer, Brockner et al. found a significant three-way interaction among process fairness, outcome favorability, and uncertainty in all six of their studies. However, the two-way interaction between process fairness and outcome favorability was not significant within five of the six studies, and the two-way interaction was not significant within all four of the studies that appear in their research report. To be sure, although the two-way interaction effect between process fairness and outcome favorability was not significant within the four studies reported by De Cremer, Brockner et al., the form of the process–outcome interaction effect was consistent with that found in previous research. Moreover, a meta-analysis conducted on the results of the four studies included in the research report showed that the two-way interaction between process fairness and outcome favorability was significant at the .05 level.

Nevertheless, it is still worth speculating about why the two-way interaction between process fairness and outcome favorability was rather weak, that is, not significant *within* the De Cremer, Brockner et al. (in press) studies. One possibility is that the average level of uncertainty (across participants within a given study) may not have been high enough to elicit an ample degree of sense-making behavior. For example, in the study in which length of tenure served as a proxy for uncertainty, participants had been members of their organizations for approximately 5 years on average. During this rather lengthy period of time, they may have resolved the sorts of uncertainties that lead people to draw on process fairness information, particularly in the face of unfavorable outcomes. Similarly, in the study in which participants came from two groups, one facing the specter of layoffs and the other not, more than half of them (55%) came from the group with no threat of layoffs, in which uncertainty was expected to be relatively low. Perhaps the average level of uncertainty across all participants in this study may not have been high enough to elicit the sense-making process that underlies the two-way interaction between process fairness and outcome favorability.

Furthermore, in all of the studies in which uncertainty was measured directly, the average level was below the scale midpoint, sometimes considerably so. For example, in one study the average level of uncertainty was 1.95 on a scale ranging from 1 to 7, in which higher scores reflected greater uncertainty. Thus, in all four of the studies reported by De Cremer, Brockner et al. (in press) that failed to produce a significant two-way interaction between process fairness and outcome favorability, the average level of uncertainty across all participants was rather low. Perhaps it was only the subgroup of people who were *relatively* high in uncertainty who experienced enough uncertainty in an *absolute* sense to trigger the sense-making process that underlies the two-way interaction between outcome favorability and process fairness. In any event, whereas it has been noted that the two-way interaction between process fairness and outcome favorability does not always materialize (Brockner & Wiesenfeld, 1996; Chen et al., 2003), the present analysis takes the important next step of offering an informed speculation about why this may be the case: The sample as a whole experienced a low level of uncertainty. Of course, this reasoning needs to be evaluated in further research.

The Uncertainty Management Model To this point, I have discussed how uncertainty may have a moderating influence on the process–outcome interaction. However, there are other ways to conceptualize the three-way interaction among process fairness, outcome favorability, and uncertainty, for example, that outcome favorability moderates the interactive relationship between process fairness and uncertainty. The uncertainty management model (Van den Bos & Lind, 2002) posits that people need to reduce or manage uncertainty about matters pertinent to their economic and psychological well-being, and that they use process fairness information to do so. Hence, the primary finding of the uncertainty management model is the two-way interaction between process fairness and uncertainty, which shows that people are more influenced by process fairness information when uncertainty is high rather than low (Van den Bos, 2001).

To the extent that outcome favorability moderates the two-way interaction between process fairness and uncertainty, it offers an empirical extension to the uncertainty management model. In fact, the consistent finding across all six studies (both the four included in the De Cremer, Brockner et al. article in press and the two that were not) was that the central finding of the uncertainty management model, namely, the tendency for the fair process effect to be magnified under conditions of greater uncertainty, was in turn even more pronounced when people's outcomes were relatively unfavorable.

Outcome Importance

People engage in sense-making not only when they are uncertain about matters pertaining to their economic or psychological well-being (i.e., when they are *unable* to make sense of things) but also when a lot is at stake (i.e., when they are more *motivated* to reduce uncertainty). Thus, the interactive relationship between outcome favorability and process fairness may be moderated not only by employees' uncertainty about their standing as organizational members, but also by the importance of the outcomes associated with their well-being. The more important the outcomes (i.e., the more that is at stake), the more likely are outcome favorability and process fairness to interact. Of course, outcomes could be more or less important for a variety of reasons, some economic and some psychological. For example, more is at stake when people's economic well-being is more affected by the favorability of their outcomes.

Furthermore, at a psychological level, more may be at stake when people have close rather than distant relationships with the other party. In addition, more may be at stake when people define themselves on the basis of their relationship with the other party. In fact, several series of studies have examined the moderating influence of (1) relationship closeness and (2) people's self-construal on the interactive relationship between outcome favorability and process fairness. These studies are described next.

Relationship Closeness

Kwong and Leung (2002) hypothesized that the interaction effect would be stronger when people had closer relationships with the other party. As they put it:

> Studies on interpersonal closeness showed that people are motivated to expand their self-identity by including the other into the self in a close relationship. ... When people feel close to another person, that person plays a significant role in their sense of self, and the importance of the relationship should be high. (p. 282)

In one study, participants recalled how happy or satisfied they felt with the resolution of an interpersonal dispute as a function of the closeness of the relationship with the other, the other's process fairness, and the favorability of the outcome of the dispute. In a second study, Kwong and Leung examined the work effort of employees as well as their intention to remain with the organization after they had been subjected to a pay cut or a pay freeze. Independent variables included the fairness of the processes used to plan and implement the pay cuts or freezes, outcome favorability (that is, the degree of economic hardship caused by the pay cuts or freezes), and employees' commitment to the organization prior to the pay cuts or freezes. Conceptually analogous findings emerged in both studies. The interaction effect between outcome favorability and process fairness (in which high process fairness reduced the effect of outcome favorability on participants' reactions relative to when process fairness was low) was stronger when people were closer to the other party, in which they presumably attached greater importance to their relationship with the other.

Self-Construal

The broader cultural context in which interactions and relationships transpire also may influence the extent to which people include others in their self-conceptions and thereby assign importance to their relationships with them. In collectivistic cultures, Markus and Kitayama (1991) suggested that people focus on

> the fundamental *connectedness* of human beings to each other. ... Experiencing interdependence entails seeing oneself as part of an encompassing social relationship and recognizing that one's behavior is determined, contingent on, and, to a large extent organized by what the actor perceives to be the thoughts, feelings, and actions of *others* in the relationship. (p. 227; emphasis added)

In contrast, they suggested that in cultures fostering independent self-construals, there is a faith

> in the inherent separateness of distinct persons. ... Achieving the cultural goal of independence requires construing oneself as an individual whose behavior is organized and made meaningful primarily by reference to one's own internal repertoire of thoughts, feelings, and actions, rather than by reference to the thoughts, feelings, and actions of others. (p. 226)

One important implication of the distinction between interdependent versus independent self-construals is that being high on the former is more likely to lead people to assign importance to their social relationships and interactions. As Markus and Kitayama put it, "Although people everywhere must maintain some relatedness with others, an appreciation and a need for people will be more important for those with an interdependent self than for those with an independent self" (p. 229).

This reasoning suggests that self-construal may moderate the interactive relationship between outcome favorability and process fairness, such that people with more of an interdependent or less of an independent form of self-construal will exhibit the interaction effect more strongly. My colleagues and I tested this hypothesis in three separate studies

(Brockner, Chen, Mannix, Leung, & Skarlicki, 2000). Independent variables in all three studies consisted of outcome favorability and process fairness. An additional independent variable in Studies 1 and 2 was whether participants came from a country with a more collectivistic culture, such as Taiwan or the People's Republic of China (PRC), which tend to foster more interdependent forms of self-construal, or whether they came from a country with a more individualistic culture, such as Canada or the United States, which tend to foster more independent forms of self-construal. Self-construal also was operationalized in Studies 2 and 3 by having participants complete a self-report measure. The dependent variable consisted of participants' support for the decision that was reached (in Study 1) and their support for the other party (in Studies 2 and 3). All three studies yielded a significant three-way interaction effect. As predicted, the tendency for high process fairness to reduce the effect of outcome favorability was more pronounced when people maintained more interdependent than independent forms of self-construal.

Implications for Cross-Cultural Theory and Research on Justice The fact that the two-way interaction between process fairness and outcome favorability was stronger among those with more of an interdependent self-construal speaks to the potentially high generality of the two-way effect itself. Virtually all of the studies included in the Brockner and Wiesenfeld (1996) review were conducted in Western countries (primarily the United States), in which people tend to have more independent forms of self-construal. The majority of the world's population, however, resides in collectivistic countries that elicit more interdependent forms of self-construal. Thus, the studies included in the Brockner and Wiesenfeld review may actually *under*estimate the magnitude of the interactive relationship between outcome favorability and process fairness worldwide.

Brockner et al. (2000, Study 2) also illustrated a more refined way for justice researchers (and organizational scholars, more generally) to evaluate cross-national differences in people's beliefs and behaviors. Globalization has raised our awareness of the notion that so-called laws of human behavior may be culturally bound. For example, the fundamental attribution error, in which people are predisposed to explain behavior as resulting from people's internal characteristics, may not be so fundamental after all. Morris and Peng (1994) found that people in more collectivistic countries are more likely to make external or situational attributions for behavior.

Similarly, pervasive organizational justice effects also are moderated by people's national culture. For example, one of the most widely replicated findings in the justice literature is that people respond better (e.g., they judge decisions to be fairer, and they are more likely to be supportive of decisions and decision makers) when they have been allowed to have greater input into the decision-making process (Lind

& Tyler, 1988; Thibaut & Walker, 1975). A series of studies showed, however, that the positive effects of voice vary as a function of cultural differences in power distance (Hofstede, 1980), which refers to the difference in power afforded to those at higher versus lower levels of formal decision-making authority. In high power distance countries (e.g., Turkey and Mexico), it is normative and legitimate for those at the top to make decisions with little or no input from those at the bottom of the hierarchy. Neither expecting nor wanting to have input, people with low levels of authority in higher power distance countries have been shown to be less likely to respond positively to higher levels of voice relative to their counterparts from lower power distance countries, such as the United States (Brockner et al., 2001).

Many studies testing for cross-cultural differences do so suboptimally. In a typical research design, people are selected from two or more countries. Differing cultural norms and values within the countries are assumed to produce systematic psychological differences, which in turn are expected to yield effects on the ultimate dependent variables. This research strategy is flawed in at least two important respects. First, it fails to verify whether people from the various countries actually differ from one another on the psychological dimensions expected to account for between-country differences on the dependent variables. Whereas systematic (between-country) differences on psychological dimensions certainly exist, there also may be a considerable amount of within-country variation on those same dimensions (e.g., see Vandello and Cohen's 1999 research on regional differences in individualism-collectivism within the United States). In any given study, the standing of participants from different countries on the relevant psychological dimensions may not conform to the researchers' prior expectations (akin to a flawed manipulation in an experimental study). Second, even if between-country differences do emerge on the relevant psychological dimensions as well as on the ultimate dependent variables, it cannot be assumed that the former accounted for the latter.

To address both of these concerns, cross-cultural researchers need to operationalize (i.e., measure or manipulate) the psychological dimension that is hypothesized to account for between-country differences on the ultimate dependent variable (Brockner, 2003). For example, Brockner et al. (2000, Study 2) examined people's desire for future interaction with their negotiation partner as a function of the partner's process fairness toward them during the negotiation and the favorability of their negotiation outcomes. Participants were drawn from two countries (the United States and the PRC), the assumption being that those from the United States would have more independent or less-interdependent forms of self-construal than their counterparts from the PRC. As predicted, the participants from the PRC were more likely than those from the United States to exhibit the interaction between outcome favorability and process fairness. That is, among those from the PRC but not among those from the United States, high process fairness reduced the effect of outcome favorability on people's desire for future interaction with their negotiation partner relative to when process fairness was low.

Participants in this study also completed a self-report measure of self-construal. As expected, the U.S. sample was more independent or less interdependent than were those from the PRC. Of greater importance, the results of a mediation analysis suggested that it was self-construal rather than participants' country that moderated the interactive relationship between outcome favorability and process fairness.

These results meaningfully extend previous demonstrations of the interaction effect between outcome favorability and process fairness. Our earlier review of studies included samples from multiple countries, but never in the same study (Brockner & Wiesenfeld, 1996). Thus, all that could be concluded was that the interaction effect is not limited to a single cultural setting. We now know that country differences in self-construal influence the magnitude of the interactive relationship between outcome favorability and process fairness. Taken together with the findings of Kwong and Leung (2002), the findings suggest that how much people assign importance to their relationship with the other party is positively related to the magnitude of the interaction effect between outcome favorability and process fairness, in which high process fairness reduces the effect of outcome favorability relative to when process fairness is low.

In summary, the process–outcome interaction has been shown to be stronger when people have a closer relationship with the other party (Kwong & Leung, 2002) and when they have more interdependent forms of self-construal (Brockner et al., 2000). Both findings lend themselves to a common interpretation: In encounters in which more is at stake for various aspects of people's sense of self (e.g., esteem, identity), the process–outcome interaction may be more likely to emerge. This interpretation is consistent with the view that the process–outcome interaction reflects people's attempts to make sense of a variety of matters relevant to their psychological well-being. Unfavorable (more than favorable) outcomes may heighten people's motivation to make sense of things, prompting them to use process fairness information to do so. Moreover, to the extent the outcomes are more important economically, psychologically, or both, the interactive relationship between outcome favorability and process fairness will be heightened even further.

The immediately preceding section of this chapter considered the moderating effect of uncertainty on the interactive relationship between process fairness and outcome favorability (De Cremer, Brockner et al., in press). When people were more uncertain of their standing as organization members, the findings suggested that people more strongly engaged in a sense-making process elicited by the receipt of unfavorable outcomes, which heightened their susceptibility to influence by process fairness information. However, the force with which sense-making is instantiated does not merely depend on uncertainty. It also may depend on the importance of the outcomes or how much is at stake. The distinction between uncertainty and outcome importance as inducements to sense-making in the face of unfavorable outcomes is analogous to the distinction between ability (or lack thereof) and motivation. More specifically, let us assume that people will initiate sense-making when (1) the status quo is such that they cannot (i.e., they are unable to) make sense of things, and (2) they are motivated to do so. Hence, higher levels of uncertainty may have induced people to engage in more of a sense-making process, thereby setting the stage for uncertainty to moderate the interactive relationship between outcome favorability and process fairness. Furthermore, the more that people's outcomes are important to them, as they presumably were for participants who attached greater importance to their relationships (Brockner et al., 2000; Kwong & Leung, 2002), the more motivated they are to engage in sense-making, setting the stage for relationship importance to moderate the interaction between process fairness and outcome favorability. Taken together, the studies on uncertainty and outcome importance help to delineate the conditions under which the interactive relationship between process fairness and outcome favorability is more versus less likely to emerge. Moreover, all of the moderator variables may be subsumed under the broader umbrella of factors that affect people's tendencies to engage in sense-making, particularly in the face of unfavorable outcomes.

Contrast Effects as Moderators of the Process–Outcome Interaction

Whereas the process–outcome interaction often has been depicted as one in which process fairness has a moderating influence on outcome favorability, it is equally accurate to say that the form of the interaction is such that people react particularly badly when they receive an unfavorable outcome accompanied by an unfair process. Thus, another way to delineate possible moderators of the process–outcome interaction is by asking the question, Might there be conditions under which the tendency to react particularly badly to the combination of an unfavorable outcome and an unfair process may be even more likely to occur? Here is one possible answer to this question: when people expected to be treated relatively positively by the decision-making authority. In other words, the more that people experience the combination of an unfavorable outcome and unfair process as an unpleasant surprise, the more likely they may be to react particularly badly.

Social judgment theory from the attitudes literature (e.g., Sherif, Sherif, & Nebergall, 1965) has suggested that people integrate their prior beliefs with their subsequent experiences in two very different ways: through assimilation or contrast. When assimilating, people judge their experiences to be consistent with their prior beliefs, in which case their experiences are not likely to be especially noticeable or impactful ("more of the same"). For example, people may continue to react positively to an authority perceived to be trustworthy as long as the authority's behavior was at least reasonably consistent with people's prior expectations, that is, when their outcomes were favorable, or when the authority exhibited high process fairness, or both. When contrasting, however, people perceive their experiences to be discrepant from their prior beliefs, in which case their experiences are more noticeable and therefore are more likely to be impactful. Thus, when people experience a contrast between how they expect to be treated (e.g., when an authority is believed to be trustworthy) and how they are actually treated (e.g., the authority doles out an unfavorable outcome with an unfair process), their typical tendency to react negatively may be heightened all the more.

This reasoning suggests that factors that lead people to "expect better" from a decision-making authority (i.e., better than the combination of an unfavorable outcome and an unfair process) may heighten people's tendencies to react particularly badly to receiving an unfavorable outcome via an unfair process. I now review research pertaining to this proposition, beginning with a series of studies by Lin, Che, and Leung (2009), who examined the moderating influence of the authority's morality on the interactive relationship between outcome favorability and process fairness. (As I explain further, Lin et al. invoked outcome or relationship importance as the key driver of the moderating influence of the authority's morality. Whereas this possibility is conceptually plausible, the authors did not directly test it. Moreover, Brockner, Bianchi et al. in 2010 evaluated the relationship importance explanation of the Lin et al. findings but found no evidence to support it.)

Lin et al. (2009) evaluated whether the morality of an organizational authority would moderate the interactive relationship between outcome favorability and process fairness, such that the interaction effect was expected to be stronger when the authority was more moral. The authors had hypothesized that people would assign more importance to their relationships with authorities who were relatively high in morality, thereby leading to the prediction that the process–outcome interaction would be shown more strongly when the authority was relatively high in morality. As Lin et al. put it:

> Leader morality is known to influence employees' feeling about the importance they attach to their relationships with leaders. ... In other words, leader morality is an important factor that determines the strength of a leader-member relationship. In addition, perceived leader morality is associated with identification with a leader ... , and perceived leader ethicality positively influences followers' organizational commitment. ... People value their relationship with moral leaders and the organizations they represent, and accord more importance to this relationship. (p. 1541)

If the morality of the decision-making authority is a proxy for the amount of importance that people assign to their relationship with the authority, then just as Kwong and Leung (2002) found for relationship closeness, it may be expected that the interactive relationship will be shown more strongly by people who perceive the decision-making authority to be higher in morality.

In two studies (conducted in Beijing), Lin et al. (2009) examined the effects of the morality of the decision-making authority, outcome favorability, and process fairness on participants' attitudes toward the organization. One study drew on a vignette used in previous research (Van den Bos, Vermunt, et al., 1997) in which participants were asked to imagine that they had applied for a desirable job in a reputable organization. Outcome favorability was varied on the basis of whether they received the job offer, and process fairness was operationalized on the basis of whether the decision maker used more accurate or less accurate information to evaluate the applicants' suitability. Prior to the outcome favorability and process fairness manipulations, participants "overheard" information about the manager who was responsible for the hiring decision. In the high-morality condition, participants were led to believe that the manager was, for example, a tolerant and responsible person who complied with the law, treasured subordinates' talent, and never abused power to pursue personal gain. In the low-morality condition, participants were told, among other things, that the manager was jealous of subordinates, scorned the law, coerced subordinates, and often abused power. The dependent variable consisted of participants' attraction to the organization.

The results revealed a three-way interaction between outcome favorability, process fairness, and leader morality, exhibited in Table 3.4. When the manager was described as high in morality, the typical interaction between outcome favorability and process fairness emerged, such that high process fairness reduced the positive relationship between outcome favorability and participants' attraction to the organization relative to when process fairness was low. When the manager was described as low in morality, there was no evidence of this particular form of interactive relationship between outcome favorability and process fairness.

Lin et al. (2009) did a second study in which participants were asked to describe a recent formal performance appraisal that they had received from their managers. Unlike in the previous study, the independent variables of outcome favorability, process fairness, and the managers' morality were measured (rather than experimentally manipulated). The dependent variable consisted of participants' pride in their organization. Again, Lin et al. found evidence of a three-way interaction, similar to the one found in the vignette study. Among those who rated their manager as higher in morality, there was a significant interaction between process fairness and outcome favorability, such that high process fairness reduced the positive relationship between outcome favorability and pride in the organization relative to when process fairness was low.

TABLE 3.4 Mean Level of Attraction to the Organization as a Function of the Morality of the Authority, Process Fairness, and Outcome Favorability (Lin, Che, & Leung, 2009, Vignette Study)

	Outcome Favorability	
Process Fairness	High	Low
High Authority Morality		
High	5.06	4.33
Low	4.36	2.00
Low Authority Morality		
High	3.58	2.64
Low	3.04	2.64

Source: The role of leader morality in the interactions effect of procedural justice and outcome favorability, *Journal of Applied Social Psychology,* 2009, Vignette Study, with permission from Wiley-Blackwell.

Note: Scores could range from 1 to 6, with higher scores reflecting greater attraction to the organization.

Among those who saw their manager as lower in morality, however, there was no hint of this interactive relationship between outcome favorability and process fairness.

Whereas Lin et al. (2009) hypothesized that relationship importance would account for the moderating effect of the authority's morality on the process–outcome interaction, they did not examine relationship importance in either of their studies. In other words, they did not provide any independent evidence that leader morality had its moderating effect via how much importance people assigned to their relationship with the authority.

Moreover, it is possible to account for the moderating effect of leader morality on the process–outcome interaction in other ways. Perhaps it was the perceived trustworthiness that accounted for the moderating effect of the authority's morality on the process–outcome interaction. For example, if the authority was seen as more moral and therefore more trustworthy, perhaps the authority's behavior (including process fairness) would be seen as more genuine or authentic. The greater the perceived authenticity of the process fairness, the more likely it may be to have a moderating influence on outcome favorability.

Yet another explanation, also based on the prospect that the authority's morality was linked to perceptions of his or her trustworthiness, is that the authority's morality influenced how much people were negatively surprised when they received an unfavorable outcome with an unfair process. Hence, when an authority who was expected to be moral (read: trustworthy) violated people's expectations (by doling out unfavorable outcomes with low process fairness), people may have felt betrayed and, as a result, reacted particularly badly.

Thus, no fewer than three explanations may account for Lin et al.'s (2009) findings that the morality of the authority moderated the interactive relationship between outcome favorability and process fairness: (1) The morality of the authority was a proxy for how much importance people assigned to their relationship with the authority (this is the explanation that Lin et al. favored), (2) the morality of the authority influenced how much people viewed the authority's behavior as authentic or genuine, and (3) the morality of the authority influenced how much people were likely to be unpleasantly surprised when they received an unfavorable outcome with an unfair process. Note that it is only the third explanation in which contrast effects are hypothesized to play a pivotal role in determining the magnitude of the interactive relationship between process fairness and outcome favorability. Let us consider each of these explanations in greater detail.

Morality as a Basis of Relationship Importance

People may assign greater importance to their relationships with authorities who are seen as more moral. Morality may be a basis of power and influence; for example, authorities high in morality are likely to have greater referent power (French & Raven, 1959) than their less-moral counterparts. Hence, more may be at stake for people in their dealings with authorities who are more moral. For example, employees may benefit more (tangibly or intangibly) when they have a positive relationship with managers who are higher in morality, and they may be harmed more when they have a negative relationship with managers who are higher in morality. Thus, if relationship importance has a moderating impact on the interactive relationship between process fairness and outcome favorability (Kwong & Leung, 2002), and if the authority's morality is a proxy for relationship importance, then the authority's morality should moderate the process–outcome interaction, such that it will be more pronounced when the authority is more moral.

Morality as a Basis of Trustworthiness: The Role of Authenticity

When authorities are seen as moral, people may do more than assign importance to their relationships with them. They may also judge the authorities' actions as more genuine or authentic and therefore may be more affected by those actions. All of us probably have had dealings with authorities in which we had reasons to doubt (that is, we did not trust) their enactment of high process fairness. In those instances, we probably reacted less positively than if we had taken the authority's high process fairness at face value. Consider, for example, two organizations, one that created fair procedures to be "in compliance" with external forces such as governmental regulations, and another that did so for more intrinsic reasons (i.e., because its leaders genuinely believed that fair procedures were the right thing to do). Whereas employees may respond more favorably in both instances if they perceive process fairness to be relatively high, this tendency may be more pronounced when the process fairness was judged to be authentic.

De Cremer and Tyler (2007) provided more formal support for this speculation, in which they tested for an interactive effect of an authority's trustworthiness and procedural fairness on subordinates' willingness to cooperate with the authority in both laboratory and field settings. Whereas main effects were found for both independent variables (as might be expected, participants were more cooperative with authorities who were high in process fairness and who were more trustworthy), an interaction effect also emerged such that the fair process effect was much more pronounced when the authority was trustworthy rather than not trustworthy.

De Cremer and Tyler (2007) did not examine outcome favorability; hence, we are unable to determine if the authorities' trustworthiness moderated the interactive relationship between process fairness and outcome favorability in the same way that the authority's morality did in the Lin et al. (2009) studies. Nevertheless, the reasoning that De Cremer and Tyler provided for their findings provides insight into how the trustworthiness of the authority may moderate the interaction effect. The process–outcome interaction effect arises from people's tendencies to use process fairness information to make sense of their environments, and more so when their outcomes are unfavorable rather than favorable. If so, then they may be likely to be more influenced by process fairness information that is judged to be more authentic. The trustworthiness of the authority in turn may be positively related to how much people judge the authority's process fairness as authentic. Thus, it stands to reason that trustworthiness will have a moderating influence on the process–outcome interaction effect, such that the interaction effect will be more pronounced when the authority is judged to be more trustworthy.

Relationship Importance Versus Trustworthiness: Distinguishing the Nature of the Underlying Process

In the previous sections of the chapter on uncertainty and on outcome importance as moderators of the process–outcome interaction, I suggested that these two factors may exert influence by affecting the extent to which people are induced to engage in sense-making by the receipt of unfavorable outcomes. That is, the strength of people's sense-making tendencies (which underlie the interaction effect) is posited to be greater when uncertainty is higher or when more is at stake.

An alternative (and not mutually exclusive) possibility is that certain factors may moderate the interaction effect not by affecting how strongly the sense-making process is instantiated, but rather by affecting people's perceptions and judgments once the sense-making process is under way. Thus, even when the intensity of people's sense-making efforts is held constant, they may be more likely to see an authority's high process fairness as more genuine or real (and hence they may be more positively affected by being treated with high process fairness) when the authority is perceived to be higher in morality and hence trustworthiness.

One way to differentiate between these two explanations is by asking people to indicate the extent to which they (1) judge their relationship with the decision-making authority as important and (2) judge the actions of the authority to be authentic, intrinsically motivated, or otherwise taken "at face value." If the relationship importance explanation were carrying the day, we would expect to find a positive relationship between people's judgments of the authority's morality and how much they valued their relationship with the authority. On the other hand, if perceived trustworthiness were the underlying mechanism, then we would expect to find a positive relationship between judgments of the authority's morality and how much their actions were judged to be genuine or authentic. Of course, these two possibilities are not mutually exclusive.

Morality as a Basis of Trustworthiness: The Role of Expectations

People's beliefs about an authority's morality generate expectations about how the authority is likely to behave, which in turn may influence their reactions to information gleaned from their actual encounters with the authority. Let us apply this reasoning to how an authority's morality may have a moderating influence on the interactive relationship between process fairness and outcome favorability. If the authority is perceived to be moral, then people's expectations of how they are likely to be treated should be relatively positive. They probably expect to receive at least reasonably favorable outcomes from their encounters with the authority, and they almost certainly expect the authority to exhibit high process fairness. As long as the authority delivers on either of the outcome favorability or process fairness dimensions, people may assimilate the authority's behavior to their preexisting beliefs of trustworthiness, in which case they should (continue to) respond relatively positively to the authority and to the authority's decisions. If, however, the authority metes out an unfavorable outcome with an unfair process, then people are likely to perceive a contrast between their prior beliefs and their actual experience. Such an experience of expectancy violation (which is akin to feeling betrayed) may cause people to react particularly badly to the authority and the authority's decisions.

I am not necessarily suggesting that the experience of violated expectations are so strong that people will react more negatively to the combination of an unfavorable outcome and an unfair process that comes from an authority previously believed to be high in morality relative to how they would react to the same unfavorable outcome and unfair process delivered by an authority low in morality. At the very least, however, it can be predicted that *among those who believed the authority to be high in morality,* reactions should be most negative when an unfavorable outcome is accompanied by an unfair process relative to all other combinations of conditions. Indeed, this is precisely what Lin et al. (2009) found in both of their studies.

Moreover, the contrast effect explanation suggests an additional contributor to Lin et al.'s (2009) three-way interaction among the authority's morality, outcome favorability, and process fairness. When people perceive the authority to be low in morality and therefore do not expect to be treated well, there is one condition that is most likely to be experienced as a contrast to their prior expectations: favorable outcomes that are delivered with high process fairness. Given the "positive contrast" between their prior beliefs and their actual experience with the authority, people may be expected to react particularly favorably to the authority and the authority's decisions when they do not believe that the authority is moral but they experience favorable outcomes along with high process fairness. In fact, Lin et al. found some evidence consistent with this reasoning, although the positive contrast effect found in their studies (when the authority was seen as low in morality; see the bottom half of Table 3.4) was not as pronounced as the negative contrast effect (when the authority was seen as high in morality; see the top half of Table 3.4).

To learn more about the mechanisms accounting for Lin et. al.'s (2009) finding that the morality of a decision-making authority moderated the process–outcome interaction, Brockner, Bianchi et al. (2010) conducted replications of their two studies. We used the same materials that Lin et al. used in their vignette study, in which we experimentally manipulated the morality of the decision-making authority, the process fairness with which the authority made the decision, and outcome favorability. In addition to the dependent variable examined by Lin et al. (participants' attraction to the organization), we collected two different measures of trustworthiness. In one, participants made ratings of the authority who had made the decision (along such dimensions as integrity, competence, morality, and well-intentioned). In another, participants judged the authenticity of the behavior of the decision-making authority. We also assessed how much participants assigned importance to their relationship with the decision-making authority.

Replicating the results of Lin et al. (2009), we found a three-way interaction among the morality of the authority, process fairness, and outcome favorability on participants' attraction to the organization. As shown in Table 3.5, when the decision maker was high in morality, participants exhibited relatively high levels of attraction to the organization with one exception: when they received an unfavorable outcome that was accompanied by an unfair process. This condition constituted

TABLE 3.5 Mean Level of Attraction to the Organization as a Function of the Morality of the Authority, Process Fairness, and Outcome Favorability (Brockner, Bianchi et al., 2010, Vignette Study)

	Outcome Favorability	
Process Fairness	High	Low
High Authority Morality		
High	6.00	4.94
Low	5.25	2.90
Low Authority Morality		
High	5.02	3.15
Low	4.02	2.97

Note: Scores could range from 1 to 7, with higher scores reflecting greater attraction to the organization.

a negative contrast between what the leader's high morality would have led participants to expect and what they actually experienced.

Different results emerged when the leader was low in morality. In this instance, participants responded negatively except in one condition: when participants received a favorable outcome via high process fairness. This condition created a positive contrast between what the leader's low morality would have led them to expect and what they actually experienced. That is, when leader morality was low, attraction to the organization in the high process fairness/high outcome favorability condition ($M = 5.02$) was significantly greater than that shown in the other low morality conditions, taken together.

We conducted additional analyses in an attempt to shed light on the mechanisms that may account for the moderating effect of the morality of the authority on the interactive relationship between process fairness and outcome favorability. First, we examined whether relationship importance played a role, which is what Lin et al. (2009) had surmised. Participants were asked questions such as, "How important is your relationship with the decision maker?" In fact, there was a significant main effect of the authority's morality on the perceived importance of the relationship, such that participants assigned more importance to the relationship when the authority was relatively high in morality. However, the results of subsequent analyses failed to support the notion that the moderating effect of the authority's morality on the interactive relationship between process fairness and outcome favorability was attributable to perceived relationship importance. For example, the relationship importance explanation predicts that there should have been a significant three-way interaction among perceived relationship importance, process fairness, and outcome favorability; however, this three-way interaction effect was trivial.

Whereas relationship importance did not play a role in helping to explain the interactive effect of the authority's morality, process fairness, and outcome favorability on participants' attraction to the organization, the related perceptions of the authority's trustworthiness and authenticity appeared to be far more explanatory. That is, the measures of both perceived trustworthiness and perceived authenticity yielded a three-way interaction effect of the authority's morality, outcome favorability, and process fairness, the forms of which were quite similar to that found on the measure of participants' attraction to the organization shown in Table 3.5. Furthermore, mediational analyses showed participants' perceptions of the trustworthiness or authenticity of the authority accounted for the three-way interaction effect on their attraction to the organization. That is, controlling for the hypothesized mediator (i.e., either trustworthiness or authenticity) eliminated the three-way interaction effect on organizational attraction shown in Table 3.5; moreover, controlling for the three-way interaction effect did not eliminate the relationship between the hypothesized mediators and organizational attraction.

In summary, the results of the vignette study replicated the findings of Lin et al. (2009) in showing that when the authority was higher in morality (but not when the authority was lower in morality), participants exhibited particularly low levels of attraction to the organization when they received an unfavorable outcome with an unfair process. Furthermore, the results extend the Lin et al. findings by providing more direct evidence of the underlying mechanism. We tested but did not find support for the factor that Lin et al. believed to be explanatory, namely, that people assigned more importance to their relationships with the authority that was relatively high in morality. However, we did find evidence that the authority's morality, in conjunction with process fairness and outcome favorability, influenced people's trust in (or perceived authenticity of) the authority, which in turn predicted how attracted they felt toward the organization.

If the factor accounting for the effect of the authority's morality was trustworthiness, then other measures of the authority's trustworthiness should behave the same way as morality did in moderating the interactive relationship between process fairness and outcome favorability. Brockner, Bianchi et al.'s (2010) second study tested this reasoning in a field setting. Participants from a variety of organizations completed an online survey that included measures of their organizational commitment (as the dependent variable) along with measures of outcome favorability, perceptions of their managers' process fairness, and the extent to which they trusted their managers. The trust measure consisted of various subscales, including a generic measure (e.g., "I believe that the managers responsible for this organization are trustworthy")

TABLE 3.6 Predicted Values of Organizational Commitment as a Function of Trust in Management, Outcome Favorability, and Process Fairness (Brockner, Bianchi et al., 2010, Survey Study)

	Outcome Favorability	
Process Fairness	**High**	**Low**
High Trust in Management		
High	6.57	6.11
Low	6.11	4.88
Low Trust in Management		
High	6.20	4.27
Low	4.61	3.51

Note: Scores could range from 1 to 7, with higher scores reflecting greater organizational commitment.

along with measures developed by McAllister, Lewicki, and Chaturvedi (2008) tapping knowledge-based trust (e.g., "Management does what they say they are going to do"), identification-based trust (e.g., "Management and I share the same basic values"), and goodwill-based trust (e.g., "Management will protect and defend me, perhaps even at their own expense"). Regardless of which trust subscale was used, we found a three-way interaction among trust, outcome favorability, and process fairness on organizational commitment. As can be seen in Table 3.6 (which shows the results based on the generic subscale), the nature of the effect was remarkably similar to the results found in the vignette study (compare Tables 3.5 and 3.6). Among the subset of participants who were relatively trusting of their managers, the lowest level of commitment was exhibited when they received unfavorable outcomes with low process fairness (suggestive of a negative contrast effect). In contrast, whereas participants who were relatively untrusting of their managers also showed the lowest organizational commitment when they received an unfavorable outcome with an unfair process, the relatively untrusting group responded almost as negatively when their outcomes were unfavorable and process fairness was high. Another way to describe the reactions of those who had relatively low trust in management is that they exhibited particularly high levels of commitment when they received favorable outcomes with high process fairness (suggestive of a positive contrast effect).

Other findings also suggest that the interactive relationship between outcome favorability and process fairness may result from the negative contrast between people's expectations about how they are likely to be treated by the other party and their actual experience with the other. Aggarwal and Larrick (2010) asked participants to imagine that they were regular customers of a take-out restaurant, toward which they were generally positively predisposed. Half of them were led to believe that they had an exchange relationship with the restaurant that emphasized the economic or transactional nature of their encounters. The other half were told that they had more of a communal relationship with the restaurant, in which their encounters were not driven solely or primarily by economic or transactional considerations. Rather, in communal relationships greater importance is assigned to offer mutual support and cooperation, to make resource allocation decisions based on people's needs rather than on their inputs, and to ensure the social and psychological well-being of the parties to the relationship.

All participants were told that one day they ordered food from the restaurant and that they were not satisfied with it; they had contacted the restaurant to lodge a complaint. The response of the restaurant varied along the dimensions of outcome favorability and process fairness. For example, in the high process fairness condition participants were treated with a high degree of respect, whereas in the low process fairness condition they were not treated with respect. Dependent variables included various measures of participants' support for the restaurant, such as how much this incident had made their relationship weaker or stronger than before, how satisfied they were with the restaurant, and the likelihood of ordering from the restaurant again.

A significant three-way interaction effect emerged on all dependent measures. The two-way interaction between outcome favorability and process fairness (in which the receipt of an unfavorable outcome with an unfair process elicited particularly negative reactions) was exhibited more strongly by those who believed that they had a communal rather than an exchange relationship with the restaurant. Whereas it is impossible to eliminate other explanations of these findings, for example, perhaps participants assigned greater importance to their relationship with the restaurant in the communal than in the exchange condition, one possibility is that participants were unpleasantly surprised (and, as a result, responded most negatively) when they believed that they had a communal relationship with the restaurant but were subsequently treated with low outcome favorability and low process fairness. Moreover, the Aggarwal and Larrick (2010) findings are noteworthy because they help to extend the generality of a moderating influence on the process–outcome interaction by showing that it may be exhibited by customers (rather than by employees) in reaction to the actions of organizational authorities.

Future Research Opportunities Taken together, the findings of Lin et al. (2009), Brockner, Bianchi et al. (2010), and Aggarwal and Larrick (2010) suggest that the process–outcome interaction in which people react particularly negatively when they receive an unfavorable outcome with an unfair process may result from a negative contrast between people's expectations and their actual experiences. It is bad enough to receive an unfavorable outcome with an unfair process. However, this painful experience of multiplying insult times injury may be heightened even further when it violates people's expectations. Further support for the "negative contrast effect" explanation emanates from the fact that all of the studies provided suggestive evidence of a positive contrast effect as well. That is, if people reacted particularly negatively to actual experiences that violated their positive prior expectancies, then they also should have reacted particularly positively to actual experiences that violated their negative prior expectancies. In fact, this is precisely what happened; see for example, the bottom halves of Table 3.4 in the Lin et al. (2009) study and Table 3.5 in the Brockner, Bianchi et al. (2010) research. When leader morality was low (in the Lin et al. study) or when trust was low (in the Brockner, Bianchi et al. study) participants probably had low expectations about how they would be treated. Note, however, that they responded most positively when they received a favorable outcome with high process fairness, which represented a positive contrast effect.

In spite of the converging evidence across these studies, however, the findings leave unanswered several important questions that need to be addressed in future research.

First, why did people only exhibit contrast effects when outcome favorability *and* process fairness differed from their prior beliefs? Perhaps it is because people's reactions depend on how much they believe the decision-making authority has the motivation *and* the ability to behave differently from what their prior beliefs about the authority would have led them to expect. For example, suppose an individual were relatively untrusting towards his/her manager but was treated by the manager with high outcome favorability and high process fairness. Both the favorable outcome and the fair process may signal to the recipient that the decision-maker is motivated to behave differently (more positively) towards him/her. The favorable outcome and the fair process also may signify that the decision-maker has the knowledge to "see the light," i.e., s/he is more capable of making decisions higher in outcome favorability and process fairness. Just as motivation interacts with ability to influence behavior, it may be that our *cognitive representations* of others' behavior also are interactively determined by judgments of others' motivation and capability to act. Of course, the latter speculation needs to be evaluated in future research.

Second, further research is needed to specify the psychological underpinnings of the contrast effects that account for the moderating influence of (1) the authority's morality or trustworthiness (Brockner, Bianchi et al., 2010; Lin et al., 2009) or (2) the nature of the relationship with the other party (Aggarwal and Larrick, 2010) on the process–outcome interaction. For example, if people react particularly badly when they receive an unfavorable outcome via an unfair process from an authority believed to be trustworthy, *why* is that the case? Moreover, even though the positive contrast effects were not as clear and consistent as were the negative effects, *why* would people react particularly positively if they received a favorable outcome through a fair process from an authority believed to be untrustworthy? One speculation about the mechanism underlying contrast effects is that when peoples' actual experiences violate their expectancies, they may see themselves as more personally responsible for their actual experiences. For example, if a trustworthy authority acts badly toward people (i.e., gives them an unfavorable outcome with an unfair process), people may believe that they must have done something to bring this on themselves. After all, the authority did not do what he or she was expected to do. To the extent that they see themselves as personally responsible for the expectancy-violating behavior of the authority, they may want to distance themselves from the authority, which may manifest itself by being less attracted to the organization that the authority represents. Relatedly, if an untrustworthy authority acts positively toward people (i.e., gives them a favorable outcome with a fair process), then people also may believe that they must have done something to warrant such a pleasant surprise. As a result, they may be particularly attracted to the organization that the authority represents.

More on the Relationship Between Trust and the Process–Outcome Interaction

Whereas further research is needed to account for the moderating influence of the authority's trustworthiness on the process–outcome interaction, the fact remains that trustworthiness had a moderating influence. This finding represents an additional way to conceptualize the role of trust in the interactive relationship between process fairness and outcome favorability. In this chapter, I provided evidence of the mediating role that trust plays in accounting for the process–outcome interaction (i.e., that it is not process fairness per se that interacts with outcome favorability to influence people's support for decisions, decision makers, and institutions). Rather, process fairness influences people's trust in a decision-making authority, which in turn interacts with outcome favorability to influence people's beliefs and behaviors (Brockner et al., 1997; see Figure 3.1A).

Fairness heuristic theory (e.g., Lind, 2001) also posits that people use process fairness information to make inferences about how much to trust a decision-making authority; moreover, once the authority's trustworthiness has been established (one way or the other), then process fairness information is far less consequential. Van den Bos, Wilke, and Lind (1998) examined the effects of orthogonal manipulations of an authority's process fairness and trustworthiness on participants' satisfaction with how resources were allocated. The trustworthiness variable consisted of three levels: One group was led to believe that the authority was trustworthy, a second group was told that the authority was not trustworthy, whereas a third group was given no information about how much to trust the authority. (Outcome favorability was not varied.) The results showed an interaction effect between process fairness and trustworthiness, such that when participants were given no information about the trustworthiness of the authority there was a strong positive relationship between process fairness and participants' satisfaction with the decision. However, when participants were informed about the trustworthiness of the authority (i.e., when they were told that the authority either was trustworthy or was not trustworthy), process fairness was unrelated to participants' satisfaction with the decision.

Whereas Brockner et al. (1997) and Van den Bos et al. (1998) examined somewhat different empirical questions, a common theme running through both studies (and others, e.g., Konovsky & Pugh, 1994) is that people use process fairness information to make inferences about an authority's trustworthiness. Both studies also showed that trustworthiness trumped process fairness in that people were more likely to be affected by their judgments of the authority's trustworthiness than by the authority's process fairness. Note, however, that Lin et al. (2009) and Brockner, Bianchi et al. (2010) found a different pattern of results. These authors discovered that when the authority was judged to be more trustworthy, people were more likely to exhibit the process–outcome interaction in which people responded particularly negatively to the receipt of an unfavorable outcome accompanied by an unfair process.

In sum, previous research has shown that trustworthiness *mediates* the effect of process fairness on people's support for decisions, decision makers, and institutions, and this mediating effect has been found in studies examining process fairness as a main effect (Konovsky & Pugh, 1994; Van den Bos et al., 1998) as well as process fairness in interaction with outcome favorability (Brockner et al., 1997). Other studies have shown that trustworthiness has a *moderating* influence on process fairness, again, in studies examining process fairness as a main effect (De Cremer & Tyler, 2007) as well as process fairness in interaction with outcome favorability (Brockner, Bianchi et al., 2010; Lin et al., 2009). Whether trust plays a mediating role or a moderating role in relation to the process–outcome interaction suggests that conceptually distinct psychological processes may be in play. If that is so, then it may be useful to delineate why this is so and, relatedly, to identify the conditions under which trust in the decision-making authority is more likely to play a mediating or moderating role.

One factor that may determine whether trust in the authority has a mediating or moderating effect on the interactive relationship between process fairness and outcome favorability is *people's certainty about how much to trust the decision-making authority.* When people have uncertain beliefs about the trustworthiness of the authority (i.e., when their beliefs are not well formed), they may rely on information that helps them to make inferences about the authority's trustworthiness. One indicator of the authority's trustworthiness, in turn, is the fairness of the processes the authority uses to plan and implement decisions. Judgments of trustworthiness in turn interact with outcome favorability to influence people's willingness to support the authority and the authority's decisions (Brockner et al., 1997). High trust in the authority reduces the impact of outcome favorability on people's willingness to support the authority and the authority's decisions relative to when trust in the authority is low. In short, when uncertainty about how much to trust an authority is high, trust may play a mediating role in the interactive relationship between outcome favorability and procedural fairness, giving rise to the pattern of results observed by Brockner et al. (1997).

What happens when people's beliefs about how much to trust an authority are more certain? Previously, I offered several explanations of why an authority's trustworthiness may have a moderating influence on the interactive relationship between process fairness and outcome favorability. Whereas the explanations differ, each is predicated on the assumption that people's trustworthiness beliefs are more well formed or certain. For example, one speculation was that people may react particularly badly when they experience a negative contrast between their prior belief that the authority was trustworthy and the receipt of an unfavorable outcome that is accompanied by low process fairness. This type of negative contrast may be experienced with greater intensity if people's beliefs about the conflicting elements (i.e., high prior trustworthiness vs. the subsequent experience of low outcome favorability and low process fairness) are maintained with greater certainty. In sum, it may be that the moderating effect of trustworthiness on the interactive relationship between process fairness and outcome favorability found by Lin et al. (2009) and by Brockner, Bianchi et al. (2010) is more likely to occur when people are more certain about their beliefs about the authority's trustworthiness.

Indeed, additional analyses of the Brockner, Bianchi et al. (2010) field study have lent preliminary support for this rather complex prediction. Previously, I mentioned that participants in this study indicated their organizational commitment, outcome favorability in the workplace, the process fairness of their managers, and how much they trusted their managers. They also indicated how certain they were of their trust perceptions. The results yielded a marginally significant ($p < .08$) four-way (amazing) interaction effect. (Lest the reader think that a four-way interaction effect is beyond interpretation, allow me to try to walk you through it.) Those who were more certain of their trust ratings exhibited a significant three-way interaction among trust, process fairness, and outcome favorability that was similar in nature to the pattern found by Lin et al. (2009) and by Brockner and Bianchi (see Tables 3.4 through 3.6). Recall the nature of this three-way interaction: When trust was higher, people were especially likely to respond negatively (i.e., with lower attraction or commitment to the organization) when they received an unfavorable outcome accompanied by low process fairness.

What about the people who were less certain of how much they trusted their managers? This group showed no trace of a three-way interaction among trust, process fairness, and outcome favorability ($F < 1$). Furthermore, there was even some evidence that the low-certainty group behaved similarly to the participants in the Brockner et al. (1997) studies, in which trust played more of a *mediating* role in the interactive relationship between process fairness and outcome favorability. For the lower-certainty group, process fairness was positively related to trust, which in turn interacted with outcome favorability to influence organizational commitment.

If uncertainty about how much to trust the authority dictates whether trust will have a moderating influence on the process–outcome interaction effect (akin to the results of Lin et al., 2009, and Brockner, Bianchi et al., 2010) or play a mediating role in the process–outcome interaction effect (akin to the results of Brockner et al., 1997), then it is important to identify the antecedents of people's level of certainty about their trust in the authority. These are precisely the factors that are likely to affect whether the authority's trustworthiness will play a moderating role or a mediating role in the interactive relationship between outcome favorability and process fairness.

For example, one factor that may be relevant is the stage of the relationship between the two parties. Early in the relationship, people's beliefs about how much to trust the authority may be relatively uncertain; they have little basis for well-formed beliefs about the trustworthiness of the decision-making authority. As a result, they may use process fairness information to make inferences about the authority's trustworthiness, particularly when their initial outcomes are unfavorable and when they have some incentive to do so, such as when the authority controls valued resources (either tangible or intangible) or when the relationship with the authority is expected to be an ongoing one. Moreover, process fairness information may come in a variety of forms. The most obvious one is how the authority behaved along dimensions known to shape people's judgments of process fairness (e.g., voice, consistency, accuracy, interactional justice, and the like). Lacking direct experience with the authority's process fairness, employees also may be affected by observations of how fairly the authority treated others, such as their coworkers (e.g., Brockner, 1990), as well as by what fellow employees say (Salancik & Pfeffer, 1978), either about the fairness with which specific decisions were implemented (Degoey, 2000) or about the climate for justice in the organization in general (Naumann & Bennett, 2000). Judgments of the authority's trustworthiness (emanating from these various forms of process fairness information) may interact with outcome favorability to influence people's willingness to support the authority and the authority's decisions. Over time, however, people are likely to develop more certain or well-formed beliefs about the authority's trustworthiness, which may set the stage for trustworthiness to moderate the interactive relationship between process fairness and outcome favorability.

Thus, an important question for future research is whether judgments of an authority's trustworthiness have different consequences at various stages of a relationship; moreover, if this is the case, why? Note that answering these questions may best be accomplished with a longitudinal design in which the constructs of process fairness, outcome favorability, and trustworthiness (as independent variables) and people's willingness to support decisions, decision makers, and institutions (as possible dependent variables) are assessed both at earlier and at later stages of a relationship. An additional challenge to doing such a study is statistical power. Note that the reasoning posits a four-way interaction among trust in the authority, process fairness, outcome favorability, and relationship stage, such that the three-way interaction among trust, process fairness, and outcome favorability observed in several studies (Brockner, Bianchi et al., 2010; Lin et al., 2009) may be more likely to emerge at a later stage of the relationship, when people are presumably more certain of their trust judgments, whereas the mediating influence of trust on the process–outcome interaction found by Brockner et al. (1997) may be more likely to occur at an earlier stage of the relationship, in which people are presumably less certain of their trust judgments. Obviously, a sizable sample would be needed to test the predicted four-way interaction with a reasonable degree of power.

While pragmatically challenging, a study of this type may not only help to resolve the intriguing question of how trustworthiness relates to the interactive relationship between outcome favorability and process fairness, but also may address matters of interest to organizational and social psychologists beyond the confines of justice theory. For example, the findings from such a study may provide insight into the process of relationship formation and development by specifying how people's beliefs and concerns change over time. The findings also may help to inform the trust literature (e.g., Kramer & Tyler, 1996) by showing the multiple ways in which people use judgments of an authority's trustworthiness to guide their own beliefs and behaviors. That is, early on people may use judgments of the authority's trustworthiness (shaped by process fairness as well as other information) to predict how the authority is likely to behave over time. Such expectations about the authority's behavior are likely to have a profound influence on people's beliefs and behaviors apart from the effect such expectations may have on the process–outcome interaction. For example, people may seek to deepen their relationships with others whose trustworthiness engenders positive expectations of how they are likely to behave in the future.

Later, people may use judgments of the authority's trustworthiness to decide how important the relationship is to them, as a basis for judging the authenticity of the authority's actions, or as a standard against which to compare their actual experiences with the authority. Moreover, these three types of judgments may have meaningful effects, extending well beyond their moderating influence on the interactive relationship between outcome favorability and process fairness. For example, Brockner, Bianchi et al. (2010) found that people assigned greater importance to their relationships with authorities who were described as higher in morality. Whereas Brockner and Bianchi did not find that the moderating effect of the authority's morality on the process–outcome interaction was attributable to relationship importance, it seems entirely possible that the greater importance that people assign to their relationships with more moral or trustworthy authorities may have other noteworthy effects. For example, people may work harder to maintain their relationships with authorities perceived to be more moral or trustworthy. Moreover, trustworthiness judgments may be used to make inferences about the authenticity of the authority's behavior on dimensions *other than* process fairness. For example, they may take at face value the authority's statements about what the organization needs to do going forward and, as a result, be more willing to go along with such statements.

It is also worth noting that people's uncertainty about how much to trust an authority may come about in multiple ways. Thus far, I have suggested that people may be uncertain because they have not acquired enough trust-relevant information to form a firm impression, one way or the other. For example, at an early stage of their relationship with an authority, people simply may not have enough to go on to generate a meaningful judgment of the authority's trustworthiness. Consequently, any trust judgment that they do form is likely to be fraught with uncertainty. Alternatively, people may be uncertain about their level of trust in authority not because they lack information but rather because the information that they have amassed may be inconsistent. For example, if an authority alternates between being fair and unfair in the course of planning and implementing decisions, those interacting with the authority are not likely to know what to think (about the authority's trustworthiness).

It is possible that uncertainty about how much to trust an authority that emanates from *inconsistent* trust-related information (rather than from a *lack* of trust-relevant information) may have different effects on how much people draw on and hence are affected by process fairness information. If information is lacking, then people may use process fairness information to make inferences about the authority's trustworthiness, which may ultimately translate into trustworthiness playing a mediating role in the process–outcome interaction, in the manner shown in Figure 3.1A and as found by Brockner et al. (1997).

On the other hand, if information is inconsistent, people may be less apt to use process fairness information as a way to reduce uncertainty, especially if the inconsistency pertains to how much the authority exhibited process fairness in the past. If the authority has a history of being inconsistent in the fairness with which he or she plans and implements decisions, then subsequent information that people learn about the authority's process fairness may not reduce their uncertainty about the authority's trustworthiness. After all, today's high process fairness may be replaced by tomorrow's low process fairness, in which case people may not believe that they are able to make informed judgments of the authority's trustworthiness on the basis of the authority's process fairness in a given instance. If that is the case, then the mediating role of trust in the process–outcome interaction observed by Brockner et al. (1997) may fail to materialize.

Thus, in the course of examining whether people's uncertainty about how much to trust an authority influences the role of trust in the process–outcome interaction, future researchers also may do well to examine these two different types of uncertainty. In so doing, they may shed further light on the nature of uncertainty. More generally, one of my goals in writing this book is to show how theory and research pertaining to the interactive relationship between process fairness and outcome favorability may deepen our understanding of phenomena outside the purview of organizational justice. Further research on the role played by an authority's trustworthiness on the process–outcome interaction provides one possible venue in which this goal may be achieved.

Future Research on Moderators of the Process–Outcome Interaction

Whereas the studies discussed help to establish several moderators of the interactive relationship between outcome favorability and process fairness (uncertainty, outcome importance, and factors that engender contrast effects), they also raise important questions for future research. For both practical and theoretical reasons, it is important to determine *when* the interactive relationship is more versus less likely to occur. For instance, the fact that high process fairness reduces the effect of outcome favorability may be useful to managers, who are trying to gain the most support for their decisions and themselves in the most economically feasible ways. I alluded to this possibility in Chapter 1, and I have more to say about it in Chapter 7. To use the interaction effect between outcome favorability and process fairness to their best advantage, managers need to know when it is more versus less likely to occur.

Moreover, whereas outcome importance, uncertainty, and factors that promote contrast effects have been shown to moderate the process–outcome interaction, they represent rather broad categories of factors. Other determinants of or proxies for outcome importance, uncertainty, and contrast effects need to be investigated to evaluate whether they have a similar moderating influence on the interactive relationship between outcome favorability and process fairness. For example, outcome importance is likely to depend on how much is at stake economically (e.g., whether one survives an organizational downsizing or whether one is given a valued scarce resource, such as a coveted promotion). The more that is at stake economically, the more likely is outcome favorability to interact with process fairness. Outcome importance also depends on the needs and values that people bring to the situation. The more the outcome is in an arena that people feel deprived of or hungry for, or the more that the outcome is in a domain that is central to people's self-concepts, the more likely may be the favorability of the outcome to interact with process fairness.

Uncertainty also may depend on situational or dispositional factors reflective of people's needs to reach closure or confidence in the correctness of their beliefs. For example, people high in uncertainty avoidance (Hofstede, 1980) or high in the need for closure (Kruglanski, Webster, & Klem, 1993) may find uncertainty aversive and therefore may be less apt to experience uncertainty (regardless of whether it is present). Indeed, one of the items from the Kruglanski et al. Need for Closure Scale is, "I do not like situations that are uncertain." People low in self-esteem, on the other hand, may be more likely to experience uncertainty than their high self-esteem counterparts. Indeed one of the reasons why people with low self-esteem are susceptible to influence by external or social cues is that they are uncertain of the correctness of their own beliefs (Brockner, 1988). One way to conceptualize the process–outcome interaction is that particularly in the face of unfavorable outcomes, people become uncertain about a variety of matters of economic and psychological significance, prompting them to draw on and hence be affected by process fairness information to help them reduce or manage their uncertainty. Perhaps people's general tendencies to experience uncertainty (as reflected by their uncertainty avoidance, need for closure, or self-esteem) will influence the amount of uncertainty that they experience in their encounters with others, particularly in the face of unfavorable outcomes. If so, then these inputs into uncertainty also may have a moderating influence on the interactive relationship between process fairness and outcome favorability.

Moreover, the extent to which people experience contrast between expectation and experience may depend on the extent to which a given event departs from the status quo. For example, let us compare two organizations, one known to be very paternalistic toward its employees and another one that is not nearly as paternalistic. Suppose both organizations were to take action that yielded unfavorable outcomes for some of its employees, and moreover, that they did so with varying degrees of process fairness. My hunch is that the process–outcome interaction, in which people who received an unfavorable outcome with an unfair process respond particularly negatively, will be stronger in the organization known to be more rather than less paternalistic. Another possible contributor to a contrast effect would be people's general proclivities to be trusting toward decision-making authorities. Those with more of an inclination to trust (Wrightsman, 1992) also may perceive more of a negative contrast between what they expected and what they experienced if they were to receive an unfavorable outcome with low process fairness, in which case people's propensity to trust may be yet another moderator of the process–outcome interaction. In short, further research on additional moderators of the interaction effect is needed, guided by the conceptualizations set forth in this chapter.

Moreover, conceptual progress may be achieved through efforts to differentiate between findings as well as to integrate them (Greenberg, 1990b). Hence, just as it is important to see whether various representations of uncertainty, outcome importance, and contrast effects similarly moderate the interactive relationship between outcome favorability and process fairness, it is worth testing for differences in the magnitude of these moderating influences. For example, whereas uncertainty prompts people to engage in information search that gives rise to the interaction effect, what is somewhat less clear is the nature of the uncertainty that elicits the interaction effect. By examining the moderating influences of different types of uncertainty *in the same research setting* (e.g., uncertainty about how much to trust the other, uncertainty about how much people believe that they are viewed favorably by the decision-making authority, and uncertainty about how to explain the reasons for one's outcomes), future researchers may better discern the nature of the uncertainty that people are seeking to address that gives rise to the interactive relationship between process fairness and outcome favorability.

CHAPTER SUMMARY

Chapter 3 addressed two questions, the answers to which shed light on the mechanisms accounting for the interactive relationship between outcome favorability and process fairness. First, why does the interaction effect occur, that is, what are its mediators? Second, when does the interaction effect occur, that is, what are its moderators? Research conducted subsequent to Brockner and Wiesenfeld's (1996) review has provided answers to both of these questions. Mediators include people's trust in decision-making authorities and how much they view the authority as responsible for their unfavorable outcomes, although the precise form of the mediating influence differs in these two instances. For the former, process fairness influences trust, which in turn interacts with outcome favorability to influence people's support for decisions, decision makers, and institutions. For the latter, outcome favorability and process fairness interact with each other to influence how much people see the authority as responsible for their outcomes, which in turn influences people's support for decisions, decision makers, and institutions.

Moderating influences include how much people are uncertain about their standing as organizational members, relationship importance, interdependent self-construal, and trust in the decision-making authority; in each instance, a higher level of the dimension is associated with a stronger interactive relationship between outcome favorability and process fairness. Along the way, I discussed the implications of the findings for the organizational justice literature as well as other literatures, and I offered a number of suggestions for further research. For example, the fact that trust has been shown to play both a mediating role (Brockner et al., 1997) and a moderating role (Lin et al., 2009) raises the important question of why this is the case and, relatedly, when trust may be expected to have a mediating influence or a moderating influence on the interactive relationship between outcome favorability and process fairness. My colleagues and I are currently doing research designed to answer these questions.

CHAPTER

4

High Process Fairness Heightens the Effect of Outcome Favorability

INTRODUCTION

Chapters 2 and 3 described some noteworthy extensions to the process–outcome interaction summarized by Brockner and Wiesenfeld (1996), which showed that high process fairness reduced the effect of outcome favorability on people's reactions to decisions relative to when process fairness was low. The years since 1996 have provided considerable evidence that the interaction effect also may take a form decidedly different from that discussed in Chapters 2 and 3. Chapter 4 discusses how high process fairness may *heighten* the effect of outcome favorability relative to when process fairness is low. To be sure, the tendency for high process fairness to heighten the influence of outcome favorability emerged in a handful of studies reported by Brockner and Wiesenfeld, who referred to such findings as "contrary interactions." Not only did the contrary interactions take a different form from the vast majority of studies reported by Brockner and Wiesenfeld, but also they emerged on different types of dependent variables, namely, those reflective of people's self-evaluations, such as their state self-esteem (Schroth & Shah, 2000) or their self-efficacy (Gilliland, 1994).

CHAPTER OVERVIEW

Chapter 4 consists of four major sections. First, I describe the psychological process through which high process fairness heightens the impact of outcome favorability on people's self-evaluations relative to when process fairness is low. Chapters 2 and 3 suggested that people use process fairness information to make a number of important inferences pertinent to their economic and psychological well-being, such as how favorable their short- and long-term outcomes are likely to be, how much to hold the other party responsible for their outcomes, how much to trust the other party, whether their relationship with the other party is more communal or transactional, and the extent to which they are held in high regard by the other party. Much of Chapter 4 is based on the premise that people use process fairness information for yet another important sense-making purpose: to determine the extent to which they are personally responsible for their outcomes.

The second section of the chapter considers two conceptually distinct ways in which process fairness may influence people's self-evaluations: (1) the relational route (Tyler & Lind, 1992), which posits that people use process fairness information to make inferences about how much they are held in high regard by the other party (higher process fairness leads people to believe that they are held in higher regard), and (2) the self-attributional route, which posits that people use process fairness information to determine how personally responsible they are for their outcomes; higher process fairness leads people to see themselves as more personally responsible for their outcomes (Van den Bos et al., 1999), and the more personally responsible people believe they are for their outcomes, the more likely is the favorability of their outcomes to influence their self-evaluations.

After considering that people's tendencies to make self-attributions for their outcomes helps us understand how high process fairness heightens the effect of outcome favorability on self-evaluations, I address two related questions: (1) Under what conditions are people more likely to embark on the relational route versus the self-attributional route? That is, what determines whether the relationship between process fairness and self-evaluations will be driven by a relational mechanism or by a self-attributional mechanism? (2) *Given that* people have embarked on one of these routes rather than the other, under what conditions will process fairness be more versus less likely to influence self-evaluations? That is, what factors have a moderating influence on the relational mechanism through which process fairness influences self-evaluations, and what factors have a moderating influence on the self-attributional mechanism through which process fairness influences self-evaluations?

Third, whereas the ubiquitous "fair process effect" posits that people generally respond more favorably to decisions that are enacted with higher process fairness, an interesting implication of the self-attributional mechanism (more so than of the relational mechanism) is that when their outcomes are unfavorable, people may actually react *less* favorably when they are treated with higher process fairness. However, this "reverse fair process effect" has proven to be somewhat elusive. Whereas some studies have shown that higher process fairness reduces people's self-evaluations in response to unfavorable outcomes, others have shown that when people's outcomes are unfavorable, the positive relationship between process fairness and self-evaluations is either attenuated or eliminated but does not actually morph into a negative relationship (Brockner et al., 2003). Hence, the third section offers theory and research designed to help reconcile the inconsistent findings in previous studies that have examined the relationship between process fairness and people's self-evaluations in the face of unfavorable outcomes.

Fourth, an interesting implication of the reverse fair process effect is that people may not always strongly prefer to be treated with higher rather than with lower process fairness. If in response to unfavorable outcomes people evaluate themselves negatively when they are treated with higher process fairness (or at least if they are less likely to evaluate themselves positively), then when they are uncertain about the favorability of their outcomes ex ante, their typical tendency to prefer high process fairness may be reduced. The self-attributional mechanism posits that outcomes derived from fair processes are more likely to influence people's self-evaluations than are outcomes derived from unfair processes. Therefore, if people do not expect their outcomes to be favorable (or if they are at least uncertain about the favorability of their upcoming outcomes), their desire to be treated with high process fairness may be reduced. Thus, the fourth section of Chapter 4 analyzes people's preferences for process fairness as a dependent variable, in particular identifying when people may be less apt to prefer being treated with high process fairness. I suggest that people's reduced preferences for high process fairness may be functionally similar to engaging in self-handicapping behavior; both serve to reduce the self-relevance of upcoming outcomes that people suspect may be unfavorable.

As in the previous chapters, I (1) sprinkle throughout all four sections of Chapter 4 suggestions for further theory and research and (2) discuss how the concepts and empirical findings presented here inform literatures other than justice, such as those pertaining to identity (Skitka, 2003), regulatory focus (Higgins, 1998), self-handicapping (Jones & Berglas, 1978), and affective forecasting (Gilbert, 2006).

HOW HIGH PROCESS FAIRNESS HEIGHTENS THE IMPACT OF OUTCOME FAVORABILITY ON SELF-EVALUATIONS

It comes as little surprise that people feel better about themselves when their outcomes are favorable rather than unfavorable. What needs further consideration, however, is why the positive relationship between outcome favorability and self-evaluations is stronger when process fairness is relatively high, as has been found in many studies (Brockner et al., 2003; De Cremer & van Knippenberg, 2003; Koper, van Knippenberg, Bouhuijs, Vermunt, & Wilke, 1993; Ployhart & Ryan, 1997; Ployhart, Ryan, & Bennett, 1999). Two forces seem to be at play. First, theory and research on achievement motivation have suggested that outcome favorability is more likely to be positively related to people's self-evaluations to the extent that they attribute their outcomes to something about themselves (e.g., Weiner, 1985). All else being equal, then, favorable outcomes lead people to feel better about themselves when they make more self-attributions for their outcomes, and unfavorable outcomes lead people to feel worse about themselves when they make more self-attributions.

Second, high process fairness leads people to make more self-attributions for their outcomes. Outcomes resulting from fair processes are likely to be seen as deserved (i.e., arrived at "fairly and squarely"). The notion that outcomes are deserved is akin to people believing that it was something about themselves (their behavior or personal qualities) that was responsible for their outcomes. Consistent with this reasoning, several studies have shown that higher process fairness leads people to make more self-attributions for their outcomes (Leung, Su, & Morris, 2001; Van den Bos et al., 1999). In the Van den Bos et al. study, for example, all participants received an unfavorable outcome based on an evaluation process that was relatively fair or unfair. They then indicated the extent to which their outcomes were due to something about themselves. As predicted, people were much more likely to make self-attributions for their outcomes when the evaluation process was fairer, and this tendency was heightened even further in a more evaluative context, in which they were probably more motivated to explain the reasons for their outcomes.

Thus, the tendency for high process fairness to heighten the influence of outcome favorability on self-evaluations results from the facts that (1) process fairness is positively related to how much people make self-attributions for their outcomes, and (2) how much people make self-attributions for their outcomes influences the magnitude of the positive relationship between outcome favorability and self-evaluations. Not only have many studies shown that higher process fairness heightens the influence of outcome favorability on self-evaluations, but also there is some support for the hypothesized mediating role of self-attributions. More specifically, Brockner et al. (2003, Study 2) had an alleged company recruiter ask participants to complete a measure of their "managerial potential." Half were told that they had a lot of potential and would have been hired by the recruiter's company based on their performance (favorable outcome condition), whereas the other half were told just the opposite (unfavorable outcome condition). Participants also rated (1) the fairness of the process used to make judgments of their managerial potential, (2) the extent to which they attributed their outcome to something about themselves (their ability and effort), and (3) their self-evaluations.

Results showed a significant interactive effect of outcome favorability and process fairness on participants' self-evaluations, such that outcome favorability was more positively related to self-evaluations when process fairness was relatively high. A separate analysis of self-evaluations also yielded a significant interaction between outcome favorability and self-attributions, such that outcome favorability was more positively related to self-evaluations when people made more self-attributions for their outcomes. Process fairness and self-attributions were positively related to one another, as expected. Moreover, the results of a mediation analysis showed that it was not process fairness per se that interacted with outcome favorability to influence people's self-evaluations. Rather, in yet another instance of "mediated moderation" (Muller et al., 2005), process fairness was positively related to people's tendencies to make self-attributions for their outcomes, which in turn interacted with outcome favorability to influence people's self-evaluations.

The fact that high process fairness heightens the influence of outcome favorability on self-evaluations relative to when process fairness is low has at least two important implications. First, it suggests yet another way (beyond those mentioned in Chapters 2 and 3) in which people use process fairness information for sense-making purposes, namely, to determine how much they are personally responsible for their outcomes. Second, it identifies an additional mechanism (beyond that provided by Tyler and Lind's 1992 relational model) through which process fairness influences people's evaluations of themselves. I turn to these two important implications next.

Linking Process Fairness With Self-Attributions for Outcomes

The initial explanation of procedural justice effects posited that people were primarily concerned with receiving favorable tangible outcomes in both the short and long term (Thibaut & Walker, 1975). According to Thibaut and Walker, people use process fairness information to make inferences about the favorability of their tangible outcomes. Thus, people prefer fair processes relative to unfair processes because the former makes them more optimistic than the latter about their chances to receive favorable tangible outcomes. Relational models of procedural justice (e.g., Tyler & Lind, 1992) focused on people's desire to experience favorable "psychological outcomes" in their interactions with others. Relational theory implies that people use process fairness information to make inferences about the other party and their relationship with the other party (i.e., neutrality, standing, and trust), which in turn influences their senses of self-esteem and self-identity. Thus, according to the relational viewpoint, people prefer high process fairness because, among other things, it communicates that the other party thinks highly of them, which in turn enables them to feel good about themselves.

The tendency for high process fairness to heighten the effect of outcome favorability on people's self-evaluations suggests an additional way in which people use process fairness information: to determine the reasons for their outcomes, in particular to evaluate the extent to which they are personally responsible for their outcomes. The results of studies presented in Chapters 2 and 3 suggested that people use process fairness information for causal attribution purposes, particularly when deciding how much to hold *the other party* responsible for their outcomes (Barclay et al., 2005; Brockner et al., 2007). Research and theory have suggested that people are more likely to attribute their outcomes (especially unfavorable outcomes) to the other party when the other exhibits lower process fairness (Brockner et al., 2007; Folger & Cropanzano, 2001). The interactive effect of outcome favorability and process fairness on self-evaluations reported in the present chapter suggests that people also are more likely to make self-attributions for their outcomes when the other exhibits higher process fairness.

At first blush, the assertions made in the last two sentences of the preceding paragraph may appear to be redundant. For example, if people are more apt to attribute their unfavorable outcomes to the other party when the other exhibits lower process fairness, would not such a tendency also suggest that they are more likely to attribute their unfavorable outcomes to themselves when the other exhibits higher process fairness? This is not necessarily so. An affirmative answer to the question assumes that attributions to the other party and attributions to the self represent the endpoints of a single continuum, such that stronger attributions to the other party are synonymous with weaker self-attributions and vice versa. Indeed, early writings on attribution theory implied that internal and external attributions of causality were unidimensional, that is, inversely related to one another (Kelley, 1973). However, more recent research has shown that internal and external attributions of causality represent two distinct dimensions rather than opposite endpoints of a single dimension (e.g., Amabile, Hill, Hennessey, & Tighe, 1994). Hence, the fact that low process fairness leads people to attribute their unfavorable outcomes to the other party does not necessarily mean that high process fairness leads people to make more self-attributions for their unfavorable outcomes. Rather, the latter is an empirical question to which the studies described in the present chapter provide a meaningful answer.

In summary, process fairness information may affect a wide variety of attitudes and behaviors precisely because people use such information for a host of sense-making purposes. The interactive effect of outcome favorability and process fairness on people's self-evaluations suggests that one such purpose is to determine how much to make self-attributions for one's outcomes. One important mandate for future research, then, is to determine when people use process fairness information for one sense-making purpose rather than the other. I discuss this matter in more detail in this chapter, for example, in the discussion of identity theory on pages 123–129.

HOW PROCESS FAIRNESS INFLUENCES SELF-EVALUATIONS

The different ways in which people use process fairness information for sense-making purposes suggest that the influence of process fairness on self-evaluations may take multiple forms and may come about through multiple mechanisms. To this point, the justice theory that has had the most to say about the effect of process fairness on people's self-evaluations is the relational model (Tyler & Lind, 1992). According to this viewpoint, process fairness informs people of several related factors that may influence their self-evaluations. For one thing, process fairness sends a message about how much the parties enacting the process ("enacters") seek to include versus exclude recipients in the collective. The greater the process fairness, the more the enacters are communicating messages of inclusion rather than exclusion, and the more that recipients feel included rather than excluded, the more likely they may be to evaluate themselves positively.

Relatedly, process fairness also symbolizes the esteem with which recipients are held in the eyes of the enacters; the greater the process fairness, the more likely are recipients to believe that they are held in high regard. The notion of "reflected appraisal" (Cooley, 1902; Mead, 1934) posits that people's self-evaluations are determined in part by their inferences of how they are viewed by important others. Thus, people may evaluate themselves more positively in response to higher levels of process fairness because they believe that important others think highly of them (i.e., value them, respect them, like them, want to include them rather than exclude them, etc.). This reasoning suggests that the relational model is well equipped to account for the positive *main effect* of process fairness on self-evaluations, which has been found on numerous occasions (e.g., Koper et al., 1993; Tyler, DeGoey, & Smith, 1996). For that matter, reflected appraisal also may account for the typically observed positive main effect of outcome favorability on self-evaluations (Koper et al., 1993). After all, people are more likely to infer that they are thought of highly when others dole out favorable rather than unfavorable outcomes.

However, the reflected appraisal mechanism seems less able to account for the *interactive effect* of process fairness and outcome favorability on people's self-evaluations, in which outcome favorability is *more* consequential when process fairness is relatively high. Instead, the link between process fairness and people's tendencies to make self-attributions for their outcomes may provide better insight into why outcome favorability has more of an impact on people's self-evaluations when process fairness is relatively high.

More on Reflected Appraisal and Self-Attributions

I am not suggesting that people's self-attributions for their outcomes is *better* equipped than reflected appraisal to account for the effect of process fairness on self-evaluations. Rather, the reflected appraisal process underlying relational theory is unlikely to provide a *complete* account of how process fairness affects people's self-evaluations. More likely, both reflected appraisal and how much people make self-attributions for their outcomes may help to account for the relationship between process fairness and self-evaluations. If that is the case, then it is worth considering when the relationship between process fairness and self-evaluations is more likely to be accounted for by one mechanism rather than the other.

For example, the various elements comprising process fairness may differ in the extent to which they influence people's self-evaluations via reflected appraisal. Bies (1987) made an important contribution to the justice literature by introducing the notion of *interactional fairness*, which refers to the quality of the interpersonal treatment that people receive in their dealings with decision-making authorities. Until that time, procedural fairness was conceptualized to consist of the formal decision-making rules used by institutions to make resource allocation decisions, such as voice (Thibaut & Walker, 1975), or the criteria set forth by Leventhal et al. (1980), such as accuracy and consistency.

Blader and Tyler (2003) recognized that interactional justice differed from procedural fairness in at least two respects, which gave rise to their four-component model of process fairness organized by the two dimensions along which interactional fairness and procedural fairness differ: (1) the source of the process (i.e., "the policies, rules, and prevailing norms of the group as a whole," or formal rules, vs. "the actions of particular representatives of the group," or informal behavior; Blader & Tyler, 2003, p. 749) and (2) the content of the process (i.e., the quality of the source's decision-making procedures vs. the quality of the source's treatment). The four components created by a factorial crossing of the source and content dimensions are presented in Table 4.1, along with a sample item used to measure each component.

Process fairness enacted through informal behavior may be more likely to influence people's self-evaluations via reflected appraisal than is process fairness enacted through formal rules. For example, within the domain of quality of treatment, some of the items measuring informal behavior include "My supervisor treats me fairly when decisions are being implemented" and "My supervisor usually gives me an honest explanation for the decisions he or she makes." In contrast, some of the measures of formal rules pertaining to quality of treatment are "The rules lead to fair treatment when decisions are being implemented" and "The rules require that I get an honest explanation for how decisions are made."

TABLE 4.1 Blader and Tyler (2003) Four-Component Model of Process Fairness

	Content of the Process	
Source of the Process	**Decision-Making Procedures**	**Treatment**
Formal rules	"The rules and procedures are equally fair to everyone."	"The rules lead to fair treatment when decisions are being implemented."
Informal behavior	"My supervisor's decisions are equally fair to everyone."	"My supervisor treats me fairly when decisions are being implemented."

Note: Sample items developed by Blader and Tyler are provided in each quadrant.

Why might informal behavior be more likely than formal rules to influence people's self-evaluations via reflected appraisal? At least two possibilities come to mind. First, formal rules apply to everybody. Thus, if the rule requires that people receive honest explanations of how decisions are made, they may be less likely to perceive the provision of an honest explanation as evidence of their worthiness (e.g., the source's desire to include them in the collective). Instead, they may attribute the honest explanation to the rule that mandated it, which is a decidedly impersonal source. In contrast, informal behavior may be (or at least may be perceived to be) less constrained, thereby giving implementers more of a say in how they are going to behave. For example, when people judge their supervisor as having provided them with an honest explanation, they may infer that their supervisor had some discretion in doing so, which may be interpreted as more of a statement of their supervisor's positive regard for them relative to whether that same explanation was perceived to have been scripted or mandated by organizational policy. Put differently, the supervisor's provision of the explanation may be perceived as more authentic or credible, in which case its symbolic message of high positive regard may be experienced to a greater extent by the recipient.

Second, possible differences in perceptual salience between informal behavior and formal rules may be relevant. As Heider (1958) suggested long ago, "Behavior engulfs the field." In other words, people's attention may be directed more naturally to others' behavior than to the context in which it occurs, at least within more individualistic cultures (Morris & Peng, 1994). Others' behavior may be symbolic of how people are viewed by those others, and the nature of rules also may be symbolic of how people are viewed by the parties who make those rules. However, if people's attention is more naturally drawn to others' behavior than to the rules that may guide such behavior, then the symbolic meaning of the former also may be more impactful than the symbolic meaning of the latter.

In fact, in a recent scenario study, Blader (S. Blader, personal communication, August 24, 2005) orthogonally manipulated each of the dimensions in the Blader and Tyler (2003) four-factor model of process fairness. Participants were led to believe that they had been treated with high or low process fairness on each of the four dimensions, and the dependent variable consisted of a self-evaluation, in which participants were asked, "How would this experience make you feel about yourself?" Scale endpoints were "very negative" and "very positive." The results showed that the manipulations of process fairness based on informal behavior had more of an impact on people's self-evaluations than did the manipulations of process fairness based on formal rules.

The mediating role of reflected appraisal in the relationship between process fairness and self-evaluations also leads to the following prediction: The tendency for informal behavior to be more likely than formal rules to influence self-evaluations via reflected appraisal may be less applicable in the domain of quality of decision-making procedures than in the domain of quality of treatment. Sample measures of informal behavior vis-à-vis decision-making procedures include "My supervisor's decisions are equally fair to everyone" and "My supervisor's decisions are consistent across people and situations." Sample measures of formal rules in the domain of quality of decision-making include "The rules and procedures are equally fair to everyone" and "The rules and procedures are applied consistently across people and situations." In both instances, the presence or absence of process fairness may say relatively little about how people are perceived by the source. Rather, in both of these instances people may be more likely to make an external attribution for the process fairness that they experienced. The reason for this is that formal rules are likely to induce an external attribution for behavior. Moreover, the highly consistent behavior of the supervisor suggests an external attribution. That is, the consistency in the supervisor's behavior may lead people to attribute the supervisor's behavior to something about the supervisor rather than to something about the supervisor's opinion of themselves, the recipients of the supervisor's actions (Kelley, 1973).

The notion that process fairness may influence self-evaluations through reflected appraisal also suggests yet another way to differentiate between the various elements of process fairness. Others have similarly distinguished between the various elements of process fairness by showing that they differentially affect certain dependent variables (Colquitt et al., 2001). For example, organizational commitment is much more strongly predicted by formal rules pertaining to the quality of decision-making procedures than it is by the informal behavior of the supervisor's quality of treatment. However, evaluations of the supervisor are much more strongly predicted by the informal behavior of the supervisor's quality of treatment than they are by formal rules pertaining to the quality of decision-making procedures (Rupp & Cropanzano, 2002). In like fashion, elements of process fairness also may differ with respect to how much they influence people's self-evaluations via reflected appraisal.

Informal behavior may differ from formal rules not only on the basis of the source of the process information but also along the dimension of how self-relevant the two constructs are perceived to be. If informal behavior is in fact seen as more self-relevant than are formal rules, then process fairness information based on the former may have more of an effect on people's self-evaluations via reflected appraisal than would process fairness information based on the latter. Consistent with this reasoning, Bies (personal communication, May 24, 2005) reported that people are more motivated to extract revenge when they have been subjected to an attack on their personal identity than when they experienced a violation of rules and procedures. Attacks on personal identity typically come in the form of informal behavior and hence may be seen as more self-relevant (i.e., "taken personally") than are violations of rules and procedures.

Viewing the relationship between process fairness and self-evaluations through the lens of theory and research on persuasive communications may shed additional light on when the reflected appraisal mechanism is likely to be operative. That is, just because the source is sending messages that *could* influence recipients' self-evaluations (e.g., about the source's desire to include rather than exclude recipients) does not mean that those messages *will* actually affect recipients' self-evaluations. As research on persuasive communications and attitude change has shown (e.g., Hovland, Janis, & Kelley, 1953), the extent to which people are influenced by communications varies as a function of the source, the nature of the communication, the recipients, and the context in which the communication takes place. Hence, people's self-evaluations may be more affected by the evaluation of them implied by process fairness information when the source of the process is of high credibility (expert, trustworthy) or is someone whose opinion is greatly valued. Moreover, people may be more likely to buy into the evaluation of them implied by process fairness information when they are more uncertain about the correctness of their self-views (De Cremer & Sedikides, 2005).

Identity Theory

Identity theory provides yet another framework useful for delineating the conditions under which reflected appraisal or self-attributions for outcomes may account for the relationship between process fairness and self-evaluations. Identity theorists have noted that people maintain different conceptions of themselves, such as their material identity, their personal identity, and their social identity. According to Skitka (2003), "Material identity consists of the body and its adornment, family members to the extent that they are contextually understood as material extensions of the self, … as well as one's home and hearth, acquisitions, and accumulated wealth" (p. 288). Personal identity "refers to the experienced self, or that aspect of identity that provides a sense of personal continuity. … People seek to define and defend their sense of personal identity through achievement, mastery, and moral authenticity" (p. 288). Social identity refers to how people define themselves on the basis of their relationships with other people, groups, and organizations. It is "shaped by the groups people belong to, their social roles in those groups, and the reflected appraisal or standing that they have vis-à-vis other group members" (p. 288). The impact of these various self-conceptions on people's beliefs and behaviors depends on their relative degree of accessibility. Accessibility in turn is a function of numerous factors, including some more distal (e.g., past experiences) and others more proximal (current expectations, desires, and goals; cues from the social environment).

Skitka (2003) has proposed an accessible identity model (AIM) that posits that how people define fairness depends on the nature of the identity that is most accessible at a given point in time. For example, people's conceptions of distributive justice are more likely to be based on equity when their material identity is most accessible, whereas they may define distributive fairness on the basis of equality or need when their social identity is most accessible. Building on Skitka's AIM, I suggest that how people use process fairness information also may depend on the nature of their identity that is most accessible at a given point in time. For example, people may use process fairness information to make inferences of how they are regarded by others when their social identity is highly accessible. Accessible social identities make relational concerns more salient, which may lead people to be concerned with judgments of the other party along the dimensions of neutrality, standing, and trust (Tyler & Lind, 1992). Alternatively, they may use process fairness information to make inferences about how much to attribute their outcomes to themselves when their personal identity is highly accessible. Accessible personal identities make achievement and mastery concerns more salient, which may thereby motivate people to determine the extent to which *they* are personally responsible for their outcomes.

Chapter 3 presented the results of several studies that tested for cross-national differences in the interactive relationship between outcome favorability and process fairness (Brockner et al., 2000). The findings showed that the interaction effect, in which high process fairness reduced the effect of outcome favorability on people's willingness to support decisions and decision makers relative to when process fairness was low was exhibited to a significantly greater extent among those with more of an interdependent than independent orientation. Culturally based differences in interdependence versus independence are likely to influence the nature of identities that are accessible to people at a given point in time. More specifically, it is likely that cultures fostering more interdependent forms of self-construal heighten the accessibility of people's social identities, whereas cultures fostering more independent forms of self-construal heighten the accessibility of people's personal identities.

In the cross-national studies reported in the previous chapter (Brockner et al., 2000), it was not simply that high process fairness was more likely to reduce the effect of outcome favorability on people's support for decisions and decision makers when they came from cultures fostering interdependence; there was also some evidence that among those from cultures fostering more independent forms of self-construal, high process fairness *heightened* the effect of outcome favorability on people's support for decisions and decision makers relative to when process fairness was low.

One interpretation of these findings is that people's national culture contributed to differences in the nature of their accessible identities. Among those from cultures fostering interdependence, social identities may have been more accessible. As a result, they may have been more concerned with determining the nature of their relationship with the other, leading them to use process fairness information to make relational inferences. Higher process fairness may have led them to define their relationship in more communal ways, whereas low process fairness may have led them to define the relationship in more transactional ways, thereby making outcome favorability considerably more consequential in the latter than in the former case.

In contrast, among those from cultures fostering independence, personal identities may have been more accessible. As a result, they may have been more concerned with determining the extent to which they were personally responsible for the outcomes that they received. People may have used process fairness information to make judgments of how much to attribute their outcomes to something about themselves. Higher process fairness may have led them to make more personal or self-attributions for their outcomes, thereby heightening the effect of outcome favorability on their support for the decisions and the decision makers. A fair process (and the self-attribution accompanying it) may have led people to be extremely satisfied with decisions and decision makers when their outcomes were favorable, whereas a fair process and accompanying self-attribution may have led people to be extremely dissatisfied with the decision and decision maker when their outcomes were unfavorable.

The notion that national culture influences the nature of people's accessible identity, which in turn may dictate the form of the interactive relationship between outcome favorability and process fairness, warrants further consideration. For example, it would be useful to evaluate whether other factors (besides national culture) that make personal and social identity differentially accessible yield results similar to those reported by Brockner et al. (2000), in which national culture may have served as a proxy for the nature of people's accessible identity. People's personal identities (i.e., their tendencies to see themselves as distinct from others) may be more accessible when (1) they are made to focus on themselves by situational cues (e.g., working in an office surrounded by mirrors or in an organization in which the culture encourages introspection; Buss, 1980) or (2) they are dispositionally inclined to focus on the private or covert aspects of themselves (Fenigstein, Scheier, & Buss, 1975). When their personal identities are highly accessible, they may be motivated to determine the role that *they* played in producing certain outcomes, in which case they may use process fairness information to determine their level of personal responsibility. Under such conditions, I would expect to find an interaction between process fairness and outcome favorability, in which high process fairness increases the effect of outcome favorability on people's self-evaluations (or on other attitudes and behaviors affected by or reflective of their self-evaluations) relative to when process fairness is low.

In contrast, people's social identities may be more accessible when (1) they are bounded together with fellow group members in a common cause, (2) the nature of their work is highly interdependent on fellow group members, and (3) they are dispositionally inclined to think of themselves as connected to others (rather than as separate and distinct from others). When their social identities are highly accessible, they may be motivated to determine the nature of their relationship with the other party, in which case they may use process fairness information to make relational inferences. Under such conditions, I would expect to observe the following effects of outcome favorability and process fairness on different types of dependent variables: (1) a positive main effect of process fairness on people's self-evaluations and (2) an interactive effect of outcome favorability and process fairness on people's support for decisions, decision makers, and institutions, such that high process fairness reduces the impact of outcome favorability on support relative to when process fairness is low.

The above reasoning was partially tested in a recent series of studies by Holmvall and Bobocel (2008). I say "partially tested" because Holmvall and Bobocel did not vary outcome favorability; rather, all of their participants received unfavorable outcomes. However, the authors did examine both the level of and the salience of people's personal and social identities. Those with a strong sense of social identity emphasize relational concerns. For example, they derive positive self-regard by connecting with others, fitting in, and believing that others evaluate them positively. As a result, they are likely to use process fairness information to make inferences about their relationship with the other party, the extent to which the other party views them favorably, and so on. Hence, even when their outcomes are unfavorable, those with a strong sense of social identity are likely to exhibit a "fair process effect"; that is, they may respond more positively when process fairness is high rather than low because high process fairness elicits more favorable relational inferences.

In contrast, those with a strong sense of personal identity emphasize more individualistic concerns. Thus, they derive positive self-regard by distinguishing themselves from others (say, by performing better than others). Consequently, they may be more likely to use process fairness information to determine the extent to which they are personally responsible for their outcomes. Thus, when their outcomes are unfavorable, they may be less likely to exhibit a fair process effect; if anything, they may actually show a "reverse fair process effect." That is, seeing themselves as more personally responsible for their unfavorable outcomes when process fairness is high rather than low, they may be inclined to respond less positively when process fairness is relatively high.

In their first study, Holmvall and Bobocel (2008) had participants complete an individual difference measure of social identity, namely, the Singelis (1994) scale tapping interdependent self-construal. They then experienced a priming manipulation designed to heighten the salience of their social identity or their personal identity. Next, they read a vignette in which they were asked to imagine that they had applied for a desirable promotion in the organization in which they were currently employed. Moreover, in all instances they did not receive the promotion, that is, the outcome was unfavorable for all participants. However, for half of the participants the unfavorable outcome was delivered with higher process fairness, whereas for the other half of the participants the unfavorable outcome was delivered with lower process fairness. The dependent variable was perceived outcome fairness. Replicating previous findings, Holmvall and Bobocel found a main effect for process fairness, such that outcome fairness was judged to be greater when process fairness was high rather than low. Of greater importance, the authors found a three-way interaction among interdependent self-construal, priming, and process fairness. Specifically, those with more interdependent self-construals showed a stronger fair process effect (see also Brockner, De Cremer, Van den Bos, & Chen, 2005), and this two-way interaction between interdependent self-construal and process fairness was significantly more pronounced when participants' social identity (rather than their personal identity) had been situationally primed.

In a second study, Holmvall and Bobocel (2008) examined participants' independent (rather than interdependent) self-construals, in particular the "vertical individualism" element of independent self-construal (Triandis, 1996), in which not only is the separateness of the self emphasized but also inequality between people is accepted. This aspect of personal identity may be particularly relevant to the self-attributional mechanism presumed to account for the reverse fair process effect in the face of unfavorable outcomes. Unlike in the previous study, in which participants were asked to imagine that they had received an unfavorable outcome, in this study participants actually experienced an unfavorable outcome. As in the previous study, (1) participants were situationally primed to make their personal identity or their social identity salient, and (2) the process fairness with which the unfavorable outcome was delivered to them was either high or low. The dependent variable referred to how satisfied participants were with their outcomes. Of greatest importance, Holmvall and Bobocel found a three-way interaction among independent self-construal, priming, and process fairness. When participants were primed such that their personal identity was made salient to them, there was a significant two-way interaction between independent self-construal and process fairness. Those high in independent self-construal showed a significant "reverse process fairness effect," that is, higher process fairness engendered lower outcome satisfaction relative to their counterparts with lower independent self-construals. In contrast, when participants' social identity had been primed, there were no effects (main or interactive) for independent self-construal and process fairness.

The two Holmvall and Bobocel (2008) studies showed that *in the face of unfavorable outcomes*, process fairness bears very different relationships with outcome judgments as a function of their social and personal identity. Those with a stronger sense of social identity showed more of a fair process effect, consistent with the notion that they used process fairness information to make relational inferences about themselves, whereas those with a stronger sense of personal identity showed more of a reverse fair process effect, consistent with the notion that they used process fairness information to make attributions of personal responsibility for their outcomes. Moreover, both of these effects were more likely to emerge when the situation made salient the form of identity that was congruent with the one that people emphasized (i.e., social identity among those with more interdependent self-construals and personal identity among those with more independent self-construals) relative to when the situation had primed an incongruent form of identity (e.g., personal identity among those with more interdependent self-construals).

It is worth noting that the effect of interdependent self-construal (moderated by priming social identity) and the effect of independent self-construal (moderated by priming personal identity) were demonstrated by Holmvall and Bobocel (2008) in separate studies. Given the countless between-study differences, this leaves open the question of whether conceptually parallel findings may be found in the same study. Thus, Holmvall and Bobocel conducted a third experiment in which they examined both forms of self-construal simultaneously, along with the situational prime and process fairness variables. Importantly, the results of this study revealed both of the three-way interactions previously described: (1) Interdependent self-construal × Priming × Process fairness, such that the stronger fair process effect shown by those with more interdependent forms of self-construal was particularly likely to emerge when their social identity had been made salient, and (2) Independent self-construal × Priming × Process fairness, such that the stronger reverse fair process effect shown by those with more independent forms of self-construal was particularly pronounced when their personal identity had been made salient.

In addition to the important contribution these findings make to the interactive relationships between outcome favorability and process fairness, the Holmvall and Bobocel (2008) findings speak to two related matters of theoretical significance in the identity literature: (1) the need to distinguish between the *level* of people's self-construal (as captured by individual differences or other factors) and the *salience* of people's self-construals (as influenced by situational primes or other factors) and (2) how the level and salience of people's self-construal combine with each other to influence people's beliefs and behaviors.

On the one hand, it is tempting to view the level and the salience of self-construal as somewhat interchangeable. In other words, perhaps making salient a particular form of identity would induce people to react like those who are dispositionally inclined to have a high level of that form of identity. For example, perhaps priming people's social identities may transform them to behave similarly to those who are dispositionally high in interdependent self-construal. If that were the case, however, then Holmvall and Bobocel should have found similar effects produced by their individual difference measures of self-construal and the corresponding situational inductions of identity. For example, if interdependent self-construal interacted with process fairness in a particular manner, then the situational prime of social identity should have interacted with process fairness in the same way. Whereas Holmvall and Bobocel found some evidence of these tendencies, they were not observed consistently across their three studies.

An alternative view posits that there is a meaningful distinction between the level of people's identity (personal, social, or otherwise) and the salience or accessibility of that identity. According to this viewpoint, captured by Skitka's (2003) AIM model of justice reasoning, among others (e.g., Verplanken & Holland, 2002), the level and salience of a particular form of identity will combine interactively to influence people's beliefs and behaviors. That is, the level of a particular form of identity (e.g., interdependent self-construal) is likely to be much more influential when that form of identity is salient relative to when it is not. Indeed, it was this last type of interactive pattern between level of identity and salience of identity that consistently emerged in all three of the Holmvall and Bobocel (2008) studies.

Future Research Opportunity

Of course, a more complete test of the hypothesis that the level and salience of people's personal and social identity will dictate the form of the interactive relationship between outcome favorability and process fairness requires that outcome favorability be included as an independent variable in the research design. When people have more of an interdependent form of self-construal, they may use process fairness information to make relational inferences, in which case high process fairness will reduce the impact of outcome favorability on people's willingness to support decisions, decision makers, and institutions relative to when process fairness is low (Brockner et al., 2000). The Holmvall and Bobocel (2008) findings suggest that this complex three-way interaction among interdependent self-construal, process fairness, and outcome favorability will be even more pronounced when people's social identities are salient.

When people have more independent self-construals, however, they may use process fairness information to evaluate how personally responsible they are for their outcomes, in which case we would expect high process fairness to heighten the impact of outcome favorability on people's willingness to support decisions, decision makers, and institutions relative to when process fairness is low. Moreover, the Holmvall and Bobocel (2008) findings suggest that this particular three-way interaction effect should be even stronger when people's personal identities have been activated.

Further Articulating the Link Between Process Fairness and Self-Attributions

The positive relationship between process fairness and people's tendencies to make self-attributions for their outcomes is pivotal to the interaction effect in which high process fairness heightens the effect of outcome favorability on people's self-evaluations relative to when process fairness is low (Brockner et al., 2003). Identity theory and related research (e.g., Holmvall & Bobocel, 2008) have helped to identify when people will be more versus less predisposed to use process fairness information to evaluate the extent to which they are personally responsible for their outcomes. Given that they are oriented to do so (e.g., if they have high independent self-construals and their personal identity is salient), further research still is needed to better understand when and why high process fairness predisposes people to make more self-attributions for their outcomes. In other words, the magnitude of the relationship between process fairness and people's tendencies to make self-attributions for their outcomes may depend on other factors, even when they are already oriented to use process fairness information for self-attributional purposes.

Possible Moderators of the Relationship (Answering the "When?" Question)

It may be that certain elements of process fairness are less well suited than others to induce people to make self-attributions for their outcomes. For example, resource allocation processes generally are considered to be fair when they are consistent or unbiased, that is, when they are based on "level playing fields" in which all parties have an equal likelihood of receiving valued resources or avoiding unwanted burdens. Perhaps the most compelling example of an unbiased decision process is when resources (or burdens) are allocated on the basis of a random drawing, such as a lottery. Whereas lotteries may reflect high process fairness, it seems relatively unlikely that people will make self-attributions for the outcomes they receive on the basis of lotteries (although Langer's 1975 classic work on the illusion of control may suggest otherwise, in that people sometimes see themselves as being able to influence outcomes that they know to be randomly determined).

Another possible moderator of the relationship between process fairness and the tendency to make self-attributions is outcome favorability. In other words, process fairness not only leads people to make self-attributions for their outcomes, which in turn interact with outcome favorability to influence their self-evaluations, but also the relationship between process fairness and the tendency to make self-attributions for one's outcomes may depend on the favorability of those same outcomes. Given that people generally prefer to feel good about themselves, they respond to evaluative information in ways that enable them to enhance their self-esteem (in the face of favorable outcomes) or to protect their self-esteem (in the face of unfavorable outcomes). For example, people generally make self-attributions for favorable outcomes and external attributions for unfavorable outcomes (Weary Bradley, 1978; Zuckerman, 1979). Note that the positive relationship between process fairness and self-attributions fosters self-enhancement in the case of favorable outcomes. However, the tendency for higher process fairness to elicit stronger self-attributions runs counter to people's needs to protect themselves in response to unfavorable outcomes. If people are more likely to make self-attributions for their favorable rather than unfavorable outcomes, it may help to explain why the magnitude (or absolute value) of the positive relationship between process fairness and self-evaluations following favorable outcomes tends to be greater than the magnitude of the inverse relationship between process fairness and self-evaluations in response to unfavorable outcomes.

An alternative explanation of the last tendency is that the operationalizations of favorable and unfavorable outcomes may not be well calibrated. That is, perhaps the magnitude of the favorable outcomes that have been examined in previous research is greater than the magnitude of the unfavorable outcomes, in which case self-attributions will lead to more of a rise in self-evaluations in the former case relative to the drop in self-evaluations that would be expected to ensue from self-attributions in the latter case. Given that "losses loom larger than gains" (Kahneman & Tversky, 1984), however, this prospect seems rather remote. A more likely possibility is that, for self-serving reasons, people prefer to make self-attributions for their favorable outcomes than for their unfavorable outcomes.

Yet another possibility, also consistent with this line of reasoning, is that even if the positive relationship between process fairness and self-attributions were equally strong in the face of favorable and unfavorable outcomes, people may find ways to incorporate and hence be influenced by the self-evaluative implications of their self-attributions more in the case of favorable outcomes than unfavorable outcomes. For example, they may see their favorable outcomes as due to the internal attribution of ability, which may be particularly self-enhancing, whereas they may judge their unfavorable outcomes to the internal attribution of lack of effort, which may not be as psychologically devastating (Dweck, 1975). Ability represents a more stable internal attribution than does effort. As a result, the perception of having received a favorable outcome because of a stable internal factor may allow people to feel good about themselves, whereas the perception of having received an unfavorable outcome because of an unstable internal factor may be less likely to engender reduced self-evaluations.

Possible Mediators of the Relationship (Answering the "Why?" Question)

Future research also needs to explain why process fairness is positively related to people's tendencies to make self-attributions for their outcomes. One line of reasoning suggests that (1) people are more likely to believe that their outcomes are deserved in the case of high process fairness than low process fairness, and (2) the perception of deservingness is essentially a self-attribution. However, this line of reasoning has not been tested. In fact, I am not aware of any research that has explicitly examined why high process fairness leads people to make more self-attributions for their outcomes, even though the positive relationship between process fairness and self-attributions has been shown in a handful of empirical studies (e.g., Van den Bos et al., 1999), and conceptual arguments designed to account for these findings have appeared in the literature (Greenberg & Cropanzano, 2001).

RESOLVING AN INTRIGUING INCONSISTENCY IN REACTIONS TO UNFAVORABLE OUTCOMES

Whereas outcome favorability and process fairness frequently have been shown to interact to influence people's self-evaluations, the precise nature of the interaction effect has not been entirely consistent across studies. To be sure, what has emerged across many studies is that the relationship between process fairness and self-evaluations is significantly *more* positive when outcomes are favorable than when they are unfavorable. The inconsistency arises in how people respond to unfavorable outcomes. Some studies found that process fairness and self-evaluations continue to be positively related to one another but significantly less so than when outcomes are favorable (an "attenuation" effect). Others showed that process fairness and self-evaluations are unrelated to one another, in contrast to the positive relationship between the two that emerges when outcomes are favorable (an "elimination" effect). Still other studies showed perhaps the most intriguing pattern of all, namely, that process fairness and self-evaluations are inversely related to one another (a "reversal" effect).

Of these three different possibilities, the reversal effect is probably the most noteworthy on both conceptual and practical grounds. At the conceptual level, it stands in stark contrast to the vast majority of theory and research associated with the "fair process effect," in which higher levels of process fairness elicit more positive reactions, including but not limited to measures of how people evaluate themselves (e.g., De Cremer & Tyler, 2005; Koper et al., 1993). At the practical level, it flies in the face of the typical prescription given to decision makers, that is, to plan and implement decisions with high process fairness, especially when they must administer unfavorable outcomes, to elicit less negative or more positive reactions (including self-evaluations) in those affected by the decision (e.g., Kim & Mauborgne, 1997).

Given the significance of the reversal effect, it is important to delineate when it may be more versus less likely to occur. One potentially necessary precondition is for the unfavorable outcomes to be significant enough to have a negative impact on people's self-evaluations. Put differently, when unfavorable outcomes are not all that consequential, that is, when they do not put much of a dent in people's self-esteem, a reversal effect (i.e., an inverse relationship between process fairness and self-evaluations) seems less likely. If this reasoning is correct, then it first behooves us to identify factors that make unfavorable outcomes more consequential for people's self-evaluations.

Accordingly, people are more likely to feel badly about themselves in response to unfavorable outcomes when they (1) assign greater psychological significance to those outcomes and (2) see themselves as more personally responsible for those outcomes. The first of these two assertions is consistent with a basic tenet of motivation theory (e.g., Vroom, 1964). For example, the receipt of unfavorable feedback in a domain central to people's sense of identity is likely to reduce people's self-evaluations, at least temporarily, more than if the same unfavorable feedback was in a domain that was less self-relevant. Losing a tennis match may be more likely to reduce the self-evaluations of those who play the game for a living than of those who are merely weekend hackers. The second of these two assertions is well supported by theory and research in the achievement motivation literature (Weiner, 1985). In short, the importance people assign to, and the self-attributions they make for, their unfavorable outcomes are posited to moderate the relationship between the receipt of unfavorable outcomes and lower self-esteem; see Figure 4.1.

Moreover, process fairness is more likely to be inversely related to people's self-evaluations precisely when the receipt of unfavorable outcomes leads to more of a reduction in self-esteem. In other words, the reversal effect may be more likely to occur when (1) people assign greater psychological significance to their unfavorable outcomes and (2) when process fairness is more strongly related to people's tendencies to see themselves as responsible for the unfavorable outcomes. The first prediction conceptualizes process fairness as a proxy for self-attributions. Thus, self-attributed unfavorable outcomes that are assigned greater importance lead to more negative self-evaluations than do self-attributed unfavorable outcomes that are assigned less importance. In

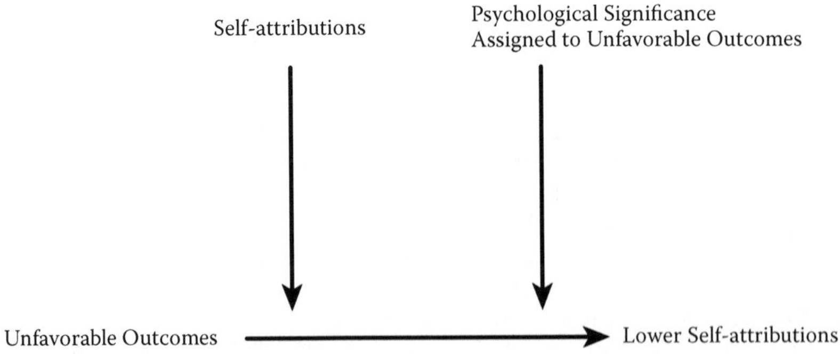

Figure 4.1 Moderators of the relationship between unfavorable outcomes and lowered self-evaluations.

the second prediction, I am suggesting that process fairness is not an invariant proxy for self-attributions. Rather, the relationship between process fairness and self-attributions will be stronger under some conditions than others. When the link between process fairness and self-attributions is stronger, process fairness is more likely to be inversely related to self-evaluations.

These predictions have been examined in recent research. Whereas the researchers did not directly examine the influence of how much people assigned psychological significance to their unfavorable outcomes or how much people used process fairness information to judge their personal responsibility for their outcomes, they did investigate factors that were likely to have influenced these two dimensions. More specifically, Brockner, De Cremer, Fishman, and Spiegel (2008) examined the moderating influence of people's prevention focus on the relationship between process fairness and self-evaluations in the face of unfavorable outcomes, the rationale being that prevention focus affects the importance that people assign to unfavorable outcomes. Holmvall and Bobocel (2008) investigated the joint effects of the salience of people's personal identity and their independent self-construal; their study was based on the notion that these two factors taken together may moderate the relationship between process fairness and how much people see themselves as responsible for their unfavorable outcomes. These studies are described next.

Regulatory Focus and the Psychological Significance Assigned to Unfavorable Outcomes

One factor that may affect the psychological significance that people assign to unfavorable outcomes is their regulatory focus orientation (Higgins, 1998), in particular their tendencies to be promotion focused and prevention focused. As suggested in Chapter 3, when people are promotion focused they assign greater significance to favorable outcomes. That is, they are more affected by perceived gains (1) relative to their prevention-focused counterparts and (2) relative to outcomes perceived as nonlosses. When people are prevention focused, however, they assign greater significance to unfavorable outcomes. Hence, they are more affected by perceived losses (1) relative to their promotion-focused counterparts and (2) relative to outcomes perceived as nongains (Idson & Higgins, 2000; Idson, Liberman, & Higgins, 2000, 2004). For example, Idson et al. (2000) examined the nature and intensity of people's affective experiences as a function of outcome favorability and their regulatory focus. As might be expected, people felt worse when their outcomes were unfavorable rather than favorable. Of greater importance, regulatory focus influenced the intensity of people's affective experiences *within* a given outcome condition. Consistent with the notion that being more prevention focused leads people to assign greater significance to unfavorable outcomes, Idson et al. found that those who were more prevention focused felt even worse about their unfavorable outcomes than did their counterparts who were less prevention focused.

The fact that prevention focus predisposes people to assign significance to unfavorable outcomes suggests that those with more of a prevention focus may be more likely to exhibit a reversal effect. We found support for this hypothesis in three separate studies (Brockner et al., 2008). In one study, people read a vignette in which they were asked to imagine that they were employees who had just received information about their pay raise for the upcoming year. Three different outcome conditions were created: unfavorable, moderate, and favorable. Moreover, both the level of process fairness information (high vs. low) and type of process fairness information (procedural vs. interactional) were varied, such that for half of the participants procedural fairness was manipulated (to be either high or low), whereas for the other half interactional fairness was manipulated to be either high or low. (See Chapter 3, pp. 62 and 67, for more detail on the nature of the process fairness manipulations.)

Participants' regulatory focus orientation was assessed as an individual difference variable based on a measure frequently used in the previous research on regulatory focus (e.g., Higgins, 1998). The dependent variable consisted of participants' state self-esteem (Heatherton & Polivy, 1991). Results showed a significant three-way interaction among outcome favorability, process fairness, and prevention focus. Within the unfavorable outcome condition, a significant two-way interaction between process fairness and prevention focus emerged. As can be seen in Figure 4.2, process fairness was inversely related to self-evaluations among those relatively high in prevention focus ($p < .10$), whereas process fairness and self-evaluations were positively related to one another among those with less of a prevention focus orientation ($p < .01$).

Different findings emerged in the moderate outcome and favorable outcome conditions (Brockner et al., 2008). For one thing, the

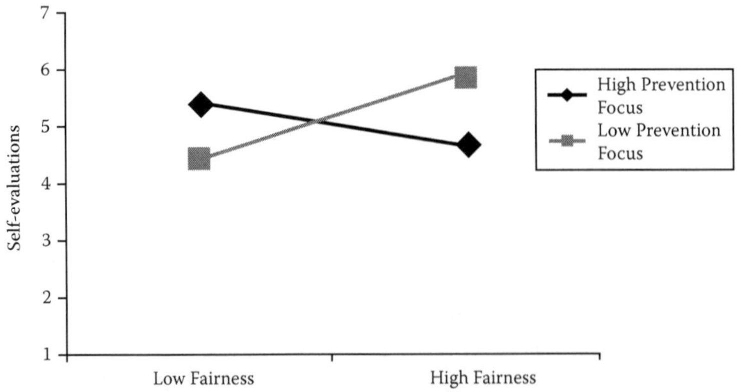

Figure 4.2 Predicted values of the relationship between process fairness and self-evaluations at high and low levels of prevention focus in the unfavorable outcome condition (Brockner et al., 2008, Study 1. Reprinted from *Journal of Experimental Social Psychology, 44*, 2, When does high procedural fairness reduce self-evaluations following unfavorable outcomes? The moderating effect of prevention focus, with permission from Elsevier.).

interaction between process fairness and prevention focus did not even approach significance in both of these conditions. In fact, the only significant finding that did emerge was the main effect of process fairness in the favorable outcome condition; as might be expected, process fairness was positively related to self-evaluations.

Brockner et al. (2008) conducted two additional studies, in which outcome favorability was not varied. Given our primary interest in clarifying the relationship between process fairness and self-evaluations in response to unfavorable outcomes, all participants in these two studies experienced an unfavorable outcome. These two studies also included several features intended to enhance the internal and external validity of the results of the first study. In Study 1, regulatory focus was operationalized as a measured individual difference variable, making it harder to discern its causal impact. To improve internal validity, we experimentally manipulated regulatory focus in the two subsequent studies, drawing on a method used in previous regulatory focus research (e.g., Cesario, Grant, & Higgins, 2004).

Four other aspects of the two subsequent studies provided us the opportunity to enhance the external validity of the results of Study 1 (Brockner et al., 2008). First, the studies were conducted in a different culture (i.e., that of The Netherlands, rather than the United States). Second, the decision-making contexts differed. Whereas Study 1 examined people's reactions to a pay raise, the two subsequent studies investigated how people reacted to a promotion decision (in both cases, to the unfavorable outcome of not receiving the promotion). Third, the

TABLE 4.2 Mean Level of Self-Evaluations as a Function of Process Fairness and Regulatory Focus (Brockner et al., 2008, Study 2)

	Regulatory Focus	
Process Fairness	**Promotion**	**Prevention**
High	5.65	4.39
Low	5.48	5.37

Source: Reprinted from the *Journal of Social Psychology, 44,* 2, When does high procedural fairness reduce self-evaluations following unfavorable outcomes? The moderating effect of prevention focus, with permission from Elsevier.

Note: Scores could range from 1 to 7, with higher scores reflecting higher self-evaluations.

substance of the process fairness manipulation was based on voice (rather than on accuracy, consistency, and interactional fairness, as had been done in the first study). Fourth, whereas Study 1 was based on a vignette, in which participants were asked to indicate how they would respond to a hypothetical situation, one of the subsequent studies examined participants' reactions to a situation that they actually experienced.

In spite of all of these differences, the results of the two subsequent studies were quite consistent with one another and with the results found in the unfavorable outcome condition of the first study described. For illustrative purposes, the results of one of the subsequent studies are presented in Table 4.2. As can be seen, a reversal effect was found in the prevention condition but not in the promotion condition.

A study by Cropanzano, Paddock, Rupp, Bagger, and Baldwin (2008) provided additional evidence that high process fairness may elicit more negative self-evaluations than low process fairness when people are prevention focused and when their outcomes are unfavorable. All participants worked on a task, in which they had the opportunity to be more rewarded for doing well rather than poorly. Prior to working on the task, they were manipulated to be either prevention focused or promotion focused based on an induction that has been used in the regulatory focus literature (Higgins, Shah, & Friedman, 1997) but was different from the one used by Brockner et al. (2008). All participants then worked on a task and were led to believe that they performed well or poorly. Moreover, the process used to arrive at their outcomes was either fair or unfair. The dependent variables included measures of participants' emotional states. Tangney and Fischer (1995) suggested that emotions differ in the extent to which they are "self-conscious" (i.e., reflective of people's feelings about themselves). Negative self-conscious emotions include guilt, shame, and embarrassment, whereas an example of a positive self-conscious emotion is pride. Cropanzano et al. found that participants reacted most negatively on *self-conscious* emotions when they were prevention focused and when they had received an unfavorable outcome through a fair process. That is, they exhibited significantly more embarrassment and significantly less pride in this condition relative to the average of all other conditions. In contrast, their reactions on measures of the less self-conscious emotions were not particularly extreme in the prevention focus/unfavorable outcome/fair process condition. For example, participants were not angrier in the prevention focus/unfavorable outcome/fair process condition than in the other conditions.

Use of Process Fairness Information to Make Self-Attributions for Outcomes

Theory and research suggest that people's tendencies to use process fairness information to make self-attributions for their outcomes may depend on both the level (or content) of their self-construals and the extent to which a particular self-construal is psychologically salient (Holmvall & Bobocel, 2008; Markus & Kitayama, 1991). Given that their personal identity has been activated or made salient, those with more independent (rather than interdependent) forms of self-construal appear to be more inclined to use process fairness information to evaluate how personally responsible they are for their outcomes. If so, then those same conditions (i.e., when people's personal identity is salient and they are high in independent self-construal) also should be more likely to elicit the reversal effect.

It is worth noting that the distinction between the salience of personal identity and the degree of independent self-construal is reminiscent of some early findings in the literature on the consequences of self-focused attention. A host of studies showed that factors related to people's inner workings, such as their attitudes or personality traits, were much more influential (e.g., predictive of behavior) when their attention was more self-directed (Brockner & Hulton, 1978; Pryor, Gibbons, Wicklund, Fazio, & Hood, 1977; Scheier, 1976). In other words, it is particularly when people's inner workings have been activated or made salient (such as when their attention is self-focused or their personal identity has been primed) that the substance of their inner workings is likely to influence their thoughts, feelings, and behaviors.

In one of the aforementioned studies by Holmvall and Bobocel (2008), the authors assessed people's state self-esteem (Heatherton & Polivy, 1991) in response to unfavorable outcomes. Independent variables included independent self-construal, whether participants' personal or social identity had been situationally primed, and process fairness. When participants' personal identity was primed to be salient, there was a significant interaction between independent self-construal and process fairness: Those relatively high in independent self-construal exhibited a reversal effect, whereas process fairness and self-esteem were unrelated among those lower in their independent self-construal.

In contrast, when participants' social identity was primed, there was no evidence of a reversal effect, regardless of people's level of independent self-construal. In fact, there was only a positive main effect of process fairness on self-evaluations, suggesting that when their social identity was salient participants may have used process fairness information to make relational inferences rather than to make inferences about their personal responsibility for their outcomes.

Theoretical Implications

The Brockner et al. (2008) and Holmvall and Bobocel (2008) findings may help to reconcile conflicting results that have emerged in studies examining the relationship between process fairness and self-evaluations in the face of unfavorable outcomes. In the Brockner et al. studies, the reversal effect was exhibited more by people who were dispositionally inclined or situationally induced to be prevention focused. In the Holmvall and Bobocel study, the reversal effect was only found among those with more independent self-construals, provided that their personal identities had been activated.

There has been considerable support for a key component of relational theories of justice (e.g., Tyler & Lind, 1992), namely, that process fairness is positively related to people's self-evaluations. What, then, are the implications of the present findings for relational theory given that process fairness may be inversely related to self-evaluations under certain conditions? Relational theory posits that people use process fairness information to make inferences about the other party or about their relationship with the other party (e.g., neutrality, standing, and trust), which in turn affect their self-evaluations. The present findings suggest that people use process fairness information for an additional sense-making purpose, namely, to determine the reasons for their outcomes, particularly the extent to which they are personally responsible for their outcomes (Brockner, 2002; Skitka, 2003). When processes are fair, people are likely to see themselves as responsible for their outcomes (Brockner et al. 2003; Leung et al., 2001; Van den Bos et al., 1999). Furthermore, the more that people make self-attributions for their outcomes, the more likely is the favorability of the outcomes to affect their self-evaluations (Weiner, 1985). So, for example, unfavorable outcomes should lead to more negative self-evaluations when people see themselves as more responsible for their outcomes.

Implicit in the last assertion, however, is that the outcomes are psychologically significant to people in the first place. The Brockner et al.

(2008) studies were based on the notion derived from regulatory focus theory that unfavorable outcomes are more psychologically significant and hence will be more impactful among those with more of a prevention focus (Higgins, 1998). Hence, it stands to reason that the inverse relationship between process fairness and self-evaluations in the face of unfavorable outcomes is more likely to be shown by those with more of a prevention focus. Moreover, the Holmvall and Bobocel (2008) findings suggest that people also may vary in the extent to which they are inclined to use process fairness information to make self-attributions for their outcomes. In particular, they may be especially apt to do so when their personal identity is salient to them and they construe themselves in more independent ways.

People's tendencies to use process fairness information for multiple sense-making purposes—that is, (1) to make judgments of how others view them, as set forth by relational theory (Tyler & Lind, 1992), and (2) to determine the causes of their outcomes, as suggested by Folger and Cropanzano (2001) and Van den Bos et al. (1999)—are not mutually exclusive. They may even both be operative in the same research setting (Brockner et al., 2003). In showing that process fairness may be inversely related to self-evaluations under certain conditions, the Brockner et al. (2008) and Holmvall and Bobocel (2008) findings do not negate or contradict relational theory. Rather, they suggest that the sense-making processes underlying relational theory (that is, people's use of process fairness information to make inferences about how they are viewed by the other party) simply do not fully account for the ways in which process fairness information influences people's evaluations of themselves.

Regulatory Focus Theory The extent to which people are promotion or prevention focused has been shown to affect a wide variety of emotions, cognitions, and behaviors (Higgins, 1998). Indeed, the validity of many well-accepted psychological principles has been shown to depend on people's regulatory focus. For example, Shah and Higgins (1997) provided evidence that the classic interactive effect of people's expectancies and valences on motivation (Vroom, 1964) is moderated by regulatory focus, being more likely to emerge when people are promotion focused. Idson et al. (2000) showed that the prospect theory notion that "losses loom larger than gains" also depends on regulatory focus, being more likely to hold when people are prevention focused.

The Brockner et al. (2008) findings suggest that regulatory focus theory also has implications for one of the most well-established principles of process fairness: People generally respond more positively to higher levels of process fairness. In fact, in the face of unfavorable outcomes, those with more of a prevention focus are likely to feel worse about themselves to the extent that process fairness is high. More generally, the present findings also are among the first to show the implications of regulatory focus theory for the procedural justice literature, thereby further broadening the reach of regulatory focus theory (see also Van Prooijen, Karremans, & Van Beest, 2006).

Future Research Opportunities In calling attention to some of the limitations of the Brockner et al. (2008) and Holmvall and Bobocel (2008) studies, we also are suggesting some avenues for further research. At the empirical level, whereas the interaction effect between prevention focus and procedural fairness in the face of unfavorable outcomes was statistically significant in all three of the Brockner et al. studies, some of the specific findings were somewhat weak. In particular, in two of the three studies the inverse relationship between process fairness and self-evaluations among those with more of a prevention focus was only marginally significant. Perhaps this was due to the possibility that the scenario methodology used in those two studies was less involving to participants than the procedure used in the third study, in which participants actually experienced unfavorable outcomes (and in which the inverse relationship between process fairness and self-esteem among those with a prevention focus was significant).

At the conceptual level, further research is needed to triangulate on the psychological processes underlying the Brockner et al. (2008) and the Holmvall and Bobocel (2008) findings. For example, the Brockner et al. studies were based on the assumption that being prevention focused predisposes people to assign greater psychological significance to unfavorable outcomes. Whereas empirical support for this assumption has been provided repeatedly in prior research (Higgins, 1998; Idson & Higgins, 2000; Idson et al., 2000, 2004), Brockner et al. did not evaluate it in their studies.

Again, it is worth noting that the simple effect examining the inverse relationship between process fairness and self-evaluations in the face of unfavorable outcomes was somewhat stronger in the study in which participants actually experienced the unfavorable outcome than in the two studies in which they were asked to read about their outcomes in the context of a hypothetical vignette. It is plausible that participants assigned greater psychological significance to the unfavorable outcome that they actually experienced than to hypothetical unfavorable outcomes. In any event, further research is needed to evaluate the reasoning underlying the Brockner et al. (2008) studies. One way to do so is by examining the influence of other factors (besides prevention focus) that may affect the degree of psychological significance that people assign to unfavorable outcomes. For example, people are likely to assign greater psychological significance to unfavorable outcome feedback pertaining to an important element of their self-concepts than to the same feedback that is less self-relevant. If Brockner et al.'s reasoning is correct, then these other factors also should interact with process fairness in the same way that prevention focus did to influence people's self-evaluations in the face of unfavorable outcomes.

One shortcoming of the Holmvall and Bobocel (2008) study is that the authors did not directly examine the extent to which people saw themselves as personally responsible for their outcomes and, perhaps more importantly, the extent to which process fairness was related to personal attributions for their outcomes. Rather, they drew on conceptual arguments from the identity literature to hypothesize that those with more of an independent self-construal would be more concerned with evaluating the extent to which they were personally responsible for their outcomes; presumably, they used process fairness information to make this judgment, particularly when their personal identity was salient. Relatedly, Holmvall and Bobocel speculated that those with more of an interdependent self-construal would use process fairness information to make relational inferences, particularly when their social identity was activated. However, in both instances Holmvall and Bobocel did not provide independent evidence that these underlying processes actually occurred.

One possible way to test for Holmvall and Bobocel's (2008) underlying reasoning is by asking people to rate the importance of various motives in their dealings with others. If the authors' theorizing is correct, then people with more of an independent self-construal should say that they are more motivated to determine the reasons for their outcomes, especially the extent to which they are personally responsible for them; moreover, their quest for self-attribution should be heightened all the more when their personal identity has been activated. Furthermore, those with more of an interdependent orientation should indicate that they are more concerned with making inferences about out how they are viewed by others, particularly when their social identity has been made salient.

Holmvall and Bobocel (2008) also posited that when people's personal identities were salient and when they had more independent forms of self-construal, they used process fairness information to make inferences about how personally responsible they were for their unfavorable outcomes. Yet another way to evaluate this reasoning is to examine other possible moderators of the relationship between process fairness and people's tendencies to see themselves as responsible for their outcomes. Those factors that cause process fairness and self-attributions to be more tightly coupled (such as when people are situationally induced or dispositionally inclined to focus on private aspects of themselves) also should be more likely to produce a reversal effect.

Moreover, not only would it be useful to vary other factors likely to influence the relationship between process fairness and self-attributions, but also it would be instructive to measure both of the "proximal" moderators of the relationship between unfavorable outcomes and reduced self-evaluations set forth in Figure 4.1, that is, how much people see themselves as responsible for their unfavorable outcomes and the degree of psychological significance that they assign to those outcomes. Holmvall and Bobocel (2008) implied that the salience of people's identity interacted with their level of independent self-construal to influence the extent to which they saw themselves as personally responsible for their unfavorable outcomes. Brockner et al. (2008) suggested that prevention focus was a proxy for how much people assigned psychological significance to their unfavorable outcomes.

However, it is possible that things may not line up quite so "neatly." For example, it could be argued that when people's personal identity is primed and they are relatively high in independent self-construal, they also may assign greater psychological significance to the receipt of unfavorable outcomes. As Bobocel (personal communication, March 8, 2008) put it in referring to the Holmvall and Bobocel studies:

> I think that our independent variables may have operated on both of these factors [that is, how much people saw themselves as personally responsible for their outcomes and the degree of importance that they assigned to those outcomes] to some degree. In our studies, we reasoned that people with a strong independent self-construal would be more likely to show the reverse fair process effect than people with a weak independent self-construal, in particular when their personal identity is primed, because these people define the self in terms of individual achievement and competition. Thus, we thought these people should be particularly motivated to understand whether they are personally responsible for the unfavorable outcome, but the unfavorable outcome had to do with achievement, which is central to their identity. So I wonder if the effects would be as strong if the feedback was less tied to an important aspect of their identity.

In summary, it was previously suggested that one of the preconditions for the intriguing reversal effect is for people to experience the unfavorable outcomes as detrimental to their self-esteem. Two factors that influence the extent to which unfavorable outcomes negatively affect self-esteem are the importance people assign to and the self-attributions they make for their unfavorable outcomes (see Figure 4.1). The findings of Brockner et al. (2008) and Holmvall and Bobocel (2008) suggest that it may be possible to extend the reasoning captured in Figure 4.1 in four respects, as illustrated in Figure 4.3:

1. Process fairness may be thought of as one input into how much people make self-attributions for unfavorable outcomes.
2. Prevention focus may be thought of as one input into how much people assign significance to unfavorable outcomes.
3. Process fairness interacts with prevention focus to influence self-evaluations in the face of unfavorable outcomes.
4. Salience of personal identity interacts with level of independent self-construal to influence the relationship between process fairness and self-attributions for unfavorable outcomes.

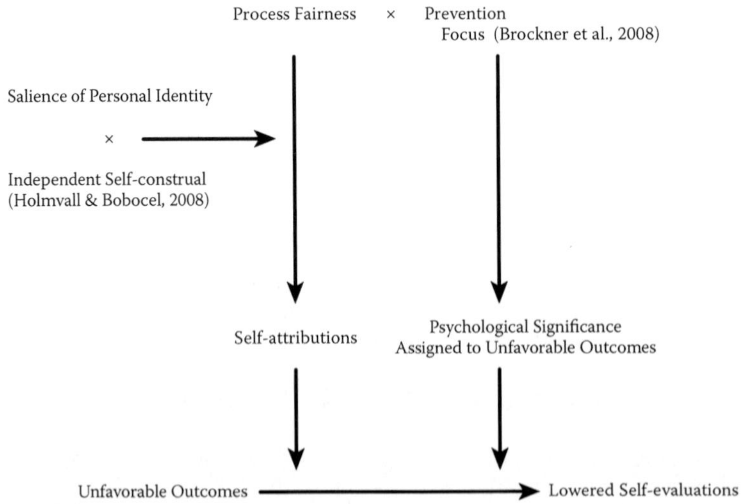

Figure 4.3 Moderators of the inverse relationship between process fairness and self-evaluations in the face of unfavorable outcomes.

PROCESS FAIRNESS PREFERENCES (OR DESIRE FOR PROCESS FAIRNESS AS A DEPENDENT VARIABLE)

In his taxonomy of organizational justice theories, Greenberg (1987b) distinguished between reactive and proactive approaches. *Reactive approaches* examine how people respond to differing levels of justice that they have experienced. The vast majority of organizational justice research has taken a reactive approach, in which fairness (distributive, process, etc.) is the independent variable, and people's reactions (e.g., organizational commitment, work motivation, etc.) serve as the dependent variable. *Proactive approaches* examine how people go about enacting fairness (or not). In proactive approaches, the level of fairness that people create serves as the dependent variable.

Of course, theory and research based on one approach may inform the other. For example, studies testing for the interactive effect of outcome favorability and process fairness on people's self-evaluations have used a reactive approach. The self-attributional mechanism that accounts for the tendency of high process fairness to heighten the effect of outcome favorability on self-evaluations has implications for when people may be more versus less likely to prefer being treated with high process fairness.

If we make the reasonable assumption that people generally like to feel good about themselves, then they should prefer processes to be fairer if they have received or anticipate receiving favorable outcomes, and they should have a reduced preference for high process fairness if they have received or expect to receive unfavorable outcomes. In the face of favorable outcomes, higher levels of process fairness, by eliciting more self-attributions, should bring about greater self-enhancement. In contrast, when outcomes are unfavorable, lower levels of process fairness, by eliciting less of a tendency to make self-attributions, should bring about greater self-protection (Weiner, 1985).

This reasoning was tested in a study examining people's preferences for decision-making processes varying in fairness (Brockner, Wiesenfeld, Siegel, & Zhang, 2010). Participants were asked to imagine that they had worked for their current employers for about a year, and that they now had an opportunity to apply for another position within the organization. They were told:

> You have been invited for an interview and have appeared before a committee. The committee told you that they have identified a list of attributes that are necessary to be successful in this position: (1) attention to detail, (2) ability to work in teams, (3) strong quantitative ability, (4) creativity, and (5) ability to cope with tight time deadlines.

Participants were also told that the organization was considering the use of two methods to make the selection decision. The information provided implied that Method 1 would be more accurate and hence fairer than Method 2. More specifically, participants were told the following about Method 1:

> The committee would collect information about the five attributes mentioned previously. Not all of this information is available in the job candidates' personnel files, and therefore the effort would require a great deal of time to gather all of the necessary information. On the other hand, having all of this information would allow the company to be very thorough in selecting the right person for the job.

Method 2 was portrayed as follows:

> The committee would collect information about the job candidates' quantitative ability only. This information is available in the job candidates' personnel files and therefore would not require nearly as much time as Method 1 requires. On the other hand, having information about candidates' quantitative ability but not the other attributes relevant to job performance would not allow the company to be nearly as thorough in selecting the right person for the job.

All participants then rated the extent to which they wanted the organization to use each of Methods 1 and 2 to make the selection decision.

To vary participants' beliefs about outcome favorability, i.e., the perceived likelihood of their chances of receiving the offer, we drew on an induction used in the self-handicapping literature (Jones & Berglas, 1978). *Self-handicapping* refers to people's tendencies to put obstacles in their way prior to engaging in an activity likely to have implications for how they feel about themselves. Examples of self-handicapping include getting drunk the night before an important exam or withholding effort at an important task. The goal of self-handicapping is to influence the attributions made for the person's task performance. If the individual performs poorly, he or she can attribute it to the handicap rather than to a more self-deflating cause such as lack of ability, whereas if the person were to perform well in spite of the handicap, he or she can attribute it to the self-enhancing cause of having an exceptionally high level of ability, one high enough to overcome the handicap. Thus, the purpose of the handicap is to reduce the self-relevance of unfavorable outcomes that may be experienced subsequent to the imposition of the handicap (by allowing people to attribute their outcomes to the handicap rather than to something more fundamental about the self) and to heighten the self-relevance of favorable outcomes that may be experienced subsequent to the handicap (by allowing them to attribute their outcomes to something about themselves, i.e., for having succeeded *in spite of* the handicap).

When people expect their outcomes to be unfavorable, or at the very least when they are uncertain about their outcomes, the presence of low process fairness may serve the same purpose as the introduction of a self-handicap. Both enable people to protect themselves by attributing unfavorable outcomes they may experience to something not fundamental to themselves, such as the handicap or, in this instance, an unfair decision process. In the absence of a self-imposed handicap or in the presence of high process fairness, people cannot as easily externalize the reasons for their outcomes and may instead be forced to make more of a self-attribution for their unfavorable outcomes, which could lead to a loss of self-esteem.

Whereas the presence of low process fairness is not exactly the same as the introduction of a self-handicap (e.g., the latter is probably more likely than the former to lower people's actual chances for success), the two may emanate from a similar psychological motivation. If so, then it is plausible that the conditions that have been shown to elicit self-handicapping also may reduce people's tendencies to prefer high process fairness. Jones and Berglas (1978) showed that self-handicapping was more likely to occur when people experienced noncontingent success rather than contingent success. Accordingly, we used the same manipulation to test the related notion that people would be less likely to prefer high process fairness when their prior success was not contingent on things that they could control. In the face of noncontingent success, people are less likely to be optimistic about their chances to maintain their success relative to if they believed that their success was contingent on things that they could control. By preferring lower levels of process fairness, those treated with noncontingent success may be able to reduce the self-relevance of an outcome that they expect to be not all that favorable. In contrast, those who believe that their prior success was contingent on things that they could control are likely to be more optimistic about their future chances for success, in which case they would prefer to introduce higher levels of process fairness; doing so would enable them to heighten the self-relevance of the anticipated favorable outcome and thereby lead to more positive self-evaluations.

All participants in the Brockner, Wiesenfeld et al. (2010) study were told the following: "You have been working at the company for one year, and you have already received a promotion while none of the other college graduates in your cohort have been promoted at all. Your pay, bonuses, and job title suggest that you have been successful." Those in the noncontingent success condition were further informed:

> Whereas you are pleased to have received the positive feedback in the form of pay, bonuses, and job title, you are very unsure about *why* you have received this positive feedback. For instance, there is no indication that you have superior capabilities to your work colleagues, and in fact when you compare yourself to them you often believe that you are weaker than them in certain fundamental ways. Further puzzling you is the fact that there doesn't seem to be much of a relationship between how hard you try and how well you perform. For example, on some projects you have not tried hard and have done well, while on other projects you have tried hard and have not done well. In short, you generally feel insecure about your ability to continue to perform well at work.

In contrast, those in the contingent success condition were told the following:

> Not only are you pleased to have received the positive feedback in the form of pay, bonuses, and job title, but also it is quite clear why you have received this positive feedback. For instance, every indication suggests that you have superior capabilities to your work colleagues. In short, you generally feel secure about your ability to continue to be successful at work.

After the manipulation of success contingency, all participants rated how strongly they wanted each of the two methods to be used as the basis for selecting the job applicant. The results showed that participants generally had more of a preference for the more fair process (Method 1) over the less-fair process (Method 2). However, their tendency to prefer Method 1 over Method 2 was significantly less pronounced when they had been pretreated with noncontingent success (*M*s = 5.28 vs. 3.78 for Methods 1 and 2, respectively, on a 7-point scale) rather than with contingent success (*M*s = 6.21 vs. 3.08, respectively).

Brockner, Wiesenfeld et al. (2010) also found that the tendency for noncontingent success to reduce people's preferences for higher process fairness depended on the extent to which they generally seek diagnostic information about themselves. That is, people are motivated not only to maintain or to protect their self-esteem but also to determine where they stand. Hence, people who want to learn about where they stand may be less motivated to engage in self-protection under conditions that may be experienced as self-threatening. The tendency to seek self-diagnostic information was measured with such items as, "I like to put myself in situations that allow me to assess my capabilities." Indeed, those more interested in learning about themselves were significantly less likely to exhibit the aforementioned tendency to prefer lower process fairness in response to noncontingent success.

In a second study, Brockner, Wiesenfeld et al. (2010) replicated the finding that being treated with noncontingent success reduces people's tendencies to prefer a fair decision-making process over an unfair one. Importantly, we operationalized process fairness in a manner differently from that which was done in our first study described above. Whereas the earlier study asked participants to rate their preferences for two decision-making methods varying in accuracy, the second study asked participants to rate their preferences for two decision-making methods varying in the amount of voice they would be allowed to have. In addition, we also found that the effect of noncontingent success on people's process fairness preferences was moderated by their regulatory focus orientation, such that the effect was stronger among those who were more prevention focused. Assigning greater psychological significance to unfavorable outcomes, those with more of a prevention focus may believe that they have more to lose psychologically if their future outcomes happen to be unfavorable. One way to "hedge their bets," that is, to reduce the self-relevance of outcomes that they think have a reasonable chance of being unfavorable, is by perceiving the process to be less fair. This may explain why those with more of a prevention focus were even more likely than their promotion-focused counterparts to show a reduced preference for high process fairness in response to having experienced noncontingent success.

Future Research Opportunities

Further research is needed to evaluate whether people's reduced preferences for high process fairness when they are uncertain about their future success may be extended to other elements of process fairness. The research done to date showed that being pretreated with noncontingent success reduced people's preference to have decisions made on the basis of accurate information or with voice. Would analogous findings emerge if process fairness were based on other elements? For example, in anticipation of unfavorable or uncertain outcomes, would the preference for reduced process fairness even extend to elements of interactional justice, which have less to do with how decisions are made and more to do with how they are carried out or communicated? People are less apt to blame others for their unfavorable outcomes when others treat them with dignity and respect (Barclay et al., 2005), which raises the possibility that they may be more apt to blame themselves (Leung et al., 2001). If others' high level of interactional fairness induces people to see themselves as more personally responsible for their unfavorable outcomes, they may paradoxically show less of a preference to be treated with high interactional fairness to ward off the threat to self-evaluations they may experience were they to see themselves as more personally responsible for their unfavorable outcomes.

Further research also is needed to evaluate if people may actually prefer an unfair process relative to a fair one. The studies done to date merely found evidence of an attenuation effect, that is, those pretreated with noncontingent success exhibited a reduced tendency to prefer a fair process over an unfair one relative to those who had been pretreated with contingent success. Under no conditions did participants actually exhibit a reversal effect, that is, a tendency to prefer an unfair process to a fair one, but they may on other occasions. For example, in advance of unfavorable outcomes that are all but ensured, and when those unfavorable outcomes have high valence (e.g., when the person is prevention focused or when the outcomes are in a domain central to people's sense of identity), people may actually prefer processes that are unfair over those that are fair.

Motivated Process Fairness Judgments

The same factors that cause people to prefer a decision process to be less fair also may motivate them to *perceive* process fairness in predictable ways. A well-known finding in the justice literature is that people's judgments of their outcomes (e.g., outcome favorability) bear a strong positive relationship with their process fairness judgments. Moreover, experimental evidence suggests that the causal arrow runs in both directions (e.g., Brockner et al., 2007). Hence, process fairness influences people's judgments of outcome favorability, and more relevant to the present discussion, outcome favorability affects people's judgments of process fairness.

People's need to feel good about themselves may account for the last finding. By viewing favorable outcomes as resulting from a fair process, people may see themselves as more personally responsible for bringing about those outcomes and thereby experience greater self-enhancement. Moreover, by viewing unfavorable outcomes as emanating from an unfair process, people may see themselves as less personally responsible for those outcomes and thereby experience greater self-protection. In other words, just as people may prefer processes that are more or less fair for self-serving reasons, they also may *perceive* the process to be more or less fair for the same reasons.

Blader (2007) tested this notion in a vignette study in which undergraduate students were asked to imagine that they had applied to be members of a valued university committee. Independent variables included (1) outcome favorability (those in the favorable outcome condition were told that their application had been accepted, whereas those in the unfavorable outcome condition were told that their application had been rejected) and (2) the extent to which process fairness was known to be low (some people were clearly informed that the process was unfair, whereas others were given no information about the process). Those clearly told that the process was unfair judged it that way, regardless of outcome favorability. However, those given no process fairness information used outcome favorability feedback to arrive at their process fairness judgments, seeing the process as much less fair when their outcomes were unfavorable rather than favorable.

Of course, people's need to protect or enhance their self-esteem is merely one of their self-related concerns. As various social psychological theories have suggested, people also need to know where they stand. For example, for self-regulatory purposes it is important for people to determine the correctness of their emotions, cognitions, and behaviors (Festinger, 1954). A clear sense of identity also is predicated on people having an accurate sense of who they are and what they represent. In certain instances, people's needs to learn about themselves may compete with, or at least lessen the impact of, their needs to protect or enhance self-esteem, as demonstrated by the Brockner, Wiesenfeld et al. (2010) finding that being pretreated with noncontingent success was less likely to reduce the preference for high process fairness among people who seek diagnostic information about themselves.

Self-theories (e.g., Markus & Kitayama, 1991; Turner, Hogg, Oakes, Reicher, & Wetherell, 1987) also recognize that people maintain multiple bases of identity, such as the private self or personal identity (which refers to beliefs about unique qualities, such as traits, beliefs, and skills and abilities) and the collective self or social identity (which refers to self-beliefs based on the groups of which people are members). Just as people need to protect or enhance their personal self-esteem, they are also motivated to protect or enhance their collective self-esteem. Whereas the needs to protect or enhance personal or collective self-esteem often work in concert, sometimes they do not.

For example, in the Blader study (2007) in which people who had not been given clear process fairness information judged process fairness to be lower when their outcomes were unfavorable rather than favorable, participants also varied in the extent to which they felt identified with the institution in which the decision was made. In other words, some participants had a strong sense of collective identity, whereas others did not. Among those with a strong sense of collective identity, judging process fairness to be low in response to an unfavorable outcome may protect their personal self-esteem, but it could have the effect of threatening their collective self-esteem. After all, they would then have to contend with feeling strongly aligned with a collective in which decisions are implemented in an unflattering manner (i.e., with low process fairness). In fact, Blader (2007) found that the relationship between outcome favorability and participants' judgments of process fairness was moderated by how strongly they identified with the institution. Those who felt more strongly identified with the institution (that is, those who had a stronger sense of collective identity) were less likely to exhibit the aforementioned positive relationship between outcome favorability and perceived process fairness relative to their counterparts who identified with the institution to a lesser extent.

Although different in many ways, the studies examining people's preference for process fairness (e.g., Brockner, Wiesenfeld et al., 2010) and their perceptions of process fairness (Blader, 2007) have a number of important common themes. Both are consistent with the results of "reactive" studies of organizational justice showing that in the face of unfavorable outcomes, there is less likely to be a positive (and there may even be a negative) relationship between process fairness and self-evaluations because unfavorable outcomes are more likely to be seen as self-threatening when process fairness is high. If so, then people should show less of a preference for process fairness in anticipation of, or in reaction to, unfavorable outcomes. Brockner, Wiesenfeld et al. showed that the tendency for people to *prefer* a fair process over an unfair one is lessened to the extent that they are uncertain about the favorability of their upcoming outcomes (i.e., if they have been pretreated with non-contingent success). Blader found that people *perceive* process fairness to be lower in response to an unfavorable than to a favorable outcome. In different ways, then, people may proactively orient themselves toward process fairness in ways that enable them to protect or enhance their self-esteem.

Moreover, both studies (Blader, 2007; Brockner, Wiesenfeld et al., 2010) remind us in different ways that people's desire to protect or enhance their personal self-esteem is one of several self-related motives that they seek to satisfy. That is, in addition to protecting or enhancing their personal self-esteem, people need to (1) determine where they stand, which may help to explain why those with more of a desire for self-diagnostic information were less apt to select an unfair process even when they were pretreated with noncontingent success (Brockner, Wiesenfeld et al., 2010), and (2) protect or enhance their collective self, which may explain why those who more strongly identified with the collective were less apt to perceive process fairness to be low even when their personal outcomes were unfavorable (Blader, 2007).

People's process fairness preferences and perceptions may not be the only venues through which their desire for self-protection may influence their attitudes toward process fairness. Just as uncertainty about future success reduced people's typical tendency to prefer a fair decision-making process over an unfair one (Brockner, Wiesenfeld et al., 2010), the same condition may heighten the perceived desirability of *decision makers* who have the reputation of being lower in process fairness. A good deal of theory and research have delineated the benefits for both employers and employees alike engendered by trustworthy organizational authorities (e.g., Kramer & Tyler, 1996). Predictably, then, people generally prefer trustworthy over untrustworthy decision-making authorities. One of the most important determinants of authorities' trustworthiness is the extent to which they use fair processes to plan and implement decisions. Hence, an intriguing implication of the following reasoning is that when people are uncertain about their future success (e.g., when they have been pretreated with noncontingent success) they may deviate from the typical tendency to prefer decision-making authorities who are trustworthy.

In the Brockner, Wiesenfeld et al. (2010) study, participants indicated, as a function of whether they had been pretreated with noncontingent success, their preferences for decision-making processes varying in fairness. Suppose, however, that participants were asked to indicate their preferences about a slightly different matter: how much they want to see decisions made by *authorities* believed to vary in their process fairness. If asked about their preferences for decision makers known to behave with varying degrees of process fairness, then the effect of being pretreated with noncontingent success may be even stronger than that found in the Brockner, Wiesenfeld et al. study, in which the dependent variable consisted of people's preferences for decision-making *processes* varying in fairness. When people are motivated by self-protection, they want to distance themselves from unfavorable outcomes, thereby heightening the desirability of lower process fairness. If the affected parties are asked to make a recommendation about how a decision should be made and they indicate having a reduced preference for lower process fairness, they may see themselves as at least somewhat responsible for the outcomes they receive, especially if the methods ultimately used by authorities were the less fair ones that they had recommended. On the other hand, if the affected parties perceive themselves as more removed from the decision process (that is, if they are asked whom they would prefer to make decisions), then they may even more strongly prefer decision-making authorities who are known to use less-fair methods.

Why might the latter be true? If people are asked about their preferences for decision makers rather than about their preferences for the decision-making methods, then they may feel less personally responsible for the outcomes of the decision process. After all, if other people make the decision to use a less-fair process, people have two reasons to feel a reduced sense of personal responsibility: (1) the fact that a less-fair process was used and (2) the fact that others were responsible for the use of that process. In contrast, if people think that their own preferences for a less-fair decision process factored into the presence of the less fair process, they may be less likely to experience the second of these two bases of reduced personal responsibility. And, when they are pretreated with noncontingent success, in which the threat of future unfavorable outcomes looms large, they may be looking to psychologically distance themselves (read: not see themselves as personally responsible) as much as possible.

Consistent with this reasoning, several sets of studies have shown that those who are likely to be more insecure about their future outcomes are less attracted to organizations in which decision-making authorities use methods that are fair (Brockner et al., 1998; Wiesenfeld, Swann, Brockner, & Bartel, 2007). All of these studies examined the interactive effect of the process fairness exhibited by organizational authorities and individuals' self-esteem on various attitudinal and behavioral measures of organizational commitment. For present purposes, let us assume that self-esteem is a proxy for how secure people feel about their future outcomes, such that those with lower self-esteem feel less secure (Brockner, 1988). Replicating the results of numerous prior studies, Wiesenfeld et al. (2007) found that employees' perceptions of the process fairness shown by organizational authorities were positively related to employees' organizational commitment. Of greater importance, employees' self-esteem moderated this tendency such that it was significantly less pronounced among those who were lower in self-esteem.

It is worth noting that the prior studies examining the interactive effect of process fairness and self-esteem on employees' organizational commitment invoked explanations to account for the findings that differ from one another and that differ from the one proposed here. In the Brockner et al. (1998) studies, process fairness always was based on voice. We posited that persons with high self-esteem were more likely to believe that their input would make a meaningful difference relative to their counterparts with lower self-esteem. Expectancy theory (Vroom, 1964) posits that motivation partly depends on the optimism of people's expectations (e.g., the extent to which people believe that their voice will make a meaningful difference). Thus, it stands to reason that persons with higher self-esteem will be more motivated to have voice, in which case the extent to which they see themselves as having voice will have more of an effect on their work attitudes and behaviors, such as their organizational commitment.

Wiesenfeld et al. (2007) examined a broad array of operationalizations of process fairness, not simply voice. The explanation invoked to account for their findings was self-verification theory (Swann, 1983), which posits that people's views of themselves (including their self-evaluations) provide them with a crucial source of coherence (Festinger, 1957; Lecky, 1945). Should people's self-views be challenged by inconsistent information, they will have been stripped of their fundamental means of knowing the world and guiding action. Thus, once people form self-views, they work to stabilize them by engaging in various acts of self-verification, which include being attracted to others who confirm their views of themselves (and being repelled by others who disconfirm their views of themselves). The relational theory of fairness (Tyler & Lind, 1992) posits that process information symbolizes to people how they are perceived by the parties enacting the process, such that fairer processes imply that they are held in higher regard. Thus, because fair treatment is more self-verifying for persons with high self-esteem than it is for those with low self-esteem, it follows that the well-established relationship between process fairness and organizational commitment will be more pronounced among those who are high rather than low in self-esteem.

The present analysis provides yet another explanation of the interactive effect of process fairness and self-esteem on employees' organizational commitment, apart from those offered by Brockner et al. (1998)

and Wiesenfeld et al. (2007). It draws on the fact that people use process fairness information as a basis for determining how much they are personally responsible for their outcomes (Brockner et al., 2003; Van den Bos et al., 1999). It also is predicated on the well-established notions that (1) people's self-esteem may be a proxy for the favorability of the outcomes that they expect to receive, and (2) people are motivated by the need for positive self-evaluations (an assumption shared by the relational theory of procedural justice; Tyler & Lind, 1992).

Given that persons with high self-esteem have relatively favorable expectations for their outcomes, they may be attracted to organizations and organizational authorities that treat them with high process fairness. That is, the high process fairness allows them to make self-enhancing internal attributions for their anticipated favorable outcomes. Moreover, after the fact (i.e., once their outcomes are known), high self-esteem people may be more likely to perceive their outcomes to be favorable than will individuals with lower self-esteem. Therein lies yet another opportunity for persons with high self-esteem to experience self-enhancement in the course of being attracted to decision makers who treat them with high process fairness; they may see themselves as personally responsible for outcomes that have been judged to be favorable.

On the other hand, when outcomes are not expected to be particularly favorable (a belief more likely to be maintained by individuals with lower self-esteem), then for self-protective reasons they may be less attracted than persons with higher self-esteem to organizations or organizational authorities that treat them with high process fairness. After all, aligning themselves with organizations and organizational authorities that treat them with high process fairness may require people with low self-esteem to make self-deflating internal attributions for their anticipated unfavorable outcomes. Furthermore, if persons with low self-esteem judge the outcomes they receive (and not simply those that they expect to receive) as relatively unfavorable, then they have an additional reason to shy away from decision makers who treat them with high process fairness; doing so will enable them to ward off the unflattering experience of seeing themselves as personally responsible for outcomes that are perceived as unfavorable.

Comparing Self-Handicapping to the Reduced Preference for High Process Fairness

Brockner, Wiesenfeld et al. (2010) hypothesized and found that the same factor that elicits self-handicapping (being pretreated with noncontingent success) reduces people's typical tendency to prefer a fair process more than an unfair one. Given the common ancestry of self-handicapping and a reduced preference for higher process fairness, it may be useful to consider how these two tendencies are related. At least two points of similarity come to mind. First, both are based on the notion that people are motivated by the desire to maintain or enhance their self-evaluations. Thus, when they are uncertain about their future chances for success, they may do things in advance that are designed to reduce the self-relevance of unfavorable outcomes that may be coming their way. Showing less of a preference for a fair decision-making process or engaging in self-handicapping allows people to see themselves as less personally responsible for unfavorable outcomes, thereby serving to protect themselves if such outcomes were to occur.

A second similarity is the somewhat paradoxical nature of both tendencies. Self-handicapping suggests that, consciously or not, people may do things that lower their chances for success. People's preference for lower process fairness flies in the face of a pervasive theme in the justice literature, namely, that high process fairness is a good thing that elicits more positive reactions on organizationally relevant dependent variables (e.g., commitment) and personally relevant dependent variables (e.g., psychological well-being) alike.

There may be, however, at least two important differences between the two tendencies. First, whereas the introduction of a self-handicap may lower people's actual or perceived chances for success (by definition), it is less clear that the introduction of an unfair process would do likewise. The more that a decision process is perceived to be fair, the more likely are people to believe that the outcome they receive is the one that they deserve. In the face of noncontingent success, people are uncertain about their chances for future success; therefore, they may be less likely to prefer a process that will provide them with the outcome that they deserve. In other words, when people are unsure that they deserve much they may prefer a process that may produce undeserved (and hence for them, possibly better) outcomes. If this reasoning is correct, then when people are uncertain about their future success, working to introduce a less-fair process may be more beneficial than is engaging in self-handicapping. That is, whereas low process fairness and the presence of a handicap both provide people with ways to ward off the self-deflating effects of an unfavorable outcome, enacting an unfair process may seem "better" in that it may not reduce people's actual chances for success.

However, the very notion that low process fairness may not reduce people's actual or perceived chances for success suggests a second difference between low process fairness and the introduction of a self-handicap; self-handicapping may provide benefits that the introduction of low process fairness does not. More specifically, in the face of noncontingent success, people who engage in self-handicapping may feel better about themselves relative to those who do not, regardless of the favorability of their outcome. That is, self-handicappers can attribute unfavorable outcomes to the handicap and thereby protect their self-esteem. Moreover, if their outcomes are favorable, they may attribute their success to something about themselves that enabled them to be successful *in spite of* the handicap (which ordinarily would have lowered people's chances for success). In short, self-handicappers may believe that they can "have it both ways" in the face of uncertainty about their future chances for success.

In contrast, those who opt for reduced process fairness in the face of uncertainty about their chances for success may only be able to "have it one way." If their outcomes prove to be unfavorable, then lower process fairness acts much like engaging in self-handicapping: Both reduce people's felt responsibility for their outcomes and thereby enable them to protect their self-esteem. However, if their outcomes prove to be favorable, lower process fairness may make it less possible (than engaging in self-handicapping) for people to have the experience of self-enhancement. After all, lower process fairness induces people to feel less personally responsible for their outcomes (Van den Bos et al., 1999). Therefore, if the outcomes are favorable, then lower process fairness makes it less likely that people will feel good about themselves.

In summary, self-handicapping makes people's unfavorable outcomes less self-relevant, and it makes their favorable outcomes more self-relevant. Therefore, in the face of uncertainty about their future success, people have two reasons to engage in self-handicapping: to protect themselves if their outcomes prove to be unfavorable and to enhance themselves if their outcomes prove to be favorable. Whereas the introduction of lower process fairness makes people's unfavorable outcomes less self-relevant, it may not necessarily make their favorable outcomes more self-relevant. Therefore, in the face of uncertainty about future success, people may only have the self-protective reason to prefer reduced process fairness. All else being equal, then, it would seem that self-handicapping will have (or people may expect it to have) a more positive impact than reduced process fairness on their self-evaluations *across* outcome favorability conditions. Therefore, if they had to choose between the two they may prefer to engage in self-handicapping than to strive for reduced levels of process fairness.

However, this possibility assumes that people assign equal value to the self-protective and self-enhancing functions of self-handicapping, which may not always be the case. For example, Tice (1991) showed that persons with high self-esteem are more likely to engage in self-handicapping to experience self-enhancement, whereas people with low self-esteem are more likely to engage in self-handicapping to experience self-protection. Whether people are promotion focused or prevention focused (Higgins, 1998) also influences the extent to which they value gains and therefore may influence the relative attractiveness of self-handicapping and reduced process fairness. Because promotion focus leads people to assign greater psychological significance to favorable outcomes, those who are more promotion focused may be more attracted to the self-enhancement opportunity provided by self-handicapping than they are to a reduction in process fairness, which may be less apt to set the stage for people to experience self-enhancement in the face of favorable outcomes. More generally, whereas a good deal of research has examined the various strategies people proactively use to protect or to enhance their self-evaluations, we know far less about the *relative* attractiveness of these strategies vis-à-vis one another. Thus, future research needs to delineate the factors that make certain strategies more appealing to people than others. For example, if after being pretreated with noncontingent success people were given a choice between engaging in self-handicapping *or* striving toward the introduction of a less-fair decision process, which would they select? Moreover, what factors might affect such a choice? These are worthwhile questions to examine in future research.

Process Fairness, Unfavorable Outcomes, and Affective Forecasting

When outcomes are unfavorable, the relationship between process fairness and how people feel about themselves sometimes takes the form of a "reversal effect" (e.g., Brockner et al., 2008; Holmvall & Bobocel, 2008). Research on affective forecasting suggests that the reversal effect may come as somewhat of a surprise not only to students of organizational justice (e.g., to the advocates of relational theory) but also to the very people who exhibit such a tendency. Implicit in people's tendencies to engage in self-handicapping or to prefer a reduction in process fairness is the strategic nature of such activity. Undergirding both tendencies is the notion that people are able to anticipate how they are likely to feel in response to their future outcomes, and that they are taking steps beforehand to protect themselves if their outcomes prove to be unfavorable and (in the case of self-handicapping) to enhance themselves if their outcomes prove to be favorable.

However, theory and research on affective forecasting have suggested that people often are not good at predicting their future emotional states, including but not limited to their feelings about themselves (Gilbert, 2006). One way in which this predictive shortcoming comes about is through people's inability to anticipate their tendencies to engage in self-protective rationalizations. Whereas people often react to unfavorable outcomes in self-protective ways, they may not be very good at knowing that they will do so *prior to* the receipt of those outcomes.

In one study (Gilbert, Pinel, Wilson, Blumberg, & Wheatley, 1998), people were asked to predict how happy they would feel if they received an unfavorable outcome as a result of a process that was either fair or unfair. More specifically, participants in a laboratory experiment were told that they would be eligible to receive $25 if they successfully completed a job-screening procedure. Half of the participants were told that the screening procedure would be relatively fair, whereas the other half was informed that the screening procedure would be relatively unfair.

All participants were asked to predict how happy they would feel (both immediately and 10 minutes later) if they received the unfavorable outcome of not successfully completing the screening procedure

(Gilbert et al., 1998). After their affective forecasts had been assessed, all participants were told that, in fact, they had not passed the screening procedure, and therefore that they would not be receiving the $25. They then rated how happy they felt immediately after receiving this bad news and 10 minutes later. Prior to receiving the unfavorable outcome, participants predicted that they would be equally unhappy (both immediately and 10 minutes later), regardless of the fairness of the screening procedure. In other words, participants' *predictions* of their emotional states appeared to be influenced by the unfavorable outcome itself and not by the fairness of the process through which the outcome was going to be decided.

Once the unfavorable outcome was in hand, however, participants reported feeling significantly happier if the decision process was unfair rather than fair, especially when the ratings were made 10 minutes later rather than immediately after participants had been told that they did not pass the screening procedure. How come? Presumably, participants who were told that the process was unfair could more easily explain away or protect themselves from the unfavorable outcome relative to those who believed that the process was fair. The Gilbert et al. (1998) findings suggest, however, that people may not be willing or able to *anticipate* their tendencies to engage in self-protection in response to an unfavorable outcome brought about by an unfair process.

When viewed in tandem, the Gilbert et al. (1998) results and the findings of Brockner, Wiesenfeld et al. (2010) pose a conundrum. On the one hand, the Gilbert et al. study suggests that people may not be able to predict, as a function of the fairness of the process that produced the outcome, how they will feel if they were to receive an unfavorable outcome. On the other hand, the Brockner, Wiesenfeld et al. study was based on people being able to predict that how they will feel about themselves in response to an unfavorable outcome *does* depend on the fairness of the process. Brockner, Wiesenfeld et al. found that when people were uncertain about whether their previously favorable outcomes would continue (i.e., when they were pretreated with noncontingent success), they showed less of a tendency to prefer a fair process over an unfair process relative to their counterparts who were more certain that their previously favorable outcomes would continue (i.e., the group that was pretreated with contingent success). On considering the possibility that their future outcomes may be unfavorable, participants pretreated with noncontingent success may have sought to reduce the self-evaluative implications of their future outcomes by showing less of a preference for the decision process to be fair. Given that the outcomes had not yet occurred, however, participants behaved as if they were well aware of how their feelings about themselves in the face of unfavorable outcomes would differ as a function of process fairness.

In light of the apparent inconsistency in the Gilbert et al. (1998) and Brockner, Wiesenfeld et al. (2010) studies, further research is needed to delineate when people may be more versus less capable of accurately predicting their reactions to unfavorable outcomes as a function of process fairness. Perhaps there were certain methodological differences in how the two studies were conducted that made participants in the Brockner, Wiesenfeld et al. study more willing or able to anticipate how they would feel about themselves in the face of an unfavorable outcome as a function of process fairness. For one thing, all participants in the Brockner, Wiesenfeld et al. study already had received evaluative feedback. Whereas all people were told that they had been successful, half were led to believe that their success was contingent on their own contributions or inputs; the other half were told that their success was noncontingent. Being pretreated with evaluative feedback may have subtly primed people to think about how they might feel about themselves in anticipation of additional evaluative information that would be coming their way later in the study. In contrast, participants in the Gilbert et al. study had not been pretreated with evaluative feedback prior to making predictions about how they would feel if they were to receive an unfavorable outcome.

Furthermore, process fairness was a within-subject variable in the Brockner, Wiesenfeld et al. (2010) study. Participants were led to believe that the favorability of their future outcomes was more versus less assured. After being told about two methods that could be used to decide on the outcomes, one more fair than the other, they were asked to indicate their degree of preference for the two processes. Being aware of both methods, participants may have been induced to think about how their reactions to the two may differ. In contrast, process fairness was a between-subject variable in the Gilbert et al. (1998) study. Half of the participants were asked to predict their reactions to a fair process; the other half were asked to predict their reactions to an unfair process. However, in light of the fact that all participants would be receiving the same unfavorable outcome, they appear to have based their predictions on the outcome and not on the process given that participants were in less of a position to compare their process to another one. In short, factors that induce people to think more deeply about the impact of process fairness on their reactions to unfavorable outcomes may heighten the accuracy of their affective forecasts. Future research needs to evaluate this reasoning and thereby possibly forge a connection between the interactive relationship between process fairness and outcome favorability and the intriguing literature on affective forecasting.

CHAPTER SUMMARY

Whereas Brockner and Wiesenfeld (1996) reported some initial findings that high process fairness heightens the effect of outcome favorability on people's self-evaluations relative to when process fairness is low, there have since been many additional demonstrations of this effect along with empirical evidence of why it occurs. People use process fairness information to judge their level of personal responsibility for their outcomes; the greater the process fairness, the more they see themselves as responsible. Judgments of personal responsibility for outcomes, in turn, interact with outcome favorability to influence people's self-evaluations (or beliefs and behaviors that may be colored by their self-evaluations), such that outcome favorability is more consequential when people see themselves as more responsible for their outcomes.

This chapter considered some conceptual and empirical implications of the fact that people use process fairness information to make self-attributions of responsibility for their outcomes. Importantly, this notion extends how we conceptualize the relationship between process fairness and self-evaluations. Previously, the predominant account of the link between process fairness and self-evaluations had been provided by relational theory (Tyler & Lind, 1992), which posits that people use process fairness information to judge how others view or evaluate them (the greater the process fairness, the more people believe that they are viewed favorably by others), which in turn shapes people's self-evaluations. Whereas relational theory provides a compelling explanation of the main effect of process fairness on people's self-evaluations, it has more difficulty accounting for the interactive effect of process fairness and outcome favorability on people's self-evaluations. The prospect that people use process fairness information to make self-attributions for their outcomes, however, may more easily account for the latter finding.

Given that the relationship between process fairness and self-evaluations may be explained at least in part by both the relational mechanism and the self-attributional mechanism, we need to better understand when each is likely to occur. Hence, this chapter considered moderating influences on these two mechanisms. For example, it was suggested that the relational mechanism may be more apt to account for the interpersonal treatment aspects of process fairness (interactional justice) than for its decision structural elements (procedural justice). I also suggested that the self-attributional mechanism may be instantiated to a greater extent when people's attention is self-directed. Furthermore, theory and research suggested that the salience of certain forms of identity (that is, whether people are cognitively representing the social versus the personal aspects of themselves) and the level of that identity (that is, whether people are high or low in their interdependent and independent self-construals) dictate whether the relational mechanism or the self-attributional mechanism is more likely to be activated.

One way to differentiate between the two mechanisms is by examining people's reactions to process fairness information in the face of unfavorable outcomes. When outcomes are favorable, both mechanisms posit "fair process effects," in which people respond more positively when process fairness is high. When outcomes are unfavorable, however, the two mechanisms make competing predictions. The relational mechanism continues to posit a fair process effect, whereas the self-attributional mechanism predicts a reversal effect, in which people respond more negatively to higher levels of process fairness. In fact, studies examining people's reactions to unfavorable outcomes have provided some evidence of a reversal effect, but the results across studies have been inconsistent. How do we account for this inconsistency? The extent to which people are prevention focused (as a possible exemplar of how much people assign psychological significance to unfavorable outcomes) is one determinant of the reversal effect, which was indeed shown to be more pronounced among those who are more prevention focused (Brockner et al., 2008). The combination of the salience of people's personal identity and their level of independent self-construal (as a possible exemplar of factors that moderate the relationship between process fairness and how much people see themselves as personally responsible for their outcomes) is another determinant of the reversal effect, shown more strongly when people's personal identity is salient and they are also high in independent self-construal (Holmvall & Bobocel, 2008).

Finally, I considered another intriguing implication of the self-attributional mechanism, namely, that in certain instances people may show less of the typical tendency to prefer to be treated with higher than with lower process fairness. Lower process fairness reduces the relevance of outcomes for people's self-evaluations. Hence, if people are uncertain that their upcoming outcomes will be favorable, they may prefer the decision to be enacted with less process fairness. In this way, if their outcomes prove to be unfavorable they can reduce seeing themselves as personally responsible for their outcomes, thereby protecting their self-evaluations in the process. The self-handicapping literature similarly suggests that when people are uncertain about their future success they may put obstacles in their way. Whereas the obstacles make unfavorable outcomes more likely to occur, they also provide people with a handy external attribution for their outcomes, thereby reducing the self-relevance of those outcomes. If low process fairness serves a similar (self-protective) purpose, then it may be expected that conditions that elicit self-handicapping may similarly reduce people's preferences to be treated with high process fairness (Brockner, Wiesenfeld et al., 2010). Finally, I discussed conceptual relationships between people's reduced preference to be treated with high process fairness and (1) their tendencies to engage in self-handicapping and (2) their (in)ability to make forecasts about their affective states.

CHAPTER

5

Accounting for Both Interaction Effects

INTRODUCTION

Chapters 2 to 4 considered two quite different forms of interactive relationships between process fairness and outcome favorability. Whereas Chapters 2 and 3 considered the tendency for high process fairness to reduce the effect of outcome favorability, Chapter 4 discussed how high process fairness may heighten the effect of outcome favorability relative to when process fairness is low. Moreover, the evidence suggests that the form of the interaction effect depends on the nature of the dependent variable. Chapters 2 and 3 showed that on measures of psychological strain or on system-referenced measures such as people's willingness to support decisions, decision makers, and organizations, high process fairness reduced the effect of outcome favorability. In contrast, Chapter 4 showed that on measures of self-evaluation, high process fairness heightened the effect of outcome favorability.

Theory and research presented in Chapters 2–4 also shed light on the reasons for the different interactive relationships between outcome favorability and process fairness. The emerging picture is that people use process fairness information to make sense of a number of matters pertinent to their economic and psychological well-being, such as

1. Making projections about how favorable their outcomes are likely to be, not only in the near term, but also over time (the fairer the process, the more likely people are to be optimistic about the favorability of their outcomes in both the short and the long term)
2. Determining the extent to which the decision-making authority may be trusted (the fairer the process, the more the authority can be trusted)
3. Evaluating the nature of their relationship with the decision-making authority (the fairer the process, the more likely they are to define the relationship as communal rather than as transactional)
4. Judging the extent to which they are held in high regard by the decision-making authority (the fairer the process, the more likely they are to infer that they are held in high regard)
5. Determining how much to see the authority and themselves as responsible for their outcomes (the fairer the process, the more likely they are to see themselves as responsible for their outcomes, and the less likely they are to see the authority as responsible for their outcomes, especially unfavorable outcomes)

With the exception of the self-attribution tendency alluded to in point 5, all of these sense-making processes give rise to the interactive pattern set forth in Chapters 2 and 3, in which high process fairness reduced the effect of outcome favorability. The self-attribution mechanism, in contrast, helps to account for the interactive pattern described in Chapter 4, in which high process fairness heightened the effect of outcome favorability. Armed with an understanding of the sense-making mechanisms underlying the two different interactive patterns, we may be able to integrate the previous findings. That is, it may be possible to delineate when one or the other interactive pattern will arise and, moreover, will arise on the *same* dependent variable within a given study. Chapter 5 provides one such integrative effort.

CHAPTER OVERVIEW

I begin by discussing how people's status or power relative to the other party may dictate the form of the interactive relationship between process fairness and outcome favorability. It is suggested that those in positions of lower status or power are more likely to exhibit the interaction effect discussed in Chapters 2 and 3, in which high process fairness reduces the effect of outcome favorability, relative to when process fairness is low. In contrast, those in positions of higher status or power are more likely to show the interaction effect discussed in Chapter 4, in which high process fairness heightens the effect of outcome favorability relative to when process fairness is low. I then describe the results of a series of studies that have tested (and lent support to) these assertions. Moreover, the same dependent variable is examined in these studies, namely, how much people prefer to do business or otherwise want to interact with the other party in the future. At first blush, people's desire to interact with the other party seems more similar to the dependent variables considered in Chapters 2 and 3 (e.g., people's willingness to support the other party) than it is to the dependent variable considered in Chapter 4, namely, people's self-evaluations. However, as I hope to make clear, these two constructs are actually linked in that how much people wish to interact with the other party may be based on how they feel about themselves in the course of doing so.

Not surprisingly, there has been much more research on one form of interactive relationship between process fairness and outcome favorability (see Chapters 2 and 3) or on the other (see Chapter 4) than there has been research devoted to reconciling the two different forms of interaction effects. Consequently, Chapter 5 is somewhat shorter than each of Chapters 2–4. Given the relative paucity of such integrative research efforts, however, there exist ripe opportunities for future study, a host of which are described in the present chapter.

THE ROLE OF RELATIVE STATUS OR POWER

Most studies of organizational justice (indeed, most studies of management or organizational behavior) look at the effects of actions taken by people in positions of higher status or power (i.e., managers) on the attitudes and behaviors of people occupying positions of lower status or power (i.e., their direct reports). This was certainly the case in the studies that examined the interactive relationship between process fairness and outcome favorability reviewed by Brockner and Wiesenfeld (1996) and in the subsequent studies set forth in Chapters 2–4. Many of these studies have taken place in organizational settings, in which the independent variables of process fairness and outcome favorability were associated with managers' behaviors, and the dependent variables consisted of the work attitudes and behaviors of their underlings. Other studies have taken place in legal settings (e.g., Lind & Tyler, 1988), in which process fairness and outcome favorability were based on the actions taken by legal authorities (the police or the courts), and the dependent variables consisted of the reactions of those affected by the authorities' actions (e.g., citizens' willingness to support the authorities). Still others consisted of controlled laboratory experiments (e.g., Folger et al., 1983), in which process fairness and outcome favorability referred to actions taken by the experimenter, and the dependent variables consisted of the reactions of research participants. It has long been known that in encounters between experimenters and research participants, it is the former who occupy the position of higher status or power (Milgram, 1974; Orne, 1962). In short, whereas the research contexts differed (organizational, legal, and experimental), in all of them researchers examined the effects of process fairness and outcome favorability emanating from those in the position of higher status or power on the beliefs and behaviors of those in the position of lower status or power. Whereas little mention was made of this built-in difference in status or power, we will soon see that it was a necessary condition for eliciting the interaction effect between process fairness and outcome favorability (reviewed by Brockner & Wiesenfeld in 1996 and discussed further in Chapters 2 and 3), in which high process fairness reduced the influence of outcome favorability.

Let me explain. As mentioned, people's use of process fairness information to make inferences about how much to trust the authority, or how to define the nature of their relationship with the authority, may account for the interaction effect in which high process fairness reduces the effect of outcome favorability. Thus, once trust is established (by virtue of the authority exhibiting high process fairness), people are less likely to be influenced by the favorability of their outcomes. Put differently, if trust is low (because the authority showed low process fairness), then people may define the relationship as less communal or more transactional, leading them to be more susceptible to influence by the favorability of their outcomes. However, all of this reasoning presupposes that establishing the trustworthiness of the decision-making authority (or, relatedly, establishing the nature of one's relationship with the authority) is a salient or meaningful concern to people.

In fact, in the case of people occupying positions of lower status or power, this appears to be exactly the case. In writing about people in positions of lower status or power, Kramer (1996) suggested that they

> lack precisely those types of information needed to make informed judgments about the trustworthiness (or lack of trustworthiness) of those exercising authority over them. Thus, from the standpoint of those on the bottom, decisions regarding how much trust should be conferred on a particular relationship become simultaneously more *consequential* and more problematic. ... Those on the bottom of a hierarchical relationship routinely encounter both vulnerability and uncertainty, and these are the conditions that *make salient concerns about trust.* (p. 223; italics added)

Given the concern of those in lower-status or lower-power positions to establish the trustworthiness of those having authority over them, they may be highly motivated to monitor (and hence be affected by) trust-related information, especially in the face of information that calls the trustworthiness of the authority into question. Enter outcome favorability and process fairness. The trustworthiness of the authority is more likely to be questioned when the authority makes decisions that yield unfavorable outcomes, such that recipients of the unfavorable outcomes may examine the authority's process fairness to make inferences about how much to trust the authority. The more that the authority is perceived to use fair processes, the more likely are those in subordinate positions to trust the authority and to react positively as a result.

For instance, subordinates are more likely to support the authority or to work to maintain their relationship with the authority. When the authority makes decisions that yield favorable outcomes, the authority's trustworthiness is less likely to be called into question, in which case subordinates are less likely to monitor and hence be affected by the authority's process fairness. Note that this reasoning provides one explanation of the interaction effect depicted in Chapters 2 and 3, in which high process fairness reduced the effect of outcome favorability on people's willingness to support decision-making authorities relative to when process fairness is low.

What about those in positions of higher status or power? What is their salient concern, and how might this concern influence the way that they are affected by the process fairness and outcome favorability exhibited by the other (lower-status or lower-power) party? Prior theory and research suggest that parties with higher status or power have somewhat different concerns in their interactions with lower-status others. Whereas the parties with lower status or power are motivated to determine how much to trust the higher-status parties (Kramer, 1996), the parties with higher status or power assign greater importance to maintaining the existing order (i.e., to affirming their higher status) because the existing order is more beneficial to them (Pfeffer, 1992). Hence, the parties having higher status or power will be more attracted to and supportive of others of lower status or power when their encounters with the latter serve to reinforce the existing social order, that is, their position of relatively high status.

Again, outcome favorability and process fairness come into play. When people are looking to have their higher status affirmed or maintained, then they should react particularly well when they receive favorable outcomes that are accompanied by high process fairness, for two reasons. First, as suggested in Chapter 4, high process fairness makes outcomes more self-relevant. People are more likely to see themselves as personally responsible for their outcomes when process fairness is relatively high, thereby explaining why high process fairness heightens the effect of outcome favorability on their self-evaluations (Brockner et al., 2003). Thus, exchanges that combine high process fairness and favorable outcomes are particularly appealing to people in the higher-status or higher-power position. Favorable outcomes affirm the existing order for people in higher-status positions, particularly when they see themselves as more responsible for having brought about those outcomes (which fair processes are apt to do). As a result, they should be particularly attracted to the lower-status others under these conditions.

Note that this reasoning is based on the notion that people are going the "self-attributional route" in response to process fairness information; that is, they are using process fairness information to judge how personally responsible they are for their outcomes. However, the fact that they also may go the "relational route" (in which people use process fairness information to make inferences about how highly the other party regards them) provides a second, not mutually exclusive, reason why people looking to have their higher status affirmed may respond particularly well when they receive a favorable outcome along with high process fairness. This is the only circumstance in which both the outcome and the process information communicate directly or symbolically that they are held in high regard. If either the outcome is unfavorable or the process is unfair, people may infer that they are not being held in high regard, in which case they may react negatively to the lower-status other.

Moreover, when people in higher-status or higher-power positions are going the self-attributional route, the combination of high process fairness and unfavorable outcomes may be particularly unappealing to them. By definition, unfavorable outcomes are a threat to the existing order for those in higher-status positions, particularly if they have to contemplate the possibility that they were personally responsible for those unfavorable outcomes (which, again, fair processes are apt to make them do). Consequently, they should be much less supportive of or attracted to those having lesser status or power under these circumstances. Furthermore, when people are going the self-attributional route, lower process fairness reduces the self-evaluative relevance of their outcomes, in which case whatever outcomes they receive have fewer implications for whether their higher status is affirmed (if their outcomes are favorable) or threatened (if their outcomes are unfavorable). In other words, when higher-status people use process fairness information to judge how personally responsible they are for their outcomes, the positive relationship between outcome favorability and attraction toward or support for the other should be attenuated when the other exhibits lower process fairness.

Hence, when people are concerned with maintaining or affirming their existing level of status or power (which those in positions of higher status or power are want to do), their reactions to outcome favorability and process fairness information may depend on how much their existing level of status or power is affirmed versus threatened by such information. The more that their encounters with the other affirms their higher status or power, the more attracted they are likely to be to the other. Both of the mechanisms through which process fairness influences people's self-evaluations (the self-attributional route and the relational route) undergird the prediction that those in positions of higher status or power will be especially attracted to the other party when they receive favorable outcomes via high process fairness. Said differently, both the self-attributional and the relational mechanisms predict that for those in positions of higher status or power, high process fairness will heighten the impact of outcome favorability on people's desire for future interaction with the other party relative to when process fairness is low.

The self-attributional and relational mechanisms differ in the predictions they make about when people with higher status or power are apt to respond most negatively (i.e., when they will be least attracted to the other party). If those in positions of higher status or power go the self-attributional route, in which they use process fairness information to judge how personally responsible they are for their outcomes, then they should respond most negatively when they receive an unfavorable outcome with a fair process. On the other hand, if they are going the relational route, in which they use process information to make inferences about how highly they are regarded by the other party, then they should respond most negatively when they receive an unfavorable outcome with an unfair process.

In summary, the moderating effect of people's relative status or power on the interactive relationship between process fairness and outcome favorability is predicated on the notion that people with varying degrees of status or power have different concerns in their encounters with one another. For those on the bottom, their concern with evaluating the trustworthiness of those on top may lead them to exhibit the interaction effect described in Chapters 2 and 3, in which high process fairness reduces the effect of outcome favorability on, say, how much they want to have future interaction with those in the higher-status position. For those on top, their concern with maintaining the existing social order (which will affirm their higher status or power) may lead them to show the interactive pattern reported in Chapter 4, in which high process fairness heightens the effect of outcome favorability on their desire for future interaction with those on the bottom. Moreover, note that, unlike in Chapters 2 through 4, these two different interactive relationships between process fairness and outcome favorability are expected to emerge on the same dependent variable (i.e., people's desire for future interaction with the other party).

EMPIRICAL EVIDENCE

This reasoning was tested in three studies (Chen et al., 2003). Negotiations provided the social context in two of them. Students pursuing a master's in business administration (MBA) from two different universities in the same metropolitan area negotiated against one another as part of a course requirement. In the first study (consisting of a dyadic negotiation), participants completed a short survey after the negotiations measuring their perceptions of the favorability of the outcome of the negotiation, the process fairness exhibited by the other party, and their desire for future interaction with the other party. The prestige of the university in which participants were enrolled served as a proxy for their perceived status (Elsbach & Kramer, 1996). Although the MBA programs at both universities are highly regarded in most public opinion polls (e.g., *Business Week* rankings), the prestige of one program is consistently rated as higher than that of the other.

The results (Chen et al., 2003) showed a significant three-way interaction among process fairness, outcome favorability, and MBA program status. Among those from the lower-status program, there was a significant interaction between process fairness and outcome favorability, the nature of which is shown in Figure 5.1A. As can be seen, high process fairness reduced the positive relationship between outcome favorability and desire for future interaction with the other relative to when process fairness was low. This pattern is similar to the interactive relationship described in Chapters 2 and 3, in which participants always had relatively lower status or power in the exchange.

Those from the higher-status program also exhibited a significant interaction between process fairness and outcome favorability, but its nature was quite different (Chen et al., 2003). As illustrated in Figure 5.1B, high process fairness heightened the positive relationship between outcome favorability and desire for future interaction with the other relative to when process fairness was low. The nature of this interactive pattern is similar to that depicted in the studies reported in Chapter 4, although unlike in Chapter 4 the dependent variable did not consist of participants' self-evaluations.

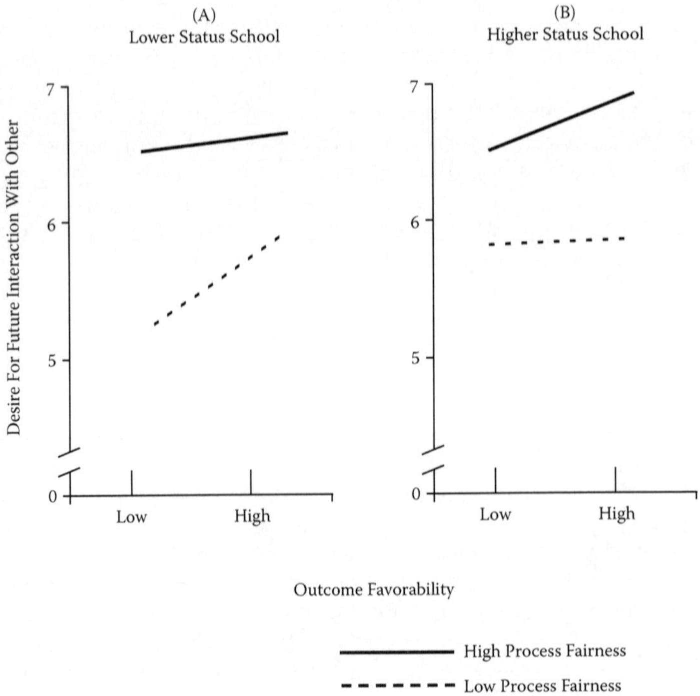

Figure 5.1 Desire for future interaction as a function of relative status of school, process fairness, and outcome favorability (Chen, Brockner, & Greenberg, 2003, Study 1. Reprinted from *Organizational Behavior and Human Decision Processes* 92, 1–2, When is it "a pleasure to do business with you?" The effects of relative status, outcome favorability, and procedural fairness, p. 21 (2003), with permission from Elsevier.).

A second negotiation study conducted by Chen et al. (2003) sought to extend these initial findings in a number of important respects. Whereas participants in the first study were drawn from MBA programs differing in prestige, there was no direct evidence that (1) the participants perceived these prestige differences, and (2) differences in perceived prestige accounted for the different interaction effects exhibited by participants from the two programs. Accordingly, participants completed a measure of the status of both their own business school and the business school represented by the other party. In fact, students from both universities perceived their relative prestige in the expected direction, such that the school with supposedly greater prestige was in fact perceived as significantly more prestigious than the school with supposedly less prestige. (Interestingly, however, the tendency for the more prestigious program to be rated more positively than the less-prestigious program was significantly less pronounced among those coming from the less-prestigious program.)

In addition, whereas the participants' encounter with each other in the first study was relatively brief, the negotiation exercise in the second study was much more involved (and involving) (Chen et al., 2003). Participants were given extensive background information related to the roles that they were to adopt during the negotiations, as well as half of a day to prepare for the upcoming negotiation; they also were given the other half of the day to complete the negotiations. Moreover, unlike the dyadic negotiations in Study 1, the exchanges were done on a team basis, in which groups of four students from one MBA program negotiated against a team of four from the other MBA program.

Again, Chen et al. (2003) found a significant three-way interaction among process fairness, outcome favorability, and program prestige. Those from the less-prestigious program showed a significant interaction between process fairness and outcome favorability along the lines of that shown in Figure 5.1A, whereas those from the more prestigious program showed a significant interaction similar to that illustrated in Figure 5.1B. In addition, when participants were sorted on the basis of the ratings of the prestige of their program relative to the other (rather than on the basis of the program in which they were enrolled), there was a significant three-way interaction among process fairness, outcome favorability, and relative status. Among those who perceived their program to be of lower status (regardless of their program), the significant interaction between process fairness and outcome favorability took the form shown in Figure 5.1A. Among those who perceived their university to be of higher status, the significant interaction between process fairness and outcome favorability took the form shown in Figure 5.1B. Moreover, Chen et al. found evidence of "mediated moderation," in that it was participants' ratings of the relative prestige of their program (and not their program per se) that moderated the interactive relationship between process fairness and outcome favorability.

Sorting participants on the basis of their ratings of the prestige of their own program relative to that of the other enabled Chen et al. (2003) to identify a third group of participants: those of relatively equal status, who perceived the prestige of their program to be similar to that of the prestige of the program of the opposing negotiation team. For this group, the interaction between process fairness and outcome favorability did not even approach significance. Perhaps this was because the mechanisms underlying the different interactive patterns shown by those of relatively lower or higher status effectively canceled one another. However, this is not to say that the relatively equal status group was unaffected by process fairness and outcome favorability. Rather than showing an interactive relationship between process fairness and outcome favorability, this group exhibited two main effects, such that they had more of a desire for future interaction with the other side when process fairness was relatively high and when outcome favorability was relatively high.

Chen et al. (2003) conducted a third study designed to conceptually replicate and extend the earlier findings in three important ways. First, the interpersonal context testing for the three-way interaction among process fairness, outcome favorability, and relative status differed from the negotiation setting used in Studies 1 and 2. All participants in Study 3 took part in a reward allocation exercise in which they played the role of recipient, and another party played the role of allocator. Second, participants' status relative to the other party was operationalized in a different way. Participants were employees of a financial services company who took part in the study in the context of a regularly scheduled training exercise. Their jobs at work consisted of being either customer service representatives or supervisors. Supervisors were one level above customer service representatives in this organization's formal hierarchical structure. Thus, participants' status relative to the allocator varied on the basis of their (and the allocator's) job title. Some of the participants who were customer service representatives were led to believe that their allocator was a supervisor in the firm (although not their supervisor). This constituted the lower-status group. Other participants who were supervisors were informed that their allocator was a customer service representative in the firm, although not one of their direct reports (higher-status group). Two other groups were paired with an allocator whom they believed to be of equal status: customer service representatives who thought their allocator also was a customer service representative (equal-low status) and supervisors who believed that their allocator also was a supervisor (equal-high status).

A third important feature is that participants were randomly assigned to be with an allocator who was of higher, lower, or equal status to themselves (Chen et al., 2003). In fact, all of the independent variables in Study 3 (process fairness, outcome favorability, and relative status) were experimentally manipulated, thereby greatly heightening the internal validity of the study relative to the negotiation studies in which all of the independent variables were measured.

In summary, all participants in Study 3 were the recipients of a reward allocation decision in a study that essentially consisted of a 2 × 2 × 2 × 2 factorial design (Chen et al., 2003). The independent variables were one's own title (supervisor or customer service representative), the allocator's title (supervisor or customer service representative), outcome favorability (favorable or unfavorable), and process fairness (high or low). As in the earlier studies, the dependent variable consisted of how much participants wanted to have future interaction with their partner, who always played the role of reward allocator.

Strikingly, the results of this study were conceptually analogous to those found in Studies 1 and 2 (Chen et al., 2003). As shown in Figure 5.2 A, among those having relatively low status (customer service representatives responding to allocation decisions made by supervisors), high process fairness reduced the effect of outcome favorability on participants' desire for future interaction with the other party relative to when process fairness was low. As seen in Figure 5.2B, among those having relatively high status (supervisors responding to decisions made by customer service representatives), high process fairness heightened the effect of outcome favorability on desire for future interaction relative to when process fairness was low. Figure 5.2 also reveals that the two equal-status groups (equal-low, Figure 5.2C, and equal-high, Figure 5.2D) showed no interaction effects but rather two main effects, such that desire for future interaction was greater when process fairness was high rather than low and when outcomes were favorable rather than unfavorable.

Other recent findings provide suggestive evidence that people's relative status may dictate the form of the interaction effect. For example, Chapter 3 described a series of studies that suggested that people's uncertainty about their standing as organizational members moderated the interactive effect of process fairness and outcome favorability on their organizational commitment (De Cremer, Brockner et al., in press). In one of these studies, length of tenure served as a proxy for uncertainty. Among those who were relatively new to the organization, high process fairness reduced the positive relationship between outcome favorability and organizational commitment relative to when process fairness was low ($p < .05$). However, among those who had greater tenure in the organization, high process fairness showed a marginal tendency to *heighten* the positive relationship between outcome favorability and organizational commitment relative to when process fairness was low ($p < .08$). In another study related to those reported by De Cremer, Brockner et al., whether employees were employed full time or part time served as a proxy for uncertainty. Among those who were employed on a part-time basis, high process fairness reduced the positive relationship between outcome favorability and organizational commitment relative to when process fairness was low ($p < .05$). However, among those who worked full time, high process fairness again showed

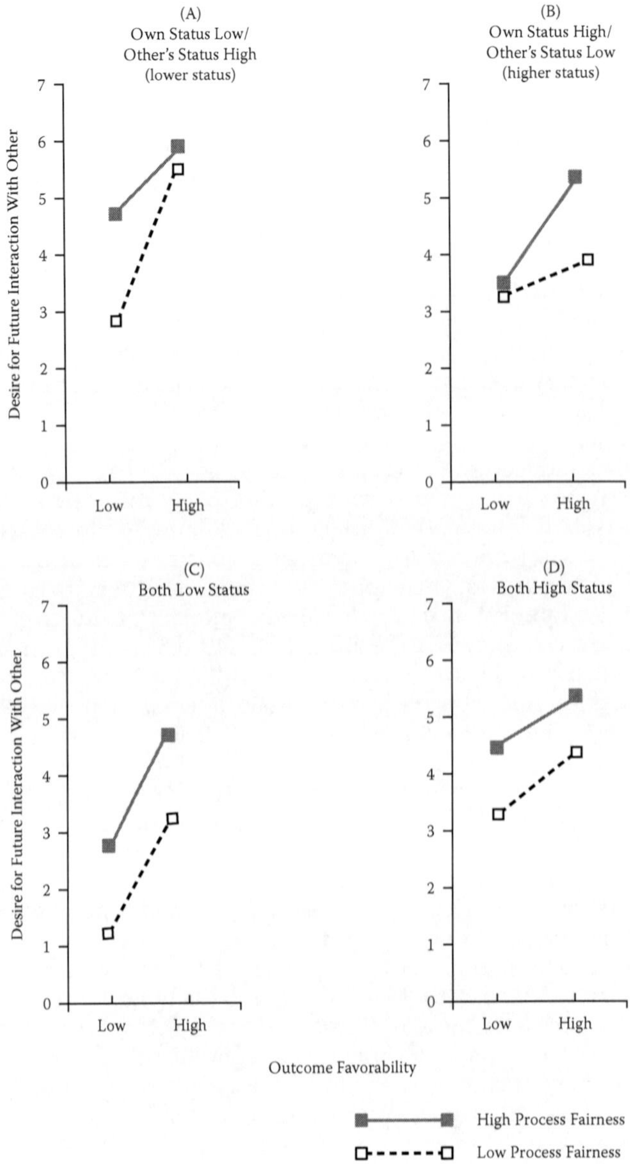

Figure 5.2 Desire for future interaction with other as a function of own and other's status, process fairness, and outcome favorability (Chen, Brockner & Greenberg, 2003, Study 2. Reprinted from *Organizational Behavior and Human Decision Processes* 92, 1–2, When is it "a pleasure to do business with you?" The effects of relative status, outcome favorability, and procedural fairness, p. 21 (2003), with permission from Elsevier.).

a marginal tendency to heighten the positive relationship between outcome favorability and organizational commitment relative to when process fairness was low ($p < .08$).

In the original presentation of these findings in Chapter 3, I suggested that length of tenure and employment status were proxies for employees' uncertainty about their standing as organizational members, which led them to draw on and hence be affected by process fairness information, particularly when their outcomes were relatively unfavorable. Conceiving of length of tenure and employment status as proxies for uncertainty also affected the way in which I presented the findings in Chapter 3. As mentioned there, those with less tenure or those who worked part time (with both groups believed to be more uncertain about their status as organization members than those with greater tenure or those who worked full time) were more likely to exhibit the tendency for high process fairness to reduce the effect of outcome favorability on organizational commitment relative to when process fairness was low. Presenting the findings in this way, however, runs the risk of underreporting the response pattern shown by those with greater tenure or those who were employed full time. That is, not only were these participants less likely to show the interactive relationship in which high process fairness *reduced* the effect of outcome favorability on organizational commitment, but also they tended toward showing a significant (albeit different) interactive relationship in their own right, in which high process fairness *heightened* the positive relationship between outcome favorability and organizational commitment relative to when process fairness was low.

In other words, whereas De Cremer, Brockner et al. (in press) conceived of length of tenure and employment status as proxies for *uncertainty about* standing or status, an alternative possibility that needs to be considered in light of the Chen et al. (2003) findings is that length of tenure and employment status also may reflect *level of* status, such that those with less tenure or those who work part time may have perceived themselves to have less status relative to their counterparts who had been around longer or who worked full time. Those with less tenure or those who work on a part-time basis may especially see themselves as having lower status in their dealings with organizational authorities, leading them to exhibit the interactive relationship shown in Figure 5.1A, in which high process fairness reduced the effect of outcome favorability. In contrast, those with more tenure or those who work full time may be more inclined to see themselves as having greater status (if not greater than organizational authorities, then probably greater than those who have less tenure or those who work part time), which may explain why their dealings with organizational authorities may give rise to the interaction effect shown in Figure 5.1B, in which high process fairness heightened the effect of outcome favorability.

A series of studies by Blader and Chen (in press) provided further replication and extension of the finding that people's relative status or

TABLE 5.1 Mean Level of Trust in and Desire for Future Interaction With Other as a Function of Process Fairness and Outcome Favorability (Blader & Chen, in press, Study 1)

	Outcome Favorability	
Process Fairness	**Unfavorable Outcome**	**Favorable Outcome**
Dependent Variable: Trust		
Low	3.92	4.06
High	3.25	4.57
Dependent Variable: Desire for Future Interaction		
Low	3.51	3.52
High	2.83	4.28

Note: Scores could range from 1 to 6, with higher scores reflecting a more positive response on the dependent variable.

power moderates the nature of the interactive relationship between procedural fairness and outcome favorability. Unlike in the work of Chen et al. (2003), in which participants' relative status served as an independent variable, *all* of the participants in some of Blader and Chen's studies (Studies 1–3) were of higher status than their interaction partners. In one study, participants were asked to recall a recent work experience in which they had dealt with others who had less status than they did (e.g., "your direct reports, colleagues from a less-influential department or division, or even colleagues at your same level who are less prominent than you are within the organization"). In a 2 × 2 factorial design (Outcome favorability × Process fairness), they were then randomly assigned to one of four conditions in which they recounted an experience in which their outcomes were either favorable or unfavorable and in which they felt that the other party treated them with high or low process fairness. The dependent variables consisted of the measure of desire for future interaction used by Chen et al. as well as a measure of how much they trusted the other party.

Both measures yielded a significant interaction effect. As can be seen in Table 5.1, and similar to the pattern shown by Chen et al.'s (2003) higher-status participants depicted in Figure 5.1B, outcome favorability was more positively related to how well participants reacted when process fairness was high rather than low.

In Blader and Chen's (in press) second study, all participants read a vignette describing an encounter in the workplace in which they were asked to imagine that they were the person of higher status. For example, in one of the vignettes they played the role of a supervisor who was receiving upward feedback from a direct report in the form of the company's annual 360-degree feedback process. Again, participants were randomly assigned to one of four conditions, varying in the

TABLE 5.2 Mean Level of Trust in and Liking for Other as a Function of Process Fairness and Outcome Favorability (Blader & Chen, in press, Study 2)

	Outcome Favorability	
Process Fairness	Unfavorable Outcome	Favorable Outcome
Dependent Variable: Trust		
Low	2.55	2.80
High	3.21	3.77
Dependent Variable: Liking		
Low	1.77	2.70
High	3.10	4.64

Note: Scores could range from 1 to 6, with higher scores reflecting a more positive response on the dependent variable.

extent to which the lower-status person acted toward them with process fairness (high or low) and outcome favorability (high or low). The dependent measures consisted of (1) the same measure of trust used in the first study described and (2) how attracted participants felt toward the other party. Significant interaction effects between process fairness and outcome favorability emerged on both measures. As can be seen in Table 5.2, high process fairness heightened the positive relationship between outcome favorability and each of trust and liking relative to when process fairness was low.

Taken together, the Blader and Chen (in press) results add considerable generality to the findings exhibited by the higher-status persons in the Chen et al. (2003) studies. Blader and Chen induced higher status in different ways in their two studies, which in turn were somewhat different from the ways in which Chen et al. operationalized higher status. Moreover, in addition to replicating the Chen et al. results on the measure of desire for future interaction, Blader and Chen extended the interactive relationship between process fairness and outcome favorability to measures of trust in and attraction toward the other party. Whereas all participants in the Blader and Chen studies had higher status than their interaction partners, it is telling that they exhibited an interactive relationship between process fairness and outcome favorability similar to the subset of participants in the Chen et al. studies who were of higher status than their interaction partners.

Several other findings in the Blader and Chen (in press) studies warrant attention. First, whereas the results were similar in the two studies, in that outcome favorability was more positively related to the dependent variables when process fairness was relatively high, there was an intriguing difference as well. Specifically, in the first study participants exhibited the most negative reactions when their outcomes were unfavorable and process fairness was high (see Table 5.1). In fact, Blader and Chen reported that participants' reactions in this study were marginally more negative in the high process fairness/unfavorable outcome condition than they were in the low process fairness/unfavorable outcome condition ($p < .10$). Note, however, that this specific aspect of the interaction effect did not emerge in the second study (see Table 5.2). Rather, participants' reactions were most negative in the low process fairness/unfavorable outcome condition; indeed, they reacted significantly more negatively on both the trust and the liking measures in the unfavorable outcome/low fair process condition than they did in the unfavorable outcome/high fair process condition.

How do we account for this between-study difference? One possibility is that people used process fairness information for somewhat different purposes in the two studies. In Study 1, people may have gone the "self-attributional route," drawing on process fairness information to determine how much they were personally responsible for their outcomes. The fairer the process, the more they may have seen themselves as responsible for their unfavorable outcomes (Brockner et al., 2003; Van den Bos et al., 1999), which could have threatened their desire to maintain their relatively high status in the situation. Put differently, unfavorable outcomes for which people felt more personally responsible (due to the other's higher process fairness) may have posed more of a threat to their relatively high status than unfavorable outcomes for which people felt less personally responsible (due to the other's lower process fairness). This may explain why participants in the first study responded more negatively to unfavorable outcomes when process fairness was high rather than low.

In Blader and Chen's (in press) second study, however, people may have gone the "relational route," using process fairness information to make inferences about how much they were held in high regard by their interaction partner (Tyler & Lind, 1992). To the extent that the other party treated them with low process fairness, participants were likely to believe that they were not viewed favorably. Thus, the combination of low process fairness and unfavorable outcomes may have threatened their desire to maintain their relatively high status in the situation, which in turn may have caused them to respond most negatively toward their partners in this condition. Future research is needed to evaluate (1) whether participants indeed used process fairness information for somewhat different sense-making purposes in Blader and Chen's two studies, (2) whether participants' use of process fairness information for the different sense-making purposes accounted for the varying results that emerged in the two studies, and (3) perhaps most important, *why* participants may have used process fairness information for different sense-making purposes in the two studies.

Regarding the third question, it may be that participants focused on different aspects of the process fairness manipulations in the two studies (Blader & Chen, in press), which led them to use the information they gleaned for somewhat different sense-making purposes. Certain elements of process fairness refer to factors that people believe could have influenced their outcomes, such as whether they were allowed to present their point of view, whether the outcomes were arrived at on the basis of accurate information, and so on (Leventhal et al., 1980). Other aspects of process fairness refer to events that accompany the receipt of outcomes but do necessarily cause the outcomes themselves, such as whether one is being treated with dignity and respect as the outcomes are being distributed. People may use the former elements of process fairness to determine the reasons for their outcomes (e.g., how much to see themselves as personally responsible), whereas they may use the latter to make inferences about how favorably they are regarded by the other party. In Blader and Chen's (in press) first study, participants were asked to recall and then respond to an experience with a lower-status other "in which they felt the process was fair or unfair." In the second study, the process fairness manipulation referred more to the interpersonal behavior of the lower-status other. For example, in one scenario participants were asked to imagine that they were the senior consultant on a work project, and the junior consultant with whom they were working treated them in either a disrespectful or a respectful manner.

If participants in Blader and Chen's (in press) first study were focused on the fairness of the process that produced their outcomes (rather than on the extent to which they were treated with dignity and respect), they may have used such information to make inferences about how much they were personally responsible for the ensuing outcomes. In contrast, participants in the second study may have used the information about the other's interpersonal behavior to make relational inferences. Seeing the self as personally responsible for unfavorable outcomes would be most threatening to one's high status, which may help to explain why participants reacted most negatively in the high process fairness/unfavorable outcome condition in Blader and Chen's first study. The receipt of both unfavorable outcomes and disrespectful treatment would also be most threatening to one's high status, which may explain why participants responded most negatively in the low process fairness/unfavorable outcome condition in Blader and Chen's second study.

It is also possible that certain features of the research settings (in addition to or instead of differences in the process fairness information that was salient) induced participants to use process fairness information for somewhat different purposes. Participants in Blader and Chen's (in press) first study were asked to describe their reactions to an actual encounter they had with a coworker. In contrast, participants in Blader and Chen's second study responded to hypothetical vignettes. These settings differed in at least two ways. First, participants were probably more ego involved in the first study than in the second study. Second, the length of time in between participants' initial exposure to process fairness and outcome favorability information and the point at which they described their reactions was far greater in the first study, in which people retrospectively described their reactions to the encounter, than in the second study, in which people read the vignette and described their reactions immediately thereafter. It is possible that either or both of these factors (1) induced participants in the first study to use process fairness information more to determine their personal responsibility for their outcomes and (2) led those in the second study to use process fairness information more to make inferences about how much the other party viewed them favorably. That is, with more on the line psychologically (in Study 1), participants may have been more motivated to understand the reasons for their outcomes, leading them to use process fairness information for more causal attributional purposes.

Furthermore, in responding to (or making sense of) unfavorable outcomes, people may use process fairness information differently over time. Shortly after encountering unfavorable outcomes, people may be more concerned with determining how safe it is to deal with the other party, in which case they may view the other's process fairness as an indicator of the extent to which they are held in high regard. Over time, however (that is, perhaps with increasing psychological distance from the encounter), people may begin to ponder the extent to which they were personally responsible for their unfavorable outcomes, which may lead them to treat process fairness information as a basis for making self-attributions for their outcomes. Clearly, these speculative accounts of the differences in the results of certain aspects of Blader and Chen's (in press) first two studies need to be examined in future research.

Another noteworthy aspect of Blader and Chen's (in press) research is that the authors unearthed additional findings (not yet mentioned) that extend the interactive relationship between process fairness and outcome favorability among higher-status persons. More specifically, Blader and Chen measured a number of individual difference variables in their second study (and in a third study, also not yet mentioned) and found that each moderated the interactive relationship between outcome favorability and process fairness. Specifically, the tendency for high process fairness to heighten the effect of outcome favorability on the various dependent measures (trust in the other, liking for the other, and desire for future interaction with the other) was stronger among people who were (1) relatively high in the need to belong (Baumeister & Leary, 1995), (2) relatively low in self-esteem, and (3) relatively low in their power distance beliefs (Hofstede, 1980).

How do we account for these findings? I offer a speculative analysis next. It is broadly consistent with the results of studies that considered when people in lower-status positions will be more versus less likely to exhibit the interactive relationship between process fairness and outcome favorability set forth in Chapters 2 and 3, in which high process fairness reduced the effect of outcome favorability relative to when process fairness was low. Recall the moderating influences described in Chapter 3: outcome importance, or how much is at stake (see pp. 85–101) and people's uncertainty about their standing as organizational members (see pp. 77–85). Similar factors may have a moderating influence on the other interactive pattern shown by those in higher-status positions.

If the interaction effect shown by higher-status persons reflects a sense-making process emanating from their desire to maintain or affirm their existing level of status, then the interaction effect should be more pronounced under the following conditions: (1) when people assign greater importance to having their higher status affirmed (i.e., when more is at stake) and (2) when people are more uncertain about the legitimacy of their higher status (i.e., when they are less comfortable about "being in the skin of" the higher-status position or role). My hunch is that the three individual difference variables that Blader and Chen (in press) examined map on to either or both of these two dimensions.

Need to belong and self-esteem were measured in the second of the two Blader and Chen (in press) studies discussed. *Need to belong* (Baumeister & Leary, 1995) refers to people's desire to form attachments to individuals and groups. One consequence of the need to belong is the tendency to monitor one's social environment for evidence of inclusion versus rejection. Higher-status individuals who are relatively high in the need to belong may assign greater importance to having their higher status affirmed relative to their counterparts who are lower in the need to belong. Indeed, when occupying a higher-status position in a dyad or in a collective, people's need to belong may be satisfied if they were to receive information suggesting that their higher status was affirmed. Information affirming their higher level of status (i.e., interpersonal encounters characterized by favorable outcomes and high process fairness) symbolizes inclusion and therefore is to be embraced (which could lead to higher levels of trust in and liking for their interaction partners).

Information that threatens their existing level of status (e.g., social interactions consisting of unfavorable outcomes and high process fairness, if the latter is used to make attributions of personal responsibility for outcomes, or social interactions consisting of unfavorable outcomes or low process fairness, if the latter is used to make relational inferences) reflects exclusion and hence will be experienced as aversive, manifesting itself in the form of lower levels of trust in and liking for the other party. In sum, when people are in higher-status positions, their need to belong may influence the importance of having their higher status affirmed. If this is the case, then it may explain why the interactive relationship between process fairness and outcome favorability shown by higher-status parties was stronger among those who were higher in the need to belong.

Like need to belong, self-esteem may be a proxy for how much importance people in higher-status positions assign to having their status affirmed. Lacking self-regard, those with lower self-esteem may be more needy of the outside world to bestow favorable (e.g., higher-status-affirming) evaluations on them. When such evaluations are forthcoming (i.e., in the form of favorable outcomes accompanied by high process fairness) people respond with great appreciation. However, when such evaluations are not forthcoming (e.g., unfavorable outcomes that emanate from fair processes, to the extent that process fairness information is used to make attributions of personal responsibility), people respond much more negatively.

In addition to being a proxy for how much people assign importance to having their higher status affirmed, self-esteem may be related to how much people experience uncertainty about the legitimacy of their higher-status position. When a higher-status position is occupied by someone relatively low in self-esteem, the occupant of that position may experience greater uncertainty about the legitimacy of occupying the higher-status role; the loftiness of their status is incongruent with the way that they evaluate themselves ("I'm not worthy"). Put differently, someone relatively high in self-esteem may feel more comfortable with being in the higher-status role, in which case they may have less of a need to have their higher status affirmed.

This reasoning suggests that people with lower self-esteem occupying a higher-status position may be more influenced than persons with higher self-esteem in that same role by the extent to which their higher status is affirmed because (1) they may assign more importance to having their higher status affirmed, or (2) they are less certain that it is legitimate for them to occupy the higher-status role. This may explain why Blader and Chen (in press) found that the process–outcome interaction effect shown by higher-status persons was significantly greater among people who were relatively low in self-esteem.

Blader and Chen (in press) also conducted a third study using the same basic procedure as that used in Study 2. The sample consisted of senior-level executives attending an executive MBA program in Beijing, China. Individual difference measures included self-esteem (as in Study 2) and power distance. *Power distance* refers to how much people believe that differences in hierarchy among people (an important basis of status) are natural and desirable (Hofstede, 1980). Those higher in power distance are much more willing to accept or even embrace hierarchical differences between people relative to their lower power distance counterparts, who are far less comfortable with the notion that those in higher-status positions are entitled to have greater power than those in lower-status positions. When higher-status positions are occupied by people with higher power distance beliefs, they are relatively unlikely to question the legitimacy of their higher status; it is just the natural social order. In contrast, when people with lower power distance beliefs occupy the higher-status position, they may be more uncertain about the legitimacy of being in the higher-status position; it goes against their personal grain.

Relative to people with higher power distance, those lower in power distance may feel that it is not legitimate to occupy the higher-status position, which led Blader and Chen (in press) to predict that those lower in power distance would be more likely than those higher in power distance to show the typical process–outcome interaction exhibited by people in higher-status positions.

Replicating the results of their second study, Blader and Chen (in press) found in Study 3 that people with lower self-esteem showed more of an interactive relationship than did people with higher self-esteem. Moreover, extending Study 2, Blader and Chen found that people with lower power distance showed more of an interactive relationship than did those higher in power distance. Both people with lower self-esteem and people with lower power distance have reasons to be uncertain about the legitimacy of being in the higher-status position, which could account for the moderating influences of both factors on the process–outcome interaction. Moreover, the nature of the uncertainty associated with being in the higher-status role that people with lower self-esteem or lower power distance experienced may have been due to different factors. For people with lower self-esteem, it may have been a matter of not feeling that they were entitled to occupying the higher-status position. For people with lower power distance, it may have been a matter of being in a situation that went against their personal values.

Whereas power distance had a moderating influence on the process–outcome interaction in Blader and Chen's (in press) Study 3, it is worth noting that the more basic two-way interaction between outcome favorability and process fairness was not significant in this study. Perhaps this was because the study was conducted in China, where people generally maintain high power distance beliefs (Hofstede, 1980). If the sample as a whole was relatively high in power distance, then participants generally may have felt little reason to question the legitimacy of occupying the higher-status role. This possibility becomes all the more reasonable when we consider that the participants in the study were senior executives with many years of experience, who were probably accustomed to occupying higher-status positions. Perhaps it was only the participants who were relatively low in power distance in this sample who felt *enough* uncertainty about the legitimacy of occupying the higher-status role to orient them to seek affirmation of their higher status, thereby giving rise to the three-way interaction among process fairness, outcome favorability, and power distance.

More generally, the moderating effects of need to belong, self-esteem, and power distance on the interactive relationship between process fairness and outcome favorability suggest that people occupying higher-status positions do not always respond in the same way. Rather, their reactions depend on how they enact their roles as the higher-status party, which in turn may be affected by individual difference variables.

Previously, I speculated that the three individual difference variables examined by Blader and Chen (in press) map on to two categories of moderating influences on the interactive relationship between outcome favorability exhibited by people occupying higher-status roles: (1) the degree of importance that people assign to having their higher status affirmed and (2) the degree of uncertainty they experience about how legitimate it is for them to occupy the higher-status role. Future research needs to examine these (and related) speculations. That is, do the individual difference variables examined by Blader and Chen relate to the two categories of moderating influences set forth? Moreover, do the hypothesized moderating influences actually have the effects that I am purporting them to have? If so, might there be other individual difference or situational factors that map on to these broader categories of moderating influences? Presumably, these other factors also should influence the magnitude of the interactive relationship between process fairness and outcome favorability exhibited by higher-status persons.

Interestingly, these two classes of moderating influences are identical to the two classes of moderating influences on the interactive relationship between outcome favorability and process fairness that people exhibit when they are in the lower-status role, as described in Chapter 3: outcome importance and uncertainty. The former reflects people's motivation to make sense of things, whereas the latter reflects their (lack of) ability to do so. The common theme for both those in lower- and higher-status positions is the following: If the interaction effect they exhibit between process fairness and outcome favorability reflects their respective sense-making tendencies, then the effect should be stronger when they are more *motivated* to make sense of things, or when they are more uncertain and therefore are less *able* to make sense of things without additional information processing. Given the different concerns of lower- and higher-status persons in their exchanges with one another, the content or substance of their sense-making activity may differ, which may explain why the interactive relationship between process fairness and outcome favorability takes different forms among lower- and higher-status persons. However, for both lower- and higher-status persons, the interaction effect that they do exhibit appears to be more pronounced when (1) more is at stake and (2) there is greater uncertainty about their respective sense-making concerns.

FUTURE RESEARCH OPPORTUNITIES

Whereas recent studies suggested that the nature of the interactive relationship between process fairness and outcome favorability depends on people's status or power relative to that of their interaction partner, many questions remain for future research. First, Kramer (1996) suggested that "those on the bottom of a hierarchical relationship routinely encounter both vulnerability and uncertainty, and these are the conditions that *make salient concerns about trust*" [italics added]. This raises an important question: What is it about being on the bottom of a hierarchical relationship that heightens people's motivation to evaluate the trustworthiness of those at the top? Is it their level of power (or lack thereof)? Is it their level of status (or lack thereof)? Might it be both? Whereas status and power are closely related, they also are conceptually distinct. *Status* refers to people's reputation or standing as seen in the eyes of relevant others. *Power* refers to people's ability to influence others. Status is one of several bases of power (French & Raven, 1959), and power is one of several bases of status. Having lower levels of power than one's interaction partner may motivate people to evaluate the trustworthiness of the interaction partner, which will manifest itself in the interactive relationship in which high process fairness reduces the effect of outcome favorability relative to when process fairness is low. Being in the lower power position makes people more dependent on the good graces (read: trustworthiness) of their interaction partner, in which case it behooves those in the lower power position to monitor the level of process fairness exhibited by their interaction partners.

Note, however, that in the three studies conducted by Chen et al. (2003), the relevant variable appeared to be status rather than power. In the negotiation studies, participants did not have a previous relationship with one another, and they were not expected to interact in the future. Instead, they came from schools differing in reputation or prestige. Whereas the students were not in differential positions of power relative to one another during the course of the negotiations, they did have differing degrees of status, to the extent that they invoked their social identity as members of the more versus less-prestigious MBA program.

Similarly, it is difficult to argue that participants in the reward allocation study (Chen et al., 2003, Study 3) maintained different degrees of power. However, they did come to the negotiation with potentially different levels of status, borne of their rank as supervisor (higher status) or as customer service representative (lower status). Moreover, participants in this study only knew one another's rank; they did not know the identity of the person with whom they were paired (e.g., people never interacted with someone with whom they had a reporting relationship), so it seems unlikely that power differences in the workplace spilled over to affect their interaction with each other during the course of the study.

Moreover, just as it could be argued that in unequal exchanges, the salient concern for people in the lesser position (of power or status) is to evaluate the trustworthiness of their interaction partner who is more advantaged, so may the salient concern for the person in the more advantaged position be to maintain the existing social order. Put differently, those in positions of higher status (power) are likely to want to maintain their existing level of status (power). Thus, future research needs to evaluate whether it is differences in status, power, or both that dictate the form of the interactive relationship between process fairness and outcome favorability.

A second important task for future research is to delineate whether the hypothesized differences in the concerns of people varying in status or power actually account for the different forms of interaction effects. Chen et al. (2003) speculated that those in the lower-status position assigned greater significance to evaluating the trustworthiness of their more advantaged interaction partner, and that those in the higher position assigned greater importance to maintaining the status quo in their dealings with their less-advantaged interaction partner. Given that this reasoning was never directly tested, however, further research is needed. For example, prior to interacting with one another, people of differing degrees of status (or power) could be asked to indicate what they are trying to accomplish in the upcoming exchange. Relative to their counterparts with lower status or power, those with higher status or power are expected to say that they are more concerned with trying to maintain the status quo and less concerned with evaluating the trustworthiness of their interaction partner. Mediation tests (or more precisely, tests of mediated moderation) could then be conducted to evaluate whether the differing concerns of those with more versus less status or power account for their different forms of process–outcome interaction effects.

An alternative (and not mutually exclusive) research strategy to evaluate whether the hypothesized differential concerns of higher- and lower-status people account for their different forms of process–outcome interactions entails testing for moderating influences. Thus, if the interaction effect shown by higher-status persons emanates from their desire to maintain or affirm their higher status, then they should be more likely to exhibit the effect when they are in fact more motivated to maintain or affirm their higher status. Evidence consistent with this line of reasoning was provided by Blader and Chen's (in press) finding that the interaction effect was stronger when people occupying the higher-status role were relatively high in the need to belong or low in self-esteem, for whom it may have been more important to have their higher status affirmed. Similarly, if the interaction effect shown by lower-status persons emanates from their need to evaluate the trustworthiness of their interaction partners, then they should be more likely to exhibit the interaction effect when they are in fact more motivated to evaluate the trustworthiness of their interaction partner. Research cited in Chapter 3, showing that relationship importance (e.g., Kwong & Leung, 2002) or people's self-construals (Brockner et al., 2000) moderate the process–outcome interaction shown by those in lower-status positions, is consistent with this line of reasoning.

Particularly integrative would be research that examines moderating influences on the process–outcome interaction effect exhibited by higher- and lower-status persons within the same study. Blader and Chen (in press, Study 4) completed such a study, in which they found that the three-way interaction effect among outcome favorability, process fairness, and relative status reported by Chen et al. (2003) was itself moderated by the degree of importance that people assigned to status. More specifically, among higher-status people, the tendency for high process fairness to heighten the effect of outcome favorability on people's desire for future interaction with the lower-status other was more pronounced when people assigned greater importance to status.

Moreover, among lower-status people, the tendency for high process fairness to reduce the effect of outcome favorability on people's desire for future interaction with the higher-status other was more pronounced when people assigned greater importance to status. Importance of status was operationalized as an individual difference variable, as reflected in the following sample item: "I find it important that others acknowledge my status."

These findings manifested themselves in the form of a four-way interaction effect (Process fairness × Outcome favorability × Relative status × Importance of status). In general, four-way interaction effects are unwieldy in several respects. For one thing, statistical tests for them tend not to be powerful; large samples often are required. Moreover, at first blush they may seem difficult to interpret. Whereas further research is clearly needed, this initial four-way interaction unearthed by Blader and Chen (in press) suggests that status concerns are central to understanding the different interactive relationships between process fairness and outcome favorability exhibited by higher-status people (who are looking to maintain their status) and lower-status people (who are looking to enhance their status).

A third avenue for future research is to evaluate yet another way to account for the moderating effect of relative status on the form of the interaction between process fairness and outcome favorability, which emanates from an alternative way of looking at the three-way interaction among outcome favorability, process fairness, and relative status. To this point, I have described the three-way interaction as follows: Among those with higher (lower) status, high process fairness heightens (reduces) the impact of outcome favorability relative to when process fairness is low. An alternative way to depict the three-way interaction is that those with higher status react most positively toward their interaction partners when process fairness is high *and* when outcomes are favorable relative to all other conditions. Said differently, the absence of either high process fairness or favorable outcomes may elicit a relatively negative response in higher-status persons toward their interaction partners. In contrast, those with lower status will react positively toward their interaction partners when process fairness is high *or* outcomes are favorable. In other words, lower-status persons react more negatively when process fairness is low and outcomes are unfavorable relative to all other conditions. Thus, among higher-status persons it is *necessary* for the process to be fair and for outcomes to be favorable for them to respond positively to their interaction partners. For those with lower status, the presence of either fair processes or favorable outcomes is *sufficient* to elicit relatively positive reactions.

Possible differences in the regulatory focus orientation (Higgins, 1998) of higher- versus lower-status persons may explain why they react differently to the combined effects of process fairness and outcome favorability. Promotion focus predisposes people to be concerned with gains, whereas prevention focus leads people to assign significance to losses. It could be argued that people's status relative to that of their interaction partner influences their regulatory focus orientation. By virtue of the possibility that they are trying to *better* their standing, lower-status persons may assign greater importance to gains and hence adopt more of a promotion focus. Hence, *any* evidence of being viewed favorably by their interaction partners (such as the receipt of favorable outcomes or being treated with high process fairness) may be sufficient to elicit positive reactions toward their partners (e.g., wanting to interact with them in the future). In contrast, higher-status or higher-power persons, who are more concerned with *maintaining* their standing, may assign greater importance to loss, consistent with that of a prevention focus orientation. In other words, relative to one another, lower-status or lower-power persons may be more concerned with winning (i.e., with *improving* their plight), whereas higher-status persons may be more concerned with not losing (i.e., with *maintaining* the status quo).

In sum, theory and research lend support to the following two propositions: First, people's relative status dictates the form of the interactive relationship between process fairness and outcome favorability. Among those of higher status, high process fairness *and* favorable outcomes are necessary to elicit favorable reactions toward their interaction partners. Thus, higher-status persons exhibit *conjunctive* thinking in that high process fairness and favorable outcomes both need to be present for them to respond positively to their interaction partners. In contrast, among those of lower status, either high process fairness *or* favorable outcomes is sufficient to produce favorable reactions toward their interaction partners. In other words, lower-status persons exhibit *disjunctive* thinking, such that either high process fairness or favorable outcomes is enough to elicit a positive response. Second, given that the existing state benefits those occupying the higher-status position more than those in the lower-status position, the former may be more prevention focused (motivated not to lose), whereas the latter may be more promotion focused (motivated to gain).

To suggest that status-induced differences in regulatory focus may account for the different forms of process–outcome interactive relationships exhibited by those of higher and lower status, there needs to be evidence that people's regulatory foci influence their tendencies to engage in conjunctive and disjunctive thinking. Indeed, recent theory and research suggest that promotion focus predisposes people to engage in disjunctive thinking (consistent with the form of the process–outcome interaction effect exhibited by lower-status persons), whereas prevention focus leads people to be more inclined toward conjunctive thinking (which is consistent with how higher-status persons manifest their form of the interaction effect).

More specifically, promotion focus may lead people to believe that any of a number of behaviors or events may be sufficient for goal attainment. As Friedman (1999) suggested:

> Consider the goal of seeking accomplishment by means of accumulating vast wealth. This promotion goal can be attained in a variety of ways, such as by becoming a successful Wall Street trader, *or* by winning the state lottery. ... Once the individual has successfully pursued one route to this promotion goal (i.e., wealth acquisition) he or she need not pursue alternative routes. ... *Any* successful route to a promotion goal is a sufficient route. (p. 25; italics added)

In contrast, prevention focus may lead people to believe that all behaviors or events are necessary for goal attainment. As Friedman (1999) put it:

> Consider the goal of securing one's home from burglars, murderers, and other societal riffraff. Means of attaining this prevention goal include keeping windows *and* doors locked while asleep or away from home. ... In prevention, danger (e.g., the prospect of a break-in) can not be averted with certainty unless *all* [italics added] paths to danger are effectively overcome. (pp. 25–26)

As Brockner, Paruchuri, Idson, and Higgins (2002) put it:

> People's regulatory focus influences their strategic orientation towards goal attainment. Promotion focus leads people to attend to the sufficiency of any of a number of courses of action to bring about goal attainment. Prevention focus leads people to attend to the necessity of multiple courses of action to bring about goal attainment. Put differently, promotion focus leads people to think disjunctively, whereas prevention focus leads people to think conjunctively. (pp. 8–9)

Moreover, Brockner et al. (2002) provided evidence consistent with this reasoning. Research in behavioral decision theory has shown that people tend to misperceive the likelihood of conjunctive and disjunctive events (Bar-Hillel, 1973), overestimating in the case of the former and underestimating in the case of the latter. For example, if each of four separate events has a 90% probability of occurring, people intuitively estimate the likelihood of *all four* events occurring to be significantly higher than the actual probability, which is $90\%^4$ or approximately 66%. Moreover, if each of four separate events has a 10% probability of occurring, people intuitively estimate the likelihood that *any one* will occur to be significantly lower than the actual probability, which is $100\% - (90\%)^4$ or 34%.

Brockner et al. (2002) replicated these findings and showed that the magnitude of these effects depended on people's regulatory foci. Those with more of a promotion focus were more accurate in their probability estimates of disjunctive events, whereas those with more of a prevention focus were more accurate in their probability estimates of conjunctive events. One interpretation of such findings is that people did better at the type of estimate that was more congruent with the way in which they naturally think. Thus, those with a prevention (promotion) focus may have done better at the conjunctive (disjunctive) estimates because they are more inclined to engage in that particular form of thinking.

In sum, if higher-status persons are more prevention focused, they may be inclined to engage in conjunctive thinking, which may explain why they react much more favorably to their interaction partners when process fairness *and* outcome favorability are high. Moreover, to the extent that lower-status persons are more promotion focused, they may be inclined to engage in disjunctive thinking, which may account for their tendency to react favorably to their interaction partners if either process fairness or outcome favorability is high.

Future research needs to evaluate the merits of this alternative interpretation. For example, it would be important to evaluate whether people's relative status or power influences their regulatory focus orientation. Are people with higher status more likely to be prevention focused relative to their lower-status counterparts? Note that such a tendency may be somewhat counterintuitive in light of evidence that being in the stronger position enables people to be more aspirational and hence promotion-like in their regulatory focus orientation (E. T. Higgins, personal communication, February 1, 2006). Moreover, the alternative interpretation is based on the notion that people use process fairness information to make judgments of how favorably they are evaluated by their interaction partners. In contrast, another explanation of the process–outcome interaction shown by those in higher-status positions is based on the notion that they use process fairness information to make inferences about the extent to which they are personally responsible for their outcomes.

Thus, future research designed to differentiate between the two different explanations of the process–outcome interaction effect shown by higher-status parties needs to evaluate whether people are using process fairness information to make inferences of how they are evaluated by others, which may directly influence their self-evaluations (the "relational" route) or whether they use process fairness information to make judgments of how personally responsible they are for their outcomes, which in combination with outcome favorability information will influence their self-evaluations (the "self-attributional" route). One way to conceptualize the two different ways in which people use process fairness information is as follows: When people use process fairness information to make inferences about how they are evaluated by their interaction partners, process fairness is likely to be directly and positively related to their self-evaluations.

In contrast, when they use process fairness information to make inferences about how much they are personally responsible for their outcomes, process fairness is likely to affect how much they see their outcomes (either favorable or unfavorable) as self-relevant, which in turn sets the stage for outcome favorability to be directly and positively related to their self-evaluations. Whereas people's tendencies to use process fairness information for these two different purposes are not mutually exclusive, the purposes themselves are conceptually distinct. Thus, future research is needed to evaluate the extent to which these processes are operating and whether they do so in ways that account for the intriguing three-way interaction among process fairness, outcome favorability, and relative status.

Equal-Status Encounters

Thus far, we have considered how process fairness and outcome favorability interact to influence people's attraction toward the other party in unequal status encounters, particularly how the process–outcome interaction effect takes different forms as a function of people's relative status. In the course of doing so, we have underemphasized the question of how process fairness and outcome favorability affect people's attraction toward one another when they are of relatively equal status or power. Note that in the studies reported by Chen et al. (2003) the encounters between equal status parties failed to elicit an interactive relationship between process fairness and outcome favorability. Rather, the equal status participants exhibited main effects of process fairness and outcome favorability, such that they were more attracted to the other party when process fairness was high rather than low and when outcome favorability was high rather than low.

Understanding how and why process fairness and outcome favorability affect those in relatively equal-status encounters is important on several counts. First, many interactions and relationships (both in and out of the workplace) take place between parties with relatively equal status, such as those among peers, colleagues, and friends. For example, the pervasive flattening of organizational hierarchies has increased the extent to which employees are interacting with each other in more equal status contexts. If more equal status encounters are becoming more prevalent, it behooves us to delineate the effects of process fairness and outcome favorability within those contexts. Second, any comprehensive explanation of the interactive relationships between process fairness and outcome favorability needs to account for those circumstances in which an interactive relationship *fails* to materialize. Thus, we may be better able to understand the different process–outcome interaction effects exhibited by lower- and higher-status parties to the extent that we can explain why *neither* interaction effect emerges among people who are of relatively equal status.

As suggested throughout, the interactive relationships between process fairness and outcome favorability reflect people's tendencies to use process fairness information to make sense of a variety of matters pertinent to their economic and psychological well-being. For example, when people use process fairness information to determine how much to trust the other, there is likely to be an interactive relationship in which high process fairness reduces the effect of outcome favorability on people's attraction to the other, relative to when process fairness is low. Alternatively, when people use process fairness information to judge their degree of personal responsibility for their outcomes, there is likely to be an interactive relationship in which high process fairness heightens the effect of outcome favorability on attraction to the other relative to when process fairness is low.

Because higher- and lower-status parties have somewhat different goals in their interactions with one another, they may use process fairness information for different sense-making purposes. Being more vulnerable and therefore seeking to enhance their level of influence, those in lower-status positions may use process fairness information to make inferences about how much to trust the other. Being more concerned about maintaining the current state, those in higher-status positions may use process fairness information to make inferences about how much they are personally responsible for the outcomes received during the encounter with the other, which in turn will inform them of the extent to which their existing status has been affirmed versus threatened.

The fact that people of relatively equal status exhibit neither form of interaction effect may be explained in at least three ways. One possibility is that equal-status persons may not be particularly motivated to attain *either* of the interaction goals that are important to lower- status and higher-status persons, in which case there is little impetus for either form of interaction effect to emerge. Perhaps interpersonal encounters and relationships in which status differences are minimal reduce people's needs to make sense of their environments for self-regulatory purposes, thereby reducing their susceptibility to influence by the interaction between process fairness and outcome favorability.

Whereas this possibility cannot be summarily dismissed, it may be counteracted on both empirical and conceptual grounds. At the empirical level, this reasoning implies that process fairness and outcome favorability should have little influence on people in equal-status encounters and relationships. However, Chen et al. (2003) did not find that process fairness and outcome favorability had no effect on the equal-status participants' desire for interaction with one another. Rather, Chen et al. discovered that among their equal-status participants, process fairness and outcome favorability failed *to interact with each other* and instead yielded main effects.

At the conceptual level, it could be argued that equal-status people have reasons to experience what it is like to be in a position of both higher and lower status and thereby perceive the interaction goals of both parties. This possibility is based on two assumptions. First, a fundamental process in many social encounters and relationships is for participants to establish some form of hierarchy (e.g., Mazur, 1985; Tuckman, 1965), which in turn is one basis of status differences. After all, if the parties have not established some form of hierarchy, they may be unlikely to accomplish the objectives that brought them together in the first place. For example, in organizational settings managers have greater formal status than their direct reports. Imagine the turmoil that would exist in the absence of such a social order. Managers would set direction, but if their direct reports did not believe that managers had a legitimate right to do so, then the two parties would probably be spending most of their energies trying to resolve their relative degrees of status, and little else would be accomplished. The second assumption is that in the status-sorting process, people generally find it more desirable to attain the position of higher rather than lower status, in that greater rewards and resources (both substantive and symbolic) typically go to those in the higher-status position.

When status differences are already present, both the higher- and lower-status parties "know their places" and can therefore devote their psychological energies to the sense-making process associated with their respective position. Being more vulnerable, those in the lower-status position are motivated to determine the trustworthiness of the higher-status other, leading them to exhibit the process–outcome interaction in which high process fairness reduces the effect of outcome favorability relative to when process fairness is low. Feeling benefited by the status quo, those in the higher-status position wish to see it maintained, leading them to exhibit another form of process–outcome interaction in which high process fairness heightens the effect of outcome favorability relative to when process fairness is low.

What about those in equal-status encounters or relationships? Because hierarchy has not been established, they may need to do so. Moreover, both parties are likely to prefer being higher rather than lower in the status hierarchy. Thus, in the status-sorting process, equal-status participants may perceive *both* of the interaction goals that are emphasized by higher- and lower-status persons, respectively. That is, if they are of equal status but aspire to be of higher status (a readily understandable aspiration), they may adopt some of the psychological tendencies of higher-status people. Moreover, if they are of equal status but are concerned that they may be relegated to a lower-status position (also a readily understandable concern), they may begin to think about what it is like to be in a lower-status position and take on or at least contemplate some of the psychological tendencies of lower-status people. These processes may be quite subtle; I am not suggesting that people are necessarily aware of them as they are holding sway. Because the social interaction goal of higher-status persons elicits one form of interactive relationship between process fairness and outcome favorability, whereas the social interaction goal of lower-status persons brings about an opposing form of interactive relationship, the possibly ensuing cancellation results in no interactive relationship at all.

Note, however, that the referenced cancellation may occur in two different ways: on a within-persons basis or on an across-persons basis. On a within-persons basis, it may be that equal-status persons are jointly affected by the two processes that elicit the different forms of interaction effects. On an across-persons basis, it may be that some people in equal-status encounters emphasize one social interaction goal that elicits one of the interaction effects, whereas others emphasize the other goal that produces the opposing interaction effect. When the reactions of these two types are pooled, they may "average out" to show no interaction effect.

In summary, equal-status persons may fail to exhibit an interactive relationship between process fairness and outcome favorability because they do not emphasize *either* of the interaction goals held by higher-status or lower-status persons. Instead, they may be more consumed by establishing social order and by trying to gain the upper hand in that process. These motives also may account for the fact that equal-status encounters yield main effects of process fairness and outcome favorability. After all, people are unlikely to believe that they will rise to the position of higher status (and therefore they will be less attracted to the other) if the other treats them with lower outcome favorability or with lower process fairness. Alternatively, equal-status parties may fail to exhibit an interactive relationship between process fairness and outcome favorability because they hold *both* of the interaction goals emphasized by higher- and lower-status persons, either on a within-persons basis or on an across-persons basis.

Future research needs to evaluate the extent to which each of these processes may account for the findings of the equal-status parties. Not only may such efforts help us to better understand when and why process fairness and outcome favorability are more versus less likely to interact with each other, but also they may more generally delineate the psychology of being in a position of equal status. One way to pursue this matter is by asking people in equal-status encounters beforehand to indicate the extent to which their goal is to (1) evaluate the trustworthiness of the other party, which is presumably the salient concern for people in positions of lower status, and (2) maintain their existing status, which is presumably the important consideration for people occupying positions of greater status. If the lack of a process–outcome interaction effect among equal-status persons reflects a cancellation emanating from two different interaction goals, then the same persons should assign importance to *both* goals. On the other hand, if the lack of an interaction effect is due to the fact that certain equal-status persons assign importance to one interaction goal whereas others assign importance to the other, then there should be an approximately equal number of persons who emphasize one goal or the other.

Of course, this reasoning assumes that participants are willing and able to report accurately their interaction goals prior to their encounter with the other party, which may not be the case. Another, although perhaps more indirect, way to discern the interaction goals of people with relatively equal status is by examining within-condition variance on the dependent variable (e.g., desire for future interaction with the other party). If people of relatively equal status fail to exhibit a process–outcome interaction because they are composed of two subgroups of people, in which one emphasizes an interaction goal that produces one form of interaction effect whereas the other assigns importance to an interaction goal that produces the opposing form of interaction effect, then they may exhibit relatively high within-condition variance. Alternatively, if the lack of interaction effect reflects the absence of both interaction goals, then the within-condition variance would not be expected to be particularly high or any higher than that shown by people whose status is different from (lower or higher) that of their interaction partner.

Thus, by better understanding the psychology of equal-status encounters, we also may shed light on the interactive relationships between process fairness and outcome favorability. Moreover, interesting questions abound if equal-status persons are found to emphasize one interaction goal rather than the other. For example, if equal-status persons consist of two subgroups, one having the interaction goal of evaluating the trustworthiness of their interaction partner and the other having the interaction goal of maintaining the status quo, then it would be important to identify the factors that led them to emphasize one goal rather than the other. Along these lines, perhaps promotion-focused individuals in equal-status encounters emphasize evaluating the trustworthiness of the other party because doing so may enable them to determine how to *gain* in stature. In contrast, prevention-focused individuals in equal-status encounters may put more emphasis on maintaining the status quo, which would fulfill their desire to ward off *loss*. Furthermore, if equal-status persons are found not to be motivated to attain either of these interaction goals, then it raises the question of what it is that *does* motivate them.

CHAPTER SUMMARY

Whereas Chapters 2–4 focused on the two different forms of interactive relationships between outcome favorability and process fairness, Chapter 5 was designed to be more integrative in its approach. If we truly understand the bases of the two different forms of interaction effects, it may be possible to specify the conditions under which one form or the other (or maybe even no interaction effect at all) should be likely to emerge, even on the same dependent variable. Chapter 5 offered theory and research to suggest that people's status relative to that of the other party plays an important role in dictating the form and even the presence of the interactive relationship between process fairness and outcome favorability. When people are of lower status, the interactive pattern highlighted in Chapters 2 and 3 manifests itself, in which high process fairness reduces the effect of outcome favorability relative to when process fairness is low. This pattern is similar to the one found in many studies reviewed by Brockner and Wiesenfeld (1996). Moreover, the participants in those studies were of lower status than the party who dispensed process fairness and outcome favorability (e.g., employees responding to the actions of organizational authorities).

The present chapter took the important next step of showing that the interaction effect reviewed by Brockner and Wiesenfeld (1996) *is contingent on* people being in the lower-status position. When people are in the higher-status position, the interactive pattern described in Chapter 4 is particularly likely to emerge, in which high process fairness heightens the effect of outcome favorability relative to when process fairness is low. And, when people are of relatively equal status, neither interaction effect emerges, although process fairness and outcome favorability do yield main effects. Finally, in the course of delineating people's relative status as key to reconciling the different forms of process–outcome interaction effects, I identified a number of potentially fruitful areas for further research.

CHAPTER

6

Casting the Process–Outcome Interaction Effects More Broadly

INTRODUCTION

The interaction effects (in which high process fairness reduces the effect of outcome favorability, see Chapters 2 and 3; or in which high process fairness heightens the effect of outcome favorability, see Chapter 4) described in previous chapters are quite robust. They have been found in many contexts, using various conceptions and operationalizations of process fairness and of outcome favorability, and across a wide variety of dependent variables. Indeed, the ubiquity of the effects makes it tempting to conclude that they represent fundamental "truisms" in social and organizational psychology. Of course, the interaction effects do not always emerge to the same degree (see Chapters 3–5 for a discussion of moderating influences); on certain occasions, such as when the parties are of equal status (Chen et al., 2003) or when the sample as a whole is relatively certain about their standing as organizational members (De Cremer, Brockner et al., in press), they may not materialize at all.

As pervasive as the interaction effects appear to be, however, they actually may be tapping into more general psychological processes. By considering how the interaction effects reflect more general psychological processes, I hope to broaden the reach (and hence the conceptual significance) of the effects. Furthermore, elucidating these more general psychological processes is a worthwhile endeavor in its own right. Thus, the primary goal of Chapter 6 is to locate the interaction effects in broader conceptual spaces and in so doing deepen our understanding of both the interaction effects and the broader conceptual spaces in which they may be located.

One way to depict the interaction effects is to say that process fairness has a moderating influence on outcome favorability. A different but equally appropriate way to present the interactions is that outcome favorability has a moderating influence on process fairness. Theory and research that address the "why questions" (i.e., why does process fairness have a moderating influence on outcome favorability? and why does outcome favorability have a moderating influence on process fairness?) provide insight into how the interaction effects may be viewed through broader conceptual lenses. In this chapter, I consider how other factors besides process fairness may have a moderating influence on outcome favorability. As the preceding chapters imply, process fairness reflects more general factors that interact with outcome favorability to influence people's beliefs and behaviors. If so, then other exemplars of those same general factors should similarly interact with outcome favorability.

Moreover, I identify factors other than outcome favorability that have a moderating influence on process fairness. Outcome favorability also may represent more general factors that interact with process fairness to influence people's beliefs and behaviors. If so, then other representatives of the same general factors should similarly interact with process fairness. Moreover, because these "general factors" do not pertain solely to matters of justice, the ensuing analyses should forge connections between the justice literature and other bodies of theory and research, thereby serving to broaden the reach of the process–outcome interaction effects.

CHAPTER OVERVIEW

First, I consider what it is about process fairness that gives rise to the interactive relationship set forth in Chapters 2 and 3, in which high process fairness reduces the influence of outcome favorability, followed by a discussion of what it is about process fairness that elicits the interaction effect described in Chapter 4, in which high process fairness heightens the impact of outcome favorability. Derived from these discussions are other dimensions (besides process fairness) that may interact with outcome favorability in the same ways that process fairness did, as reported in Chapters 2–4.

I then direct the why question to outcome favorability; that is, I consider what it is about outcome favorability that causes it to have a moderating influence on process fairness. Theory and research reported in Chapters 2 and 3 have suggested that the "fair process effect" (that is, the tendency for people to respond more positively when they are treated with higher process fairness) is stronger when their outcomes are relatively unfavorable. Accordingly, I consider other factors (besides unfavorable outcomes) that magnify the fair process effect.

WHAT IS IT ABOUT PROCESS FAIRNESS (I)? OR WHY HIGH PROCESS FAIRNESS REDUCES THE IMPACT OF OUTCOME FAVORABILITY

Chapters 2 and 3 provided evidence that people use process fairness information to make a host of related but conceptually distinct inferences, each of which may account for the tendency of high process fairness to reduce the effect of outcome favorability on people's willingness to support decisions, decision makers, and institutions relative to when process fairness is low (Cropanzano, Byrne, Bobocel, & Rupp, 2001). That is, people may use process fairness information to make inferences about (1) how much to hold the decision-making authority accountable or responsible for their outcomes, especially those that are unfavorable, (2) the extent to which they are favorably regarded by the decision-making authority or by the institution that the authority represents (i.e., their perceived standing); (3) how favorable their outcomes are likely to be, not only in the short term but also over the long term; and (4) the nature of their relationship with the decision-making authority (or the institution that the authority represents). For each of these four types of inferences, I first remind you briefly of the role it plays in accounting for the process–outcome interaction, in which high process fairness reduces the effect of outcome favorability. I then suggest how these inferences may be affected by dimensions other than process fairness. These other dimensions in turn are hypothesized (or have already been shown) to behave similarly to process fairness in interacting with outcome favorability. Thus, the ensuing analyses identify a number of factors that may interact with outcome favorability in the same way that process fairness does.

The subsequent analyses are based on five reasonably straightforward assumptions. First, people are likely to be more supportive of decisions, decision makers, and institutions to the extent that they receive more favorable outcomes (e.g., Blau, 1964). Second, the concerns people have that underlie the interactive relationship set forth in Chapters 2 and 3 may be organized by two dimensions: the time frame to which the concern refers (short term vs. long term) and the substance or nature of the concern itself, that is, the concern may be economic/tangible (e.g., compensation) or psychological/intangible (e.g., feeling valued or included) (see Table 6.1).

Third, whereas people care about both their short-term and their long-term outcomes, under some conditions they may assign importance to short-term outcomes virtually exclusively, whereas on other occasions they may assign importance to short- and long-term outcomes to varying degrees. One obvious determinant of the extent to

TABLE 6.1 Types of Concerns That Underlie the Interactive Relationship Between Process Fairness and Outcome Favorability Set Forth in Chapters 2 and 3

	Nature of Concern	
Time Frame of Concern	**Economic (Tangible)**	**Symbolic (Intangible)**
Short term		
Long term		

which people assign importance to short- and long-term outcomes is the extent to which they anticipate interacting with the other party in the future; the greater the anticipated future interaction, the less likely are people to assign importance to their short-term outcomes or the more likely they are to assign importance to their long-term outcomes (Tyler & Sears, 1977; Wiesenfeld et al., 2007).

Fourth, whereas people care about both tangible outcomes and intangible outcomes, under certain conditions they may assign importance to tangible *or* to intangible outcomes virtually exclusively, whereas in other instances they may assign importance to tangible and to intangible outcomes to varying degrees. One determinant of how much people assign importance to tangible and intangible outcomes is the perceived nature of their relationship with the other party; the more that they see themselves as having a communal/relational rather than an exchange/transactional relationship with the other party, the less likely they are to assign importance to tangible outcomes or the more likely they are to assign importance to intangible outcomes (Mills & Clark, 1982; Rousseau & McLean Parks, 1993). Fifth, and finally, the sense-making process that leads people to use process fairness information to make these sorts of inferences is more likely to be triggered when people perceive their outcomes to be unfavorable rather than favorable (e.g., Wong & Weiner, 1981).

Moreover, based on this reasoning (most notably, Assumptions 2–4), it is possible to generate different conditions (varying in the complexity of people's concerns), in which the interaction effect may result from people using process fairness information to make different types of inferences. The situation in which people's concerns are the least complex is the one in which they primarily care about tangible outcomes in the short term. The most complex situation is the one in which people care about some combination of tangible and intangible outcomes across some combination of the short and the long term. Situations of moderate complexity include the one in which people assign importance to some combination of tangible and intangible outcomes primarily in the short term and the one in which they assign virtually exclusive importance to one type of outcome across some combination of the short and long term.

In trying to broaden the reach of the interaction effect in which high process fairness reduces the effect of outcome favorability relative to when process fairness is low, I consider how people may use process fairness information to make various sorts of inferences, ranging from those in which their concerns are the most simple to those in which their concerns are the most complex. Let us begin with the simplest situation, in which people primarily assign importance to their short-term, tangible outcomes.

Judgments of the Authority's Responsibility

Folger (2001) suggested that the process–outcome interaction may arise even when there is no "shadow of the future" and even when people are likely to care only about their tangible outcomes. How might this happen? As suggested by attribution theory and research, it is not only the favorability of outcomes but also how much people judge the other party as responsible for their outcomes that affect the beliefs and behaviors that they direct toward the other party (Kelley, 1973). When an organizational authority makes a decision that yields unfavorable outcomes, people are much less likely to support the decision, the authority, and the organization as a whole to the extent that they perceive the authority as responsible. One factor that influences people's tendencies to see the authority as responsible for their outcomes, in turn, is process fairness. The lower the process fairness, the more likely are people to see the authority as responsible for their outcomes, particularly when their outcomes are unfavorable.

As set forth in fairness theory (Folger & Cropanzano, 1998, 2001), process fairness influences people's judgments of the authority's responsibility for their outcomes, especially unfavorable outcomes, via counterfactual thinking about what "could" have happened and what "should" have happened (see pp. 59–61 in Chapter 3 for further elaboration of these points). Particularly when their outcomes are unfavorable, the perception that the process was relatively unfair (i.e., less fair than it could or should have been) leads people to see the authority as more responsible, which in turn will lead them to react more negatively to decisions, decision makers, and institutions. Said differently, the perception that an authority acted with high process fairness will reduce the extent to which people see the authority as responsible for their unfavorable outcomes, which in turn will minimize the negative impact of the unfavorable outcomes on people's reactions to the authority's decisions.

This reasoning suggests that factors other than process fairness that influence how much people judge the authority as responsible for their unfavorable outcomes may have the same moderating effect on outcome favorability that process fairness has. In particular, information that shapes people's attributions of causality, namely, consensus, consistency, and distinctiveness (Kelley, 1973), may be germane. For example, if organizational authorities choose to downsize their workforce, they are likely to be seen as far less responsible for the decision (and its related outcomes) if other companies in the industry also are downsizing than if the company that they represent is the only one to be downsizing (consensus information). Furthermore, if a company that has long been committed to a no-layoff policy credibly claims that its first layoff in company history is due to external factors beyond its control, it is likely to be seen as less responsible for the layoffs than is a company that has historically made layoffs a regular part of its management practices (consistency information). Moreover, if authorities choose to downsize all of their business units they are likely to be seen as less responsible for the layoffs than if they were to make the decision to downsize certain units and to grow others (distinctiveness information).

These or other factors that affect how much people judge authorities to be responsible for decisions and their associated outcomes should behave similarly to process fairness in their moderating influence on outcome favorability. When, for whatever reason, people judge authorities as less responsible for decisions, the less likely is the favorability of the outcomes associated with the decisions to influence people's reactions to the authorities. For example, layoff survivors who may be feeling the sting of unfavorable outcomes brought on by layoffs (e.g., the loss of former colleagues and friends) may react less negatively to the organizational authorities who made the decision to downsize if many other companies in the industry also are downsizing relative to if theirs was the only company to do so.

Moreover, just as people maintain locus-of-control beliefs pertaining to the perceived contingencies between their *own* behaviors and the ensuing outcomes (e.g., Rotter, 1966), they are likely to have beliefs about whether *other people's behaviors* directly affect their outcomes. Those with strong beliefs in fate ("que sera, sera") may believe that outcomes are due to forces beyond people's control. If an organizational authority were to make a decision that yielded unfavorable outcomes, those with stronger beliefs in fate may be less likely to hold the authority responsible for their unfavorable outcomes and, as a result, may be less likely to show a reduced willingness to support the authority and the authority's decisions. Research showed that there are cross-national differences in how much people believe that outcomes are due to fate (Leung et al., 2002). Therefore, those from cultures with strong beliefs in fate may be relatively unlikely to hold an organizational authority responsible and, correspondingly, be less likely to show a decline in their willingness to support the authority if they were to receive an unfavorable outcome that was associated with the authority's decisions.

For that matter, there also may be cultural differences in the extent to which organizational authorities are expected to behave with process fairness; what may be "common courtesy" in one culture may not be in another. As a result, differences in cross-cultural beliefs may influence not only the extent to which people judge a decision-making authority to be responsible for their unfavorable outcomes but also people's judgments of the authority's process fairness and therefore their perceptions of how much they see the authority as responsible for their outcomes. Said differently, in the face of unfavorable outcomes, culture may have a direct effect on how much people hold the decision maker responsible as well as an indirect effect operating through perceptions of process fairness.

Theory and research have suggested that the inverse relationship between process fairness and how much people hold the authority responsible for their outcomes is stronger in the case of unfavorable than favorable outcomes. As mentioned in Chapter Three (see pages 61-62), this may come about for two reasons. First, people are more motivated to understand the reasons for unfavorable than for favorable outcomes (Pyszczynki & Greenberg, 1981; Wong & Weiner, 1981). When people are asking why (they received an outcome) in the first place, process fairness information, which may help them answer the why question, is more likely to be drawn upon and hence be influential.

Second, unlike in the case of unfavorable outcomes, people may not be so quick to attribute their favorable outcomes to the other party. Instead, they may prefer to see *themselves* as responsible. In other words, a self-serving bias may influence the extent to which people use process fairness information to make attributions of responsibility for their outcomes. Attribution research has shown that people prefer to make external attributions for their unfavorable outcomes to minimize a loss of self-esteem and to make internal attributions for favorable outcomes to maximize a gain of self-esteem (e.g., Zuckerman, 1979). Therefore, when outcomes are unfavorable, low process fairness provides people with the handy external attribution for which they may have been looking. When outcomes are favorable, however, they are less likely to be looking for an external attribution, which may explain why there is less likely to be an inverse relationship between process fairness and how much people see the authority as responsible for their favorable outcomes.

Evidence suggests, however, that in the face of unfavorable outcomes the inverse relationship between process fairness and how much people see the authority as responsible for their outcomes is not part of a more general tendency to make self-protective external attributions for unfavorable outcomes (Brockner et al., 2007). Participants in these studies were asked to indicate the extent to which they attributed their outcomes to a variety of external and internal factors as a function of process fairness and outcome favorability. The more favorable the outcomes, the more likely they were to see themselves (i.e., their ability and effort) as responsible. Moreover, the results of all three studies supported fairness theory (Folger & Cropanzano, 1998, 2001) by showing that process fairness was inversely related to how much participants judged the decision-making authorities to be responsible for their unfavorable outcomes.

In none of the Brockner et al. (2007) studies, however, was process fairness related to *other* possible external attributions for their unfavorable outcomes, such as bad luck, the economy, the "natural course of events" following the organizational change that they had just experienced, or external factors "in general." At first blush, the facts that (1) people saw themselves as more responsible for their favorable outcomes than for their unfavorable outcomes and (2) people saw the authority as more responsible for their outcomes when the other's process fairness was low suggest that their attributions of responsibility for their outcomes were driven by self-serving concerns (i.e., to take credit when things go well and to deflect blame when they do not). However, the findings on the measures of external attributions (other than to the authority) suggest that their attributions of responsibility were not entirely attributable to self-serving motivations. That is, if people who had been treated with lower process fairness were looking to protect their self-esteem in the face of unfavorable outcomes, they could have latched on to any external attribution. This did not happen, however. Process fairness was inversely related to how much people saw the authority as responsible for their unfavorable outcomes, but it was unrelated to other external reasons for their unfavorable outcomes.

The fact that people were willing to hold a procedurally unfair authority as responsible for their unfavorable outcomes but that they did not make other types of external attributions for those same outcomes is worthy of further consideration. Taken together, these findings suggest that people's attributions for their outcomes not only may be in the service of protecting or enhancing their self-esteem but also may be undertaken to heighten people's sense of control. After all, many unfavorable outcomes refer to events over which people would like to gain a sense of control to make those events less likely to recur. Whereas certain external attributions for unfavorable outcomes may protect people from self-blame, they are not particularly controllable (Weiner, 1979). This seems to apply to the other external attribution dimensions provided to participants in the Brockner et al. (2007) studies: (1) luck, (2) the economy, (3) the "natural course of events," and (4) external factors "in general."

In contrast, holding the procedurally unfair authority as responsible for their unfavorable outcomes may allow people to feel relatively more in control. For example, they may try to influence the authority to use alternative (i.e., fairer) procedures the next time around. Or, if they see their unfavorable outcomes as resulting from the authority's low process fairness, they may try to regain control by extricating themselves from the relationship. In contrast, there may be "no escape" if the unfavorable outcome is seen as due to luck, to the economy, or to the natural course of events. Further research designed to understand the *set* of attributional findings observed by Brockner et al. (2007) may shed much-needed light on the basis of people's causal attributions for their outcomes, especially their unfavorable outcomes.

Judgments of Standing

The receipt of unfavorable outcomes does more than induce people to determine the extent to which to hold the decision maker responsible. Another immediate question or concern that people are likely to have in response to receiving an unfavorable outcome pertains to their standing, that is, the extent to which they are held in high regard by the decision-making authority (Van den Bos & Lind, in press). Again, information about the other's process fairness may be used to address this concern (Tyler & Lind, 1992). Being treated with high process fairness symbolically communicates to people that they have greater standing in the eyes of the other, more so than does being treated with low process fairness. Consider, for example, the process fairness element of providing an explanation for one's actions (Bies, 1987). When an authority offers an explanation of why certain decisions were made, the symbolic message being sent is that the recipients were thought highly enough of to warrant receiving an explanation.

Alternatively, when an authority fails to explain why certain decisions were made, the authority may be seen as saying that the recipients of the decision are not worthy of being treated in a dignified and respectful manner. As a result, recipients are likely to feel excluded and devalued, thereby suffering a blow to their self-esteem or to their identity. The prospect that the recipients' self-esteem could be threatened is reasonably straightforward. Moreover, a blow to their identity could come about, for example, if they previously strongly identified themselves with a collective in which the authority subsequently behaved badly, that is, with a lack of process fairness (e.g., Tyler & Degoey, 1995). Dissociating themselves from the authority and the institution he or she represents could come at the expense of people's sense of collective identity.

This reasoning may help to explain why process fairness is positively related to people's willingness to support an authority and the authority's decisions, more so when outcomes are unfavorable (in which people's concerns about their standing may be more likely to be aroused) than when outcomes are favorable. People use process fairness information to make inferences about how much they are valued by the decision-making authority; the greater the process fairness, the more likely are people to believe that they are held in high regard or in good standing (Tyler & Lind, 1992). Judging themselves as being in good standing when process fairness is high, people are likely to respond by supporting the authority and the authority's decisions relative to when process fairness is low (again, especially in the face of unfavorable outcomes, which are more likely to engender concerns about standing).

This reasoning suggests that other factors besides process fairness that influence people's judgments of their standing in the eyes of decision-making authorities should similarly moderate the influence of outcome favorability on people's willingness to support organizational authorities, their decisions, and the institutions that they represent. When for whatever reason people's judgments of their standing are more positive, outcome favorability is less likely to have an impact on their support for organizational authorities. People's judgments of their standing in the eyes of decision-making authorities, moreover, may be driven by both dispositional and situational factors. At the dispositional level, the trait of self-esteem may be relevant. Related to the long-held view that people's self-esteem is influenced by their perceptions of how favorably they are regarded by significant others (Cooley, 1902; Mead, 1934), Leary's (1999) more recent sociometer theory suggests that people's self-esteem functions mainly as an indicator of their beliefs about how they are viewed by others, that is, whether others value them or reject them. People with high self-esteem believe that others hold them in higher regard relative to their counterparts with low self-esteem. Therefore, the willingness of people with high self-esteem to support organizational authorities may be less affected by outcomes or cues that have self-evaluative implications. Just as high process fairness may buffer against the negative impact of unfavorable outcomes on people's support for organizational authorities and their decisions, so may high trait self-esteem (Brockner, 1988).

For example, Mossholder, Bedeian, and Armenakis (1982) found that the relationship between how much people felt supported by their peer group and their desire to remain with the organization was moderated by their self-esteem. Employees with high self-esteem were relatively unaffected by the supportiveness of their peer group. Their desire to remain with the organization and their job performance were just as high when the peer group was seen as unsupportive as when it was seen as supportive. In contrast, the desire to remain with the organization and the job performance of employees with low self-esteem were much more dependent on peer group supportiveness, such that they reacted more negatively when the peer group was seen as relatively unsupportive.

If anything, the Mossholder et al. (1982) findings may underestimate the moderating effect of employees' self-esteem on the relationship between outcome favorability (peer group supportiveness) and their willingness to support an organizational authority and the authority's decisions. After all, outcome favorability in the Mossholder et al. study was based on the supportiveness of the *peer group* rather than being in reference to an action taken by an organizational authority. The referent for the dependent variable of desire to remain with the organization was the *organization*. Theory and research have established that employees' attitudes and behaviors are more strongly related when they are in reference to the same target rather than to different targets (e.g., Lavelle et al., 2008; Rupp & Cropanzano, 2002). Thus, if outcome favorability was perceived to be associated with the actions of an organizational authority (e.g., whether one's manager doled out a favorable pay raise decision), then the moderating influence of employees' self-esteem may be particularly pronounced on dependent variables in which the authority is the referent, such as people's willingness to engage in citizenship behavior directed toward the authority.

Situational factors also may influence the extent to which people believe that they are held in high regard by organizational authorities. Whereas many firms publicly espouse that "people are our most important asset," the policies, practices, and cultures of some organizations do a much better job of credibly communicating this message than do those of others. Pfeffer (1995) vividly described the organizational practices that lead to sustainable competitive advantage through the effective management of people. Whereas it is beyond the scope of the current analysis to discuss all of the 13 practices that Pfeffer uncovered, suffice it to say that some seem likely to influence employees' *desire or motivation* to perform well on behalf of their organizations, such as (1) rewarding employees with high wages, (2) having an incentive pay plan, and (3) enacting a policy of promotion from within. Other policies are likely to affect employees' *ability* to perform, such as (1) sharing information (e.g., Pfeffer described a high-technology firm in which "there are computer terminals throughout the plant that every employee has been trained to use in order to obtain information about product yields, development progress, production rates, or any other aspect of the operation," p. 60) and (2) showing commitment to employees' skill development, such as by training them for new tasks that need to be accomplished or by offering them incentives to acquire new skills.

Whereas the substance of these various practices may differentially influence employees' motivation or ability to perform, all are likely to convey a powerful symbolic message: Employees are held in high regard. For example, high wages "send a message that the organization values its employees" (Pfeffer, 1995, p. 59). The presence of an incentive pay plan makes it more likely that employees experience distributive justice, in which top performers are affirmed by the fact that they are rewarded more handsomely than their counterparts who did not contribute as much. Promotion from within (as opposed to going outside to find people for more coveted positions) also reflects a strong statement about distributive justice and, relatedly, the extent to which the firm values its people. Sharing information implies that employees are thought of highly enough (i.e., as trustworthy and as competent) to use the information toward the accomplishment of the firm's goals. Furthermore, the symbolic messages in showing commitment to employees' skill development include (1) the firm believes that employees are capable of acquiring the new skills needed to perform different activities and (2) the firm cares about employees' career development. In a day and age in which most firms cannot offer job security, they can contribute to their workers "employability" (internal or external to the organization) by offering them opportunities to enhance their skill sets.

Pfeffer's (1995) analysis was at a more macrolevel; he was primarily interested in showing that firms that enact more of the 13 management practices that he identified were more likely to outperform their competitors. However, the practices of which he spoke also may be influential at a more microlevel of analysis, in shaping people's reactions to the outcomes associated with myriad decisions (e.g., receiving a favorable performance appraisal or not, being benefited or harmed by a new human resource policy, or taking on an expatriate assignment in which family members are adjusting well or poorly). Just as high process fairness has been shown to reduce the effect of outcome favorability on employees' willingness to support an organizational authority and the authority's decisions (in particular, high process fairness buffers against the adverse effects of unfavorable outcomes), many if not most of the practices identified by Pfeffer may interact with outcome favorability in a similar fashion. Assuming that the practices identified by Pfeffer influence employees' judgments of their standing as organization members, I would expect the presence of these practices to reduce the effect of the outcome favorability associated with a particular decision on employees' willingness to support the decision, the authority who made it, and the institution as a whole relative to when the practices identified by Pfeffer were less present.

Beliefs About Longer-Term Outcomes

An important assumption guiding the early work on procedural justice (e.g., Thibaut & Walker, 1975) is that people care about tangible outcomes. In organizational settings, for example, employees covet pay, career opportunities, interesting and engaging work, stimulating and constructive colleagues, and aesthetically pleasing work environments, to name a few. Moreover, in ongoing relationships people care about these tangible outcomes in both the short term and in the long term. Whereas a view of human nature as "people as outcome maximizers" suggests that we want short- and long-term outcomes to be favorable, we also are realistic enough to know that it is unreasonable to expect all outcomes (both short and long term) to be favorable. Hence, people may be willing to accept (and hence not be especially adversely affected by) unfavorable outcomes in the short term, provided that they believe that their outcomes will be at least reasonably favorable over the longer haul. Witness, for example, the importance that people often assign to the long-term outcomes associated with choosing a particular job, that is, whether the position is likely to be "dead end" at one extreme or "fast track" at the other.

Process fairness information is important in that people may use it to make inferences about the favorability of their tangible, long-term outcomes. In general, the greater the process fairness, the more likely are people to be reassured about the favorability of their long-term outcomes. For example, if people are allowed to have voice they may believe that they can influence the decision process to yield outcomes that will be more favorable to them relative to what they may expect to receive in the absence of voice. Moreover, if decisions are made consistently, without bias, and on the basis of accurate information, people may be more likely to believe that they will receive their "fair share" of outcomes over time relative to if the decision process was not perceived to be fair in these ways. Of course, there may be exceptions. Thus, if people believe that they are benefiting *precisely because* of the unfairness of the decision process (e.g., an "unlevel playing field" that happens to favor them), then they may feel reassured about the favorability of their longer-term outcomes when process fairness is low rather than high. Usually, however, high process fairness is more likely than is low process fairness to reassure people about the favorability of their longer-term outcomes. Furthermore, the more optimistic people are about their long-term outcomes, the less likely they may be to assign importance to the favorability of their current outcomes, which may explain why high process fairness may reduce the influence of outcome favorability on people's support for decisions, decision makers, and institutions relative to when process fairness is low.

This reasoning suggests that factors other than process fairness that influence how much people feel reassured about the favorability of their long-term outcomes should have a similar moderating influence on the favorability of their short-term outcomes. Studies have shown that people generally are optimistic about their future outcomes, often more than they have a right to be (e.g., Weinstein, 1980). As an example of what has come to be known as the "Lake Wobegon effect," if the members of a group are asked whether they believe they are in the top 30% of the group in their ability to drive cars, approximately 80% of them say yes (Svenson, 1981). Similarly, if a classroom full of students is asked to indicate whether they believe they will earn a course grade that will put them in the top 50% of the class, approximately 80% of them indicate that they will. The notion that people are generally optimistic about their future outcomes may help to explain why they sometimes are relatively unaffected by the favorability of their current outcomes; in particular, they may be willing to go along with current decisions that yield unfavorable outcomes.

Whereas people generally may be optimistic about their future outcomes, their beliefs about the favorability of their future outcomes also vary as a function of numerous individual or situational factors. Individual-level factors include the related but distinct dimensions of self-efficacy (Bandura, 1994), locus of control (Rotter, 1966), and dispositional optimism (Scheier & Carver, 1985; Seligman, 2006). How to differentiate among these three factors? Think of things in the following way: People perform behaviors, which lead to certain outcomes, which may be more or less favorable. *Self-efficacy* pertains to people's beliefs about their ability to enact the behaviors. *Locus of control* refers to their beliefs about *the relationship between* their behaviors and their outcomes. People with an internal locus-of-control orientation believe that their outcomes are contingent on their behavior, whereas those with an external locus of control believe that their outcomes are determined by factors outside their control, such as fate, luck, or powerful others. People with greater self-efficacy or with more of an internal locus of control are likely to be more optimistic about the favorability of their longer-term outcomes than are their counterparts who have less self-efficacy or who have more of an external locus of control.

Whereas self-efficacy and locus of control are likely antecedents of people's beliefs about their outcomes, *dispositional optimism* directly refers to those outcome beliefs. Moreover, given that dispositional optimism is a generalized expectancy, it reflects people's beliefs about their longer-term outcomes, in contrast to *situational optimism*, which typically pertains to people's beliefs about their immediate or short-term outcomes in a given situation. By definition, people who are more dispositionally optimistic have more positive beliefs about the favorability of their longer-term outcomes. Relatedly, it even may be that dispositional optimism mediates the hypothesized relationships between each of self-efficacy and internal locus of control and how much people feel reassured about the favorability of their longer-term outcomes.

A host of situational factors also may influence people's optimism about their longer-term outcomes. For example, employees who receive unfavorable outcomes in the short term but who are encouraged by their managers to attribute their unfavorable outcomes to temporary or situation-specific factors are likely to be more reassured about the favorability of their longer-term outcomes relative to their colleagues whose managers elicit in them a more pessimistic attributional style (Seligman, 2006). Social information-processing theory suggests that people often take cues from their coworkers about how to think, feel, and behave (Salancik & Pfeffer, 1978). Thus, being surrounded by coworkers with positive beliefs about their future outcomes may "rub off" on employees. Furthermore, the location of the group, subunit, or organization in its respective life cycle may influence members' beliefs about their future outcomes. Collectives often go through cyclical periods of growth and decline (Quinn & Cameron, 1983). When a collective is in a growth stage, its members are much more positive about their longer-term outcomes relative to when the collective is in a period of decline.

In summary, the various individual and situational factors that affect people's beliefs about the favorability of their longer-term outcomes may be expected to interact with the favorability of their current or short-term outcome to influence people's willingness to support decisions, decision makers, and institutions. Just as high process fairness may induce people to be more optimistic about their longer-term outcomes and thereby reduce the impact of the favorability of their current outcomes on their willingness to support decisions and decision makers, so may various individual and situational factors affect people's tendencies to be optimistic about their longer-term outcomes. Among people who are dispositionally optimistic, say, the effect of the favorability of their current outcomes on their willingness to support organizational authorities may be less pronounced relative to those who are less dispositionally optimistic.

A related empirical question for future research is whether the moderating effect of beliefs about the favorability of long-term outcomes on reactions to current outcome favorability is contingent, in turn, on people's tendencies to delay gratification. Implicit in the notion that people may be willing to engage in trade-offs between their current and future outcomes is that they are capable of delaying gratification (Mischel, 1966). Put differently, being low in the tendency to delay gratification may represent a boundary condition for the prediction that more positive beliefs about longer-term outcomes will reduce the influence of the favorability of more immediate, short-term outcomes. Those low in delay of gratification may not exhibit the expected tendency to absorb the short-term "hit" of unfavorable current outcomes when their longer-term outcomes are perceived to be favorable. Whereas their longer-term outcome expectancies may be bright, their difficulty intuiting or waiting for the future may have the effect of making the favorable expected outcomes "fall on deaf ears."

The Nature of the Relationship: The Critical Role of Trust

The most complex set of concerns consists of people caring about some combination of tangible and intangible outcomes over some combination of the short and long term. When people receive unfavorable outcomes in organizational settings, in which the shadow of the future looms large, it behooves them to determine the nature of their relationship with organizational authorities and the institutions that the authorities represent. Psychological contract theorists have distinguished between "relational" and "transactional" relationships between employees and employers (Rousseau, 1995). Relational contracts are characterized by a high degree of mutual trust between employees and organizational authorities, much more so than in the case of transactional contracts.

One of the major determinants of employees' trust in organizational authorities is the process fairness used by authorities to plan and implement decisions (e.g., Konovsky & Pugh, 1994). The trustworthiness of authorities, in turn, has been shown to interact with outcome favorability to influence people's willingness to support authorities and their decisions, such that trust and support are more positively related to one another when outcomes are unfavorable. Indeed, it is not process fairness per se but rather the trust in authorities elicited by process fairness that interacts with outcome favorability to influence support for authorities (Brockner et al., 1997). As suggested in Chapter 3, the interactive effect of trust and outcome favorability may be explained by several related mechanisms. First, people's trust judgments reflect expectations of how the authority is likely to behave over time on both process and outcome dimensions. Just as process fairness is positively related to trust, trust is positively related to expectations about the authority's future process fairness (Lind & Tyler, 1988). Moreover, trust in the authority is likely to be positively related to people's expectations about the favorability of their outcomes associated with their future dealings with the authority. And, as mentioned, the more favorable people's beliefs are about their future outcomes, the less likely they are to be affected by the favorability of their current outcomes.

Second, how much people trust the other party may reflect the importance that they assign to various outcomes that they receive in their dealings with the other party. People care about economic or tangible types of outcomes (e.g., how much an organizational authority's decisions make them financially better or worse off), and they care about psychological or intangible outcomes, such as how much they derive a sense of esteem, identity, or inclusion as a result of the processes and outcomes associated with the authority's decisions (Lind & Tyler, 1988). Thus, when employees perceive that they have a relational psychological contract with organizational authorities, they may experience relatively favorable psychological outcomes. For example, interacting with an authority deemed to be trustworthy is likely to foster greater feelings of inclusion than is interacting with an authority perceived to be untrustworthy. Feeling more rewarded along psychological dimensions, people may be less inclined to assign importance to economic outcomes. Moreover, if economic outcomes are less important, then it may help to explain why high trust in the other party reduced the impact of outcome favorability on employees' support for decisions, decision makers, and institutions (Brockner et al., 1997); the outcomes in those studies were economic in nature.

As with the explanation of the interaction effect emanating from people's judgments of their standing (see pp. 205–209 in this chapter), the interactive relationship between process fairness and outcome favorability is predicated on the notion that people care about their psychological well-being. However, note that process fairness information plays a conceptually distinct role in the two explanations. In the prior explanation pertaining to standing, I suggested that particularly in the face of unfavorable outcomes, people use process fairness information to make inferences about the extent to which *they are held in high regard by organizational authorities*. The greater the process fairness, the more likely are people to infer high standing, and therefore the more likely they are to respond with greater support for organizational authorities and their decisions. In the present explanation pertaining to trust, I suggest that people's trust in authorities (elicited by process fairness information or other factors) may influence the extent to which *they assign importance to different types of outcomes*; the greater the trust (i.e., the more employees see themselves as having a relational rather than transactional psychological contract with their employers), the more importance they may assign to their psychological well-being or the less importance they may assign to their economic well-being. If people assign less importance to economic or tangible outcomes when process fairness is relatively high, then it stands to reason that outcome favorability will have a reduced influence on people's support for decisions, decision makers, and organizations when process fairness is relatively high, especially when the outcome has an economic or tangible basis to it.

If it is the trust elicited by process fairness information that interacts with outcome favorability to influence employees' support for decisions, decision makers, and organizations, then factors other than process fairness that influence or reflect people's trust in the other may be expected to behave similarly to process fairness in interacting with outcome favorability. When trust (however arrived at) in the other party is relatively high, the favorability of current outcomes may be less likely to influence employees' support for decisions, decision makers, and institutions relative to when trust in the other party is relatively low.

Numerous factors may influence people's tendencies to perceive an authority as trustworthy, such as the authority's reputation, which may in turn be shaped by the authority's previous behavior or by what others have to say about the authority (Salancik & Pfeffer, 1978). Thus, when the process fairness with which authorities have planned or implemented a given decision is either ambiguous or unknown, those who have already established a reputation for being true to their word are likely to be trusted. Similarly, particularly in the face of ambiguity about an authority's trustworthiness, people may draw on the beliefs of similar others (e.g., their coworkers) or of respected others (e.g., star performers) to infer how much to trust the authority. The more that similar others or respected others judge the authority to be trustworthy, the more likely are people to do likewise.

Furthermore, the tendency to trust an authority may be affected by characteristics of the perceiver. People have varying views or philosophies about human nature. Wrightsman (1992) has shown that one of the dimensions along which people's philosophies of human nature differ is the tendency to trust. Some of us are more likely to view people in general as trustworthy. Relatedly, people differ in their attitudes toward authorities, with one relevant dimension the extent to which authorities may be trusted. Much of the research on attitudes toward authorities has been conducted among adolescents and young adults (e.g., Heaven, 1988). (Speaking to his fellow youth in the 1960s, Bob Dylan famously proclaimed, "Never trust anyone over 30.") Nevertheless, even older adults are likely to have varying attitudes toward authorities, which are likely to shape their tendencies to perceive authorities as trustworthy.

A series of studies by De Cremer and Tyler (2007) drew on the notion that people's tendencies to trust authorities may be determined by multiple factors other than the authority's process fairness. In several laboratory studies De Cremer and Tyler experimentally manipulated participants' trust in the decision-making authority. In one study, trust was varied on the basis of manipulating the psychological set that participants were instructed to adopt, such that some were asked to imagine that they were generally trusting, whereas others were asked to imagine that they were generally not trusting. In a second study, trust in the authority was varied based on information about the authority's previous behavior. For example, participants received a note that was allegedly written by another person who had previously interacted with the authority, which indicated that the authority was either trustworthy or untrustworthy.

Just as process fairness has been shown to influence trust in authorities (Konovsky & Pugh, 1994), which in turn interacts with outcome favorability to influence people's willingness to support the authority and the authority's decisions (Brockner et al., 1997), other antecedents of trust may be expected to have a similar moderating influence on outcome favorability. Factors that bring about high trust in the authority (such as social cues from coworkers suggesting that the authority is trustworthy or people's general propensities to see authorities as trustworthy) should reduce the influence of outcome favorability on people's support for the authority and the authority's decisions, relative to when people see the authority as relatively untrustworthy.

Relatedly, the extent to which people see process fairness information as indicative of the authority's trustworthiness is not hard and fast; it also may depend on other factors. For example, the positive relationship between an authority's process fairness and judgments of the authority's trustworthiness may be moderated by the perceived authenticity of the authority's process fairness. In other words, people may be affected not only by the level of process fairness that they see in an authority but also by their perceptions of the authority's underlying motivation. High process fairness that is judged to be authentic or intrinsically motivated is more likely to lead to the inference that the authority may be trusted than is the same high process fairness behavior that is perceived to be extrinsically motivated. As suggested in Chapter 3, when decision makers change their unfair ways because of some external impetus (e.g., a court order), they are less likely to receive credit (e.g., in the form of being judged as more trustworthy) than if those same behavioral changes were perceived to have come from within.

Thus, moderators of the positive relationship between an authority's process fairness and judgments of the authority's trustworthiness also may moderate the interactive relationship between process fairness and outcome favorability (Lin et al., 2009). The tendency for high process fairness to reduce the influence of outcome favorability on people's support for an authority and the authority's decisions should be more likely to occur under the same conditions in which process fairness is more positively related to judgments of the authority's trustworthiness (e.g., when the authority's process fairness is seen as more authentic or intrinsically motivated).

In attempting to expand the scope of the interactive relationship between process fairness and outcome favorability, I have identified many other factors that may affect people in the same way that process fairness does. Further research is needed to evaluate whether these other factors have the same moderating influence on outcome favorability that process fairness already has been shown to have. Future research also needs to delineate the conditions under which (or the people for whom) the interaction effect is undergirded by people's use of process fairness information for one sense-making purpose rather than another. For example, consider the psychological process in which people use process fairness information to make inferences about the favorability of their longer-term outcomes. When process fairness is high, people may be more optimistic about their longer-term outcomes, which in turn may lead them to be less concerned with (and therefore less influenced by) the favorability of their current outcomes. Note that this reasoning process may require a nontrivial amount of deliberative thinking, in which people may ask themselves something like, "What does this unfavorable outcome say about what I can expect to receive over the longer term?" People may then draw on process fairness information to help answer this question and then engage in further deliberative thinking (e.g., "Well, if the process is fair, then I am pretty optimistic about my longer-term outcomes, which means that I can 'lighten up' about my current unfavorable outcome").

On the other hand, consider the nature of the psychological process in which people use information about another party's process fairness to make judgments of how much to hold the other party responsible for their outcomes. According to Folger and Cropanzano (1998), when people receive an unfavorable outcome they are more likely to hold the other party responsible (and, as a result, react more negatively to the other) when the other exhibits relatively low process fairness. Folger and Cropanzano suggested that the inverse relationship between process fairness and judgments of the other's responsibility results from counterfactual thinking, in which an unfair process may be judged as different from what the other could have done or should have done. On the one hand, the depiction of the counterfactual processes in Folger and Cropanzano's analysis seems to suggest that people may be engaging in deliberative or systematic thinking in which, particularly in response to the receipt of unfavorable outcomes, they ask themselves questions such as, "*Could* the other party have done things in a different way?" and "*Should* the other party have done things in a different way?" On the other hand, the tendency for people to see the other as more responsible when the other uses an unfair process may reflect an automatic or heuristic thought process, especially when we consider the possibility that the unfavorable outcome may be priming people to look for parties other than themselves on which to assign blame.

This reasoning suggests that factors affecting people's tendencies to engage in heuristic versus systematic thinking (Chaiken, 1980) may be one thing that helps to explain when one mechanism rather than another better accounts for the process–outcome interaction. For example, people differ in their need for cognition, which refers to the extent to which they "engage in and enjoy effortful cognitive endeavors" that are typical of systematic thinking (Cacioppo, Petty, & Kao, 1984, p. 306). Hence, those higher in need for cognition would be less likely to agree with statements such as, "I would rather do something that requires little thought than something that is sure to challenge my thinking abilities." To the extent that the various explanations of the process–outcome interaction differ in the extent to which they reflect systematic versus heuristic thinking, they may be more or less applicable to people as a function of their need for cognition, in that those higher in need for cognition are more likely to engage in systematic than in heuristic thinking. In other words, it is entirely possible to arrive at the same interactive relationship between process fairness and outcome favorability through psychological mechanisms that differ not only in their substance or content (e.g., whether the key construct is judgments of the authority's responsibility, judgments of one's standing in the eyes of the authority, and the like) but also on the basis of the underlying process (i.e., whether the interaction effect is the result of systematic vs. heuristic thinking).

Other Determinants of Process Fairness: The Role of Regulatory Fit

Another way to expand the scope of the process–outcome interaction is by evaluating whether dimensions outside the justice literature may shape people's perceptions of process fairness. *Process fairness* has hitherto referred to people's perceptions of the legitimacy or moral correctness with which another party (e.g., an organizational authority) has gone about planning or implementing decisions. Thus, the other party is likely to be seen as exhibiting high process fairness (or as doing things in a "morally correct" way) when the authority (1) allows people to have input into the decision; (2) explains the reasons for decisions; (3) utilizes the Leventhal et al. (1980) principles such as consistency, accuracy, correctability, bias suppression; and (4) treats people with dignity and respect, to name a few.

Findings in the regulatory focus literature suggest that people's judgments of the fairness (or, at least, the moral correctness) of a process also may depend on regulatory fit, that is, the extent to which people's tendencies toward promotion or prevention match the degree of promotion or prevention that is salient in their environments. Higgins (2000) showed that people are more drawn to, find more satisfying, and are more motivated to perform in situations in which they experience regulatory fit. For example, promotion-focused people find situations that emphasize gains versus nongains to be more appealing, whereas prevention-focused people prefer or are more drawn to environments in which the salient concern is loss avoidance.

Of course, the notion that people are more drawn to, satisfied with, and motivated by situations that are congruent with their personal values is hardly new. Theory and research on person-job or person-organization fit have shown that employees tend to fare better when their skills match those needed to succeed in their jobs and organizations and when their values are congruent with those of their organizations (e.g., Chatman, 1989). What *is* new is the prospect that the phenomenology of regulatory fit may be similar to how people feel when they are treated with high process fairness. In both instances, people may experience "moral correctness."

The last speculation comes from a series of studies by Camacho, Higgins, and Luger (2003), who examined people's perceptions of the moral correctness of various events as a function of the fit between their own regulatory focus orientation and the one made salient in their environments. In the language of signal detection theory, people who are more promotion focused are more concerned with ensuring correct hits and with avoiding errors of omission, whereas those who are prevention focused are more concerned with ensuring correct rejections and with avoiding errors of commission (Crowe & Higgins, 1997). It therefore follows that promotion-focused people will be more bothered by making errors of omission than will prevention-focused people, whereas prevention-focused people will be more bothered by making errors of commission than will promotion-focused people. Camacho et al. found support for these hypotheses in two studies. Importantly, the measure of "bother" consisted of felt guilt, which reflects people's sense of having violated a moral code. In other words, promotion-focused people seemed to have felt that they had done something morally incorrect when they committed an error of omission, whereas prevention-focused people appeared to have felt that they had done something morally incorrect when they committed an error of commission.

In a third study, Camacho et al. (2003) examined how much another person's conflict resolution style "felt right" as a function of the degree of fit between the conflict resolution style itself (i.e., whether it emphasized promotion or prevention) and people's regulatory focus orientation. Those in the promotion resolution style condition were asked to "think back to a time when you had a conflict with your parent or guardian and s/he resolved the conflict by encouraging desired behaviors," whereas those in the prevention resolution style condition were asked to "think back to a time when you had a conflict with your parent or guardian and s/he resolved the conflict by safeguarding against undesired behaviors." In both conditions, participants were asked to write about how the conflict was resolved. Those who were more promotion focused judged the promotion conflict resolution style as more "right," whereas those who were more prevention focused judged the prevention conflict resolution style as more right.

Of course, regulatory fit may feel right for any of a number of reasons. A fourth study conducted by Camacho et al. (2003) suggested that the feelings of rightness elicited by regulatory fit have moral underpinnings, perhaps similar to how people may feel when they have been treated with high process fairness. In this study, participants rated how much a proposed change in policy was "right from a moral point of view" as a function of regulatory fit, that is, the relationship between whether the change emphasized promotion or prevention and people's own regulatory focus orientation. All participants read a short essay arguing for a policy change in which a new city tax would be applied toward the development and implementation of a special after-school program for public grade- and high-school students. Participants were told different things about the benefits of the afterschool program. In the promotion condition, they were told that the program will advance children's education and support more children in general, whereas in the prevention condition participants were told that the program "will secure children's education and prevent more children from failing." Again, judgments of moral correctness were significantly influenced by regulatory fit, such that participants rated the program as more "right from a moral point of view" when its benefits were framed in a way that was congruent rather than incongruent with their own regulatory focus orientation.

Taken together, the Camacho et al. (2003) findings suggest that how people come to experience a process as fair (or at least morally correct) may depend on factors other than the aforementioned antecedents of process fairness. That is, process fairness may not simply refer to how another party went about planning and implementing decisions along the dimensions of voice, consistency, accuracy, interactional justice, and so on. Rather, the notion of "process" also may refer to how individuals go about the task of self-regulation, even if no other people happen to be present or happen to be directing any behavior toward the target individuals. The extent to which this particular type of process is seen as right from a moral point of view depends on the degree of fit between the environmental emphasis on promotion versus prevention and the target individuals' own regulatory focus orientation.

Brockner and Higgins (2001) described many factors that may affect the extent to which employees perceive their work environments as emphasizing promotion versus prevention. Depending on how much these factors fit their own regulatory focus orientation, employees may perceive their work environments and the process of navigating through them as more or less "correct from a moral point of view," which may be psychologically similar to what they experience as a function of the process fairness with which they are treated by organizational authorities. For example, certain managers may dole out feedback in ways that emphasize promotion, whereas others may do so in ways that highlight prevention. Promotion-eliciting feedback focuses on gains, in which direct reports receive praise (gains) when they do well and do not receive praise (nongains) when they do poorly. Prevention-focused feedback centers on losses, in which employees receive criticism (losses) when they do poorly and avoid criticism (nonlosses) when they do well.

Organizational cultures may differ more generally in the extent to which they emphasize promotion versus prevention. The culture of an entrepreneurial start-up (which may be concerned with realizing the dreams of its founders) is more likely to emphasize promotion, whereas that of an established electrical utility (which makes money by minimizing power outages) is more likely to value prevention. Employees who are dispositionally inclined toward promotion are likely to experience regulatory fit when feedback is based on the presence or absence of praise (or if they work in the entrepreneurial start-up), whereas those who are dispositionally prevention focused are likely to experience regulatory fit when feedback consists of the presence or absence of criticism (or if they are employed by the electrical utility).

If regulatory fit is psychologically similar to being treated with high process fairness, then regulatory fit may interact with outcome favorability in much the same way that process fairness does. Transactions undertaken in a context of regulatory fit, much like being treated by an authority with high process fairness, are psychologically rewarding (e.g., value affirming). Feeling more psychologically rewarded by the process of self-regulation, people may be less likely to be influenced by outcome favorability, especially when the outcomes have more of a tangible or economic basis. Another conceptual basis for positing an interactive relationship between regulatory fit and outcome favorability goes as follows: Authorities who create environments that fit with the regulatory focus orientation of their direct reports may be seen as morally correct (read: trustworthy). The trustworthiness of an authority, in turn, has been shown to interact with outcome favorability, such that high trustworthiness reduces the influence of outcome favorability on people's willingness to support the authority and the authority's decisions relative to when trustworthiness is low (Brockner et al., 1997).

In summary, people may use process fairness information for a variety of purposes as a function of whether their concerns are relatively simple, in which they are trying to reduce uncertainty about their short-term and tangible outcomes, or complex, in which they are trying to make sense of both their tangible and intangible outcomes in both the short and long term. For each purpose, factors other than process fairness may influence its accompanying sense-making process in much the same way that process fairness does. If so, then these other factors, which on the surface seem to have little to do with process fairness, may interact with outcome favorability in the same way that process fairness does. *Whatever* causes people to (1) see the other party as less responsible for their unfavorable outcomes, (2) infer that the other party holds them in greater standing, (3) be relatively optimistic about their longer-term outcomes, and (4) see the other party as more trustworthy should reduce the influence of outcome favorability on, say, their willingness to support the other party and his or her decisions. Future research that tests (and finds support for) these hypotheses may go a long way toward broadening the scope of the interactive relationship between process fairness and outcome favorability.

The scope of the process–outcome interaction is not necessarily limited to contexts in which we examine people's reactions to another as a function of the other's process fairness and the favorability of the outcomes associated with the encounter. As recent theory and research on regulatory fit suggest, it may not even be necessary for an interaction partner to be present to produce the psychological state elicited by process fairness information. Much like what people are likely to experience in reaction to the process fairness with which another treats them, the process of engaging in self-regulation may feel more or less morally right as a function of regulatory fit (Camacho et al., 2003); this last speculation raises the intriguing hypothesis that regulatory fit may interact with outcome favorability to influence people's beliefs and behaviors in the same way that process fairness does.

WHAT IS IT ABOUT PROCESS FAIRNESS (II)? OR, WHY HIGH PROCESS FAIRNESS HEIGHTENS THE IMPACT OF OUTCOME FAVORABILITY

In Chapters 2 and 3, I considered the interactive relationship between process fairness and outcome favorability in which high process fairness *reduced* the influence of outcome favorability; the preceding section of this chapter identified a host of other factors that may be expected to behave similarly to process fairness in how they interact with outcome favorability. In Chapter 4, I considered the interactive relationship between process fairness and outcome favorability in which high process fairness *heightened* the impact of outcome favorability. This particular form of interactive relationship emanates from yet another way in which people use process fairness information: to determine how much to make self-attributions (i.e., to see themselves as personally responsible) for their outcomes. Studies have shown that people are more likely to make self-attributions for their outcomes when process fairness is relatively high (e.g., Leung et al., 2001; Van den Bos et al., 1999).

Outcome favorability is more likely to influence people's self-evaluations for better or worse when people see themselves as more personally responsible for their outcomes (Weiner, 1985). By influencing how much people see themselves as responsible for their outcomes, process fairness interacts with outcome favorability to influence self-evaluations, such that outcome favorability is more likely to affect self-evaluations (and the beliefs and behaviors influenced by self-evaluations) when process fairness is relatively high (Brockner et al., 2003).

One way to broaden the scope of this particular form of interactive relationship between process fairness and outcome favorability is by delineating other factors (besides process fairness) that influence the extent to which people see themselves as responsible for their outcomes.

Presumably, these other factors should behave similarly to process fairness in how they interact with outcome favorability, such that outcome favorability will be more influential when people see themselves as more personally responsible for their outcomes. For example, Ployhart, Ehrhart, and Hayes (2005) asked undergraduate students to indicate how they would feel about themselves after being informed of college application decisions. Half of them were told that they were admitted (favorable outcome condition), and half were told that they were rejected (unfavorable outcome condition).

The authors (Ployhart et al., 2005) also varied consensus information, which Kelley (1973) theorized to influence people's tendencies to make self-attributions for their outcomes. Those in the high-consensus conditions were led to believe that their outcome was similar to that of most applicants (thus, those in the favorable outcome condition were told that most applicants were admitted, while those in the unfavorable outcome condition were told that most applicants were rejected), whereas those in the low-consensus conditions were told that their outcome was different from that of most applicants; that is, those in the favorable outcome condition were told that most applicants were rejected, while those in the unfavorable outcome condition were told that most applicants were accepted). Given Kelley's suggestion that low consensus information induces people to see themselves as more personally responsible for their outcomes, outcome favorability should have been more likely to influence the self-evaluations of those in the low-consensus conditions than in the high-consensus conditions. Indeed, this is precisely what Ployhart et al. found.

Thus, process fairness information may affect one factor that influences people's tendencies to perceive outcomes as self-relevant: the extent to which they see themselves as personally responsible for their outcomes. However, this particular form of process–outcome interaction may be cast even more broadly by delineating other factors that influence people's tendencies to perceive their outcomes as *self-relevant*. For example, employees may *assign* greater self-relevance to their outcomes when their attention is self-directed. Research has shown that people's causal attributions are directly linked to their focus of attention (e.g., Storms, 1973). Therefore, if people focus on their external environment, they are likely to attribute their outcomes to the environment. If, however, their attention is self-directed, their outcome attributions are likely to follow suit. Just as high process fairness makes people more likely to make self-attributions for their outcomes (which in turn may interact with outcome favorability to influence self-evaluations), so may other factors that focus people's attention on themselves.

In a related vein, the degree to which people *experience* their outcomes as self-relevant also may depend on self-directed attention. Studies have shown that self-focused attention increases the intensity of people's internal experiences. For example, people experience their emotions more intensely when their attention is more self-focused (Scheier &

Carver, 1977). Thus, if outcome favorability influences people's self-evaluations, then the felt intensity of that experience (and hence the impact of outcome favorability on their self-evaluations) is likely to be greater when their attention is self-directed.

Numerous factors may influence people's tendencies to direct attention inward, including their dispositional tendencies toward self-focused attention (Fenigstein et al., 1975) as well as situational inducements, such as (1) being new to the organization or to their position within the organization, (2) being demographically different from the majority of their coworkers, and (3) receiving feedback that is inconsistent with their performance history (Brunot, Huguet, & Monteil, 1999). The various determinants of self-focused attention may behave similarly to process fairness in how they interact with outcome favorability to influence people's self-evaluations. For example, outcome favorability may have more of an influence on the self-evaluations of people who are (1) relatively new to the organization or to their position within the organization or (2) demographically different from rather than similar to the majority of their coworkers.

The perceived self-relevance of outcomes also may depend on the domain to which they refer. Certain domains are more central to people's self-concepts than are others. For example, some employees may take great pride in their abilities or interests, to the point of having them inextricably linked to their sense of who they are. The receipt of outcome feedback in those domains is more likely to influence their self-evaluations, for better or worse, than would be the case if the outcomes were less central to people's identity. For example, in an individualistic culture, in which people's self-construals tend to be relatively independent, the favorability of individual outcomes may affect their self-evaluations (Brockner & Chen, 1996). In collectivistic cultures, however, in which people have more interdependent forms of self-construal, it could be the favorability of their in-group's outcomes that are particularly likely to influence their self-evaluations (Markus & Kitayama, 1991).

In summary, in the process of interacting with others or when engaged in self-regulation on a more nonsocial basis, various factors may influence the extent to which people perceive their outcomes as self-relevant. One elicitor of self-relevance is the other party's process fairness, which affects how much people see themselves as personally responsible for their outcomes (Van den Bos et al., 1999). Other factors besides process fairness may influence people's tendencies to see themselves as personally responsible for their outcomes, and other factors (besides making personal attributions for their outcomes) may influence the extent to which outcomes are perceived as self-relevant. All of these factors are posited to act like process fairness in interacting with outcome favorability. *Whatever* causes people to see their outcomes as more self-relevant may heighten the influence of outcome favorability on their self-evaluations or on beliefs and behaviors that are influenced by their self-evaluations.

WHAT IS IT ABOUT OUTCOME FAVORABILITY? OR, WHY FAIR PROCESS EFFECTS MAY BE STRONGER WHEN OUTCOMES ARE UNFAVORABLE

Another way to expand the scope of the process–outcome interaction effect is by considering why outcome favorability has a moderating influence on process fairness. As suggested by Table 6.1, let us assume that people care about their economic or psychological well-being in the short term or in the long term. If so, then in the face of information that poses a potential threat to one or more of these aspects of well-being, people are likely to be vigilant about (and thus susceptible to influence by) information that helps them to evaluate the extent of the potential danger and whether anything can be done about it (Lazarus & Folkman, 1984). Process fairness is one such source of information that enables people to evaluate the extent to which they are viewed favorably by the other party, the extent to which their longer-term outcomes may be favorable, the extent to which the other party may be trusted, and so on. Moreover, people are more likely to experience unfavorable outcomes than favorable outcomes as a threat to their well-being, thereby leading them to be more affected by process fairness information when outcomes are unfavorable rather than favorable.

This reasoning suggests that other factors besides the receipt of unfavorable outcomes that people experience as a potential threat to their well-being should similarly make them more susceptible to influence by process fairness information. Moreover, in studies showing outcome favorability to have a moderating influence on process fairness, participants typically *received* outcomes of varying degrees of favorability, which led them to feel more or less of a threat to their well-being. The ensuing discussion suggests that even in the absence of receiving an *actual* outcome, it is plausible for people to experience more or less of a threat to their well-being, which in turn will dictate the extent to which they draw on, and hence be affected by, process fairness information.

Mortality Salience

People are likely to experience a sense of threat to their well-being when they contemplate their own death (Becker, 1973). According to terror management theory (Greenberg, Solomon, & Pyszczynski, 1997), the fear of death emanates from the instinct for self-preservation, an instinct that people share with other species. Unlike other species, however, people also are aware of the inevitability of death. The juxtaposition of these two forces has the potential to elicit a paralyzing form of terror that would threaten virtually every aspect of our psychological existence. The theory further posits that people buffer themselves against existential terror in two related but conceptually distinct ways. First, we may affirm our basic values or worldviews (known as the *cultural worldview mechanism*). Second, we may seek to bolster our self-esteem (known as the *self-esteem mechanism*). Thus, people may cope with the anticipation of threat to their physical selves by affirming or calling to mind core elements of their psychological selves (i.e., their sense of identity, which is derived at least in part from their values, and their sense of esteem).

Terror management theory has been tested by examining the effects of making people aware of their mortality (known as *mortality salience*) on their thoughts, feelings, and behaviors. For example, studies testing the cultural worldview mechanism have shown that people have more negative reactions to those who threaten their values (and that they have more positive reactions to those who support their values) when their mortality has been made more salient (Rosenblatt, Greenberg, Solomon, Pyszczynski, & Lyon, 1989). Studies consistent with the self-esteem mechanism have shown that people with higher self-esteem are less likely to deny the possibility that they may die at a relatively early age. Presumably, self-esteem serves to buffer against the anxiety that people may feel if they were to contemplate that they may die young, thereby allowing persons with higher self-esteem to be more accepting of this rather unpleasant possibility (Greenberg et al., 1993).

Both the cultural worldview mechanism and the self-esteem mechanism suggest that process fairness information may be particularly relevant to people whose mortality concerns are salient. For one thing, fairness in general (and process fairness in particular) is highly valued in most people's cultural worldviews. The notion that fairness is an extremely important cultural value is central to many conceptualizations in the justice literature (Lerner & Simmons, 1966; Lind & Tyler, 1988; Mark & Folger, 1984). Thus, when people's mortality has been made salient they are particularly hungry for information that affirms their basic values. Process fairness is one such source of information (Folger & Cropanzano, 1998, 2001); hence, when process fairness is high people are more likely to experience affirmation of a basic value and therefore react much more positively than when process fairness is low. Moreover, when people's mortality is salient they need information that affirms or bolsters their sense of self-esteem. The fact that being treated with process fairness is positively related to how people feel about themselves (Tyler & Lind, 1992) provides yet another reason that people react better when process fairness is relatively high.

This reasoning suggests that people should be more influenced by process fairness information to the extent that their mortality has been made salient. In fact, a spate of studies has found support for this proposition. Drawing on the method used in previous tests of terror management theory, Van den Bos and Miedema (2000) made mortality salient by asking participants to write about: (1) the emotions that the thought of your death arouses in you, and (2) what you think will happen to you as you physically die. Participants in the control condition were not asked to contemplate these matters. Moreover, half of the participants were allowed to voice their opinion regarding how a reward should be divided between them and another person (high process fairness condition); half were not allowed to have voice (low process fairness condition). Dependent variables assessed across three different studies included positive affect, negative affect, and relational judgments of the experimenter (e.g., how much the experimenter had respect for them and perceived them to be a full-fledged group member). Replicating previous findings in the justice literature, Van den Bos and Miedema found that people responded much more favorably on all dependent measures when they had voice relative to when they did not. Of greater importance, mortality salience had a moderating influence on voice, such that the well-established tendency for people to respond more favorably to higher levels of voice was significantly more pronounced when their mortality had been made salient. Van den Bos et al. (2005) provided further evidence of this tendency, and Van den Bos (2001) reported that mortality salience had a moderating influence on distributive fairness, such that the tendency for people to show more negative affect when their outcomes were more unfair was heightened when mortality salience was relatively high.

Without necessarily discounting the cultural worldview mechanism, a variety of additional findings suggests that the moderating influence of mortality salience on the fair process effect may be accounted for by the self-esteem mechanism. For one thing, prior research has shown that making people's mortality salient reduces their state self-esteem (Koole, Dechesne, & van Knippenberg, 2000). If thinking about their death reduces people's self-esteem, then they may be more in need of a boost to their self-esteem, thereby explaining why mortality salience heightens the influence of process fairness information, which, as mentioned, has been shown to be positively related to people's self-evaluations (Tyler & Lind, 1992).

Further support for the self-esteem mechanism is the finding that the interactive relationship between mortality salience and process fairness is moderated by whether people have engaged in self-affirmation (Steele, 1988). If mortality salience heightens people's need for positive self-evaluation (which in turn is more likely to be satisfied when they are treated with higher process fairness), then giving people an opportunity to engage in self-affirmation subsequent to thinking about their own death should make them less susceptible to influence by process fairness information. To test this reasoning, Van den Bos (2001) had half of his participants think about their own death, whereas the other half did not. Prior to manipulating whether participants were allowed to have voice in an upcoming decision, Van den Bos varied whether participants were given the opportunity to engage in self-affirmation. In the absence of self-affirmation, participants in the Van den Bos study exhibited the previously established interactive relationship between mortality salience and voice: when mortality salience was high, the presence or absence of voice had more of an impact on participants' negative affect relative to when mortality salience was low. However, when participants had engaged in self-affirmation (and therefore were presumably less in need of the positive self-evaluation elicited by higher process fairness), there was no hint of an interactive effect of mortality salience and process fairness on negative affect.

Finally, if the self-esteem mechanism accounts for the interactive relationship between mortality salience and process fairness, then other ways of threatening people's self-esteem (besides mortality salience) should have a similar moderating influence on process fairness.

To test this reasoning, Miedema, Van den Bos, and Vermunt (2006) experimentally manipulated self-threat by having some of their participants describe the emotions that they experience when they contemplated others not believing that they were intelligent (self-threat condition), whereas other participants were asked to describe the emotions they experience when they contemplated others believing that they were intelligent (no self-threat condition). Next, participants were either given or not given voice about an upcoming decision. Whereas participants' judgments of process fairness were higher when they had voice relative to when they did not, this tendency was significantly more pronounced in the self-threat condition than in the no self-threat condition.

In a second study, Miedema et al. (2006) found that inducing self-threat led to an even stronger effect of distributive justice on perceptions of fairness and negative affect than did inducing mortality salience. In other words, it may be the threat to self-esteem elicited by mortality salience rather than mortality salience per se that heightens people's need to be treated in a way that reaffirms their sense of self-worth. The fact that higher process fairness engenders more positive self-evaluations (Tyler & Lind, 1992) may explain why people are particularly likely to respond more favorably to higher levels of process fairness when their self-esteem was previously threatened, either indirectly (e.g., via mortality salience) or directly.

Process Fairness × Trait Self-Esteem

If the self-esteem mechanism set forth by terror management theory helps to account for the interactive relationship between mortality salience and process fairness, it would seem to suggest that process fairness effects should be exhibited to a greater extent by those with relatively low trait self-esteem. Presumably, those lower in self-esteem are more in need of information that shines favorably on them. Hence, they may be expected to react more positively when they are treated with high process fairness and more negatively when they are treated with low process fairness relative to their counterparts with high self-esteem. In fact, a handful of studies have shown that process fairness effects are stronger among those with lower self-esteem (De Cremer, 2003; De Cremer, van Knippenberg, Bos & van Dijke, 2004; Vermunt, van Knippenberg, van Knippenberg, & Blaauw, 2001).

However, two independent streams of research (each consisting of five separate studies) provided evidence of an opposite tendency, in which persons with high self-esteem responded more favorably to higher levels of process fairness relative to their counterparts with low self-esteem (Brockner et al., 1998; Wiesenfeld et al., 2007). I now describe the studies that showed stronger fair process effects among persons with higher self-esteem, followed by speculative remarks about how to reconcile the results of studies, some of which have shown stronger fair process effects among persons with high self-esteem and others that have shown stronger fair process effects among persons with lower self-esteem.

Why might process fairness information more strongly influence the beliefs and behaviors of persons with higher self-esteem? At least two reasons come to mind. First, certain antecedents of process fairness may make other concerns salient, which in turn may have more of an influence on those with higher self-esteem. More specifically, consider the antecedent of process fairness that probably has been studied more widely than any other: voice. One of the most well-replicated effects in the justice literature is that when people are allowed to have input into a decision process, they will judge the process as more fair, and as a result, they will be more willing to support the decision that was reached, the parties responsible for planning and implementing the decision, and the organization in which the decision was made (Lind & Tyler, 1988; Thibaut & Walker, 1975). One way to explain these findings is through the language of expectancy-valence theory or, at least, the "valence" part of expectancy-valence theory (Vroom, 1964). That is, people are more motivated to have voice because of the greater rewards (either tangible or intangible) that they believe may come their way when they are allowed to provide input relative to when they are not (Thibaut & Walker, 1975). Being more motivated to have voice ex ante, they will respond more positively when voice is high rather than low ex post.

People's motivation to have voice (and hence, the extent to which they will be affected by having had it) may depend not only on the valence associated with having voice, but also on how much they believe in the efficacy of their voice, that is, the extent to which they believe that their voice may make a meaningful difference in an upcoming decision. Perceptions of the efficacy of voice in turn may be influenced by multiple factors. For example, if subordinates are working for managers who have more of a history of taking their subordinates' views into account when making decisions, then subordinates are more likely to believe that their voice will make a meaningful difference (Shapiro & Brett, 1993). Believing their voice to be more efficacious, such subordinates are expected to be more motivated to have voice ex ante and to be more affected by the extent to which they had it ex post. Even more relevant to the present discussion, people's beliefs in the efficacy of their voice also may be affected by their self-esteem. Those with higher levels of self-esteem may be more likely to believe that their voice will make a meaningful difference. As a result, persons with higher self-esteem may be more motivated to have voice ex ante and therefore may be more influenced by the extent to which they believe that they had it ex post.

In four field studies, Brockner et al. (1998) examined the interactive effect of voice and trait self-esteem on a variety of dependent variables (participants' organizational commitment, work motivation, and satisfaction with how they were treated by the other party). Whereas voice was positively related to the dependent variables in all four studies, in each instance the voice effect was more strongly pronounced among those with higher levels of trait self-esteem.

Moreover, Brockner et al. (1998) conducted a fifth study that differed in two important ways from the field studies and that enabled them to evaluate further the mechanism presumed to account for the moderating effect of trait self-esteem on reactions to voice. First, rather than sorting people on the basis of their trait self-esteem, the authors directly examined the variable that was believed to account for the effect of trait self-esteem: the extent to which people believed that they were capable of providing meaningful input into an upcoming decision process. Second, both of the independent variables (capability of providing meaningful input and degree of voice) were experimentally manipulated, thereby imbuing the findings with a high degree of internal validity. The dependent variable consisted of people's satisfaction with the decision that was reached. The results were conceptually analogous to those found in the field studies. Perceived capability and voice interacted to influence participants' satisfaction with the decision that was reached, such that having voice led to significantly higher levels of satisfaction when they thought that they were highly capable of providing meaningful input into the decision, whereas having voice had no effect on satisfaction when people were led to believe that they were less capable of providing meaningful input into the decision.

At first blush, it could be argued that there may have been something specific to voice that elicited these findings. Perhaps unlike other determinants of process fairness, voice may make salient to people concerns about their competence. In other words, allowing people to take part in a decision process not only may influence perceptions of process fairness but also may induce them to evaluate whether they have the wherewithal to make a meaningful contribution. People's concerns about their competence may be less likely to arise as a function of other determinants of process fairness that have less to do with their capabilities, such as (1) whether decisions are made on the basis of accurate information, (2) whether decisions are made consistently, (3) whether decision makers provide a clear and adequate explanation of the rationale for their actions, and (4) whether decision makers provide recipients with ample advance notification of their decisions. Perhaps trait self-esteem would be less apt to have the moderating influence on these other determinants of process fairness than Brockner et al. (1998) found it to have on voice.

In rebuttal to this possibility, however, we need to take into account another psychological motivation that people maintain, which leads us to a second reason why process fairness effects may be stronger among persons with higher self-esteem. Whereas people are motivated by self-enhancement (i.e., the desire to feel good about themselves), we also know that they seek to maintain a consistent and coherent picture of themselves. As set forth by self-verification theory (e.g., Swann, 1999), people want to be perceived by others in the same ways that they perceive themselves. Thus, people are drawn to relationships and interaction partners in which the other party sees them in the same way that they see themselves. Moreover, in response to self-discrepant information received from the other party, people will actively work to bring the other party's views in line with their self-views (Swann & Read, 1981; Swann, Wenzlaff, Krull, & Pelham, 1992).

People's self-verification strivings may influence the relationship between their perceptions of how fairly they are being treated by another party and how attracted they feel toward that party. Process fairness provides symbolic information about how favorably people are viewed by the other. The more that the other exhibits process fairness, the more likely are people to infer that they are viewed favorably by the other (Tyler & Lind, 1992). For people with higher levels of self-esteem, self-enhancement and self-verification strivings work hand in hand, such that people will be more attracted to the other party when the other exhibits higher process fairness. The picture for lower levels of self-esteem, however, is considerably more muddied. On the one hand, their self-enhancement strivings should lead them to be more attracted to others who treat them with higher process fairness, in much the same way that people with higher self-esteem may be expected to behave; if anything, it could be argued that persons with lower self-esteem may have even more of a need to be viewed favorably by others and thus will be even more appreciative of the positive evaluation conveyed by high process fairness (and more unappreciative of the negative evaluation conveyed by low process fairness) relative to their counterparts with high self-esteem. On the other hand, the self-verification strivings of persons with low self-esteem should reduce the attractiveness of other people who treat them with greater process fairness.

Wiesenfeld et al. (2007) examined the interactive effect of process fairness and self-esteem on employees' attraction toward their organizations. Across four different field settings, the authors operationalized process fairness in a variety of ways. In fact, most of the survey items used to measure process fairness consisted of elements other than voice, such as (1) the Leventhal et al. (1980) criteria of accuracy, bias suppression, and consistency; (2) how much people were treated with dignity and respect; and (3) more general measures (e.g., how much they agreed with survey items such as, "The selection process for new positions in this division has been managed in the fairest way possible"). Attraction to the organization also was measured in different ways, such as self-reported organizational commitment and a behavioral measure of absenteeism. All four studies yielded evidence of the same interactive effect of process fairness and self-esteem on attraction. Among persons with high self-esteem, process fairness was positively and significantly related to attraction. Among persons with low self-esteem, the relationship between process fairness and attraction was trivial.

In a fifth study conducted under more controlled conditions, Wiesenfeld et al. (2007) measured people's trait self-esteem and then randomly assigned them to be treated with either higher or lower process fairness. All of the participants were students at a large state university in the United States. They read about a veridical breach of computer security that had recently taken place at their university. Half of the participants were told that the university was handling the breach with relatively high process fairness, whereas the other half were told that the breach was being handled with relatively low process fairness.

Consistent with the results of their field studies, Wiesenfeld et al. (2007) found that among those higher in self-esteem, process fairness was positively and significantly related to participants' commitment to the institution, whereas among those lower in self-esteem, process fairness and commitment were unrelated to one another. Wiesenfeld et al. also measured how much participants experienced self-verification in their encounter with the institution, as measured by their agreement with items such as, "The administration of the university sees me as I see myself." Participants with high self-esteem reported feeling significantly more self-verified when the university handled the breach with higher than with lower process fairness, whereas participants with low self-esteem reported experiencing significantly greater self-verification when the university handled the breach with lower than with higher process fairness.

Whereas participants with low self-esteem felt significantly more self-verified when the university handled the breach with low process fairness than with high process fairness, process fairness was unrelated to their level of commitment. Thus, self-verification strivings among people with lower self-esteem led to an *elimination* of the positive relationship typically found between the organization's process fairness and people's attraction or commitment to the organization. However, the desire for self-verification among persons with low self-esteem did not produce a *reversal* of the typical positive relationship between process fairness and their attraction or commitment to the organization. Perhaps this is due to the fact that there are other factors besides self-verification that account for the relationship between process fairness and attraction or commitment to the organization. For example, people's need to feel good about themselves (the self-enhancement motive) applies to people with low self-esteem, which would argue for a positive relationship between process fairness and attraction or commitment. Moreover, the positive relationship between process fairness and attraction or commitment probably is not entirely driven by self-related motives. People may be more attracted or committed to organizations that treat them with higher process fairness because they believe that such treatment is inherently morally correct (Folger, 2001). Perhaps self-verification and these other motives (e.g., self-enhancement, morality) cancelled each other out among individuals with lower self-esteem, thereby producing a nonsignificant rather than inverse relationship between process fairness and organizational commitment.

Toward Reconciliation: The Case of Voice

Given that trait self-esteem has been shown to interact with process fairness in different ways across studies, an intriguing conceptual and empirical challenge is to delineate when process fairness effects may be stronger among those lower in trait self-esteem and when they may be more pronounced among those higher in trait self-esteem. As always, the challenge of reconciling conflicting predictions or findings may be facilitated by grounding the main variables (in this case, process fairness and trait self-esteem) in a broader theoretical context. That is, theoretical accounts of findings that have already emerged may provide insight into when the opposite results are apt to arise.

Accordingly, Brockner et al. (1998) drew on expectancy theory to account for the tendency of voice effects to be stronger among people with higher self-esteem. People with higher self-esteem are likely to believe that they are more capable of providing meaningful input into a decision process. Expectancy theory posits that one basis of people's motivation is the belief that they are capable of making a meaningful difference. The more that people believe in their capabilities, the greater their motivation is. Furthermore, the more motivated they are (in this case, to have voice), the more likely is the actual level of voice that they have to influence their attitudes and behaviors (e.g., their satisfaction with a decision).

This reasoning suggests that when people with lower capabilities are more motivated to have voice, then they will be more influenced by the level of voice that they experience. Moreover, expectancy theory posits that people's motivation depends not only on their beliefs about their efficacy to bring about certain outcomes, but also on the extent to which they value or assign importance to those outcomes. In other words, there may be conditions under which it is more important for people of lower capability to have voice into a decision process. When this is the case, those with less capability to provide meaningful input may be more motivated to have voice and, as a result, may be more affected by the actual level of voice that they experience.

When might people with less capability assign greater importance to having voice in a decision process? Consider, for example, the cultural dimension of masculinity-femininity (Hofstede, 1998), which refers to how much members of a given culture assign significance to the values of achievement and competition (masculinity) versus the value of nurturing those with less capability (femininity). In cultures valuing femininity, greater importance may be assigned to allowing the less-capable people to have voice or input into a decision process. After all, inviting the less-capable people to express their views may be the nurturing thing to do; it may allow them to feel included in the group's activities. In contrast, in cultures valuing masculinity, the more capable people would be expected to play a more active role in a decision process, whereas the less capable would play a less-active role. After all, this type of arrangement should enable the group to accomplish that which it values: achievement. Consistent with this reasoning, Brockner et al. (1998) found in their study conducted in the United States that the positive effect of voice on satisfaction was stronger among the more capable participants; furthermore, the United States has a culture that is relatively high in masculinity (Hofstede, 1998).

This reasoning suggests that if the interactive relationship between capability and voice were examined in a culture emphasizing femininity, then the results may be different. In a context emphasizing femininity, the positive effect of voice on satisfaction may be stronger among those who see themselves as less capable of providing meaningful input. One country that is relatively high in femininity is the Netherlands (Hofstede, 2007; Van de Vliert & Janssen, 2002). Indeed, one book chapter that described the experience of American business students studying in the Netherlands was titled, "Femininity Shock" (Vunderink & Hofstede, 1998).

Cultural differences in masculinity-femininity are not the only determinant of how much people value competition and achievement versus nurturing those with lower capability. These values may be situationally malleable as well. For example, even in the masculinity-oriented United States, people sometimes may find themselves in situations in which the femininity-related value of nurturing the development of those who are less well off is emphasized. Moreover, even in the femininity-oriented Netherlands, people may encounter instances in which the masculinity-related values of competition and achievement are given prominence. Whereas Brockner et al. (1998) found that the positive effect of voice on satisfaction was shown to a greater extent by those who saw themselves as more capable, it may be that when cultural or situational factors emphasize nurturing the development of those with less capability, the interactive relationship between capability and voice may take a different form. More specifically, it could be the less-capable people (rather than the more capable people) who will be more motivated to have voice and therefore more likely to respond with greater satisfaction when they have greater voice in a decision process.

A series of studies tested this reasoning (Van den Bos, Brockner et al., in press). The procedure was modeled after the laboratory experiment conducted by Brockner et al. (1998), in which participants were led to believe that they were more or less capable of providing meaningful input into an upcoming decision. Also, as in the earlier study, participants either were allowed to have voice or were not, with the dependent variable consisting of their satisfaction with the decision. Study 1 was conducted in the United States; participants were expected to assign importance to the masculinity-related value of competitive achievement.

The third independent variable (Van den Bos, Brockner et al., in press) was whether participants were induced to focus on the femininity-related value of nurturing the development of those with lower capability. In the experimental (femininity) condition, the value of nurturing those with lower capability was made salient. Participants were told that the researchers were striving to create a climate in which those with more capabilities should pay close attention to the needs and opinions of those with lower capabilities. In the control condition, nothing was said to participants about nurturing those with lower capability.

The results (Van den Bos, Brockner et al., in press) yielded a three-way interaction effect among capability to provide meaningful input, voice, and the experimental manipulation of values. As can be seen in Table 6.2, in the control condition, which essentially procedurally replicated the method used by Brockner et al. (1998) in their U.S. sample, the results resembled those found previously: The positive effect of voice on satisfaction was stronger among those who believed that they were more capable of providing meaningful input into the upcoming decision. On the other hand, in the experimental condition, in which participants were induced to value the development of those with lower

TABLE 6.2 Decision Satisfaction as a Function of the Values Manipulation, Voice, and Capability of Providing Meaningful Input (Van den Bos, Brockner et al., in press)

	Capability of Providing Meaningful Input	
Voice	**High**	**Low**
Experimental Condition (Emphasizing Nurturance of Those Less Capable)		
Low	5.12	3.96
High	4.46	5.00
Control Condition		
Low	4.24	4.20
High	5.21	4.12

Note: Scores could range from 1 to 9, with higher scores reflecting greater satisfaction with the decision.

capability, the interaction between capability and voice took a different form: The positive effect of voice on satisfaction was stronger among those who believed that they were *less* capable of providing meaningful input into the decision.

Whereas these results are consistent with the notion that those who see themselves as more capable of providing meaningful input show a stronger voice effect on satisfaction when the masculine values of competition and achievement are emphasized, the findings are merely suggestive. As in the previous study conducted in the United States (Brockner et al., 1998, Study 5), when nothing was said to participants about what they should value, voice was more positively related to satisfaction among those who believed that they were more capable of providing meaningful input (Van den Bos, Brockner et al., in press). As an extension of the earlier findings, the results showed that when people were induced to value the nurturance of those with lower capability, it was the participants with lower capability who exhibited more of a positive relationship between voice and satisfaction.

The logic underlying the Van den Bos, Brockner et al. (in press) study was that, in the absence of saying anything to participants about what they should value, they would default to the predominant values in their culture. The United States is more of a masculine culture, in which people assign importance to competitive achievement (Hofstede, 1998). Thus, people's motivation to have voice (and hence the positive relationship between voice and satisfaction) may not simply depend on their perceived capability to provide meaningful input. Rather, it also may be necessary for those who saw themselves as more capable to assign importance to competitive achievement, a value that is typical of people in masculine cultures. Indeed, the results showed that when people are led to value nurturing those with lower capability, the findings of Brockner et al. (1998, Study 5) actually reversed themselves, in that those who saw themselves as less capable were more apt to exhibit a positive relationship between voice and satisfaction.

Whereas the results of Van den Bos, Brockner et al.'s (in press) initial study were consistent with this reasoning, further research is needed. In fact, it may be useful to make explicit the assumptions on which this initial study is based and then to conduct additional research to evaluate the adequacy of these assumptions. Indeed, three assumptions guided the previous study: (1) the American participants examined in Study 1 valued masculinity, such that they assigned importance to achievement and outperforming their peers (Hofstede, 1998, 2007); (2) in the absence of instructing participants to assign importance to any values (that is, in the control condition), they were expected to default to the values predominant in their culture; and (3) through experimental induction, people could be led to focus on "countercultural" values, in which case the results would reverse those found in the control condition (in which nothing was said about what they should value).

One way to evaluate these assumptions is by examining participants from a different culture, particularly one that emphasizes more feminine values such as nurturing those who are less capable (see Hofstede, 1998, 2007). Furthermore, participants from the new culture should be exposed to two different conditions: one in which nothing is said about what they should value (as in the control condition in Study 1) and another in which they are instructed to assign importance to countercultural values, which in this instance would be the masculinity-oriented ones of competitive achievement (the experimental condition). If the reasoning underlying the results of Van den Bos, Brockner et al.'s (in press) initial study is correct, then in the control condition participants should default to the values that are predominant in their culture. That is, the satisfaction of those who saw themselves as less capable of providing meaningful input should be more affected by whether they had voice. Moreover, in the condition in which participants were led to emphasize the countercultural masculine values of achievement and outperforming their peers, we would expect the satisfaction level of those who saw themselves as more capable of providing meaningful input to be more affected by whether they had voice.

To test this reasoning, Van den Bos, Brockner et al. (in press) conducted a second study in the Netherlands, where people are more likely than in the United States to emphasize the feminine value of nurturing the less capable (Hofstede, 1998, 2007). As in the previous study, the authors manipulated people's beliefs of how capable they were of providing meaningful input into an upcoming decision as well as whether they were allowed to have voice in the decision. Furthermore, the third independent variable consisted of whether participants were led to assign importance to values contrary to the predominant ones in the culture. The predominant cultural values in the initial study were assumed to be more masculine, hence the countercultural condition emphasized femininity. In the second study, the predominant cultural values were assumed to be more feminine, hence the countercultural condition in this instance emphasized the masculine value of competitive achievement.

In summary, Van den Bos, Brockner et al.'s (in press) second study was conducted in the Netherlands and consisted of a 2 (capabilities: higher vs. lower) × 2 (procedure: voice vs. no voice) × 2 (values: competitive achievement emphasized or not) factorial design. As in the initial study, Van den Bos et al. predicted a three-way interaction effect. In the control condition, in which nothing was said about what participants should value, it was expected that the satisfaction of those who saw themselves as less capable of providing meaningful input would be more affected by whether they had been given voice. In the experimental condition, in which participants were led to assign importance to outperforming their peers, we expected the satisfaction level of those who saw themselves as more capable to be more affected by whether they had been given voice. As can be seen in Table 6.3, the results lent strong support to these predictions.

TABLE 6.3 Decision Satisfaction as a Function of the Values Manipulation, Voice, and Capability of Providing Meaningful Input (Van den Bos, Brockner et al., in press)

	Capability of Providing Meaningful Input	
Voice	**High**	**Low**
Experimental Condition (Emphasizing Competitive Achievement)		
Low	3.65	4.06
High	5.14	4.38
Control Condition		
Low	4.57	3.52
High	4.38	4.56

Note: Scores could range from 1 to 9, with higher scores reflecting greater satisfaction with the decision.

In summary, the findings of Van den Bos, Brockner et al. (in press) provide insight into the question of whether process fairness effects are likely to be stronger among those higher or lower in self-esteem. When process fairness is in reference to voice, whether those higher or lower in self-esteem show stronger process fairness effects depends on people's motivation to have voice. When people are more motivated to have voice, they will be more influenced by the level of voice that they experience. The key, then, is to delineate the conditions under which people's self-esteem is positively versus negatively related to their motivation to have voice. One basis for people with high self-esteem to be more motivated to have voice is their greater confidence about being able to provide meaningful input relative to their counterparts with low self-esteem. Motivation depends on expectancies, such that those who maintain more positive expectancies generally show greater motivation. Thus, when the motivation to have voice is driven by expectancies, that is, the belief that one's input will be more efficacious, persons with high self-esteem will be more motivated to have voice and hence will be more influenced by the level of voice that they experience.

However, motivation does not solely depend on expectancies. Valence also matters, such that the more that is at stake, the greater the motivation is (Vroom, 1964). As the Van den Bos, Brockner et al. (in press) studies suggest, sometimes it may be more important for those who see themselves as less capable to have voice, in which case people with lower self-esteem will be more motivated to have voice and hence will be more influenced by the level of voice that they experience.

Taken together, the Van den Bos, Brockner et al. (in press) findings suggest that when the value of competitive achievement is emphasized, persons with higher self-esteem (who see themselves as more capable) will show a stronger voice effect, whereas when the value of nurturing the development of those with lower capability is salient, persons with lower self-esteem (who see themselves as less capable) will show a stronger voice effect. Van den Bos et al. used national culture and an experimental manipulation as proxies for the values that may be emphasized in a given situation. It is important to keep in mind that these values refer to central constructs in several areas of social and organizational psychology, such as the distinction between task orientation versus relationship orientation in the leadership literature (e.g., Hersey & Blanchard, 1969) and the distinction between competence versus warmth in the person perception literature (e.g., Judd, James-Hawkins, Yzerbyt, & Kashima, 2005). As such, it is possible that numerous factors may influence the relative prominence of these related sets of values. For example, leaders may adopt more of task orientation in certain instances, with resulting emphases on competitive achievement, and they may adopt more of a relationship orientation on other occasions, with resulting emphases on nurturing those with lower capability. Similarly, depending on their interaction goals, people sometimes may value being seen as competent (in which case they are likely to assign importance to competitive achievement), or they may value being seen as warm (in which case they assign importance to nurturing those with lower capability). My hunch is that when, for whatever reason, greater emphasis is placed on competitive achievement, people's motivation to have voice will be positively related to how much they believe that their voice will make a meaningful difference, in which case the positive effect of having voice is likely to be stronger among people with higher self-esteem. Alternatively, when, for whatever reason, the nurturing or development of those less capable to provide meaningful input is more important, then the motivation to have voice will be inversely related to how much people see themselves as capable of providing meaningful input, in which case the positive effect of having voice is likely to be stronger among those with lower self-esteem.

Toward Reconciliation (in Cases Other Than Voice)

The preceding analysis may be particularly applicable to those instances in which process fairness is based on voice. As we saw, voice makes relevant people's beliefs about their competence to provide meaningful input, which in different ways may influence their motivation to have voice and hence the extent to which they are affected by voice. However, most other elements of process fairness do not make salient people's beliefs about their ability to provide meaningful input. Therefore, additional theorizing may be necessary to delineate the conditions under which fair process effects are shown more strongly by persons with higher or lower self-esteem when process fairness is not based on voice.

Toward that end, recall that outcome favorability was considered to be an exemplar of a broader category of factors that affect the extent to which people experience a threat to their well-being and, more specifically, to their self-esteem. In the face of a threat to self-esteem, people may become more susceptible to influence by information that is relevant to their self-esteem, such that they will react more positively (negatively) to information that shines favorably (unfavorably) on them relative to those who do not feel as self-threatened. Process fairness is one such source of information in that it conveys how people are viewed by the party enacting the process (e.g., whether they are viewed favorably by the enacting party, whether they are being included or excluded by the enacting party, etc.). In short, process fairness information is particularly relevant to people's sense of their *social* self-esteem, that is, the extent to which they believe that they are viewed favorably by others (Leary, 1999).

This reasoning suggests that process fairness information may be particularly influential when people are low in social self-esteem. In other words, to the extent that trait self-esteem is in reference to the social self (as opposed to being in reference to a more achievement-oriented basis of self-esteem, such as judgments of one's competence), it may be that process fairness effects will be more pronounced among those who are relatively low in self-esteem. Interestingly, in three previously referenced studies in which process fairness effects were shown to be stronger among those lower in trait self-esteem, the content of the self-esteem measures always was in reference to the social self, for example, "I worry about what other people think of me" (De Cremer, 2003; De Cremer et al., 2004; Vermunt et al., 2001).

In contrast, the content of the self-esteem measures was less social in at least some of the studies in which persons with high self-esteem showed stronger fair process effects. For example, in several of their studies Brockner et al. (1998) used the Rosenberg (1965) self-esteem scale, which is more of a measure of global self-worth (including sample items such as, "I feel that I am a person of worth, at least on an equal basis with others"). Wiesenfeld et al. (2007) used the Heatherton and Polivy (1991) state self-esteem scale in several of their studies, in which only a small portion of items referred to social self-esteem, and in another of the Wiesenfeld et al. studies the self-esteem measure consisted of Tafarodi and Swann's (2001) self-liking scale, which taps into people's evaluations of themselves rather than how they think they are viewed by others (e.g., "I feel great about who I am").

Moreover, recall the results of studies in which threat to self-esteem was experimentally manipulated (Miedema et al., 2006) and examined as a moderator of the fair process effect. In their Study 1, the effect of process fairness on perceptions of fairness was significantly stronger in the self-threat condition than in the no-threat control condition. In their Study 2, the effect of process fairness on perceptions of fairness and negative affect was greater in the self-threat condition relative to a condition in which participants' mortality had been made salient. A careful examination of the self-threat induction in these studies suggests that it was participants' *social* self-esteem that may have been manipulated. In Study 1, part of the self-threat induction consisted of asking participants to describe the emotions they experience when they think of other people believing that they (the participants) are not at all intelligent, whereas in Study 2 part of the self-threat induction consisted of having participants describe the emotions that arise in them when they think of other people judging them in a very negative way. In contrast, the Brockner et al. (1998) study that manipulated participants' self-perceptions did so more in the domain of perceived competence than in the arena of how appealing they were in the eyes of others. Specifically, some participants were led to believe that they were capable of providing meaningful input into an upcoming decision, whereas others were not. Brockner et al. found that participants with more favorable self-perceptions (i.e., those led to believe that they were more capable) showed a stronger fair process effect (i.e., were more influenced by the degree of voice that they had in the decision).

Thus, another factor that may affect the form of the moderating influence of self-esteem on the fair process effect is the nature of the self-esteem. The greater the "sociality" of the self-esteem (i.e., the more that it refers to people's beliefs about how they are evaluated by others), the more likely it may be for people with lower self-esteem to show a stronger fair process effect. Being low in social self-esteem increases the importance and hence the impact of information that is relevant to people's social self-esteem, such as whether they are treated with higher or lower process fairness.

Moreover, just as self-esteem may vary in its sociality, so may process fairness information differ in how much it is directly relevant to people's social self-esteem. Whereas all elements of process fairness symbolically convey the extent to which people are held in high regard, it is possible that certain determinants of process fairness communicate this message more directly than others. For example, if decisions are made transparently or on the basis of accurate information, then people may infer that they are respected by decision makers. However, they may be even more likely to infer that they are respected or held in high regard if decision makers treat them with a high degree of interactional justice (Bies, 1987). Colquitt (2001) suggested that one aspect of Bies's original conceptualization of interactional justice, namely, interpersonal sensitivity, is virtually synonymous with respectful interpersonal treatment.

In several of the studies in which process fairness effects were more pronounced among individuals with lower self-esteem (De Cremer et al., 2004; Vermunt et al., 2001), not only was it social self-esteem that was measured, but also process fairness consisted of factors that were likely to be highly relevant to people's social self-esteem. More specifically, in both the De Cremer et al. and the Vermunt et al. studies, process fairness referred to the interpersonal sensitivity with which they were treated. De Cremer et al. used Colquitt's (2001) four-item measure of interpersonal sensitivity (e.g., "To what extent have you been treated with respect"), and Vermunt et al.'s measure consisted of very similar items that stressed the relational component of procedures, such as those used by Tyler et al. (1996). In contrast, the studies in which persons with high self-esteem showed stronger fair process effects tended not to operationalize process fairness on the basis of the interpersonal sensitivity with which participants were treated (Brockner et al., 1998; Wiesenfeld et al., 2007).

In the De Cremer (2003) studies, in which individuals with lower self-esteem showed stronger fair process effects, the process fairness element consisted of the consistency with which the authority made decisions. In the first of three studies, De Cremer provided evidence to suggest that the authority's consistency influenced people's inferences about how favorably they were regarded by the authority. Participants read a vignette in which they were asked to imagine that their supervisor was either inconsistent (thereby making it difficult to know the standards the supervisor used to make decisions) or consistent (in which case it was not difficult to know the standards the supervisor was using). Participants reported that they would feel a greater degree of self-uncertainty in their relationship with the supervisor who was inconsistent rather than consistent.

If the degree of self-uncertainty experienced in the relationship with the authority reflects people's beliefs about how favorably they are regarded by the authority (such that greater self-uncertainty is akin to believing that one is regarded less favorably by the authority), then it stands to reason that the influence of the authority's consistency will be greater among those with lower social self-esteem. In fact, this is precisely what De Cremer (2003) observed in his second and third studies. Rather than being asked to read about the consistency with which the authority made decisions (as had been done in De Cremer's first study), participants in both studies directly experienced the authority's decision-making consistency. Dependent variables included judgments of procedural fairness and participants' desire to replace the authority (in Study 2) and the extent to which they would feel badly about themselves in their interaction with the authority (in Study 3). All three measures showed that social self-esteem had a moderating influence on consistency, such that the tendency for participants to respond more favorably when the authority was consistent rather than inconsistent was exhibited to a greater extent by those with lower social self-esteem.

Whereas the preceding discussion identified several factors that may predispose the fair process effect to be stronger among persons with lower self-esteem, it is also important to consider the conditions under which the fair process effect may be exhibited to a greater extent by individuals with higher self-esteem. The mechanism accounting for the finding that voice effects are more pronounced among individuals with high self-esteem (Brockner et al., 1998) may be less applicable to other determinants of process fairness. As suggested, the receipt of voice may activate people's concerns about whether they are competent to provide meaningful input; other antecedents of process fairness may be less likely to make salient people's concerns about their personal competence.

However, the mechanism accounting for the stronger effects of voice among persons with higher self-esteem is not the only one that may explain why people with higher self-esteem exhibit stronger fair process effects. As Wiesenfeld et al. (2007) found, people's self-verification strivings also may explain why the positive effects of being treated with greater process fairness may be shown more strongly by individuals with higher self-esteem individuals. If so, then the conditions that heighten people's tendencies to engage in self-verification should be precisely those in which fair process effects should be more pronounced among individuals with higher self-esteem. For example, people are more likely to engage in self-verification to the extent that their self-views are firmly held (Swann, 1999). If people were to experience a situational or temporary threat to their self-esteem but then be treated by another person with high process fairness, they may be unlikely to be repelled by the other's high process fairness. If anything, after being situationally self-threatened people may be attracted to the other party who treated them with high process fairness, which may have provided them with a much-needed opportunity for self-enhancement.

When people are chronically low in self-esteem, however, self-verification strivings may be salient. As a result, they may be considerably less attracted to another party who treats them with high process fairness. Swann (1999) has found that to show the self-verification effect in which people with unfavorable self-conceptions are more attracted to those who evaluate them negatively rather than positively, it is necessary to select people at the extremely low end of a self-evaluative dimension, say, the bottom 20%. In other words, because most people evaluate themselves relatively positively, the bottom half of a distribution may not be sufficiently convinced of their negative self-appraisals to make self-verification their primary concern. Wiesenfeld et al. (2007) provided evidence that self-verification accounted for the tendency of people with lower self-esteem to show no fair process effect. Consistent with this reasoning, Wiesenfeld et al. examined participants who were one standard deviation above or below the mean in process fairness and *two* standard deviations above or below the mean in self-esteem.

Self-verification theory also posits that people's self-verification strivings are likely to be more pronounced in ongoing relationships (Swann, 1999). In more temporary relationships, people with negative self-conceptions may allow themselves to engage in self-enhancement when they receive positive evaluations from another. However, if the relationship is expected to endure, then people with negative self-conceptions may not feel that they can afford to deceive themselves by accepting positive (read: self-enhancing) information from another party; they may believe that such self-deception is only likely to be dashed in the future. Consistent with this reasoning, it should be noted that self-verification effects often have been tested for and observed in the context of ongoing relationships. For example, it has been shown that married people with low self-esteem reject spouses who see them positively. Relatedly, people are more likely to divorce partners who perceived them favorably to an excessive degree (Cast & Burke, 2002). Conceptually analogous results have been found among college roommates (Swann & Pelham, 2002). In each of these instances, regardless of the level of their self-evaluations, people were attracted to others who provided them with evaluations that confirmed their views of themselves and were repelled by others who did not.

This reasoning suggests that the interactive relationship between process fairness and self-esteem (in which the positive relationship between another party's process fairness and people's attraction toward that party is stronger among persons with higher self-esteem) should be more likely to emerge if people see themselves as having a relatively enduring relationship with the other party. This hypothesis was tested and confirmed in one of Wiesenfeld et al.'s (2007) studies, as illustrated in Figures 6.1 and 6.2. Among those who perceived their relationship with the organization to be more enduring, there was a significant interaction between process fairness and self-esteem, such that when self-esteem was high, process fairness was strongly and positively related to organizational commitment, whereas when self-esteem was

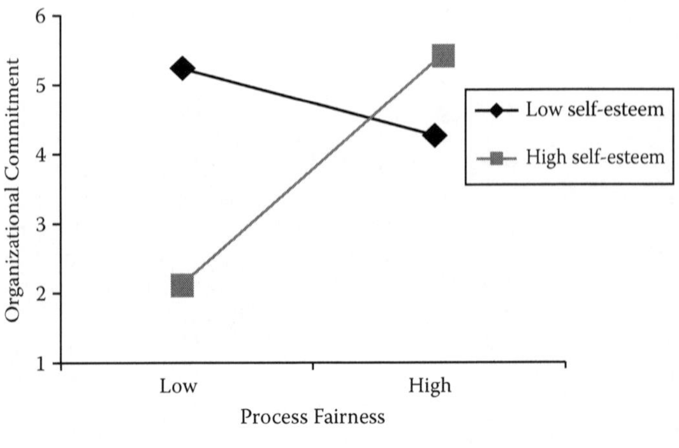

Figure 6.1 Organizational commitment as a function of self-esteem and process fairness among those who saw the relationship as more enduring (Wiesenfeld et al., 2007. From *Academy of Management Journal, 50,* 1235–1253. With permission.).

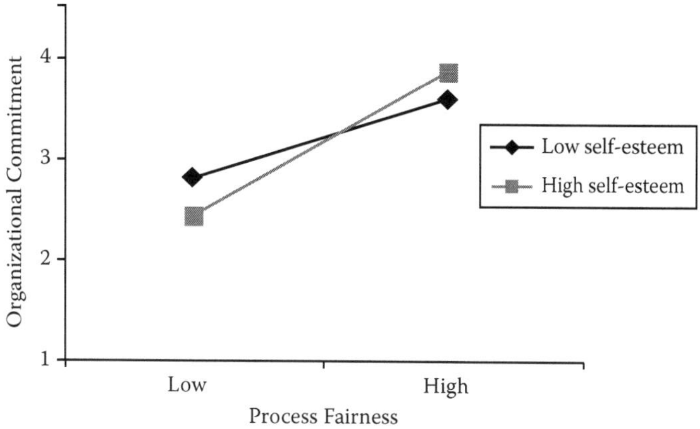

Figure 6.2 Organizational commitment as a function of self-esteem and process fairness among those who saw the relationship as less enduring (Wiesenfeld et al., 2007. From *Academy of Management Journal, 50,* 1235–1253. With permission.).

low, process fairness and organizational commitment were unrelated. No such interaction emerged, however, among those who did not see their relationship with the organization as relatively enduring. Rather, process fairness was positively related to organizational commitment for both people with high and people with low self-esteem.

In summary, people's reactions to the self-evaluative information conveyed by process fairness may be affected by two fundamental motivations: the desire for self-enhancement and the desire for self-verification. When self-enhancement holds sway, the fair process effect may be more pronounced among those with lower self-esteem (especially, lower social self-esteem) because they are likely to be more hungry for information that enhances their social self relative to their counterparts higher in social self-esteem. When self-verification predominates, the fair process effect is likely to be more pronounced among those with higher self-esteem because being treated with high process fairness is more self-verifying for those who view themselves positively. Thus, whether fair process effects are exhibited to a greater extent by persons with lower self-esteem or persons with higher self-esteem may depend on the relative importance of people's self-enhancement motive versus their desire for self-verification.

One rather broad-reaching factor that may reflect the significance that people assign to these two motives is the extent to which they are open to having their self-conceptions changed. When people are less open to having their self-concepts changed, self-verification may prevail, whereas when they are more open, self-enhancement may carry the day. Openness to self-concept change in turn may be captured or caused by numerous factors. For example, having an extremely positive or extremely negative self-view is likely to reflect less openness. So are self-views that are maintained with a high degree of certainty. Moreover, people may be less open to self-concept change (i.e., they may believe that it is important to be seen by others in the same way that they see themselves) in relatively enduring relationships to ease the process of interacting with the other party. After all, if others with whom we have enduring relationships do not see us in the way that we see ourselves, then we will constantly have to negotiate with them about what we can or cannot do, what we like or dislike, and so on. This may explain the somewhat paradoxical finding that people with more negative self-evaluations may actually be more attracted to others who evaluate them negatively rather than positively (Swann, 1999). In contrast, if the relationship is not expected to endure, then people with negative self-evaluations may show more of a self-enhancement effect, preferring to be with others who evaluate them more positively (e.g., treat them with higher process fairness).

This reasoning suggests that other factors that either reflect or have an influence on people's openness to self-concept change also may dictate the nature of the interactive relationship between process fairness and trait self-esteem. For example, certain elements of the big five personality dimension, "openness to experience" (Goldberg, 1993), may be influential. Open people prefer novelty to familiarity. They are less likely to be resistant to change, which may include more of a willingness to "reinvent" themselves or at least see themselves differently. Moreover, people's openness to self-concept change may grow out of more general beliefs they maintain about the malleability of human nature. According to Dweck and Leggett (1988), some people believe that human nature (including their self-concepts) is basically fixed ("entity theorists"), whereas others believe that it is more malleable ("incrementalists"). For example, entity theorists are more likely than incrementalists to endorse the statement, "The kind of person that someone is, is something basic about them, and it can't be changed very much."

Future research may test for the moderating effects of both openness to experience and belief in the malleability of human nature on the interactive relationship between process fairness and trait self-esteem. I would expect the interactive relationship between process fairness and trait self-esteem set forth by self-verification theory (in which people with high self-esteem show a stronger fair process effect than individuals with low self-esteem) to be more pronounced among those who are less open or among those who are less likely to believe in the malleability of human nature. Put differently, those who are more open to experience or those who are more likely to believe in the malleability of human nature may be likely to respond more positively to being treated with higher process fairness, perhaps even more so if they are relatively low in (social) self-esteem.

Further research that dictates the form of the interactive relationship between process fairness and trait self-esteem represents yet another opportunity for justice scholars to inform other literatures. Social psychologists have provided compelling evidence that people's beliefs and behaviors often are in the service of satisfying their desire to feel good about themselves (self-enhancement) and their desire to be known (self-verification, which in turn reflects a broader desire for self-consistency; Leary, 1999; Swann, 1999). Although fundamental, these two motives are conceptually distinct, and as we saw in the case of people with more negative self-evaluations, they give rise to very different effects. Rather than concerning themselves with the question of whether one motive is summarily more important than the other, future researchers may do well to delineate the conditions under which (or the people for whom) self-enhancement and self-verification or self-consistency may be more versus less influential. Thus, future research that examines when process fairness will have more of an effect on those who are higher or lower in trait self-esteem may inform the important and long-standing question of when different self-related motives are more versus less likely to be activated (Jones, 1973; Shrauger, 1975).

Relatedly, for a variety of reasons, including their greater need for self-enhancement, people with low self-esteem often have been found to be more susceptible to influence by events in their external environments relative to their counterparts with high self-esteem; I have referred to this elsewhere as the "plasticity effect" (Brockner, 1988). Thus, research that delineates when people with high versus low self-esteem are more affected by the process fairness with which they have been treated may deepen our understanding of the plasticity effect, for example, by identifying when the opposite results (i.e., in which people with high self-esteem are more affected by process fairness) may be apt to occur.

Outcome Favorability as a Symbol of Alarm

In trying to broaden the scope of the process–outcome interaction effect, I have portrayed level of outcome favorability as a proxy for how much people experience threat to their economic or psychological well-being. Particularly in response to unfavorable outcomes, people use process fairness information to evaluate the degree of threat that they experience or to determine how to cope with it. That is, since people perceive greater threat when outcomes are relatively unfavorable, process fairness and outcome favorability interact such that the fair process effect is stronger when outcomes are more unfavorable. This reasoning suggests that other factors besides outcome favorability that represent threat to well-being (which also can be addressed by process fairness information) should similarly have a moderating influence on process fairness, such as uncertainty (Van den Bos & Lind, 2002), mortality salience (Van den Bos et al., 2005), and threat to people's self-esteem (Miedema et al., 2006), especially their social self-esteem.

In all of these instances, however, people were exposed to (or were asked to contemplate) information that actually threatened their well-being, such as an unfavorable outcome or writing about how they would feel if they thought about their mortality. A series of studies suggested that it may not even be necessary for people to be exposed to or even to contemplate information that actually threatens their well-being for fair process effects to be heightened. Merely encountering cues that symbolically represent danger or alarm may do the trick. This prediction is grounded in the literatures on close relationships and social neuroscience, which posit that exposure to threatening events activates a "human alarm system," which leads people to be more vigilant about (and therefore more susceptible to influence by) information that enables them to make sense of or cope with their environments (Eisenberger, Lieberman, & Williams, 2003).

Van den Bos, Ham, et al. (2008) reported a series of studies in which they examined whether exposing people to stimuli that are merely symbolic of alarm has a moderating influence on process fairness. In one study, participants looked at their computer screens for 1 minute prior to being exposed to process fairness information. Half of the participants saw an exclamation mark on their computer screen (the alarm condition), whereas the other half faced a blank computer screen (no alarm condition). Participants then read a vignette in which they were asked to imagine that they had applied for a job, and that they had gone through a standard selection procedure in which they were treated with higher or lower process fairness. Whereas participants generally rated the process as more fair in the high process fairness condition than in the low process fairness condition, this tendency was significantly more pronounced when participants had previously been exposed to the cue that symbolized alarm (the exclamation mark).

Van den Bos, Ham et al. (2008) conducted two other studies in which distributive (rather than process) fairness was experimentally manipulated, along with the presence or absence of cues symbolic of alarm. In one study, participants read a vignette in which they were treated with higher or lower distributive fairness. The manipulation of the alarm-related cue was similar to that in the first study, with one exception. In the no alarm condition, rather than facing a blank computer screen for the minute prior to reading the vignette, participants saw a screen in which the elements of the exclamation mark were scrambled. A typical exclamation mark consists of a vertical line with a point directly below it. In the no alarm condition, participants saw a horizontal line with a point directly below it (at the midpoint of the line). Consistent with the results of their first study, Van den Bos et al. found that participants' judgments of distributive justice were significantly more affected by the manipulation of distributive justice in the alarm condition than in the no alarm condition.

In a third study Van den Bos, Ham et al. (2008) varied the presence or absence of a different cue symbolic of alarm. Participants were approached by an experimenter while they were walking in a shopping area in a Dutch city. An orange light was directly behind the experimenter. In the alarm condition, the orange light flashed on and off, whereas in the no alarm condition it was always off. Participants then read a brief vignette (different from the one used in the previous studies) in which they were asked to imagine that they had been treated with higher or lower distributive fairness. Again, the effect of manipulated fairness on perceived fairness was significantly greater in the alarm condition than in the no alarm condition.

Importantly, Van den Bos, Ham et al. (2008) provided additional evidence in all three studies that participants were more alert in the alarm condition than in the no alarm condition. Specifically, in the studies in which the alarm cue consisted of the exclamation mark, participants took less time to make their fairness ratings in the alarm condition than in the no alarm condition. Moreover, in the study in which the alarm cue consisted of the flashing light, participants reported themselves to be significantly more alert and attentive in the alarm condition than in the no alarm condition.

An important task for future research is to evaluate whether merely exposing people to alarm-related cues heightens the influence of fairness information in contexts in which they actually experience more versus less fair treatment rather than merely reading about it in a hypothetical vignette, which was the case in the Van den Bos, Ham et al. (2008) studies. Nevertheless, the findings already in hand provide further support for some relatively novel ways of conceptualizing the process–outcome interaction. First, they provide additional evidence that the interactive relationship between process fairness and outcome favorability may generalize to circumstances in which the process and outcome factors do not refer to the same event. Chapter 2 also described studies showing process–outcome interaction effects in which the two dimensions referred to different events. For instance, Garonzik et al. (2000) found that the favorability of expatriates' nonwork outcomes (e.g., how well they and their family members had adjusted to their living conditions) interacted with the process fairness with which organizational authorities made decisions to influence how much the expatriates were thinking seriously about departing prematurely from their overseas assignments. Elovainio et al. (2007) discovered that people's experiences of process fairness in the workplace interacted with whether a family member had recently suffered a serious illness to influence their sickness-related absences from work. Siegel et al. (2005) reported that work–life conflict interacted with employees' perceptions of the process fairness with which organizational authorities *generally* made decisions to influence employees' organizational commitment.

These findings suggest that outcome favorability may have "carry-over" effects, leading it to interact with process fairness even when the two have different referents. To cite yet another example of a carryover effect, employees who join an organization after having experienced an unfavorable outcome in their previous work situation (such as being abruptly dismissed) may be particularly vigilant about the extent to which the new work environment is psychologically safe. One indicator or determinant of the safety of the new work environment is the process fairness shown by organizational authorities. Thus, new hires joining an organization on the heels of an unpleasant departure from their former employers may be more vigilant about and hence more influenced by the process fairness exhibited by their new employers relative to new hires who join in the absence of an unpleasant departure from their former employers.

In all of these instances, however, outcome favorability is represented in concrete ways (i.e., how well expatriates and their family members had adjusted to their new environments, whether a family member had encountered a serious illness, the extent to which employees were experiencing work–life conflict, and whether people had a bad experience with their former employers). The Van den Bos, Ham et al. (2008) findings suggest that outcome favorability may have a moderating influence on process fairness even when the two dimensions have different referents *and* when people cognitively represent outcome favorability in symbolic rather than in concrete ways.

The conceptual foundation for the Van den Bos, Ham et al. (2008) studies also is reminiscent of how it may be possible to account for the process–outcome interaction by invoking the Lazarus and Folkman (1984) model of stress and strain. As suggested in Chapter 2, the primary appraisal (pertaining to the experience of felt threat) may interact with the secondary appraisal (of whether people think anything can be done to control or counteract the threat) to influence their psychological strain. Indeed, the conceptual rationale put forth by Van den Bos et al. in their introduction seems to draw on the Lazarus and Folkman reasoning. As they wrote, "The alarm system is responsible for detecting cues that might be harmful to survival and, after activation, for recruiting attention and coping responses to minimize threat" (p. 203). The symbol of alarm that Van den Bos et al. varied may be a proxy for the primary appraisal (in which people cognitively represent the experience of threat), whereas the process fairness manipulation may be a proxy for the secondary appraisal (which shapes people's inferences about how much it is possible to control or counteract the threat). Again, however, the Van den Bos et al. findings suggest that merely symbolically representing the primary appraisal of felt threat may be sufficient for it to interact with factors that reflect the secondary appraisal, such as process fairness.

Yet another important implication of the Van den Bos, Ham et al. (2008) findings is that they call attention to a distinction between two broad categories of factors that make people more versus less affected by process fairness. On the one hand, certain factors may influence the magnitude of fair process effects by polarizing (i.e., inducing more extreme) perceptions of process fairness. For example, in the Van den Bos et al. studies fairness was both experimentally manipulated as an independent variable and assessed as a dependent variable (process fairness was examined in one of the three studies described here, and distributive fairness was examined in the other two). Whereas the manipulations of fairness within a given study were identical in the alarm and no alarm conditions, they were *perceived* more strongly (i.e., with greater extremity) in the alarm conditions than in the no alarm conditions. Van den Bos et al. did not include any other dependent variables besides perceived fairness. However, it stands to reason that if (1) certain conditions cause fairness to be perceived more extremely and (2) fairness is known to influence subsequent feelings (e.g., negative affect) or behaviors (e.g., willingness to support a decision), then the same conditions that cause fairness to be perceived more strongly also should have more of an influence on subsequent feelings or behaviors. For example, Miedema et al. (2006) found that an experimental manipulation of fairness (in this case, distributive fairness) was experienced more strongly when participants had been self-threatened relative to when their mortality had been made salient, and that their negative affect was more strongly affected by the fairness manipulation when they had been self-threatened relative to when their mortality had been made salient. One possibility is that the manipulation of fairness interacted with self-threat to influence perceptions of fairness, which in turn influenced negative affect.

On the other hand, it could be differences in people's *reactions to* (rather than differences in their *perceptions of*) fairness that cause process fairness effects to be more pronounced under certain conditions than others. For example, in many, if not most, of the studies testing for the moderating influence of uncertainty on process fairness, the results on manipulation check measures actually showed that people's perceptions of process fairness are *not* more influenced by the manipulation of process fairness when uncertainty has been made salient relative to other conditions (mortality salience or other types of control conditions; Van den Bos et al., 2005). However, those same studies showed that when uncertainty was aroused, the manipulation of process fairness had more of an impact on the ultimate dependent variable (e.g., negative affect) relative to when uncertainty was not aroused.

Thus, unfavorable outcomes may heighten the *influence* of process fairness without necessarily affecting people's *perceptions* of process fairness. Throughout the book we have considered ways in which people may use process fairness information for a variety of sense-making purposes (e.g., to determine the nature of their long-term outcomes, to determine how much to hold the authority as responsible for their outcomes, and so on). Since these sense-making concerns are likely to be instantiated more strongly by unfavorable outcomes than by favorable outcomes, the *effects of perceived process fairness* may be more pronounced when outcomes are unfavorable, even though people's *perceptions of process fairness* may be equivalent to those experienced when outcomes are favorable.

Of course, the two mechanisms accounting for the influence of process fairness are not mutually exclusive. For example, unfavorable outcomes may heighten the effect of process fairness by eliciting more extreme perceptions of process fairness or by leading people to have stronger reactions to their existing perceptions. Much like exclamation marks and flashing lights, the receipt of unfavorable outcomes may activate the human alarm system, causing people to be more sensitized to the process fairness information that they encounter, such that a fair process seems all the more fair, and an unfair process seems all the more unfair. Alternatively, unfavorable outcomes may motivate people to make greater use of the process fairness information that they encounter. Whereas these two mechanisms are not mutually exclusive, they are conceptually distinct. Hence, it behooves us to delineate the extent to which one mechanism, the other, or both may be at play.

More specifically, in studies in which process fairness is operationalized (i.e., manipulated or measured) through its various antecedents (voice, accuracy, consistency, etc.), it is worth examining whether the impact of these elements on people's perceptions of process fairness varies as a function of other factors (e.g., outcome favorability, uncertainty, and mortality salience). Suppose researchers were to find a moderating influence of outcome favorability on the relationship between the elements of process fairness (as independent variables) and people's perceptions of process fairness (as dependent variables), such that the relationship between the elements of process fairness and perceptions of process fairness was stronger when outcomes were relatively unfavorable. Furthermore, suppose that in the same study the elements of process fairness interacted with outcome favorability to influence one of the typical dependent variables (e.g., people's willingness to support an authority's decision). If the elements of process fairness interacted with outcome favorability to influence both perceived fairness and support for the decision, then further analyses should be conducted to evaluate whether perceptions of fairness mediated the interactive effect of the elements of process fairness and outcome favorability on support for the decision. Alternatively, if an interaction effect emerged on the measure of support but not on the measure of perceived fairness, then we would be left to conclude that outcome favorability influenced people's *reactions to* their process fairness perceptions without necessarily influencing the perceptions themselves.

Substituting for Process Fairness and Outcome Favorability Simultaneously

In another section of this chapter (pp. 201–217) in which we considered why process fairness had a moderating influence on outcome favorability, we identified many other factors that may interact with outcome favorability in the same way that process fairness does (e.g., judgments of the authority's responsibility for their outcomes, trust in organizational authorities, etc.). I suggested that substituting any of these factors for process fairness should lead to an analogous interaction effect with outcome favorability. For example, when for whatever reason people judge an authority to be more responsible for their unfavorable outcomes, they should be more likely to react negatively to the authority and the authority's decisions (Folger et al., 1983). Similarly, when people are less trusting of organizational authorities, their attitudes toward them are more likely to be affected by outcome favorability (Brockner et al., 1997).

Subsequent sections (pp. 224–227 and 246–251), which analyzed why outcome favorability has a moderating influence on process fairness, identified other factors that interact with process fairness in the way that outcome favorability does (e.g., mortality salience, threat to the self, and symbols of alarm). Thus, substituting any of these factors for outcome favorability produces an analogous interaction effect with process fairness. For example, threat to the self interacts with process fairness, such that when people feel more self-threatened they are more influenced by subsequent process fairness information (Miedema et al., 2006).

Whereas different factors may substitute for process fairness in having a moderating influence on outcome favorability and different factors may substitute for outcome favorability in having a moderating influence on process fairness, the conceptual advance is the same: locating the interactive relationships between process fairness and outcome favorability in a broader theoretical space. Moreover, both sets of analyses suggested that it is possible to substitute other factors for *either* process fairness *or* outcome favorability to generate interaction effects accounted for by the same mechanisms underlying the interactive relationships between process fairness and outcome favorability.

An intriguing implication of the self-esteem mechanism of terror management effects is that it may be possible to substitute other factors for *both* process fairness and outcome favorability simultaneously. For example, making people more or less aware of their mortality, like outcome favorability, may influence the extent to which they experience a threat to their sense of self. All else being equal, people are likely to feel more self-threatened when their mortality has been made salient and when their outcomes are unfavorable rather than favorable. Those who are feeling more self-threatened (who presumably are more in need of self-enhancing information) are therefore likely to be more affected by self-evaluative information, for better or worse. Process fairness is one source of self-evaluative information (such that people's sense of self is more likely to be enhanced when process fairness is relatively high), but it is not the only source. When people's mortality has been made salient or, more generally, when they are experiencing a threat to self, factors other than process fairness (which also affect people's self-evaluations) should have effects similar to those elicited by process fairness.

In short, process fairness has certain psychological effects but so do other factors. Outcome favorability may elicit other types of psychological effects but so do other factors. One way to broaden the scope of the interactive relationship between process fairness and outcome favorability even further is by showing that other factors besides process fairness (which have the same psychological effects as process fairness) may interact with other factors besides outcome favorability (which have the same psychological effects as outcome favorability). In other words, the interactive relationship between process fairness and outcome favorability may simply be an exemplar of interaction effects produced by factors from two *different* and *more general* categories of variables.

For example, Van den Bos et al. (2005, Experiment 2) examined the effects of process fairness (voice) on felt anger under three different conditions: one in which mortality had been made salient, one in which uncertainty had been made salient (by asking participants to write about the emotions that the thought of being uncertain arouses in them), and a control condition in which neither mortality nor uncertainty had been made salient. Relative to what was observed in the control condition, the anger of those whose mortality had been made salient was more affected by process fairness (i.e., whether they were given voice). Interestingly, the anger of those for whom uncertainty was made salient was even more affected by voice relative to those for whom mortality had been made salient. If the effect of voice were due to its self-evaluative implications, then other factors with self-evaluative implications should elicit the same effects as voice. That is, when mortality has been made salient, and perhaps even more so when uncertainty has been made salient, these other factors should have the same consequences as voice.

In fact, Van den Bos et al. (2005) conducted further research that provided a partial test of this reasoning. In one study, participants had either uncertainty or their mortality made salient to them (which could be thought of as a substitute for outcome favorability in the sense that people may have felt more self-threatened by uncertainty than by mortality salience, given the previous finding that the former elicited more of an effect of voice on anger than did the latter). Subsequently, they read a passage that either praised or derogated the group of which they were members (which could be thought of as a substitute for process fairness in that people were likely to feel more positively evaluated when their group was praised). According to social identity theory (e.g., Brewer & Gardner, 1996), people define and evaluate themselves partly on the basis of the collectives to which they belong. Therefore, people are likely to experience greater self-enhancement when their group is praised rather than derogated. The main dependent variable was the extent to which people agreed with the passage (which had either praised or derogated their group). When their mortality had been made salient, participants were significantly more likely to agree with the passage that praised rather than derogated their group. Moreover, this effect was even stronger when uncertainty had been made salient. Unfortunately for the present purposes, the study did not include a control condition in which potential sources of self-threat (such as mortality and uncertainty) had not been made salient. In the absence of self-threat, I would expect the effect of the nature of the passage (i.e., whether it praised or derogated people's group) on agreement with the passage to be significantly weaker than that observed when mortality and uncertainty had been made salient. If such findings were to occur, they would provide even more definitive evidence that the interactive relationship between process fairness and outcome favorability may be part of a broader set of interactive relationships between the psychological dimensions instigated by outcome favorability (e.g., the degree to which the self is threatened) and process fairness (e.g., the degree to which the self is subsequently enhanced [when process fairness is high] or demeaned [when process fairness is low]).

Even more generally, the interactive effect of outcome favorability and process fairness (on at least certain dependent variables) may exemplify Lazarus and Folkman's (1984) two-factor model of psychological strain. As suggested in Chapter 2, the extent to which people experience psychological strain may be an interactive function of (1) how much they feel threatened and (2) how much they believe that they will be able to deal effectively with the threat. In the presence of felt threat (e.g., when outcomes are relatively unfavorable), factors that influence people's perceptions of being able to deal with it (e.g., process fairness) become far more consequential than when threat is not perceived. Hence, outcome favorability (as a proxy for primary appraisal) and process fairness (as a proxy for secondary appraisal) interact, especially on measures of psychological strain, such as negative affect. Along these lines, it is noteworthy that in many of the studies cited in this section for which I have tried to delineate why outcome favorability has a moderating influence on process fairness, the dependent variable has indeed consisted of negative affect (Miedema et al., 2006; Van den Bos, 2001; Van den Bos & Miedema, 2000; Van den Bos et al., 2005). Viewed through the lens of Lazarus and Folkman's theory, then, the interactive relationship between outcome favorability and process fairness, at least as it manifests itself on measures of psychological strain, may be reflective of a more general interactive relationship between primary appraisal and secondary appraisal.

It is worth keeping in mind, however, that a similar interactive relationship between outcome favorability and process fairness (in which high process fairness reduces the effect of outcome favorability) also has frequently emerged on dependent variables that do not obviously reflect psychological strain, such as people's willingness to support decisions, decision makers, and institutions (see Chapters 2 and 3 as well as Brockner & Wiesenfeld, 1996). In other words, it seems unlikely that the tendency for high process fairness to reduce the influence of outcome favorability, relative to when process fairness is low, can be entirely explained by Lazarus and Folkman's (1984) two-factor model of stress.

CHAPTER SUMMARY

This chapter sought to locate the process–outcome interaction effects in broader conceptual spaces. Chapters 2 and 3 considered how high process fairness reduces the influence of outcome favorability on people's support for decisions, decision makers, and institutions, as well on their experience of psychological strain, relative to when process fairness is low. In addressing what it is about process fairness that is responsible for the findings described in Chapters 2 and 3, we see that other factors may similarly have a moderating influence on outcome favorability, such as the extent to which people hold the other as responsible for their unfavorable outcomes and the extent to which people are optimistic about their longer-term outcomes, to name a few. Chapter 4 showed that high process fairness may heighten the effect of outcome favorability on people's self-evaluations relative to when process fairness is low. In considering the reasons for the interaction effect covered in Chapter 4, we identified other factors that were expected to behave similarly to process fairness in interacting with outcome favorability to influence people's self-evaluations, such as their tendencies to see themselves as personally responsible for their outcomes.

Another way to describe the interactive relationship between process fairness and outcome favorability set forth in Chapters 2 and 3 is that the fair process effect is more likely to emerge when people's outcomes are relatively unfavorable. People use process fairness information in a variety of ways to make sense of and adapt to their environments. Moreover, they generally are more motivated to make sense of their environments in the face of threats to their economic and psychological well-being. If outcome favorability serves as a proxy for threat to well-being, such that people feel more threatened when their outcomes are relatively unfavorable, then other factors that elicit threats to well-being (that process fairness information is well-suited to address), such as mortality salience or uncertainty, should behave similarly to outcome favorability in their moderating influence on the fair process effect. Moreover, we saw that a heightening of the fair process effect may not even require people to be subjected to an actual threat to their well-being. Studies have suggested that the presence of abstract symbols reflecting alarm has a moderating influence on process fairness.

In the course of considering why fair process effects tend to be stronger in the face of unfavorable outcomes, this chapter also identified an intriguing inconsistency in the justice literature, namely, whether individuals with low or high self-esteem are more likely to exhibit fair process effects. Given that previous studies have supported both tendencies (reviewed here), I described the kind of further research that may help to reconcile these conflicting results. Finally, I attempted to broaden the scope of the interactive relationships between process fairness and outcome favorability by showing how analyzing them helps to forge connections between justice theory and other literatures in social and organizational psychology, including attribution theory, trust, regulatory focus theory, terror management theory, and self-verification theory.

CHAPTER

7

Practical Applications

INTRODUCTION

Whereas the preceding chapters emphasized the conceptual and empirical importance of the interactive relationships between process fairness and outcome favorability, this chapter deals with their practical implications. In particular, I consider how theory and research may be brought to bear on matters about which practitioners are likely to care. Of course, how we academics can best make connections with practitioners is a long-standing question of considerable complexity and significance. In recent years, writers such as Malcolm Gladwell (the author of *Blink*), Daniel Goleman (the author of *Working With Emotional Intelligence*), and James Surowiecki (the author of *The Wisdom of Crowds*) have been able to distill the essence of well-conceived but somewhat technical theory and research into works that are accessible to the more general public. Furthermore, several organizational scholars (e.g., Max Bazerman, Chip Heath, and Jeffrey Pfeffer) have written trade book versions of their and others' academic work in an attempt to make the ideas of academics known to larger audiences, including practitioners of management.

It is beyond the scope of this book to delineate how researchers may cross the practice divide most effectively; for a more detailed discussion of this matter, see the October 2007 issue of the *Academy of Management Review*. It seems safe to say, however, that if we are not working on matters that practitioners care about, whether we can cross the divide is not likely to be consequential. Hence, this chapter considers some of the more attention-worthy practical considerations implicit in the interactive relationships between outcome favorability and process fairness.

Among the parties who most stand to benefit by drawing on the practical implications of the interaction effects are (1) people in positions of authority (e.g., managers in work organizations), who are trying to gain support for their decisions, themselves, and the institutions that they represent, and (2) those who are affected by the authorities' decisions (e.g., the direct reports of those managers). In seminars with executive audiences, I often show them the process–outcome interaction effect illustrated in Figure 1.1 (see Chapter 1) and engage them in dialogue about how such findings may be applicable to their work. They always "get it," albeit in different ways.

Some focus on the message that high outcome favorability reduces the impact of process fairness relative to when outcomes are unfavorable. Consistent with the age-old adage, "all's well that ends well," the takeaway for these executives is that as long as they can give their people the outcomes they want, they do not need to attend *as much* to how they go about doing so. Implementing decisions with high process fairness often takes time and psychological energy, which may be in short supply for decision-making authorities. For example, allowing people to have input may slow a decision-making process, as may the interactional fairness elements of providing explanations or treating people with dignity and respect. I recently attended a leadership lecture given by a senior executive in the Fire Department of New York. In a semi-humorous defense of the sometimes-brusque behavior of firefighters when they are in the "heat of battle," this executive said something to the effect of, if we are doing something as important as saving people's lives, we don't have to concern ourselves with how courteously or politely we behave when doing so.

Other managers focus on the message that high process fairness reduces the influence of outcome favorability relative to when process fairness is low. In other words, the takeaway is that if the process is done fairly they do not have to concern themselves as much with whether people will be satisfied with the outcomes of the decision. Given that it could be quite economically costly to implement decisions with high outcome favorability, the practical relevance of this observation virtually speaks for itself. In short, whereas I have yet to hear executives utter the words, "interactive relationship between outcome favorability and process fairness," they nevertheless are able to conceptualize the interaction effect in ways that are meaningful to them.

At first blush, these two ways in which executives assign meaning to the interaction effect depicted in Figure 1.1 seem to suggest that outcome favorability and process fairness are interchangeable, in that implementing decisions with a high level of one of these dimensions reduces the need to do so with a high level of the other dimension. However, there is more to it than that, which managers also are quick to realize. Usually, the economic costs of giving many people the outcomes that they want far outweigh the economic costs of implementing decisions to many people with high process fairness. Thus, when done on a large-scale basis, the enactment of high outcome favorability is usually much more cost prohibitive than is implementing decisions with high process fairness. This is an important consideration for managers, whose jobs, after all, often entail gaining the greatest employee support in ways that are least financially costly to their organizations (Brockner, 2006).

CHAPTER OVERVIEW

Drawing on empirical evidence, I begin by making the business case for why it is important for managers to practice high process fairness. Studies examining the interaction effect set forth in Chapters 2 and 3 contribute mightily to this case. They show that particularly in the face of unfavorable outcomes, high process fairness (which may be relatively inexpensive financially) engenders employee attitudes and behaviors that contribute positively to the bottom line. The next section of the chapter elaborates on a paradox embedded in the preceding sentence, that is, if high process fairness in the face of unfavorable outcomes makes such good business sense, then why is high process fairness not practiced even more regularly? Drawing on expectancy theory, I cite a variety of motivational forces that may impede the practice of high process fairness. The emerging picture is one in which managers may be experiencing a good deal of ambivalence. On the one hand, practicing high process fairness is both a business imperative and a moral imperative. On the other hand, managers are subjected to a host of forces that make it difficult for them to practice high process fairness.

Given these conflicting influences, I next consider some of the individual and organizational factors that make managers more versus less likely to exhibit high process fairness. The chapter concludes by considering two points of intrigue: (1) Managers are likely to experience a dilemma when they have to deliver unfavorable outcomes. On the one hand, meting out unfavorable outcomes with an unfair process may cause the recipients to feel resentful towards management. On the other hand, doling out unfavorable outcomes with a fair process may cause the recipients to feel badly about themselves. (2) It seems likely that enacting high process fairness may become more important in the future than it is now (and it is hardly unimportant now). Given the technological advances that have made it easier to record and publicize people's behavior, the stakes associated with whether people in authority positions exhibit high process fairness may be even greater in the years ahead.

PRACTICING HIGH PROCESS FAIRNESS: MAKING THE BUSINESS CASE

Whereas some managers readily see how the process–outcome interaction has applied relevance, others may need a bit more persuading.

For example, it is one thing to say that high process fairness does not cost much (relative to high outcome favorability). It is another thing to illustrate how managers and the organizations that they represent stand to benefit by planning and implementing decisions with high process fairness. Fortunately, the latter type of evidence is beginning to build, based on studies examining or related to the interactive relationship between outcome favorability and process fairness considered in Chapters 2 and 3. Some of these studies showed how high process fairness helps to "soften blows" that would otherwise have a negative impact on the organization's bottom line. Other studies suggested that once outcome favorability has reached a moderate level, companies may be better advised to focus on high process fairness than to enact the typically more expensive strategy of trying to provide outcomes that are more than moderately favorable. I explain both of these points further.

High Process Fairness as Blow Softener

Organizations sometimes inflict unfavorable outcomes on their employees, which could lead employees to respond in ways that are economically harmful to the organization. By reducing the sting associated with unfavorable outcomes, high process fairness makes people less likely to engage in retaliatory behaviors that may be costly to the organization.

Employee Dismissals and Wrongful Termination

Lind, Greenberg, Scott, and Welchans (2000) found that one of the strongest predictors of whether employees file a wrongful termination lawsuit is their perception of the fairness with which the termination process was implemented. The more that employees felt that their former managers (1) were concerned about being fair, (2) were sympathetic to their needs, (3) explained the reasons for the termination, and (4) were honest and up-front in dealing with them, the less likely they were to file suit. More specifically, only 1% of ex-employees who felt that they were treated with high process fairness (in which they gave ratings of 5 on a 5-point scale) filed a wrongful termination lawsuit. However, those who believed that they were not treated with process fairness (those who gave ratings of 1 on the same 5-point scale) filed lawsuits at a much greater rate: 17%.

Based on a 20-year-old (and hence conservative) estimate of what it costs a company to defend itself against a wrongful termination suit ($80,000), for every 100 employees that a company dismisses, the expected cost savings of practicing high process fairness is $1,280,000. This figure is calculated as the difference in expected costs when process fairness is low ($1,360,000; i.e., $80,000 times 17) versus high ($80,000; i.e., $80,000 times 1). Moreover, inflation during these past 20 years alone would cause the $80,000 figure to swell to more than $120,000 today. Of course, what is less clear is the financial cost of practicing high process fairness in the termination process. Given the nature of high process fairness in this study (e.g., expressing genuine concern to the dismissed employees and treating them with dignity and respect), it seems quite likely that the costs of enacting high process fairness are considerably lower than $1,280,000 for every 100 dismissed employees (or, nearly $13,000 for each dismissed employee).

The relationship between process fairness and the filing of lawsuits is not limited to exchanges between employers and their former employees. Customers also are more likely to file suit against a service provider when they are not treated with process fairness. Levinson, Roter, Mullooly, Dull, and Frankel (1997) found that patients typically do not sue their doctors for malpractice simply because they believe that they received poor medical care. A more telling factor is whether the doctor took the time needed to explain his or her treatment plan (those less likely to be sued took 18.3 minutes with each patient whereas those more likely to be sued took 15.0 minutes, a mere difference of slightly more than 3 minutes) and to answer the patient's questions with care and concern, in short, to treat patients with high process fairness. In comparing the doctors who were more versus less likely to be sued for malpractice, Gladwell (2005) reported that, "There was no difference in the amount or quality of information they gave their patients; they didn't provide more details about medication or the patient's condition. The difference was entirely in *how* they talked to their patients" (p. 42; italics in original).

Pay Cuts, Employee Theft, and Voluntary Turnover

Whereas theft and turnover clearly differ (in that the former is unethical, whereas the latter usually is not), both are costly to an organization's bottom line. Theft is obviously costly. Moreover, a 2004 study by the Employment Policy Foundation showed that the average cost of turnover for a full-time worker in the private sector is more than $13,000 (and is many times larger than that among managers). Greenberg (1990a) studied the effects of process fairness on theft and turnover in the face of the unfavorable outcome of temporary pay cuts that employees had to endure in two manufacturing plants. Employees in one of the plants were treated with relatively little process fairness. A company vice president simply called a meeting at the end of the work week in which he took 15 minutes to announce the pay cut, explain why it was necessary, thank employees, and answer a few questions.

In the other plant, the *identical* pay cut was implemented with higher process fairness (Greenberg, 1990a). The meeting in which this pay cut was announced was run by the company president. Employees were told at that time that other cost-saving options had been considered, such as layoffs, but that the pay cuts were deemed to be the least unpalatable choice. Much like the doctors who were less likely to be sued for malpractice, the company president in this instance took more time to address employees' questions and concerns (the meeting lasted for 90 minutes rather than for 15). Furthermore, the company president repeatedly expressed regret about having to reduce employees' pay.

The results showed that the rate of both employee theft and voluntary turnover in the plant treated with higher process fairness was significantly less than that shown by those who had the same pay cut delivered with lower process fairness (Greenberg, 1990a). Again, it is difficult to assess the economic costs to the company to enact the pay cut with higher process fairness. However, it seems safe to say that a 90-minute meeting held by the company president (relative to the 15-minute meeting held by a vice president) more than paid for itself in the form of reducing employee theft and voluntary turnover.

Work–Life Conflict and Organizational Commitment

Whereas layoffs and pay cuts refer to relatively discrete or infrequent "unfavorable outcomes" that may cause people to behave in ways that are costly to their employers, certain conditions cause employees to experience unfavorable outcomes on a more continual basis. Consider work–life conflict as a case in point. Many organizations do little to help employees manage their work–life conflict, perhaps figuring that the responsibility rests on employees' shoulders. Organizations that do try to lend a helping hand often do so in the form of costly programs or policies. As described in Chapter 2, studies by Siegel et al. (2005) revealed an additional strategy for dealing with work–life conflict: high process fairness. Siegel et al. discovered that work–life conflict had no effect on employees' organizational commitment, provided that they felt that senior executives (1) generally provided good reasons for organizational decisions and (2) generally treated them with dignity and respect. Again, high process fairness softened the blow associated with unfavorable outcomes, in that employees were willing to remain committed to their organizations when work–life conflict was high if (and only if) executives in their organizations practiced high process fairness.

"Show Me the High Process Fairness"

In the movie *Jerry Maguire*, the character played by Cuba Gooding Jr. uttered the now-famous line, "Show me the money." Indeed, when it comes to dealing with certain human resource management problems, some companies (presumably the more well-off ones) appear to have heeded this advice. For example, downsizing organizations sometimes offer much in the way of tangible resources to the people who are losing their jobs, such as severance pay, assistance in finding other jobs (including but not limited to outplacement counseling), and continuation of health insurance or other kinds of benefits until people become gainfully reemployed. And, as discussed in Chapter 2, companies sometimes expend huge resources to help their expatriate employees adjust to their overseas assignments. The results of several studies suggest, however, that there may be a more cost-effective way to handle things. As long as executives practice high process fairness, they may be able to reduce dramatically (note: not eliminate) the amount of tangible and costly assistance that their firms need to offer.

Survivors' Reactions to Downsizing In a series of studies, my colleagues and I examined whether the perceived size of the severance package given to those who lost their jobs affected the organizational commitment of the employees who remained (Brockner et al., 1994). One might have expected that survivors would be committed to the organization when they believed that the severance package was large (i.e., that there would be a positive main effect of the perceived size of the package given to the layoff victims on the organizational commitment of those who remained). Instead, we found an interactive relationship between process fairness and outcome favorability. Specifically, the perceived size of the package was weakly or not at all related to survivors' organizational commitment when the organization handled the layoffs with high process fairness. Thus, whether survivors believed that companies spent a large amount or only a moderate amount in providing for the terminated employees did not lead to differences in survivors' organizational commitment, provided that the layoffs were implemented with high process fairness. It was only the survivors who believed that the layoffs were handled with low process fairness who showed a positive relationship between the perceived size of the package and their organizational commitment.

Managing Expatriates When expatriates depart prematurely from their overseas assignments, it may be extremely costly to their organizations (and often to the expats themselves). Conventional wisdom has it that expats are prone to depart prematurely if they or their family members have not adjusted well to their living conditions. Accordingly, companies often go to great expense to facilitate the adjustment of expats and their family members. As described in Chapter 2, Garonzik et al. (2000) evaluated how much expatriates' and their family members' adjustment to various aspects of their lives outside work (e.g., housing, schooling, and health care) was related to the expats' intention to depart prematurely from their overseas assignments. The results showed that how well expatriates and their family members had adjusted to their living conditions had little effect on expatriates' intentions to depart prematurely, provided that the expats believed that their bosses *generally* treated them with high process fairness (e.g., allowed them to have input into decisions). In other words, even when they or their family members had not adjusted particularly well to their living conditions, high process fairness provided them with an impetus to "tough it out" and not return prematurely from their overseas assignments. In contrast, when process fairness was low, expats were much more likely to think seriously of departing prematurely if they (or their family members) were less rather than more well adjusted to their living conditions.

I do not mean to suggest that when managing survivors' reactions to downsizing or expatriates' adjustment to their overseas assignments, organizational authorities should unilaterally provide high process fairness *instead of* offering tangible support. Rather, the takeaway message from theory and research is that organizations need to provide *some* tangible support even as its authorities practice high process fairness. How much tangible support to offer is perhaps best captured by the expression "the law of diminishing returns." *Once a moderate level of tangible support has been offered,* it may be much more cost-effective for organizations to practice high process fairness than it is for them to allocate additional tangible resources to the challenge at hand. For example, to address employees' work–life conflict, organizations have invested in many costly policies and programs, including day care centers, stress reduction programs, gymnasiums, concierge services, dependent care, and elder care allowances. These are worthwhile endeavors that may increase employees' commitment to their jobs and organizations. However, companies may not need to "go overboard" in providing tangible support (which is financially costly), provided that the practice of high process fairness is integral to their organizational culture.

THE PARADOX OF PROCESS FAIRNESS

To authorities seeking to gain support for their decisions and the organizations that they represent, high process fairness seems to have many desirable features. The behaviors that comprise high process fairness usually are not financially prohibitive. Moreover, as I suggested in the preceding section, high process fairness has positive effects on employees' attitudes and behaviors that directly or indirectly influence the bottom line. In addition to these sound business reasons for managers to practice high process fairness, doing so will help them to satisfy the moral imperative. For every element of process fairness (e.g., voice, giving explanations, etc.), the more that it is practiced, the more that the agent is behaving in an ethically appropriate fashion. Indeed, one of Leventhal et al.'s (1980) six elements of procedural justice is the *ethicality rule,* which refers to how much decision makers use procedures that are compatible with existing moral and ethical standards.

Given all that high process fairness has going for it, one might expect managers to practice it to a high or even to a very high degree. The paradox, however, is that this appears not to be the case. For example, in an executive education program at Columbia Business School (which has been attended by more than 500 managers from organizations and industries all over the world), we ask participants to complete a 360-degree feedback exercise in which they rate themselves (and are rated by their boss, peers, direct reports, and customers) as agents of organizational change. This 34-item instrument covers various elements of successful change implementation, including surfacing dissatisfaction with the status quo, providing a vision of the future, having a process in place to move people from the dissatisfying status quo to the more alluring future state, and helping organizational members work through their resistance to change. Of 34 items, there is only 1 in which people rate themselves significantly more positively than how they are rated by each of the other rater groups: "When managing change, I make extra efforts to treat people with dignity and respect." These findings suggest that when they are planning and implementing change, managers practice process fairness (or, at least, the interactional justice element of process fairness) far less than others think that they do.

Further evidence that process fairness is not practiced nearly enough came from a spate of studies (seven at last count; for a review, see Skarlicki & Latham, 2005) conducted on literally thousands of managers, which have investigated the effects of training managers in process fairness. Study after study showed that managers who completed the training not only were perceived by their subordinates as showing greater process fairness than their untrained counterparts, but also that the subordinates of the trained managers responded more positively than the subordinates of the untrained managers, as measured by their willingness to go the extra 9 yards in doing their work and their commitment to remain with the organization. Several studies even have shown that employees whose managers underwent process fairness training were significantly less insomniac in the face of stressful work conditions (pay cuts and layoffs) relative to employees whose managers had not undergone the training (e.g., Greenberg, 2006). The good news from these studies is that managers *can* improve their process fairness. The bad news is that, in the absence of training, many if not most managers leave a lot to be desired vis-à-vis the practice of process fairness.

Accounting for the Paradox of Process Fairness

The evidence that managers often do not practice high process fairness is somewhat circumstantial; further research is needed to evaluate just how widespread its underperformance is. If, however, high process fairness is at least somewhat underperformed, then for both practical and theoretical reasons it is important to delineate why this is the case. As with any behavior, acting with high process fairness while doling out unfavorable outcomes depends on the motivation and ability levels of the implementers of decisions. Thus far, I identified some of the motivational factors that induce decision implementers to behave with high process fairness: It may cost relatively little financially, it may lead to positive results on the bottom line, and it is the "morally correct" thing to do. Provided that the implementer has the requisite abilities needed to enact high process fairness (e.g., social skill in delivering bad news), then high process fairness should be likely to ensue. This reasoning suggests that it may be worthwhile to consider the motivation- or ability-based factors that explain why executives do *not* practice high process fairness.

Motivational Deterrents: An Expectancy Theory Analysis

Based on the expectancy-valence theory of motivation (e.g., Vroom, 1964), there may be at least three sets of motivation-based deterrents to the practice of high process fairness. First, people need to believe that the effort that they put forth in trying to behave with high process fairness while delivering unfavorable outcomes will bear fruit. In the terminology of expectancy theory, this is the E (for effort) that leads to P (for performance) belief. The belief that "E leads to P" is influenced by or reflects people's perception that they have the ability to perform the focal behavior. If people do not think that they have the ability to perform a certain behavior, they are unlikely to believe that by trying hard they will perform the behavior well. Second, people need to believe that behaving with high process fairness while delivering unfavorable outcomes will elicit certain outcomes. In the language of expectancy theory, this is the belief that "P leads to O" (for outcomes). Third, people need to assign positive value to the outcomes that are perceived to be contingent on the performance of high process fairness. In the terminology of expectancy theory, this is the belief that "O is valued." Moreover, the expectancy-valence framework is a multiplicative one, suggesting that if any of these three elements is not in place, then the behavior is relatively unlikely to occur. I now consider how each of the three elements of expectancy theory helps us to identify obstacles to the practice of high process fairness.

Obstacles to Believing That E Leads to P Molinsky and Margolis (2005) suggested that the delivery of unfavorable outcomes with high process fairness requires three sets of skills: technical, interpersonal, and intrapersonal. For example, managers delivering the unpleasant news of layoffs have to ensure that they can communicate the message properly rather than sugarcoating or downplaying what is happening (technical), that they are able to handle smoothly the unpleasant behaviors and emotions that may be hurled their way by the pained recipients of the message (interpersonal), and that they can tolerate the various sources of internal discomfort (e.g., guilt and anxiety) they are likely to experience by being the bearer of bad news (intrapersonal). Molinsky and Margolis (2006) provided a vivid example of the intrapersonal challenge experienced by one manager in the course of implementing layoffs:

> Internally, there is a nervous stomach, you feel on edge. Sometimes you get physically nauseous or a headache. Very often the night before or after you have very bad dreams that are not necessarily related to the downsizing itself, but from that stress. There is a degree of nervousness

> that almost makes you have to step back and say, "I have to be calm, I can't show that I am nervous about delivering this message." (p. 149)

Being able to meet the intrapersonal challenge, let alone all three of these challenges, is no simple task. Understandably, many managers may doubt their abilities to do what is necessary, which is to deliver the unfavorable outcome with high process fairness.

A study by Cole and Latham (1997) provided evidence that managers may fail to practice high process fairness when delivering unfavorable outcomes because they do not believe that they have the capability to do so. The purpose of the study was to evaluate whether managers who had been trained to deliver unfavorable outcomes with high process fairness would be more likely to do so relative to a control group of managers who had not been trained. The training consisted of a blend of lectures, group discussions, and role-playing exercises, in which the goal was to increase the likelihood that managers would display the behaviors comprising high process fairness (e.g., providing a clear and adequate explanation of why certain decisions were made, allowing the affected parties to express their points of view, and treating the affected parties with dignity and respect). Managers were randomly assigned to be trained or not. Subsequent to the training manipulation, all of them asked one of their subordinates to take part in a hypothetical disciplinary situation in which participants had to administer an unfavorable outcome to the subordinate because of the subordinate's subpar behavior (e.g., being absent from work on account of taking a second job or not performing well in the afternoon after drinking alcohol during the lunch break).

Managers who were trained were seen as significantly higher in process fairness while taking the disciplinary action relative to their counterparts in the control group who had not been trained. What accounted for the higher process fairness shown by the trained managers? Both prior and subsequent to the training manipulation, all participants completed a measure of their self-efficacy beliefs pertaining to the behaviors comprising high process fairness. As might be expected, managers who had undergone the training developed stronger feelings of self-efficacy pertaining to their ability to enact high process fairness relative to the untrained group. Moreover, these self-efficacy beliefs mediated the effect of the training on the process fairness exhibited by participants when taking disciplinary action (i.e., when delivering unfavorable outcomes).

The flip side of doubting one's ability to deliver the unfavorable outcome with high process fairness is to be overly confident about one's ability (or at least tendency) to do so. However, neither bode well for the likelihood that high process fairness will be exhibited. Those who doubt their ability to enact high process fairness are unlikely to be motivated to do so, as Cole and Latham (1997) found. Instead, they may distance themselves from (or otherwise avoid) the recipients of the unfavorable outcomes, which typically leads to behaviors that are antithetical to high process fairness. Those who overestimate the frequency with which they practice high process fairness (a high percentage, as suggested by the results of the previously described survey of managers attending the Columbia executive education program) either may "come on too strong" (that is, fail to deliver the unfavorable outcome with interpersonal sensitivity) or may not be motivated to improve their process fairness, figuring that they are already enacting it.

Why managers overrate themselves in the practice of process fairness is itself an intriguing question, one worthy of further research. Perhaps they have more access than do outside observers to their *intentions* to treat others with dignity and respect; unfortunately, they simply may not be very good in reading how those intentions come across in the eyes of others. Another, more self-serving, possibility is wishful thinking. Managers may view treating others with dignity and respect as akin to showing them "*common* courtesy" (my emphasis). Since most people think that they are better than average (ironically, more than 50% think this to be the case; e.g., Kruger, 1999), they may believe that they generally do better than that which is common. Whatever the reasons, managers' blind spots about *themselves* may be yet another barrier to the practice of process fairness.

Obstacles to Believing That P Leads to O Those who implement decisions may fail to exhibit process fairness because its resulting benefits sometimes may not be obvious. As described in Chapter 2, a study of more than 25,000 Finnish employees examined the relationship between how much they had experienced significant negative life events specifically, the onset of severe illness of a close family member, and the frequency of their sickness-related absences from work over the next 30 months (Elovainio et al., 2007). Participants also rated the extent to which managers in their workplace exhibited process fairness. Consistent with previous research on the health consequences of negative life events, the onset of serious illness of a family member elicited more frequent sickness-related absences relative to that shown by people who did not experience such an unfortunate event (e.g., Holmes & Rahe, 1967). Of greater relevance to the present discussion is the moderating influence of process fairness on the negative life event. That is, the tendency for the negative life event to translate into sickness-related absences depended on how much process fairness employees experienced in the workplace. When process fairness was high, the negative life event was much less likely to lead to sickness-related absences than when process fairness was low. Moreover, this effect lasted for 30 months after the onset of the event. Said differently, *not* being pretreated with process fairness led to "absences waiting to happen" (i.e., when employees subsequently encountered negative life events). The fact that high process fairness may have this positive type of spillover effect may not be obvious to organizational authorities, thereby reducing their tendencies to practice high process fairness.

On a related note, recall the aforementioned studies that showed that high process fairness reduced the relationships between (1) how well expatriates and their family members adjusted to their overseas assignments and the expats' intentions to depart prematurely (Garonzik et al., 2000) and (2) employees' work–life conflict and their organizational commitment (Siegel et al., 2005). In both of these instances, process fairness referred to employees' perceptions of how decisions were made *in general,* not simply about their expatriation experience in the former case or about their work–life conflict in the latter case. The fact that process fairness in contexts other than the focal one may nevertheless spill over to affect people's reactions to outcomes received in the focal context may not be apparent to managers, which also may explain why high process fairness may be underperformed.

Perhaps the positive spillover effects are attributable to trust (Brockner et al., 1997). That is, when managers generally implement decisions with high process fairness, they are likely to be seen as trustworthy. The perception of trustworthiness in turn may carry over to other situations and thereby have a moderating influence on the favorability of the outcomes received in those situations, such that high trustworthiness reduces the influence of outcome favorability on people's support for decisions, decision makers, and institutions relative to when trustworthiness is low (Brockner et al., 1997). In any event, the nonobviousness of possible spillover effects of high process fairness may reduce decision makers' tendencies to practice it.

Homo Economicus, Run Amok Sometimes, implementers' guiding assumptions may lead them to overlook the possibility that behaving with high process fairness when doling out unfavorable outcomes will be beneficial to their organizations. Thus, when companies are accused of or criticized for some wrongdoing, all too often they try to address the concern by focusing on outcomes, or "what" they do (e.g., adopting an environmentally friendly policy when none existed beforehand), to the relative exclusion of processes, or "how" they go about trying to address the concern. Relatedly, Oberholzer-Gee and Frey (1996) analyzed "siting" decisions, which refers to the act of locating hazardous waste facilities in certain communities. Among their findings is that those who make siting decisions (senior government officials) often do not pay adequate attention to the fairness of the process used to make these decisions (e.g., ensuring the input of various parties who will be affected by the decision, such as residents of the communities in which the facilities will be located) and instead focus almost entirely on outcomes (i.e., giving the residents more compensation for having the facility located in their community).

To cite another example, driven by outcome- or economically based assumptions, managers who wish to minimize the negative effects of layoffs may believe that they can best reduce the sting of job loss by providing a generous severance package to those who lose their jobs. At a cocktail party not so long ago, the chief executive officer of a major international bank proudly told me about the hefty severance package that his company provided to the people who had been recently downsized from his organization. I expressed admiration for his organization's obvious show of concern for the layoff victims and then proceeded to ask him the (conversation-ending) question of whether the company had said anything to or done anything for the people who remained. What I had in mind, of course, was whether the organization showed process fairness toward the employees who remained (e.g., explaining why the layoffs were necessary, listening to and trying to respond to their concerns going forward, etc.). Somewhat defensively, he said that he and his senior management team believed that it was only necessary to do something for the employees who were "affected" by the layoffs because, after all, the remaining employees were "lucky enough to still have their jobs."

On a related note, it is striking how often executives at downsizing companies use the word *affected* when referring to the people who had lost their jobs. The use of this word—perhaps an Orwellian version of "organizational Newspeak"—is misleading in its implication that the employees who remain somehow are *not* affected. In short, it is not that outcome- or economically based solutions are wrong as much as they reflect an *incomplete* understanding of what needs to happen when authorities implement important decisions. It is possible that managers who focus on outcome-based solutions (i.e., the economics of the situation) may do so *in lieu of* process-based solutions (i.e., the psychology of the situation), thereby failing to appreciate fully the benefits of behaving with high process fairness due to their "managerial myopia." The two types of solutions, however, are not mutually exclusive. Moreover, in a downsizing context, not only does high process fairness elicit more favorable reactions among those who remain, but also it can lead to less unfavorable reactions among those who leave, as indicated by the Lind et al. (2000) finding that employees were much less likely to sue for wrongful termination when they believed that they were treated with interpersonal sensitivity when told that they were being let go.

Homo Legalicus, Run Amok It is one thing to say that high process fairness is not practiced because the benefits of doing so may not be obvious. Yet another explanation is that implementers actually may believe that they or their organizations could suffer harmful consequences if they were to behave with high process fairness. Authorities exhibit process fairness by providing explanations of their decisions and, more generally, by making themselves available to their people. However, legal counsel may discourage companies from providing explanations or from having their managers make themselves available on the grounds that disclosure of information could make the firm vulnerable to lawsuits.

This logic has it that it is better not to say anything at all rather than to risk having the information come back to haunt the firm in the courtroom. Of course, by not saying anything at all process fairness is less likely to be exhibited. Legal considerations about what to communicate are important, of course, but they should not be taken to unnecessary extremes. All too often, firms may withhold information (e.g., that they had considered alternatives to downsizing) when they may have been far better off revealing such information to their employees.

Obstacles to Believing That O Is Valued I suggested that authorities may be motivated to practice high process fairness because doing so (1) could be financially prudent (i.e., in exchange for behaviors that may cost them and their organizations relatively little money, they may elicit employee attitudes and behaviors that contribute positively to the bottom line) and (2) may help them to satisfy the "moral imperative." However, this analysis overlooks the possibility that authorities also have other needs, which they may believe are unlikely to be satisfied if they were to behave with high process fairness (Brockner, Wiesenfeld, & Diekmann, 2009). I now discuss three such needs: (1) the desire to wield power and influence, (2) the desire to maintain a positive view of themselves, and (3) the desire to reduce their cognitive loads. In discussing each of these needs, I provide a basis for understanding how managers may believe that the practice of high process fairness may be costly rather than beneficial to them.

Wielding Power and Influence Authorities may believe that engaging in process fairness represents a threat to their power. One of the main elements of process fairness is allowing those affected by a decision to have input. However, a long-standing obstacle to involving employees in decision making is managers' beliefs that their own power and influence may be reduced when employees are given a say in how things should be done (Klein, 1984). Moreover, managers who unwaveringly believe that "knowledge is power" may be unwilling to share information, in which case they are unlikely to provide explanations or make themselves available for two-way communications with their direct reports.

Clearly, managers sometimes do run the risk of losing power when they show high process fairness by involving others in decision making or by providing information about why certain decisions were made. Perhaps even more often, however, the practice of process fairness is likely to increase managers' power and influence. When managers involve their direct reports in decision making or make decisions on the basis of the criteria set forth by Leventhal et al. (1980), such as accuracy and consistency, the direct reports are likely to be *intrinsically* supportive of (rather than merely compliant with) decisions, their bosses, and the organization as a whole. Indeed, research by Zapata-Phelan, Colquitt, Scott, and Livingston (2008) provided evidence that being treated with high process fairness engenders many of the psychological states that undergird intrinsic motivation, such as perceived control, positive self-regard, and a sense of belonging (Deci & Ryan, 2002). Consequently, managers who practice high process fairness and thereby intrinsically motivate their direct reports actually may increase rather than decrease their degree of power and influence over their direct reports (Hill, 1994). Admittedly, building one's power and influence by practicing high process fairness does not happen overnight; it requires managers to be willing to make investments in time or psychological energy that they may be unwilling or unable to do.

Maintaining a Positive Self-View In their roles as organizational agents, managers typically have incentive to do that which is in the best financial interests of their firms. In addition (and sometimes in conflict with this motive), they want to act in ways that will enable them to enhance or at least protect their self-esteem. Molinsky and Margolis (2005) suggested that decision-making authorities have several reasons to experience the self-esteem-threatening emotion of guilt when doling out unfavorable outcomes. Whereas moderate levels of guilt may induce prosocial behavior, including high process fairness, high levels of guilt may lead authorities to engage in self-protective behaviors, such as psychologically distancing themselves from or avoiding the recipients of the unfavorable outcomes, the very antitheses of high process fairness.

For example, managers may feel guilty if they see themselves as responsible for creating the conditions that made it necessary for them to administer the unfavorable outcomes to the recipients. As Molinsky and Margolis (2005) suggested, "a manager who has failed to coach a poorly performing employee will feel more personal responsibility for creating conditions that necessitate firing that employee than will a manager who has tried, albeit unsuccessfully, to change an employee's behavior through feedback and mentoring" (p. 251). Folger and Skarlicki (1998) found that when managers were led to believe that others had lost their jobs because of the managers' mistakes rather than because of market conditions that were beyond the managers' control, managers were more likely to distance themselves from the people whose jobs were lost. Much like the doctors who were more likely to be sued for malpractice (Levinson et al., 1997), managers who believed that the job loss was caused by their own mistakes (rather than market conditions beyond their control) were not willing to spend much time meeting privately with the layoff victims to discuss their dismissals. Furthermore, even if managers do not see themselves as responsible for creating the conditions that made it necessary to administer unfavorable outcomes, they may experience responsibility and hence guilt to the extent that they played a role in the *planning or implementation* of the decisions that brought about the unfavorable outcomes.

Molinsky and Margolis (2005) suggested that managers' guilt in delivering unfavorable outcomes also depends on the justifiability of the harm produced in relation to the good achieved: the lower the justifiability, the greater the guilt. Thus, if people receive unfavorable outcomes through no fault of their own, then it is harder for managers to justify delivering them. Or, if the delivery of the unfavorable outcomes is a relatively unusual event (e.g., a previously paternalistic organization that chooses to lay off some of its employees for the first time), it may be seen as less legitimate, less necessary, and therefore less justifiable.

A series of studies by Grant, Molinsky, Margolis, Kamin, and Schiano (2009) provided evidence of how managers may distance themselves from the recipients of unfavorable outcomes (in the form of reduced process fairness) as a way to reduce their guilt. In one study, participants were asked to imagine that they had to deliver the bad news to students that the scholarships that they were expecting to receive were being cut back. (Participants had no say in the making of this decision but rather had to deliver it.) The authority responsible for actually making the decision did so either procedurally fairly or unfairly. Cross-cutting the manipulation of the authority's procedural fairness was whether participants' prosocial identities had been made salient to them. For example, those whose prosocial identities had been made salient to them were asked to respond to questions about the extent to which behaving prosocially is central to their sense of identity.

The dependent variables consisted of how much participants experienced negative self-relevant emotions such as guilt and shame and the extent to which they expressed compassion toward the parties who were unfavorably affected by the decision in communicating with them about it. Consistent with previous research on the reactions of the recipients of decisions yielding unfavorable outcomes, when participants' prosocial identities had not been made salient they experienced more negative affect when the authority who made the decision was procedurally unfair rather than fair (Brockner et al., 2007; Cropanzano & Folger, 1989). Although participants had no say in the making of the procedurally unfair decision, they may have felt badly about being associated with its delivery, causing them to feel worse about themselves. Moreover, the letters that they wrote to the recipients of the decision were more compassionate (i.e., higher in interactional fairness) than when the authority had been procedurally fair.

What about those whose prosocial identities had been made salient to them? Presumably, these participants would not want to violate their now-activated self-concepts that emphasized not doing harm to others. However, by virtue of being in a position in which they had to deliver unfavorable outcomes to others, they were likely to experience a dissonance-arousing, self-threatening psychological state ("I think of myself one way, but I am being asked to behave in a different way"). If the authority responsible for making the decision was procedurally unfair, participants may reduce dissonance by seeing the *authority* as responsible for the unfavorable outcomes associated with the decision (Folger & Cropanzano, 1998, 2001), thereby freeing them from feeling badly about themselves (e.g., guilty) and correspondingly reducing their impetus to behave compassionately toward the recipients of the decision. If the authority was procedurally fair, however, then participants were less able to reduce dissonance by blaming the authority for the unfavorable outcomes that they have to deliver. One way to behave consistently with their prosocial identity when the authority was procedurally fair is by delivering the unfavorable outcome with greater compassion. This reasoning suggests that when people's prosocial identities had been made salient, they may deliver the news to the affected parties with greater compassion (process fairness) when the authority responsible for making the decision was procedurally fair rather than unfair; in fact, this is exactly what Grant et al. (2009) discovered.

Moreover, in a second study, Grant et al. (2009) replaced the measure of compassion expressed, which is more of an indicator of process fairness, with a measure of how much the harmed parties should be compensated, which is more reflective of distributive fairness. Analogous results emerged: When people's prosocial identity had not been made salient, the harmed parties received greater compensation when the authority making the decision was procedurally unfair rather than fair, whereas just the opposite occurred when people's prosocial identity had been made salient.

Reducing Cognitive Load Molinsky and Margolis's (2005) analysis also suggests that it is psychologically draining for people to deliver unfavorable outcomes to others, inducing a state known as *high cognitive load* ("the mentally taxing experience of maintaining heightened awareness and focused attention," p. 253). Most people do not enjoy being the bearer of bad news (Tesser & Rosen, 1975), and yet the role of delivering unfavorable outcomes requires them to be exactly that. They may find themselves caught between wanting to make things better for the recipients and knowing that doing so is not possible. To make matters worse, the reactions of the recipients may be quite palpable, for example, when the people who have to deliver the unfavorable outcomes identify with the recipients personally or with the situation in which the recipients find themselves (Brockner, 1990; Molinsky & Margolis, 2005).

While delivering unfavorable outcomes, implementers have to decide whether to do so with higher or lower process fairness. The former typically requires them to make themselves psychologically available, that is, to reduce the psychological distance between themselves and the recipients. Unfortunately, there is a price to pay in reducing psychological distance, namely, an increase in cognitive load. Consequently, they may choose to distance themselves to reduce their cognitive load. Moreover, implementers may distance themselves from the recipients even in the absence of feeling responsible for the recipients' plights. The receipt of unfavorable outcomes is likely to elicit a host of unpleasant emotions, such as anxiety, anger, and sadness. Studies of emotional contagion have shown that people sometimes take on the emotional states of those around them (Barsade, 2002). Consequently, managers may go into avoidance mode and as a result fail to exhibit high process fairness so they do not "catch" the painful emotions that are being experienced by the recipients of the unfavorable outcomes.

Furthermore, there is even evidence that cognitive load may short-circuit people's tendencies to experience the very emotions that may predispose them to act with high process fairness, such as sympathy (Skitka, Mullen, Griffin, Hutchinson, & Chamberlin, 2002). Hence, when it comes to delivering unfavorable outcomes with high process fairness, implementers may be "caught between a rock and a hard place." If they experience high levels of emotionality, for example, through the related factors of palpability and contagion, then implementers may expend psychological resources trying to manage their own emotions. Moreover, the inherent complexity of dealing with the technical, intrapersonal, and interpersonal requirements of the task at hand, by heightening cognitive load, may block the onset of the emotions that engender high process fairness. Either way, the chances for unfavorable outcomes to be delivered with high process fairness become remote.

Ability-Based Deterrents to the Practice of Process Fairness

Expectancy theory helps to identify some of the reasons why people may not be motivated to practice process fairness. One of these is the belief that E leads to P, which is affected by or reflects people's *beliefs about* their abilities to perform the appropriate behavior. Whereas having confidence in their ability to perform the appropriate behavior makes people more motivated to engage in it, it does not ensure that the behavior will be properly enacted. In addition to considering the other two expectancy-theory-based elements of motivation, we need to take into account whether people *actually have* the abilities needed to perform the behaviors successfully. All behaviors are a function of people's motivation *and* ability to enact them. Hence, even if people are motivated to behave with high process fairness, they may or may not have the ability to do so.

As Molinsky and Margolis (2005) pointed out, doling out unfavorable outcomes with high process fairness requires technical, interpersonal, and intrapersonal skills. It is entirely possible that implementers will be dispositionally deficient in one or more of these skill sets. Moreover, even if they have the requisite skills, the motivational and emotional challenges associated with delivering unfavorable outcomes with high process fairness may make it difficult for them to utilize their skills. As Molinsky and Margolis put it:

> Guilt, sympathy, performance anxiety and cognitive load … tax an individual's capacity to perform. … Capacity refers to the intrapsychic resources available to a performer at the moment of task execution for handling the technical, interpersonal, and intrapersonal demands of performing the task. … Psychological resources are finite and can be depleted

> by competing demands that arise. … Even if performers are highly motivated to behave in a pro-social manner [a questionable assumption, given the above analysis] this motivation must be matched with sufficient available psychological capacity. That capacity is increasingly depleted as guilt, sympathy, performance anxiety, and cognitive load rise. (p. 255; brackets added)

In summary, given that behavior is a function of motivation times ability (which suggests that the behavior is unlikely to be performed if either motivation or ability is relatively low), it becomes more understandable why high process fairness may not be exhibited by those responsible for the delivery of unfavorable outcomes.

Motivational and Emotional Ambivalence

The picture emerging from the motivational analysis set forth is that the implementers of unfavorable outcomes are subjected to multiple forces with competing effects on their likelihood of exhibiting high process fairness. On the one hand, practicing high process fairness makes good economic sense for organizations in that behaviors that are not financially expensive to implement elicit outcomes that positively contribute to the bottom line. Moreover, practicing high process fairness may help implementers satisfy the moral imperative. On the other hand, implementers may lack confidence in their abilities to deliver unfavorable outcomes with high process fairness, they may not necessarily believe that the positive consequences of being process fair are more likely to occur than are the negative consequences, and they may assign greater value to the consequences of not behaving with high process fairness than to the consequences of behaving with high process fairness.

Molinsky and Margolis (2005) artfully described the emotional experience (or "internal drama") associated with the motivational ambivalence experienced by the implementers of unfavorable outcomes. On the one hand, feelings of sympathy and guilt, at least when experienced to moderate degrees, would predispose implementers to do the prosocial thing of behaving with high process fairness. On the other hand, strong feelings of sympathy and guilt, along with performance anxiety and cognitive load, may make them less likely to exhibit process fairness. Whereas expectancy theory delineates some of the factors that deter managers from practicing high process fairness, Molinsky and Margolis (2006) provided an analysis of the various ways in which managers' failure to practice high process fairness manifests itself, in an insightful article, "The Emotional Tightrope of Downsizing." Their analysis focused on how managers fail to exhibit process fairness when implementing organizational downsizing. However, it is likely to apply to a broader range of situations in which managers have to deliver unfavorable outcomes (e.g., when planning or implementing threatening organizational changes other than downsizing or when called on to deliver unflattering performance appraisals).

More specifically, implementers sometimes may come on "too soft." Their discomfort as the bearer of bad news may cause them to understate or cushion its enormity. Or, the unfavorable outcomes may be presented in ways that make them seem open for bargaining and negotiation. Whereas both of these strategies may have the desired effect of at least temporarily reducing the emotional strain for both parties, they violate the process fairness rule of being honest and up-front in dealing with others. Moreover, to the extent that actual bargaining does take place, it invites inconsistency (e.g., some people slated to be laid off may negotiate to be retained longer than others, even though all were originally targeted to be dismissed at the same time), which represents yet another violation of high process fairness (Leventhal et al., 1980).

On other occasions, implementers may come on "too strong." That is, if they feel emotionally distraught by the task before them, they may unload their emotions in the course of delivering the bad news. For example, overcome by sadness, they may cry excessively while delivering the news. Or, feeling resentful about having to be the bearer of bad news, they may lash out against the organization during the delivery. In either case, the focus is on the deliverers' emotional state rather than on the recipients', in which case the latter are less likely to feel that they were treated with dignity and respect. Implementers also may come on too strong in how they respond to the recipients' reactions. For example, it is not uncommon for recipients to respond to unfavorable outcomes in ways that anger the implementers, for example, by holding the implementers responsible. To the extent that implementers take the bait and start arguing with the recipients, high process fairness also is unlikely to be exhibited.

A third type of reaction that makes high process fairness less likely to occur is the tendency for implementers to distance themselves psychologically from the recipients. Rather than trying to soften the blow or going on the offensive, this strategy is designed to reduce the intensity with which implementers experience their own negative emotions associated with delivering the bad news (e.g., anxiety, guilt) or the negative emotions elicited in recipients by the bad news (e.g., anger, sadness). It may take the form of delivering the unfavorable outcome in a very mechanical, awkward fashion or in doing so with great dispatch, neither of which is likely to make recipients feel that they were treated with dignity and respect.

Getting to High Process Fairness

Given the huge upsides associated with delivering unfavorable outcomes with high process fairness, and given the many motivational or emotional obstacles that may stand in the way, we need to learn more about the factors affecting whether unfavorable outcomes are delivered with high process fairness. As Molinsky and Margolis (2005) implied, it is critical to understand the motivational and emotional experience of the deliverers as they contemplate and execute the task before them. Simply showing them the benefits and encouraging them to "just do it" are unlikely to be sufficient. In a qualitative study of how to overcome the motivational and emotional obstacles to delivering unfavorable outcomes with high process fairness, Molinsky and Margolis (2006) found that managers used a number of different cognitive and behavioral strategies. For example, to reduce the likelihood of coming on too soft, they justified the correctness of the decision. Thus, managers who had to implement layoffs told themselves that people who lose their jobs often go on to "bigger and better" things subsequently (a "silver lining" justification). Or, they convinced themselves that the layoffs were necessary to ensure the viability of the company as a whole.

To make it less likely that they would come on too strong, managers found ways to release emotion before or after but *not during* their meeting with the recipients of unfavorable outcomes. One manager described how talking to close others prior to the difficult conversation better enabled her to prepare for it: "We will sit and we will talk about, 'Gee, isn't it awful that we have to layoff all these good people and I feel bad for this person,' or 'I have to tell three pregnant women today that they are getting laid off.'" Another method used by some to ward off the likelihood of coming on too strong was to divert attention away from the negative emotion that they were experiencing. As one manager put it, "I try to think about other things. My family, you know, the games that my kids are going to or playing that evening. I try as best as I can not to bring too much of that back to the house with me" (Molinsky & Margolis, 2006, p. 156).

Still others used a method that reduced their tendencies to engage in the distancing behaviors that are noxious to the recipients of the unfavorable outcomes. This technique, which Molinsky and Margolis (2006) called "quarantining," entails managers distancing themselves *temporarily* from the negative emotions that they were experiencing. Users of quarantining offered expressions such as "putting on a game face" and "putting emotion on the back burner" to describe it. At first blush, quarantining sounds similar to the psychological distancing that may translate into a *lack* of process fairness in delivering unfavorable outcomes. Quarantining differs from distancing, however, in that the implementers are intentionally using it to be psychologically available to the recipients. One manager who drew on this strategy said, "I've ... taken a step back and tried to remove myself emotionally from the meeting ... yet maintaining enough empathy with the person to be able to make them feel like they've been treated with dignity and respect" (p. 155).

The various strategies used by managers illustrate just how precarious it is for unfavorable outcomes to be delivered with high process fairness. In enacting each strategy, managers walk a fine line between behaving versus failing to behave with high process fairness (e.g., the aforementioned subtle distinction between quarantining and psychological distancing). Moreover, if the justification strategy used as an antidote to coming on too soft is taken too far, managers run the risk of delivering the unfavorable outcomes coldly and callously, that is, of coming on too strong. Similarly, if the methods used to ward off coming on too strong are overdone, managers may make the opposite mistake of coming on too soft. For example, either releasing or distracting may cause managers to underestimate the magnitude of the situation as it is experienced by the recipients of unfavorable outcomes.

In summary, the analyses of Molinsky and Margolis (2005, 2006) illustrated (1) the various ways in which implementers of unfavorable outcomes may fail to exhibit high process fairness and (2) the cognitive and behavioral strategies they use to cope with their predicaments, such that some strategies are more likely to lead them to practice high process fairness than are others. Whereas it is useful to know *how* implementers of unfavorable outcomes may fail to practice high process fairness and *how* they cope with the predicament of having to deliver unfavorable outcomes, it is also important to identify the factors that make them more versus less likely to practice high process fairness in the course of delivering unfavorable outcomes. For example, Margolis and Molinsky (2008) examined whether the deliverers of unfavorable outcomes tended to psychologically distance themselves from, versus engage with, the recipients. They discovered a nearly even split between these two tendencies, with those who distanced themselves less likely to exhibit high process fairness. Thus, even though deliverers *may* distance themselves from the recipients of unfavorable outcomes does not mean that they *will* do so. Further research on what makes it go one way or the other is clearly needed.

Both individuals and organizations may have a part to play in this regard. Moreover, some factors are likely to influence or reflect implementers' *motivation* to practice high process fairness, whereas others are likely to influence or reflect their *ability* to practice high process fairness.

What Individuals Can Do

Some people may naturally have the emotional intelligence (Goleman, 1998) needed to deliver unfavorable outcomes with high process fairness. For example, they may have the abilities to (1) regulate their negative emotions such as guilt and anxiety and (2) keep a "cool head" in the face of others' negative emotions, such as sadness and anger. Cole (2004) examined how managers behave when delivering unfavorable outcomes in the context of having disciplinary discussions with their unionized employees. The results were noteworthy in two respects. First, Cole identified an extensive set of behaviors that predicted the extent to which managers were seen as exhibiting high process fairness in the course of the disciplinary discussions. Among the strongest predictors of perceived fairness were (1) transformational leadership, that is, how much managers acted in ways that enhanced their employees' self-worth, how much they encouraged employee participation, and the extent to which they shared information; (2) active listening; (3) "conversational maintenance," which referred to the extent to which they were attentive to the employee; and (4) fact finding, that is, how much they sought facts or clarification from employees. Whereas there have been numerous discussions of the elements that comprise process fairness (e.g., voice, the Leventhal et al., 1980, criteria, and interactional justice), the Cole findings lend even greater specificity to what managers need to do if they want to be seen as behaving with high process fairness.

Second, Cole (2004) also discovered that there were highly significant differences between male and female managers in their tendencies to express the four (and other) predictors of perceived fairness, such that the female managers were rated higher than their male counterparts on all of the dimensions. The study did not delineate the cognitive or behavioral strategies that women managers used to enable them to behave in ways that were judged as more process fair than the men; delineating such strategies represents an important question for future research (e.g., Gross, 2001). However, the findings suggest that the likelihood that unfavorable outcomes will be delivered with high process fairness may depend on characteristics of the implementers, which raises the question of whether there may be other attributes of the implementers that may be influential.

For example, delivering unfavorable outcomes with high process fairness would seem to require not only emotional intelligence (Goleman, 1998) but also interpersonal or political savvy. Ferris, Davidson, and Perrewé (2005) identified four key dimensions of political skill: social astuteness, interpersonal influence, networking ability, and apparent sincerity. Those who score high on any or all of these dimensions may be more apt to deliver unfavorable outcomes with higher process fairness. For example, to the extent unfavorable outcomes are delivered with apparent sincerity (e.g., in which concerns for the recipients' well-being are expressed), recipients are likely to believe that they were treated with dignity and respect.

In summary, individuals who have more of the technical, interpersonal, or intrapersonal skills needed to practice high process fairness (Molinsky & Margolis, 2005) are more likely to do so for two reasons: First, these people have more of the *ability* needed to practice process fairness. Second, to the extent that they accurately perceive their skill sets, they are likely to maintain more positive beliefs that E leads to P and, as a result, be more *motivated* to practice process fairness.

What Organizations Can Do

Factors residing within work organizations also may affect how well managers handle the various negative emotions they may experience while delivering unfavorable outcomes, which in turn may affect the extent to which they exhibit high process fairness. Moreover, different sorts of workplace factors may influence the various ways in which implementers fail to exhibit high process fairness. For example, suppose that the implementers' guilt about being the bearer of bad news causes them to come on too soft (via cushioning or appearing to leave matters open for negotiation). If senior managers can induce implementers to believe that the unfavorable outcomes are absolutely necessary, then the implementers may engage in the justification process, enabling them to deliver the message in a forthright manner (Molinsky & Margolis, 2006).

For example, if senior managers convincingly demonstrate to the implementers that they carefully considered alternatives to the chosen action and that the chosen action clearly dominated the alternatives (by minimizing costs and maximizing benefits), then implementers may be less likely to come on too soft. Moreover, if senior managers communicated how, in the course of selecting the chosen alternative, they experienced some of the negative emotions that implementers are likely to be feeling (e.g., guilt and performance anxiety), then implementers also may be less likely to come on too soft in their delivery of the unfavorable outcomes. By sharing their own emotional struggles in selecting the chosen course of action, senior managers are likely to convey that it is appropriate for the implementers to have mixed feelings about what they have to do, but at the end of the day they need to deliver the message forthrightly. In short, if senior managers were to behave in the ways described, then lower-level managers may be motivated to deliver unfavorable outcomes with high process fairness.

Other factors may make it less likely for implementers to act out their emotional discomfort (e.g., guilt, performance anxiety, or cognitive load) in the form of coming on too strong. Molinsky and Margolis (2006) suggested that some implementers coped by distracting themselves from the emotional pain of delivering unfavorable outcomes, instead focusing their attention on other positive aspects of their lives. Just as some managers may proactively redirect attention on their own, organizations may make activities available to managers that facilitate this process. Moreover, managers' likelihood of coping successfully with the emotional turmoil may be further enhanced if the activities provided by the organization are self-affirming (Steele, 1988). Implementers may come on too strong because they are unable to manage the threat to self-integrity elicited by or reflected in the negative emotions that they are experiencing. For example, guilt resulting from seeing themselves as responsible for the unfavorable outcomes may threaten implementers' self-conceptions as kind and caring people who do not inflict harm on others. Furthermore, performance anxiety emanating from the difficulty of the task at hand may threaten their sense of competence and control.

If this reasoning is correct, then the deliverers of unfavorable outcomes may be better able to cope with their emotional turmoil by engaging in self-affirmation. One type of self-affirming activity that organizations may be able to provide is corporate volunteerism. Research has shown that employees who participated more in corporate volunteer programs were more committed to the organization. In one series of studies, the beneficiaries of employees' volunteer efforts were external to the organization (Brockner, Senior, & Welch, 2010), whereas in another study the beneficiaries were internal to the organization (Grant, Dutton, & Rosso, 2008). Furthermore, the positive relationship between employees' tendencies to take part in corporate-sponsored volunteer programs and their organizational commitment was mediated by the experience of self-affirmation. In sum, certain types of distractions may better enable implementers to cope with the emotional pain brought on by having to deliver unfavorable outcomes. If implementers' emotional pain (and corresponding tendencies to come on too strong when delivering unfavorable outcomes) emanates from threatened self-integrity, then it behooves organizations to ensure that its implementers of unfavorable outcomes have opportunities to experience self-affirmation.

As self-affirmation theory has suggested, people can counteract the threat to their self-integrity (i.e., reduce the impact of the threat on their beliefs and behaviors) by doing something that reaffirms their self-integrity (Steele, 1988). If the failure to deliver unfavorable outcomes with high process fairness is the result of implementers feeling self-threatened, then they may be more likely to deliver unfavorable outcomes with high process fairness when they can do so in ways that allow them to affirm their self-integrity. Unfortunately, the protocol in most organizations (even well-intentioned ones) makes this unlikely to happen. When unfavorable outcomes need to be delivered, organizational authorities often provide the implementers with tightly choreographed scripts on how to do so. Whereas tight and well-crafted scripts may serve to ensure that at least a baseline level of process fairness is enacted, and whereas they may satisfy legalistic concerns that recipients are not to be told "too much," they are hardly a recipe for implementers to experience self-affirmation. Perhaps giving implementers some freedom in how they choose to go about practicing high process fairness (even if that were to mean allowing them to choose from a range of options deemed acceptable by organizational authorities) may make them more likely to exhibit process fairness precisely because the act of doing so will be more self-affirming (Margolis & Molinsky, 2008).

Furthermore, implementers' failure to exhibit high process fairness when delivering unfavorable outcomes may take the form of distancing themselves from the recipients. To offset this possibility, organizations may find it helpful to provide implementers beforehand with a realistic preview of the emotional turmoil that delivering unfavorable outcomes often elicits. People are better able to tolerate negative events (and their psychological reactions to those events) if they have been forewarned about them (Janis & Mann, 1977). Put differently, negative events and emotions are much less tolerable when they catch people unaware. A common reaction to experiencing *unexpected* negative events and emotions is to flee from the scene relative to when those same events and emotions had been anticipated.

For example, one of the main reasons for employee turnover, especially the costly sort that emerges shortly after people have joined the organization, is "reality shock," in which employees discover that their job and organizational environments are less desirable than what they expected them to be. Because employers want to be wanted by prospective employees, recruiters tend to present the organization in a desirable light. Unfortunately, this practice is shortsighted. Whereas it may attract people to the firm, it also sets the stage for them to be disillusioned when their actual experience falls short of their prior expectations. The irony is that certain features that employees find undesirable may have been quite tolerable if only they had been told about them in advance. Studies showed that employee turnover is significantly reduced when new recruits are given a realistic job preview (RJP), which tells them not only about the upsides but also about the downsides associated with taking a position in the firm (Phillips, 1998; Wanous, 1980).

Just as providing would-be employees with an RJP reduces their tendency to withdraw behaviorally from the firm in the form of turnover, giving would-be deliverers of unfavorable outcomes a realistic preview of the painful or at least conflicting emotions they are likely to experience may reduce the likelihood of them psychologically withdrawing, manifested by distancing themselves from the recipients of the unfavorable outcomes. Perhaps knowing in advance about the emotional challenges associated with delivering unfavorable outcomes will motivate implementers to develop ways to meet these challenges if they were to arise. For example, implementers may find it useful to form a "self-help" group in which they validate one another's feelings ("misery loves company") as well as provide guidance to one another on how to cope with the emotional challenges. Then, when the emotional challenges actually do arise, implementers may be better equipped to deal with them relative to their counterparts who had not anticipated them. The net effect may be a reduced likelihood of fleeing from the scene psychologically, that is, less of a tendency to distance themselves from the recipients of unfavorable outcomes and, with that, an increased chance of them delivering unfavorable outcomes with high process fairness.

Delineating the essence of the emotional challenges associated with delivering unfavorable outcomes has implications for process fairness training programs. Promisingly, numerous studies have shown that managers can be trained to improve the extent to which they practice process fairness, which is particularly important when they have to deliver unfavorable outcomes (Skarlicki & Latham, 2005). As Molinsky and Margolis's (2005, 2006) analyses of the psychology of delivering unfavorable outcomes suggest, an important element of a process fairness training program may be to help implementers manage the emotional and motivational challenges they experience when deciding how to deliver unfavorable outcomes. Whereas this element may be present in some process fairness training programs, it is possible that the training programs could be enhanced even further if this particular element were to be given greater emphasis.

In summary, organizational authorities may help to create the conditions that make lower-level executives more likely to implement unfavorable outcomes with high process fairness. Some of these conditions may exert influence by heightening implementers' motivation to practice high process fairness; others may exert influence by heightening their ability to do so, and still others may heighten implementers' motivation *and* ability. For example, process fairness training programs have been shown to heighten managers' self-efficacy beliefs about practicing process fairness (Cole & Latham, 1997), which may heighten their motivation to practice process fairness by establishing more positive beliefs that E leads to P. Furthermore, process fairness training programs also may enhance trainees' *actual* ability to practice process fairness.

TOWARD A MORE NUANCED VIEW OF PRACTICAL IMPLICATIONS

Thus far, this chapter has considered some practically important matters associated with the process–outcome interaction effect discussed in Chapters 2 and 3, in which high process fairness *reduces* the effect of outcome favorability on employees' support for decisions, decision makers, and institutions relative to when process fairness is low. Practical implications grow out of the fact that (financially inexpensive) high process fairness accompanying the delivery of unfavorable outcomes has positive effects on employee attitudes and behaviors that directly contribute to the bottom line. Given this prospect, we need to understand better the motivational factors and emotional challenges that prevent implementers from practicing high process fairness, particularly when they are delivering unfavorable outcomes.

Further complicating matters are the practical implications emanating from the process–outcome interaction considered in Chapter 4, in which high process fairness *heightens* the impact of outcome favorability. That is, when delivering unfavorable outcomes managers would like to gain the support of recipients for their decisions, for themselves, and for the institutions that they (the managers) represent. Moreover, they want to gain the recipients' support in the most economically prudent ways, suggesting that it is wise for managers to deliver unfavorable outcomes with high process fairness. Note, however, that delivering unfavorable outcomes with high process fairness may have other effects on the recipients, which may or may not be preferred. For example, in Chapter 4 we saw that high process fairness heightens the influence of outcome favorability on people's self-evaluations, for better or for worse. Favorable outcomes delivered with higher process fairness engender more positive self-evaluations than do those same outcomes delivered with lower process fairness. However, unfavorable outcomes delivered with higher process fairness may actually cause people to feel worse about themselves, especially when they assign more psychological significance to their unfavorable outcomes or when the higher degree of process fairness induces them to see themselves as more responsible for their unfavorable outcomes (Brockner et al., 2008; Holmvall & Bobocel, 2008).

Given that process fairness may be inversely related to people's self-evaluations in the face of unfavorable outcomes, implementers need to consider several questions carefully prior to delivering unfavorable outcomes. First, how troubled would they be if recipients were to feel worse about themselves in response to the unfavorable outcomes? Under certain conditions, implementers may not be especially bothered by this prospect and may even welcome it. For example, it could be argued that if people were to receive negative feedback (in the form of unfavorable outcomes), they may not be motivated to change unless they also were induced to take the feedback seriously (read: personally). As numerous studies suggested, people are more likely to take unfavorable outcomes seriously or personally when the outcomes are delivered with higher process fairness (e.g., Schroth & Shah, 2000). On other occasions, however, managers may prefer to minimize the self-esteem loss caused by delivering unfavorable outcomes. If so, then delivering unfavorable outcomes with high process fairness may have the unwanted effect of reducing the recipients' self-esteem.

This raises another set of questions. If implementers prefer to minimize the recipients' loss of self-esteem in response to unfavorable outcomes, how may they best achieve this goal? Should they practice high process fairness? My advice is that implementers should practice high process fairness but simultaneously remain vigilant about the possibility that recipients may feel worse about themselves (than if the implementers did not practice high process fairness). For one thing, when outcomes are unfavorable, process fairness may be unrelated (rather than inversely related) to people's self-evaluations: no harm, no foul. Moreover, if and when process fairness *is* inversely related to people's self-evaluations, then implementers may be able to take other steps to counteract the reduction in self-esteem felt by recipients in response to high process fairness. For example, giving recipients an opportunity to reaffirm their self-integrity (Steele, 1988) may be particularly useful under such conditions.

In short, herein lies yet another way in which implementers may find themselves caught between a rock and a hard place when they have to dole out unfavorable outcomes. Delivering the unfavorable outcomes with low process fairness makes it quite likely that recipients will feel resentful toward the decision makers and fail to support them, their decisions, and the organizations that they represent. Alternatively, delivering the unfavorable outcomes with high process fairness runs the risk that recipients will become down on themselves. Of these two types of downsides, the ones associated with behaving with low process fairness seem to be more serious. For one thing, it is not even certain that process fairness will be inversely related (rather than unrelated) to recipients' self-esteem. As suggested in Chapter 4, an inverse relationship between process fairness and self-evaluations in the face of unfavorable outcomes is much more likely to arise when people assign significance to their unfavorable outcomes, such as when they are prevention rather than promotion focused (Brockner et al., 2008) or when they see themselves as more personally responsible for their outcomes (Holmvall & Bobocel, 2008).

Moreover, even if higher process fairness does reduce people's self-evaluations in response to unfavorable outcomes, they still may be able to restore their sense of self-worth by experiencing self-affirmation. For example, if managers were to deliver an unfavorable performance review with high process fairness, the recipients may be motivated to take the feedback seriously; they could not easily externalize the negative feedback as resulting from an unfair process. If, however, such a performance review also included constructive and personalized feedback on how to improve, then recipients may respond positively for several reasons related to self-affirmation. For one thing, constructive feedback may help them to attain the knowledge, skills, and abilities needed to improve, thereby bolstering their sense of self-efficacy or self-confidence. Moreover, the symbolic message associated with being given personalized feedback communicates that their needs are taken seriously by the source of the feedback, which also may bolster their feelings of self-worth.

It has long been known that people are more likely to engage in constructive behavioral change when they are threatened *and* when they can see a clear and attainable path forward (e.g., Dabbs & Leventhal, 1966; Rogers & Prentice-Dunn, 1997). Delivering unfavorable outcome feedback to people with high process fairness may cause them to experience self-threat. If, however, such a delivery were to be accompanied by clear information on what they need to do to improve (i.e., how to counteract the threat), people are likely to respond constructively. This analysis also reminds us that implementers need to concern themselves with other things besides whether they deliver unfavorable outcomes with high process fairness; helping the recipients who may feel self-threatened determine how to respond constructively also is important.

THE IMPORTANCE OF PRACTICING HIGH PROCESS FAIRNESS: NOW MORE THAN EVER?

The age-old expressions with which I began this book (e.g., "It's not only what you do, but also how you do it") suggest that the importance of the *process* of behavior, quite apart from its substance, has long been recognized. This book has elaborated on the importance of process in two respects. First, I shined the spotlight on one particular element of process: its perceived fairness. Second, I considered *when* process fairness is particularly likely to be influential (e.g., when outcomes are unfavorable).

An interesting op-ed piece by Thomas Friedman in *The New York Times* (June 27, 2007) suggested that how we behave is likely to be, if anything, increasingly important in the years ahead. Friedman described an incident that had transpired years earlier, in which he was misperceived as having behaved with low process fairness.

> I was catching a plane at Boston's Logan Airport and went to buy some magazines for the flight. As I approached the cash register, a woman coming from another direction got there just behind me—I thought. But when I put my money down to pay, the woman said in a very loud voice: "Excuse me! I was here first!" And then she fixed me with a piercing stare that said, "I know who you are." I said I was very sorry, even though I was clearly there first. (p. A23)

Whereas Friedman (2007) was courteous enough to apologize, he went on to say that if this situation happened today rather than years ago, he would be even more motivated to treat the woman with dignity and respect. Why? Friedman suggested that technological advances have given us the capability of publicizing others' behavior. Celebrities, of course, have known this for years. They have to be vigilant about paparazzi catching them in the act of doing something that would shine unfavorably on them and then publicizing their behavior. Now, however, the fear of exposure applies to all of us, celebrities and noncelebrities alike. As Friedman put it:

> I'd be thinking there is some chance this woman has a blog or a camera in her cellphone and could, if she so chose, tell the whole world about our encounter—entirely from her perspective—and my utterly rude, boorish, arrogant … behavior. When everyone has a blog, a MySpace page or Facebook entry, everyone is a publisher. When everyone has a cellphone with a camera in it, everyone is a paparazzo. When everyone can upload video on YouTube, everyone is a filmmaker. When everyone is a publisher, paparazzo, or filmmaker, everyone else is a public figure. We're all public figures now. (p. A23)

Quoting Dov Seidman (2007), the author of the recent book, *"How,"* Friedman (2007) went on to say: "In the information age, life has no closets or chapters; you can leave nothing behind, and you have nowhere to hide your skeletons. Your past is your present" (p. A23).

So, Friedman (2007) suggested, "Whether you're selling cars or newspapers (or just buying one at the newsstand), get your hows right—how you build trust, how you collaborate, how you lead and how you say you're sorry. More people than ever will know about it when you do—or don't" (p. A23).

Together, Friedman (2007) and Seidman (2007) provided two somewhat different reasons why the stakes associated with practicing process fairness have never been higher. One of these reasons, described in this chapter, is prevention focused (Higgins, 1998). As Friedman's anecdote suggests, the costs of treating others with low process fairness may be heightened to the extent that such behavior can be easily made public. To minimize such costs, then, we would be well advised to behave with high process fairness. In the truest sense, the ounce of "prevention" may be worth the pound of cure. The other reason, not mentioned thus far, is promotion focused. That is, in addition to preventing bad things from happening, high process fairness may actually make positive things more likely to occur. As Friedman put it:

> But this also creates opportunities. Today "what" you make is quickly copied and sold by everyone. But, "how" you engage your customers, "how" you keep your promises, and "how" you collaborate with partners—that's not so easy to copy, and that is where companies can now really differentiate themselves. (p. A23)

Quoting Seidman (2007) again, Friedman (2007) wrote: "When it comes to human conduct there is tremendous variation, and where a broad spectrum of variation exists, opportunity exists, … the opportunity to *outbehave the competition*" (p. A23; italics in original). Friedman then provided several examples of how to outbehave the competition, including one in which a "hospital taught its doctors to apologize when they made mistakes, and dramatically cut their malpractice claims" (p. A23).

I rest my case.

CHAPTER SUMMARY

This chapter explicitly considered several practical concerns emanating from the interactive relationships between process fairness and outcome favorability to which we researchers should devote our energies. For example, the interaction effect depicted in Chapters 2 and 3, in which high process fairness reduced the effect of outcome favorability relative to when process fairness is low, suggests that a strong business case may be made for managers to practice high process fairness. More specifically, when employees' outcomes are unfavorable, managers may be able to elicit high support and thereby enhance the organization's bottom line by enacting the (typically financially inexpensive) behaviors that constitute high process fairness. High process fairness may soften the blow associated with receiving unfavorable outcomes, thereby lessening employees' tendencies to retaliate in ways that could be materially harmful to the organization. Moreover, once organizations have delivered outcomes that are at least moderately favorable to their constituents, they may be better served not by giving out even more in the way of favorable outcomes (which could be rather financially expensive) but rather by putting more of an emphasis on practicing high process fairness.

Given the strong economic incentives managers have to practice high process fairness, and given the moral imperative for them to do so, it is intriguing that many decisions are not implemented with relatively high levels of process fairness. This chapter analyzed why this is the case. Three principles central to expectancy theory helped to delineate some of the countervailing forces to the practice of high process fairness. Managers may not believe (1) that they have the wherewithal to practice high process fairness, (2) that the benefits of practicing high process fairness are more likely to arise than are the costs, and (3) that the benefits outweigh the costs (quite apart from the perceived likelihood of both).

Behavior is a function of motivation and ability. Thus, in addition to the aforementioned motivational factors that may impede the practice of high process fairness, managers' tendencies to practice high process fairness may be compromised if they lack ability, for example, if the cognitive load imposed on them reduces their capacity to meet the various challenges that delivering high process fairness entails. In short, managers have reasons to practice high process fairness, but they also have reasons not to do so. Given this state of affairs, it is important to delineate the factors that make the practice of high process fairness more versus less likely, as I have tried to do in this chapter. The chapter also called attention to the conundrum managers are likely to experience when they dole out unfavorable outcomes. On the one hand, to the extent that they deliver unfavorable outcomes with an unfair process, the affected parties are likely to feel angry and resentful. On the other hand, to the extent that they deliver unfavorable outcomes with a fair process, the affected parties may feel worse about themselves. Ways for managers to deal with this conundrum also were considered. Finally, I offered the conjecture that whereas practicing high process fairness always has been worthwhile, it may become even more important in the years to come given the growing ease of recording and publicizing people's behavior.

APPENDIX TO CHAPTER 1—OUTCOME FAVORABILITY AND OUTCOME FAIRNESS: RELATED AND YET DISTINCT

Outcome fairness refers to the extent to which the outcome is consistent with the prevailing norm or basis for making allocation decisions, such as equity, equality, and need (Deutsch, 1985). *Outcome favorability* refers to how much people stand to benefit (economically, psychologically, or both) as a result of the decision that was reached. Whereas there are obvious conceptual distinctions between outcome fairness and outcome favorability, the two constructs also are related to one another. When equity is the fairness norm (which is often the case in work organizations), outcome fairness is present when the relationship between people's benefits and contributions is similar to the benefits-to-contributions relationship of the appropriate targets of comparison, which typically but not always consist of their coworkers (Adams, 1965). To the extent that people rate their own contributions highly, they also are likely to believe that they are entitled to receive favorable outcomes. In other words, favorable outcomes are fairer than unfavorable outcomes provided that people have relatively positive views of their own contributions. Research has shown, moreover, that people generally have positive views of their contributions toward collective action (e.g., Messick & Sentis, 1979), often to an unjustified extent (Taylor & Brown, 1988). This reasoning may help to explain why people's estimates of outcome fairness tend to be strongly related to their judgments of outcome favorability. In fact, correlations tend to be in the neighborhood of .70 (Brockner et al., 2003; Skitka, Winquist, & Hutchinson, 2003).

Other empirical findings (in particular, research on the interactive relationships between process fairness and each of outcome fairness and outcome favorability) provide further evidence of the overlap between outcome favorability and outcome fairness. Some studies have examined the interactive relationship between process fairness and outcome fairness (e.g., McFarlin & Sweeney, 1992), whereas others have investigated the interaction between process fairness and outcome favorability (e.g., Schaubroeck, May, & Brown, 1994). Across studies, the interactive relationship between process fairness and each of outcome fairness and outcome favorability took the same basic form as that described in

Chapters 2 and 3, such that high process fairness reduced the effect of outcome fairness/favorability on people's support for decisions, decision makers, and institutions relative to when process fairness was low.

A few studies included both outcome fairness and outcome favorability. For example, Brockner et al. (2003, Study 1) looked at the interactive effect of process fairness and outcome fairness/favorability on participants' self-evaluations. Some of the items in the outcome measure tapped fairness (e.g., "The outcome was fair"), whereas others referred to favorability (e.g., "The outcome of this encounter benefited me"). In one regression analysis, we examined the interaction between outcome fairness and process fairness. In a separate regression analysis, we tested the interaction between outcome favorability and process fairness. The interaction effects were significant in *both* instances and took the form set forth in Chapter 4: High process fairness heightened the positive relationship between each of outcome fairness and outcome favorability and self-evaluations, relative to when process fairness was low. We then conducted an additional regression in which both interaction effects were entered simultaneously. This time, *neither* interaction effect was significant, suggesting that outcome fairness and outcome favorability were virtually interchangeable in how they interacted with process fairness to influence people's self-evaluations. Put differently, it was what outcome favorability and outcome fairness had *in common* that interacted with process fairness to influence self-evaluations.

Conceptual and empirical considerations suggest, however, that outcome fairness and outcome favorability are not always interchangeable. After all, even correlations as high as .70 suggest that at least half of the variance in one factor cannot be accounted for by variance in the other. Other findings provided further evidence that outcome fairness and outcome favorability are meaningfully separable. Skitka et al. (2003) conducted meta-analyses of the antecedents and consequences of outcome fairness and outcome favorability, finding important differences in both cases. For example, whereas various elements of process fairness (other than voice) were significantly predictive of people's judgments of outcome favorability and outcome fairness, the relationship between process fairness and outcome favorability was considerably stronger than was the relationship between process fairness and outcome fairness. Moreover, as main effect predictors of other factors, outcome fairness and outcome favorability were shown to behave differently. For instance, outcome fairness was more strongly related to organizational commitment, organizational citizenship behavior, and task satisfaction than was outcome favorability.

In one study of the antecedents of black engineers' attraction to an organization as a function of the organization's affirmative action policies, Cropanzano et al. (2005) provided a different type of evidence attesting to the distinction between outcome fairness and outcome favorability. The independent variables included people's judgments of the following elements of the organization's affirmative action policy: outcome fairness, outcome favorability, procedural justice, and interactional justice. The dependent variables included an attitudinal measure of the perceived attractiveness of the organization as well as an assessment of participants' intention to apply to the organization.

One purpose of the study was to examine how procedural justice and interactional justice interacted with each of outcome fairness and outcome favorability to influence the dependent variables. Accordingly, a regression analysis was conducted in which the following three-way interaction effects were entered simultaneously: (1) Outcome fairness × Procedural justice × Interactional justice and (2) Outcome favorability × Procedural justice × Interactional justice. If outcome fairness and outcome favorability were behaving similarly, then both of the three-way interaction effects should be nonsignificant when they were entered into the regression equation simultaneously. This did not happen. On the attitudinal measure, the three-way interaction involving outcome fairness was significant, whereas the three-way interaction involving outcome favorability was not. On the intention-to-apply measure, both three-way interactions were significant. Whereas the different findings on the two dependent measures are of some interest in their own right, the more important conclusion for present purposes is that outcome fairness and outcome favorability did not behave interchangeably.

In summary, conceptual reasoning and empirical evidence suggest that outcome fairness and outcome favorability are at once strongly related to and meaningfully distinct from one another. An important mandate for future theory and research is to predict when and explain why outcome fairness and outcome favorability have similar versus different effects. Skitka et al. (2003) took an important first step in addressing whether outcome fairness and outcome favorability differ as main effects. A logical next step is to learn more about when and why outcome fairness and outcome favorability behave similarly versus differently in how they interact with process fairness.

FUTURE RESEARCH OPPORTUNITY

To guide such thinking, it may be useful to return to basic theoretical accounts of why outcomes interact with process fairness. For example, the cognitive appraisal theory of stress (Lazarus & Folkman, 1984) gives reason to believe that outcome fairness and outcome favorability may interact similarly with process fairness. After all, the receipt of either an unfair outcome or an unfavorable outcome could lead to the perception of threat during the primary appraisal process. In contrast, fair outcomes or favorable outcomes are much less likely to elicit the perception of threat. Information pertaining to process fairness in turn may be used for secondary appraisal purposes, which enables people to determine whether they will be able to counteract the threat.

Primary appraisal (perceived threat) and secondary appraisal (perceived control) interact with each other to influence felt stress (a notion considered in greater detail in Chapter 2). Hence, when the primary appraisal leads to the perception of threat (due either to low outcome fairness or to low outcome favorability), the secondary appraisal shaped by process fairness information will have much more of an effect on felt stress relative to when the primary appraisal process does not lead to the perception of threat (i.e., when outcomes are relatively fair or favorable). This reasoning leads to the expectation of an interactive effect of outcome *fairness* and process fairness on stress like that found in the studies by Greenberg (2006) and Tepper (2001), and it leads to the expectation of a similar interactive effect of outcome *favorability* and process fairness on stress like that found in studies by Vermunt and Steensma (2003) and Elovainio et al. (2007).

Alternatively, outcome fairness and outcome favorability sometimes may behave differently in how they interact with process fairness due to the fact that unfair outcomes and unfavorable outcomes may represent different kinds of threat. Unfair outcomes may raise people's concerns about how *fairly* they will be treated by the other party over the longer haul. Unfair outcomes may be somewhat less apt to arouse people's concerns about whether they will receive *favorable* outcomes over the longer haul. For example, consider the case of "positive inequity" (Adams, 1965), in which people's outcomes are unfair, in that they are receiving more than they deserve if resources had been allocated on the basis of their contributions, but also are favorable. If the threat elicited by unfair outcomes is concern about fair treatment over the longer haul, then process fairness information should be highly relevant and therefore likely to have a highly significant effect on felt stress.

In contrast, unfavorable outcomes may represent a different kind of threat, namely, how much people may expect to receive favorable outcomes over the longer haul. Whereas process fairness information may be somewhat informative (such that people are likely to be more reassured about the favorability of their longer-term outcomes when process fairness is high rather than low), it also may be that process fairness information will be judged as saying less about the *favorability* of future outcomes than it says about the *fairness* of future treatment. Consequently, felt stress may be less affected by the interaction between outcome favorability and process fairness than by the interaction between outcome fairness and process fairness.

The last prediction assumes that people do not assign greater significance to the receipt of favorable outcomes over the long term than they do to the receipt of fair treatment over the longer haul. If, however, long-term outcome favorability were more important to people than long-term outcome fairness, then a larger portion of the variance in felt stress may be accounted for by the interaction between outcome favorability and process fairness than by the interaction between outcome fairness and process fairness. That is, even though process fairness may be less indicative of long-term outcome favorability than of long-term outcome fairness, the greater importance assigned to outcome favorability may make people's felt stress more susceptible to the moderating influence of process fairness on outcome favorability than to the moderating influence of process fairness on outcome fairness. In any event, further research is needed to delineate when and why outcome fairness and outcome favorability interact similarly versus differently with process fairness.

REFERENCES

Adams, J. S. (1965). Inequity in social exchange. In L. Berkowitz (Ed.), *Advances in experimental social psychology* (Vol. 2, pp. 267–299). New York: Academic Press.

Affleck, G., Tennen, H., Pfeiffer, C., & Fifield, J. (1987). Appraisals of control and predictability in adapting to a chronic disease. *Journal of Personality and Social Psychology, 53*, 273–279.

Aggarwal, P., & Larrick, R. P. (2010). *The interaction of relationship norms and fairness norms: When interpersonal fairness matters more.* Manuscript submitted for publication.

Aiken, L. S., & West, G. S. (1991). *Multiple regression: Testing and interpreting interactions*. Newbury Park, CA: Sage.

Amabile, T. M. (1996). *Creativity in context.* Boulder, CO: Westview Press.

Amabile, T. M., Hill, K., Hennessey, B. A., & Tighe, E. (1994). The Work Preference Inventory: Assessing intrinsic and extrinsic motivational orientations. *Journal of Personality and Social Psychology, 66*, 950–967.

Aryee, S., Budhwar, P. S., & Chen, Z. X. (2002). Trust as a mediator of the relationship between organizational justice and work outcomes: Test of a social exchange model. *Journal of Organizational Behavior, 23*, 267–286.

Bacharach, S. B., Bamberger, P., & Conley, S. (1991). Work–home conflict among nurses and engineers: Mediating the impact of role stress on burnout and satisfaction at work. *Journal of Organizational Behavior, 12*, 39–53.

Bandura, A. (1994). Self-efficacy. In V. S. Ramachaudran (Ed.), *Encyclopedia of human behavior* (Vol. 4, pp. 71–81). New York: Academic Press.

Barclay, L., Skarlicki, D. P., & Pugh, S. D. (2005). Exploring the role of emotions in injustice perceptions and retaliation. *Journal of Applied Psychology, 90*, 629–643.

Bar-Hillel, M. (1973). On the subjective probability of compound events. *Organizational Behavior and Human Performance, 9*, 396–406.

Barsade, S. (2002). The ripple effect: Emotional contagion and its influence on group behavior. *Administrative Science Quarterly, 47*, 644–675.

Baumeister, R. F., & Leary, M. (1995). The need to belong: Desire for interpersonal attachments as a fundamental human motivation. *Psychological Bulletin, 117*, 497–529.

Becker, E. (1973). *The denial of death*. New York: Free Press.

Bies, R. J. (1987). The predicament of injustice: The management of moral outrage. In L. L. Cummings & B. M. Staw (Eds.), *Research in organizational behavior* (Vol. 9, pp. 289–319). Greenwich, CT: JAI Press.

Black, J. S., & Gregersen, H. B. (1999). The right way to manage expats. *Harvard Business Review, 77*, 52–61.

Black, J. S., Gregersen, H. B., & Mendenhall, M. E. (1992). *Global assignments*. San Francisco: Jossey-Bass.

Blader, S. L. (2007). What determines people's fairness judgments? Identification and outcomes influence procedural justice evaluations under uncertainty. *Journal of Experimental Social Psychology, 43*, 986–994.

Blader, S. L., & Chen, Y. (in press). What influences how higher status people respond to lower status others? Effects of procedural fairness, outcome favorability, and concerns about status maintenance. *Organization Science.*

Blader, S. L., & Tyler, T. R. (2003). A four component model of procedural justice: Defining the meaning of a "fair" process. *Personality and Social Psychology Bulletin, 29*, 747–758.

Blau, P. M. (1964). *Exchange and power in social life*. New York: Wiley.

Bond, J. T., Galinsky, E., & Swanberg, J. E. (1998). *The 1997 national study of the changing workforce*. New York: Families and Work Institute.

Brewer, M. B., & Gardner, W. L. (1996). Who is this "we"? Levels of collective identity and self representations. *Journal of Personality and Social Psychology, 71*, 83–93.

Brockner, J. (1988). *Self-esteem at work: Research, theory, and practice.* Lexington, MA: Lexington Books.

Brockner, J. (1990). Scope of justice in the workplace: The case of survivors' reactions to co-worker layoffs. *Journal of Social Issues, 46*, 95–106.

Brockner, J. (2002). Making sense of procedural fairness: How high procedural fairness can reduce or heighten the influence of outcome favorability. *Academy of Management Review, 27*, 58–76.

Brockner, J. (2003). Unpacking country effects: On the need to operationalize the psychological determinants of cross-national differences. In R. M. Kramer & B. M. Staw (Eds.), *Research in organizational behavior* (Vol. 25, pp. 333–367). Oxford, UK: Elsevier Press.

Brockner, J. (2006). Why it's so hard to be fair. *Harvard Business Review, 84*(3), 122–129.

Brockner, J., Ackerman, G., Greenberg, J., Gelfand, M., Francesco, A. M., Chen, Z. X., et al. (2001). Culture and procedural justice: The influence of power distance on reactions to voice. *Journal of Experimental Social Psychology, 37*, 300–315.

Brockner, J., Bianchi, E., Van den Bos, K., Miles, P., Seifert, M., Shannon, L., & Moon, H. (2010). *Trust in decision-making authorities dictates the form of the interactive relationship between outcome favorability and procedural fairness*. Manuscript submitted for publication.

Brockner, J., & Chen, Y. (1996). The moderating effects of self-esteem and self-construal in reaction to a threat to the self: Evidence from the People's Republic of China and the United States. *Journal of Personality and Social Psychology, 71*, 603–615.

Brockner, J., Chen, Y., Mannix, E., Leung, K., & Skarlicki, D. (2000). Culture and procedural fairness: When the effects of what you do depend upon how you do it. *Administrative Science Quarterly, 45*, 138–159.

Brockner, J., Davy, J., & Carter, C. (1985). Layoffs, self-esteem, and survivor guilt: Motivational, affective, and attitudinal consequences. *Organizational Behavior and Human Decision Processes, 36,* 229–244.

Brockner, J., De Cremer, D., Fishman, A., & Spiegel, S. (2008). When does high procedural fairness reduce self-evaluations following unfavorable outcomes?: The moderating effect of prevention focus. *Journal of Experimental Social Psychology, 44,* 187–200.

Brockner, J., De Cremer, D., Van den Bos, K., & Chen, Y. (2005). The influence of interdependent self-construal on procedural fairness effects. *Organizational Behavior and Human Decision Processes, 96,* 155–167.

Brockner, J., Fishman, A. Y., Reb, J., Goldman, B., Spiegel, S., & Garden, C. (2007). Procedural fairness, outcome favorability, and judgments of an authority's responsibility. *Journal of Applied Psychology, 92,* 1657–1671.

Brockner, J., Heuer, L. B., Magner, N., Folger, R., Umphress, E., Van den Bos, K., et al. (2003). High procedural fairness heightens the effect of outcome favorability on self-evaluations: An attributional analysis. *Organizational Behavior and Human Decision Processes, 91,* 51–68.

Brockner, J., Heuer, L., Siegel, P., Wiesenfeld, B., Martin, C., Grover, S., et al. (1998). The moderating effect of self-esteem in reaction to voice: Converging evidence from five studies. *Journal of Personality and Social Psychology, 75,* 394–407.

Brockner, J., & Higgins, E. T. (2001). Regulatory focus theory: Its implications for the study of emotions in the workplace. *Organizational Behavior and Human Decision Processes, 86,* 35–66.

Brockner, J., & Hulton, A. J. B. (1978). How to reverse the vicious cycle of low self-esteem: The importance of attentional focus. *Journal of Experimental Social Psychology, 14,* 564–578.

Brockner, J., Konovsky, M., Cooper-Schneider, R., Folger, R., Martin, C., & Bies, R.J. (1994). The interactive effects of procedural justice and outcome negativity on the victims and survivors of job loss. *Academy of Management Journal, 37,* 397-409.

Brockner, J., Paruchuri, S., Idson, L. C., & Higgins, E. T. (2002). Regulatory focus and the probability estimates of conjunctive and disjunctive events. *Organizational Behavior and Human Decision Processes, 87,* 5–24.

Brockner, J., Senior, D., & Welch, W. (2010). *Corporate volunteerism, the experience of a positive self-concept, and organizational commitment: Evidence from two field studies.* Manuscript submitted for publication.

Brockner, J., Siegel, P. A., Daly, J. P., Tyler, T. R., & Martin, C. (1997). When trust matters: The moderating effect of outcome favorability. *Administrative Science Quarterly, 42,* 558–583.

Brockner, J., & Wiesenfeld, B. M. (1996). An integrative framework for explaining reactions to decisions: The interactive effects of outcomes and procedures. *Psychological Bulletin, 120,* 189–208.

Brockner, J., Wiesenfeld, B. M., & Diekmann, K. (2009). Towards a "fairer" conception of process fairness: Why, when, and how more may not always be better than less. *The Academy of Management Annals, 3,* 183–216.

Brockner, J., Wiesenfeld, B., Siegel, P., & Zhang, S. (2010). *Hedging your bets: Uncertainty about continued success reduces people's desire for high procedural fairness.* Manuscript submitted for publication.

Brunot, S., Huguet, P., & Monteil, J-M. (1999). Performance feedback and self-focused attention in the classroom: When past and present interact. *Social Psychology of Education, 3*, 271–293.

Buss, A. H. (1980). *Self-consciousness and social anxiety.* San Francisco: Freeman.

Cacioppo, J. T., Petty, R. E., & Kao, C. F. (1984). The efficient assessment of need for cognition. *Journal of Personality Assessment, 48*, 306–307.

Camacho, C. J., Higgins, E. T., & Luger, L. (2003). Moral value transfer from regulatory fit: What feels right *is* right and what feels wrong *is* wrong. *Journal of Personality and Social Psychology, 84*, 498–510.

Campbell, J. (1990). Self-esteem and clarity of the self-concept. *Journal of Personality and Social Psychology, 59*, 538–549.

Carr, J., Gregory, B. T., Ensley, M. D., & Tepper, B. J. (2005, November). *Effects of procedural justice on the relationships between work status congruence and organizational commitment and citizenship behaviors.* Paper presented at the Southern Management Association Conference, Charleston, SC.

Cast, A. D., & Burke, P. J. (2002). A theory of self-esteem. *Social Forces, 80*, 1041–1068.

Cesario, J., Grant, H., & Higgins, E. T. (2004). Regulatory fit and persuasion: Transfer from "feeling right." *Journal of Personality and Social Psychology, 86*, 338–404.

Chaiken, S. (1980). Heuristic versus systematic information processing and the use of source versus message cues in persuasion. *Journal of Personality and Social Psychology, 39*, 752–766.

Chatman, J. A. (1989). Improving interactional organizational research: A model of person-organization fit. *Academy of Management Review 14*, 333–349.

Chen, C. C., Choi, J., & Chi, S-C. (2002). Making justice sense of local-expatriate compensation disparity: Mitigation by local referents, ideological explanations, and interpersonal sensitivity in China-foreign joint ventures. *Academy of Management Journal, 45*, 807–817.

Chen, Y., Brockner, J., & Greenberg, J. (2003). When is it "A pleasure to do business with you"? The effects of relative status, outcome favorability, and procedural fairness. *Organizational Behavior and Human Decision Processes, 92*, 1–21.

Clark, M. S., & Mills, J. (1993). The difference between communal and exchange relationships: What it is and is not. *Personality and Social Psychology Bulletin, 19*, 684–691.

Cohen-Charash, Y., & Spector, P. E. (2001). The role of justice in organizations: A meta-analysis. *Organizational Behavior and Human Decision Processes, 86*, 278–321.

Cole, N. D. (2004). Gender differences in perceived disciplinary fairness. *Gender, Work and Organization, 11*, 254–279.

Cole, N. D., & Latham, G. P. (1997). Effects of training in procedural justice on perceptions of disciplinary fairness by unionized employees and disciplinary subject matter experts. *Journal of Applied Psychology, 82*, 699–705.

Colquitt, J. (2001). On the dimensionality of organizational justice: A construct validation of a measure. *Journal of Applied Psychology, 86*, 386–400.

Colquitt, J. A., Conlon, D. E., Wesson, M. J., Porter, C. O. L. H., & Ng, K. Y. (2001). Justice at the millennium: A meta-analysis of 25 years of procedural justice research. *Journal of Applied Psychology, 86*, 425–445.

Cook, T. D., & Campbell, D. T. (1979). *Quasi-experimentation: Design and analysis for field settings.* Chicago: Rand McNally.

Cooley, C. H. (1902). *Human nature and social order.* New York: Scribner's.

Cropanzano, R., Byrne, Z. S., Bobocel, D. R., & Rupp, D. E. (2001). Moral virtues, fairness heuristics, social entities, and other denizens of organizational justice. *Journal of Vocational Behavior, 58,* 164–209.

Cropanzano, R., & Folger, R. (1989). Referent cognitions and task decision autonomy: Beyond equity theory. *Journal of Applied Psychology, 74,* 293–299.

Cropanzano, R., Goldman, B., & Folger, R. (2003). Deontic justice: The role of moral principles in workplace fairness. *Journal of Organizational Behavior, 24,* 1019–1024.

Cropanzano, R., & Konovsky, M. A. (1995). Resolving the justice dilemma by improving the outcomes: The case of employee drug screening. *Journal of Business and Psychology, 10,* 221–243.

Cropanzano, R., Paddock, L., Rupp, D. E., Bagger, J., & Baldwin, A. (2008). How regulatory focus impacts the process by outcome interaction for perceived fairness and emotions. *Organizational Behavior and Human Decision Processes, 105,* 36–51.

Cropanzano, R., Slaughter, J., & Bachiochi, P. (2005). Organizational justice and black applicants' reactions to affirmative action. *Journal of Applied Psychology, 90,* 1168–1184.

Crowe, E., & Higgins, E.T. (1997). Regulatory focus and strategic inclinations: Promotion and prevention in decision making. *Organizational Behavior and Human Decision Processes, 69,* 117–132.

Dabbs, J. M., & Leventhal, H. (1966). Effects of varying the recommendations in a fear-arousing communication. *Journal of Personality and Social Psychology, 4,* 525–31.

Dalton, D. R., & Mesch, D. J. (1990). The impact of flexible scheduling on employee attendance and turnover. *Administrative Science Quarterly, 35,* 370–387.

Daly, J. P., & Tripp, T. M. (1996). Is outcome fairness used to make procedural fairness judgments when procedural information is inaccessible? *Social Justice Research, 9,* 327–349.

Davis, M. (1971). That's interesting! Towards a phenomenology of sociology and a sociology of phenomenology. *Philosophy of the Social Sciences, 1,* 309–344.

Deci, E., L., & Ryan, R. M. (2002). *Handbook of self-determination research.* Rochester, NY: University of Rochester Press.

De Cremer, D. (2003). Why inconsistent leadership is regarded as procedurally unfair: The importance of social self-esteem concerns. *European Journal of Social Psychology, 33,* 535–550.

De Cremer, D., Brockner, J., Fishman, van Dijke, M., van Olffen, W., & Mayer, D. (in press). When do procedural fairness and outcome favorability interact to influence organizational commitment?: The moderating effect of uncertainty. *Journal of Applied Psychology.*

De Cremer, D., & Sedikides, C. (2005). Self-uncertainty and responsiveness to procedural justice. *Journal of Experimental Social Psychology, 41,* 157–173.

De Cremer, D., & Sedikides, C. (2008). Reputational implications of procedural fairness for personal and relational self-esteem. *Basic and Applied Social Psychology, 30,* 66–75.

De Cremer, D., & Tyler, T. R. (2005). Managing group behaviour: The interplay between fairness, self, and cooperation. In M. P. Zanna (Ed.), *Advances in experimental social psychology* (Vol. 37, pp. 151–218). San Diego, CA: Academic Press.

De Cremer, D., & Tyler, T. R. (2007). The effects of trust in authority and procedural fairness on cooperation. *Journal of Applied Psychology, 92*, 639–649.

De Cremer, D., & van Knippenberg, D. (2003). Cooperation with leaders in social dilemmas: On the effects of procedural fairness and outcome favorability in structural cooperation. *Organizational Behavior and Human Decision Processes, 91*, 1–11.

De Cremer, D., van Knippenberg, D., Bos, A., & van Dijke, M. (2004). How self-relevant is fair treatment? Social self-esteem moderates interactional justice effects. *Social Justice Research, 17*, 407–419.

Degoey, P. (2000). Contagious justice: Exploring the social construction of justice in organizations. In B. Staw and R. Sutton (Eds.), *Research in organizational behavior* (Vol. 22, pp. 51–102). Greenwich, CT: JAI Press.

Deutsch, M. (1975). Equity, equality, and need: What determines which value will be used as the basis of distributive justice? *Journal of Social Issues, 31*, 137–150.

Deutsch, M. (1985). *The resolution of conflict: Constructive and destructive processes.* New Haven, CT: Yale University Press.

Dunham, R. B., Pierce, J. L., & Castenada, M. B. (1987). Alternative work schedules: Two field quasi-experiments. *Personnel Psychology, 40*, 215–242.

Dweck, C. S. (1975). The role of expectations and attributions in the alleviation of learned helplessness. *Journal of Personality and Social Psychology, 31*, 674–685.

Dweck, C. S., & Leggett, E. L. (1988). A social-cognitive approach to motivation and personality. *Psychological Review, 95*, 256–273.

Eisenberger, N. I., Lieberman, M. D., & Williams, K. D. (2003). Does rejection hurt? An fMRI study of social exclusion. *Science, 302*, 290–292.

Elovainio, M., Vahtera, J., Kivimäki, M., Linna, A., van den Bos, K., Greenberg, J., et al. (2007, August). *Procedural and interactional justice as determinants of employee health following the severe illness of a family member: A study of "absences waiting to happen."* Paper presented at the Academy of Management Conference, Philadelphia.

Elsbach, K., & Kramer, R. M. (1996). Members' responses to organizational identity threats: Encountering and countering the *Business Week* rankings. *Administrative Science Quarterly, 41*, 442–476.

Fazio, R. H., & Zanna, M. P., (1981). Direct experience and attitude-behavior consistency. In L. Berkowitz (Ed.), *Advances in experimental social psychology* (Vol. 16, pp. 161–202). San Diego, CA: Academic Press.

Feldman, D. C. (1995). Managing part-time and temporary employment relationships: Individual needs and organizational demands. In M. London (Ed.), *Employees, careers, and job creation* (pp. 121–141). San Francisco: Jossey-Bass.

Fenigstein, A., Scheier, M. F., & Buss, A. H. (1975). Public and private self-consciousness: Assessment and theory. *Journal of Consulting and Clinical Psychology, 43*, 522–527.

Ferguson, T. J., & Rule, B. G. (1983). An attributional perspective on anger and aggression. In R. G. Geen & E. I. Donnerstein (Eds), *Perspectives on aggression: Theoretical and empirical reviews* (Vol. 1, pp. 41–74). New York: Academic Press.

Ferris, G. R., Davidson, S. L., & Perrewé, P. L. (2005). *Political skill at work*. Palo Alto, CA: Davies-Black.

Festinger, L. (1954). A theory of social comparison processes. *Human Relations, 7*, 117–140.

Festinger, L. (1957). *A theory of cognitive dissonance*. Stanford, CA: Stanford University Press.

Folger, R. (1986). Rethinking equity theory: A referent cognitions model. In H. W. Bierhoff, R. L. Cohen, & J. Greenberg (Eds.), *Justice in social relations* (pp. 145–162). New York: Plenum Press.

Folger, R. (1993). Reactions to mistreatment at work. In J. K. Murnighan (Ed.), *Social psychology in organizations: Advances in theory and research* (pp. 161–183). Englewood Cliffs, NJ: Prentice-Hall.

Folger, R. (2001). Fairness as deonance. In S. W. Gilliland, D. D. Steiner, & D. P. Skarlicki (Eds.), *Research in social issues in management* (pp. 3–31). Greenwich, CT: Information Age.

Folger, R., & Cropanzano, R. (1998). *Organizational justice and human resource management*. Thousand Oaks, CA: Sage.

Folger, R., & Cropanzano, R. (2001). Fairness theory: Justice as accountability. In J. Greenberg & R. Cropanzano (Eds.), *Advances in organizational justice* (pp. 1–55). Stanford, CA: Stanford University Press.

Folger, R., & Martin, C. (1986). Relative deprivation and referent cognitions: Distributive and procedural justice effects. *Journal of Experimental Social Psychology, 22*, 531–546.

Folger, R., Rosenfield, D., Grove, J., & Corkran, L. (1979). Effects of "voice" and peer opinions on responses to inequity. *Journal of Personality and Social Psychology, 37*, 2253–2261.

Folger, R., Rosenfield, D., & Robinson, T. (1983). Relative deprivation and procedural justification. *Journal of Personality and Social Psychology, 45*, 268–273.

Folger, R., & Skarlicki, D. P. (1998). When tough times make tough bosses: Managerial distancing as a function of layoff blame. *Academy of Management Journal, 41*, 79–87.

French, J. R. P., & Raven, B. H. (1959). The bases of social power. In D. Cartwright (Ed.), *Studies in social power* (pp. 150–167). Ann Arbor: Institute for Social Research.

Friedman, R. S. (1999). *The phenomenological correlates and consequences of distinct self-regulatory systems*. Unpublished doctoral dissertation, Columbia University, New York.

Friedman, T. L. (2007). The whole world is watching. *The New York Times*, June 27, 2007, p. A23.

Frone, M. R., Russell, M., & Cooper, M. L. (1997). Relation of work-family conflict to health outcomes: A four-year longitudinal study of employed parents. *Journal of Occupational and Organizational Psychology, 70*(4), 325–335.

Garonzik, R., Brockner, J., & Siegel, P. A. (2000). Identifying international assignees at risk for premature departure: The interactive effect of outcome favorability and procedural fairness. *Journal of Applied Psychology, 85*, 13–20.

Gilbert, D. T. (2006). *Stumbling on happiness.* New York: Knopf.

Gilbert, D. T., Pinel, E. C., Wilson, T. W., Blumberg, S. J., & Wheatley, T. P. (1998). Immune neglect: A source of durability bias in affective forecasting. *Journal of Personality and Social Psychology, 75*, 617–638.

Gilliland, S. W. (1994). Effects of procedural and distributive justice on reactions to a selection system. *Journal of Applied Psychology, 79*, 691–701.

Gladwell, M. (2005). *Blink: The power of thinking without thinking.* New York: Little, Brown.

Goldberg, L. R. (1993). The structure of phenotypic personality traits. *American Psychologist, 48*, 26–34.

Goldman, B. (2003). An application of referent cognitions theory to legal-claiming by terminated workers: The role of organizational justice and anger. *Journal of Management, 29*, 705–728.

Goleman, D. (1998). *Working with emotional intelligence.* New York: Bantam.

Gouldner, A. W. (1960). The norm of reciprocity: A preliminary statement. *American Sociological Review, 25*, 161–78.

Grant, A., Dutton, J. E., & Rosso, B. D. (2008). Giving commitment: Employee support programs and the prosocial sensemaking process. *Academy of Management Journal, 51*, 898–918.

Grant, A. M., Molinsky, A., Margolis, J., Kamin, M., & Schiano, W. (2009). The performer's reactions to procedural injustice: When prosocial identity reduces prosocial behavior. *Journal of Applied Social Psychology, 39*, 319–349.

Greenberg, J. (1987a). Reactions to procedural injustice in payment allocations: Do the ends justify the means? *Journal of Applied Psychology, 72*, 55–61.

Greenberg, J. (1987b). A taxonomy of organizational justice theories. *Academy of Management Review, 12*, 9–22.

Greenberg, J. (1990a). Employee theft as a reaction to underpayment inequity: The hidden cost of pay cuts. *Journal of Applied Psychology, 75*, 561–568

Greenberg, J. (1990b). Organizational justice: Yesterday, today, and tomorrow. *Journal of Management, 16*, 399–432.

Greenberg, J. (1993). Stealing in the name of justice: Informational and interpersonal moderators of theft reactions to underpayment inequity. *Organizational Behavior and Human Decision Processes, 54*, 81–103.

Greenberg, J. (2005). Stress fairness to fare no stress: Managing workplace stress by promoting organizational justice. *Organizational Dynamics, 33*, 352–365.

Greenberg, J. (2006). Losing sleep over organizational injustice: Attenuating insomniac reactions to underpayment inequity with supervisory training in interactional justice. *Journal of Applied Psychology, 91*, 58–69.

Greenberg, J., & Cropanzano, R. (2001). *Advances in organizational justice.* Stanford, CA: Stanford University Press.

Greenberg, J., Pyszczynski, T., Solomon, S., Pinel, E., Simon, L., & Jordan, K. (1993). Effects of self-esteem on vulnerability-denying defensive distortions: Further evidence of an anxiety-buffering function of self-esteem. *Journal of Experimental Social Psychology, 29*, 229–251.

Greenberg, J., Solomon, S., & Pyszczynski, T. (1997). Terror management theory of self-esteem and cultural worldviews: Empirical assessments and conceptual refinements. In M. P. Zanna (Ed.), *Advances in experimental social psychology* (Vol. 29, pp. 61–139). Orlando, FL: Academic Press.

Gross, J. J. (2001). Emotion regulation in adulthood: Timing is everything. *Current Directions in Psychological Science, 10*, 214–219.

Grover, S. L., & Crooker, K. J. (1995). Who appreciates family-responsive human resource policies: The impact of friendly-family policies on the organizational attachment of parents and nonparents. *Personnel Psychology, 48*, 271–288.

Heatherton, T., & Polivy, J. (1991). Development and validation of a scale for measuring state self-esteem. *Journal of Personality and Social Psychology, 60*, 895–910.

Heaven, P. C. L. (1988). Locus of control and attitudes to authority among adolescents. *Personality and Individual Differences, 9*, 181–183.

Heider, F. (1958). *The psychology of interpersonal relations.* New York: Wiley.

Hersey, P., & Blanchard, K. H. (1969). Life cycle theory of leadership: Is there a best style of leadership? *Training and Development Journal, 33*, 26–34.

Higgins, E. T. (1998). Promotion and prevention: Regulatory focus as a motivational principle. In M. P. Zanna (Ed.) *Advances in experimental social psychology* (Vol. 30, pp. 1–46). San Diego, CA: Academic Press.

Higgins, E. T. (2000). Making a good decision: Value from fit. *American Psychologist, 55*, 1217–1230.

Higgins, E. T., Friedman, R. S., Harlow, R. E., Idson, L. C., Ayduk, O. N., & Taylor, A. (2001). Achievement orientations from subjective histories of success: Promotion pride versus prevention pride. *European Journal of Social Psychology, 31*, 3–23.

Higgins, E., T., Shah, J., & Friedman, R. (1997). Emotional responses to goal attainment: Strength of regulatory focus as a moderator. *Journal of Personality and Social Psychology, 72*, 515–525.

Hill, L. (1994). *Managing your team.* Boston, MA: Harvard Business School.

Hofstede, G. (1980). *Culture's consequences: International differences in work-related values.* Newbury Park, CA: Sage.

Hofstede, G. (Ed.). (1998). *Masculinity and femininity: The taboo dimension of national cultures.* Thousand Oaks, CA: Sage.

Hofstede, G. (2007). Trust and transparency in supply netchains. In W. Y. C. Wang, M. S. H. Heng, & P. Y. K. Chau (Eds.), *Supply chain management: Issues in the new era of collaboration* (pp. 105–126). Hershey, PA: IGI Global.

Holmes, T. H., & Rahe, R. H. (1967). The social readjustment rating scale. *Journal of Psychosomatic Research, 11*, 213–218.

Holmvall, C. M., & Bobocel, D. R. (2008). What fair procedures say about me: Self-construals and reactions to procedural fairness. *Organizational Behavior and Human Decision Processes, 105*, 147–168.

Holtom, B. C., Lee, T. W., & Tidd, S. T. (2002). The relationship between work status congruence and work-related attitudes and behaviors. *Journal of Applied Psychology. 87*, 903–915.

Homans, G. (1961). *Social behaviour: Its elementary forms*. London: Routledge and Kegan Paul.

Hovland, C. I., Janis, I. L. and Kelley, H. H. (1953). *Communications and persuasion: Psychological studies in opinion change*. New Haven, CT: Yale University Press

Idson, L. C., & Higgins, E. T. (2000). How current feedback and chronic effectiveness influence motivation: Everything to gain versus everything to lose. *European Journal of Social Psychology, 30*, 583–592.

Idson, L. C., Liberman, N., & Higgins, E. T. (2000). Distinguishing gains from non-losses and losses from non-gains: A regulatory focus perspective on hedonic intensity. *Journal of Experimental Social Psychology, 36*, 252–274.

Idson, L. C., Liberman, N., & Higgins, E. T. (2004). Imagining how you'd feel: The role of motivational experiences from regulatory fit. *Personality and Social Psychology Bulletin, 30*, 926–937.

Isen, A. M., & Baron, R. A. (1991). Positive affect as a factor in organizational behavior. In L. L. Cummings & B. M. Staw (Eds.), *Research in organizational behavior* (Vol. 13, pp. 1–53). Greenwich, CT: JAI Press.

Janis, I. L., & Mann, L. (1977). *Decision making: A psychological analysis of conflict, choice and commitment*. New York: Free Press.

Janssen, O. (2004). How fairness perceptions make innovative behavior more or less stressful. *Journal of Organizational Behavior, 25*, 201–215.

Jones, S. C. (1973). Self and interpersonal evaluations: Esteem theories versus consistency theories. *Psychological Bulletin, 79*, 185–199.

Jones, D. A., & Skarlicki, D. P. (2003). The relationship between perceptions of fairness and voluntary turnover among retail employees. *Journal of Applied Social Psychology, 33*, 1226–1243.

Jones, E. E., & Berglas, S. (1978). Control of attributions about the self through self-handicapping strategies: The appeal of alcohol and the role of underachievement. *Personality and Social Psychology Bulletin, 4*, 200–206.

Jones, E. E., & Davis, K. E. (1965). From acts to dispositions: The attribution process in person perception. In L. Berkowitz (Ed.), *Advances in experimental social psychology* (Vol. 2, pp. 219–266). New York: Academic Press.

Judd, C. M., James-Hawkins, L., Yzerbyt, V., & Kashima, Y. (2005). Fundamental dimensions of social judgment: Understanding the relations between judgments of competence and warmth. *Journal of Personality and Social Psychology, 89*, 899–913.

Kahneman, D., & Tversky, A. (1984). Choices, values and frames. *American Psychologist, 39*, 341–350.

Kelley, H. H. (1973). The processes of causal attribution. *American Psychologist, 28*, 107–128.

Kickul, J., Lester, S. W., & Finkl, J. (2002). Promise breaking during radical organizational change: Do justice interventions make a difference? *Journal of Organizational Behavior, 23*, 469–488.

Kim, W. C., & Mauborgne, R. (1997). Fair process: Managing in the knowledge economy. *Harvard Business Review, 75*, 65–75.

Klein, J. (1984). Why supervisors resist employee involvement. *Harvard Business Review, 62*, 87–96.

Konrad, A. M., & Mangel, R. (2000). The impact of work-life programs on firm productivity. *Strategic Management Journal, 21*, 1225–1237.

Konovsky, M. A., & Pugh, S. D. (1994). Citizenship behavior and social exchange. *Academy of Management Journal, 37*, 656–669.

Koole, S. L., Dechesne, M., & Van Knippenberg, A. (2000). *The sting of death: Evidence that reminders of mortality undermine implicit self-esteem.* Unpublished manuscript.

Koper, G., van Knippenberg, D., Bouhuijs, F., Vermunt, R., & Wilke, H. (1993). Procedural fairness and self-esteem. *European Journal of Social Psychology, 23,* 313–325.

Kramer, R. M. (1996). Divergent realities and convergent disappointments in the hierarchic relation: Trust and the intuitive auditor at work. In R. M. Kramer & T. R. Tyler (Eds.), *Trust in organizations: Frontiers of theory and research* (pp. 216–245). Thousand Oaks, CA: Sage.

Kramer, R. M. (2001). Identity and trust in organizations: One anatomy of a productive but problematic relationship. In M. A. Hogg & D. J. Terry (Eds.), *Social identity processes in organizational contexts* (pp. 167–180). Philadelphia: Psychology Press.

Kramer, R. M., & Tyler, T. R. (1996). *Trust in organizations: Frontiers of theory and research.* London: Sage.

Krehbiel, P. J., & Cropanzano, R. (2000). Procedural justice, outcome favorability, and emotion. *Social Justice Research, 13,* 339–360.

Krosnick, J. A., Boninger, D. S., Chuang, Y. C., Berent, M. K., & Carnot, C. (1993). Attitude strength: One construct or many related constructs? *Journal of Personality and Social Psychology, 65,* 1132–1151.

Kruger, J. (1999). Lake Wobegon be gone! The "below-average effect" and the egocentric nature of comparative ability judgments. *Journal of Personality and Social Psychology, 77,* 221–232.

Kruglanski, A. W., Webster, D. M., & Klem, A. (1993). Motivated resistance and openness to persuasion in the presence or absence of prior information. *Journal of Personality and Social Psychology, 65,* 861–876.

Kwong, J. Y. Y., & Leung, K. (2002). A moderator of the interaction effect of procedural justice and outcome favorability: Importance of the relationship. *Organizational Behavior and Human Decision Processes, 87,* 278–299.

Lambert, S. J. (2000). Added benefits: The link between work–life benefits and organizational citizenship behavior. *Academy of Management Journal, 43,* 801–815.

Langer, E. J. (1975). The illusion of control. *Journal of Personality and Social Psychology, 32,* 311–328.

Lavelle, J. J., Brockner, J., Konovsky, M., Price, K. H., Henley, A. B., Taneja, A., et al. (2008). Commitment, procedural fairness, and organizational citizenship behavior: A multi-foci analysis. *Journal of Organizational Behavior, 30,* 337–357.

Lavelle, J., Rupp, D., & Brockner, J. (2007). Taking a multi-foci approach to the study of justice, social exchange, and citizenship behavior: The target similarity model. *Journal of Management, 33,* 841–866.

Lawler, E. E. (1968). Equity theory as a predictor of productivity and work quality. *Psychological Bulletin, 70,* 596–610.

Lazarus, R. S., & Folkman, S. (1984). *Stress, appraisal, and coping.* New York: Springer.

Lazarus, R. S., & Launier, R. (1978). Stress-related transactions between person and environment. In L. A. Pervin & M. Lewis (Eds.), *Perspectives in interactional psychology* (pp. 287–327). New York: Plenum.

Leary, M. R. (1999). The social and psychological importance of self-esteem. In R. M. Kowalski & M. R. Leary (Eds.), *The social psychology of emotional and behavioral problems: Interfaces of social and clinical psychology* (pp. 197–221). Washington, DC: American Psychological Association.

Lecky, P. (1945). *Self-consistency: A theory of personality.* New York: Island Press.

Lerner, M. J., & Simmons, C. H. (1966). The observer's reaction to the "innocent victim": Compassion or rejection? *Journal of Personality and Social Psychology, 4,* 203–210.

Leung, K., Bond, M. H., de Carrasquel, S. R., Munoz, C., Hernandez, M., Murakami, F., et al. (2002). Social axioms: The search for universal dimensions of general beliefs about how the world functions. *Journal of Cross-Cultural Psychology, 33,* 286–302.

Leung, K., Su, S., & Morris, M. W. (2001). When is criticism not constructive? The roles of fairness perceptions and dispositional attributions in employee acceptance of critical supervisory feedback. *Human Relations, 54,* 1155–1187.

Leventhal, G. S., Karuza, J., & Fry, W. R. (1980). Beyond fairness: A theory of allocation preferences. In G. Mikula (Ed.), *Justice and social interaction* (pp. 167–218). New York: Springer-Verlag.

Levinson, W. L., Roter, D. L., Mullooly, J. P., Dull, V. T., & Frankel, R. M. (1997). Physician–patient communication: The relationship with malpractice claims among primary care physicians and surgeons. *Journal of the American Medical Association, 277,* 553–559.

Lin, X. W., Che, H. S., & Leung, K. (2009). The role of leader morality in the interaction effect of procedural justice and outcome favorability. *Journal of Applied Social Psychology, 39,* 1536–1561.

Lind, E. A. (2001). Fairness heuristic theory: Justice judgments as pivotal cognitions in organizational. relations. In J. Greenberg & R. Cropanzano (Eds.), *Advances in organizational justice* (pp. 56–88). Stanford, CA: Stanford University Press.

Lind, E. A., Greenberg, J., Scott, K. S., & Welchans, T. D. (2000). The winding road from employee to complainant: Situational and psychological determinants of wrongful-termination claims. *Administrative Science Quarterly, 45,* 557–590.

Lind, E. A., & Lissak, R.I. (1985). Apparent impropriety and procedural fairness judgments. *Journal of Experimental Social Psychology, 21,* 19–29.

Lind, E. A., & Tyler, T. R. (1988). *The social psychology of procedural justice.* New York: Plenum Press.

Magner, N., Welker, R., & Johnson, G. (1996). The interactive effects of participation and outcome favorability in performance appraisal on turnover intentions and evaluations of supervisors. *Journal of Occupational and Organizational Psychology, 69,* 135–143.

Margolis, J. D., & Molinsky, A. L. (2008). Navigating the bind of necessary evils: Psychological engagement and the production of interpersonally sensitive behavior. *Academy of Management Journal, 51,* 847–872.

Mark, M. M., & Folger, R. (1984). Responses to relative deprivation: A conceptual framework. In L. Wheeler & P.R. Shaver (Eds.), *Review of personality and social psychology* (Vol. 5, pp. 192–218). Beverly Hills, CA: Sage.

Markus, H., & Kitayama, S. (1991). Culture and the self: Implications for cognition, emotion, and motivation. *Psychological Review, 98*, 224–253.

Mazur, A. (1985). A biosocial model of status in face-to-face primate groups. *Social Forces, 64*, 377–402.

McAllister, D. J. (1995). Affect and cognition-based trust as foundations for interpersonal cooperation in organizations. *Academy of Management Journal, 38*, 24–59.

McAllister, D. J., Lewicki, R. J., & Chaturvedi, S. (2010). *Trust in developing relationships: From theory to measurement.* Working paper.

McFarlin, D. B., & Sweeney, P. D. (1992). Distributive and procedural justice as predictors of satisfaction with personal and organizational outcomes *Academy of Management Journal, 35*, 626–637.

McGuire, W. J. (1973). The yin and yang of progress in social psychology: Seven koan. *Journal of Personality and Social Psychology, 26*, 446–456.

McGuire, W. J. (1997). Creative hypothesis generation in psychology: Some useful heuristics. *Annual Review of Psychology, 48*, 1–30.

McLeod, P., Lobel, S., & Cox, T. H. (1996). Ethnic diversity and creativity in small groups. *Small Group Research, 27*, 248–264.

Mead, G. H. (1934). *Mind, self, and society.* Chicago: University of Chicago Press.

Messick, D., & Sentis, K. (1979). Fairness and preference. *Journal of Experimental Social Psychology, 15*, 418–34.

Miedema, J., Van den Bos, K., & Vermunt, R. (2006). The influence of self-threats on fairness judgments and affective measures. *Social Justice Research, 19*, 228–253.

Milgram, S. (1974) *Obedience to authority. An experimental view.* New York: HarperCollins.

Mills, J., & Clark, M. S. (1982). Exchange and communal relationships. In L. Wheeler (Ed.), *Review of personality and social psychology* (Vol. 3, pp. 121–144). Beverly Hills, CA: Sage.

Mischel, W. (1966). Theory and research on the antecedents of self-imposed delay of reward. In B. A. Maher (Ed.), *Progress in experimental personality research* (Vol. 3. pp. 85–131). New York: Academic Press.

Molinsky, A. L., & Margolis, J. D. (2005). Necessary evils and interpersonal sensitivity in organizations. *Academy of Management Review, 30*, 245–268.

Molinsky, A. L., & Margolis, J. D. (2006). The emotional tightrope of downsizing: Hidden challenges for leaders and their organizations. *Organizational Dynamics, 35*, 145–159.

Morris, M. W., & Peng, K. (1994). Culture and cause: American and Chinese attributions for social and physical events. *Journal of Personality and Social Psychology, 67*, 949–971.

Mossholder, K. W., Bedeian, A. G., & Armenakis, A. A. (1982). Group process-work outcome relationships: A note on the moderating impact of self-esteem. *Academy of Management Journal, 25*, 575–585.

Muller, D., Judd, C. M, & Yzerbyt, V. Y. (2005). When moderation is mediated and mediation is moderated. *Journal of Personality and Social Psychology, 89*, 852–863.

Naumann, S., & Bennett, N. (2000). A case for procedural justice climate: Development and test of a multi-level model. *Academy of Management Journal, 43*, 881–889.

Oberholzer-Gee, F., & Frey, B. S. (1996). Fair siting procedures: An empirical analysis of their importance and characteristics. *Journal of Policy Analysis and Management, 15*, 353–376.

Ohbuchi, K., Kameda, M., & Agarie, N. (1989). Apology as aggression control: Its role in mediating appraisal of and response to harm. *Journal of Personality and Social Psychology, 56*, 219–227.

Orne, M. T. (1962). On the social psychology of the psychological experiment: With particular reference to demand characteristics and their implications. *American Psychologist, 17*, 776–783.

Pfeffer, J. (1992). *Managing with power: Politics and influence in organizations.* Boston: Harvard Business School Press.

Pfeffer, J. (1995). Producing sustainable competitive advantage through the effective management of people. *Academy of Management Executive, 9*, 55–69.

Phillips, J. (1998). Effects of realistic job previews on multiple organizational outcomes: A meta-analysis. *Academy of Management Journal, 41*, 673–690.

Pierce, J. L., Gardner, D. G., Cummings, L. L., & Dunham, R. B. (1989). Organization-based self-esteem: Construct definition, operationalization, and validation. *Academy of Management Journal, 32*, 622–648.

Ployhart, R. E., Ehrhart, K. E., & Hayes, S. C. (2005). Using attributions to understand the effects of explanations on applicant reactions: Are reactions consistent with the covariation principle? *Journal of Applied Social Psychology, 35*, 259–296.

Ployhart, R. E., & Ryan, A. M. (1997). Toward an explanation of applicant reactions: An examination of organizational justice and attribution frameworks. *Organizational Behavior and Human Decision Processes, 72*, 308–335.

Ployhart, R. E., Ryan, A. M., & Bennett, M. (1999). Explanations for selection decisions: Applicants' reactions to informational and sensitivity features of explanations. *Journal of Applied Psychology, 84*, 87–106.

Pryor, J. B., Gibbons, F. X., Wicklund, R. A., Fazio, R. H., & Hood, R. (1977). Self-focused attention and self-report validity. *Journal of Personality, 45*, 513–527.

Pyszcznski, T. A., & Greenberg, J. (1981). Role of disconfirmed expectancies in the instigation of attributional processing. *Journal of Personality and Social Psychology, 40*, 31–38.

Quick, J. C., Cooper, C. L., Nelson, D. L., & Gavin, J. H. (2003). Stress, health and well-being at work. In J. Greenberg (Ed.), *Organizational behavior: The state of science* (pp. 53–89). Mahwah, NJ: Erlbaum.

Quinion, M. (2004). *World wide words.* http://www.worldwidewords.org/weird-words/ww-jan1.htm

Quinn, R. E., & Cameron, K. (1983). Organizational life cycles and some shifting criteria of effectiveness. *Management Science, 29*, 31–51.

Rogers, R. W., & Prentice-Dunn, S. (1997). Protection motivation theory. In D. Gochman (Ed.), *Handbook of health behavior research* (pp. 113–32). New York: Plenum.

Rosenberg, M. (1965). *Society and the adolescent self-image.* Princeton, NJ: Princeton University Press.

Rosenblatt, A., Greenberg, J., Solomon, S., Pyszczynski, T., & Lyon, D. (1989). Evidence for terror management theory I: The effects of mortality salience on reactions to those who violate or uphold cultural values. *Journal of Personality and Social Psychology, 57*, 681–690.

Rotter, J. B. (1966). Generalized expectancies for internal versus external control of reinforcement. *Psychological Monographs, 80* (Whole No. 609).

Rousseau, D. M. (1995). *Psychological contracts in organizations: Understanding written and unwritten agreements.* Newbury Park, CA: Sage.

Rousseau, D. M. (2005). *I-deals: Idiosyncratic deals employees bargain for themselves.* Armonk, NY: Sharpe.

Rousseau, D. M., & McLean Parks, J. (1993). The contracts of individuals and organizations. In L. L. Cummings & B. M. Staw (Eds.), *Research in organizational behavior* (Vol. 15, pp. 1–45). Greenwich, CT: JAI Press.

Rupp, D. E., & Cropanzano, R. (2002). Multifoci justice and social exchange relationships. *Organizational Behavior and Human Decision Processes, 89,* 925–946.

Rupp, D., & Spencer, S. (2006). When customers lash out: The effects of customer interactional injustice on emotional labor and the mediating role of discrete emotions. *Journal of Applied Psychology, 91,* 971–978.

Salancik, G. R., & Pfeffer, J. (1978). A social information processing approach to job attitudes and task design. *Administrative Science Quarterly, 23,* 224–253.

Schaubroeck, J., May, D. R., & Brown, F. W. (1994). Procedural justice explanations and employee reactions to economic hardship: A field experiment. *Journal of Applied Psychology, 79,* 455–460.

Scheier, M. F. (1976). Self-awareness, self-consciousness, and angry aggression. *Journal of Personality, 44,* 627–644.

Scheier, M. F., & Carver, C. S. (1977). Self-focused attention and the experience of emotion: Attraction, repulsion, elation, and depression. *Journal of Personality and Social Psychology, 35,* 625–636.

Scheier, M. F., & Carver, C. S. (1985). Optimism, coping, and health: Assessment and implications of generalized outcome expectancies. *Health Psychology, 4,* 219–247.

Schroth, H., & Shah, P. (2000). Procedures, do we really want to know them? *Journal of Applied Psychology*, 85, 462–471.

Seidman, D. (2007). *How: Why how we do anything means everything … in business (and in life).* New York: Wiley.

Seligman, M. E. P. (1991). *Learned optimism.* New York: Knopf.

Seligman, M. E. P. (2006). *Learned optimism: How to change your mind and your life.* New York: Knopf.

Shaffer, M. A., & Harrison, D. A. (1998). Expatriates' psychological withdrawal from international assignments: Work, nonwork, and family influences. *Personnel Psychology, 51,* 87–118.

Shah, J., & Higgins, E. T. (1997). Expectancy X value effects: Regulatory focus as determinant of magnitude *and* direction. *Journal of Personality and Social Psychology, 73,* 447–458.

Shapiro, D.L, & Brett, J.M. (1993). Comparing three processes underlying judgments of procedural justice: A field study of mediation and arbitration. *Journal of Personality and Social Psychology, 65,* 1167–1177.

Shaver, K. G. (1985). *The attribution of blame: Causality, responsibility, and blameworthiness.* New York: Springer-Verlag.

Sherif, C., Sherif, M., & Nebergall, R. (1965). *Attitude and attitude change: The social judgment-involvement approach.* Philadelphia: Saunders.

Shrauger, J. S. (1975). Responses to evaluations as a function of initial self-perceptions. *Psychological Bulletin, 82*, 581–96.

Siegel, P. A., Post, C., Brockner, J., Fishman, A., & Garden, C. (2005). The moderating influence of procedural fairness on the relationship between work-life conflict and organizational commitment. *Journal of Applied Psychology, 90*, 13–24.

Singelis, T. M. (1994). The measurement of independent and interdependent self-construals. *Personality and Social Psychology Bulletin, 20*, 580–591.

Skarlicki, D., & Folger, R. (1997). Retaliation in the workplace: The roles of distributive, procedural, and interactional justice. *Journal of Applied Psychology, 82*, 434–443.

Skarlicki, D. P., & Latham, G. P. (2005). Can leaders be trained to be fair? In J. Greenberg & J. Colquitt (Eds.), *Handbook of organizational justice* (pp. 499–524). Mahwah, NJ: Erlbaum.

Skitka, L. J. (2003).An accessible identity approach to why and how people think about justice. *Personality and Social Psychology Review, 7*, 286–297.

Skitka, L. J., Mullen, E., Griffin, T., Hutchinson, S, & Chamberlin, B. (2002). Dispositions, scripts, or motivated correction? Understanding ideological differences in explanations for social problems. *Journal of Personality and Social Psychology, 83*, 470–487.

Skitka, L. J., Winquist, J., & Hutchinson, S. (2003). Are outcome fairness and outcome favorability distinguishable psychological constructs? A meta-analytical review. *Social Justice Research, 16*, 309–341.

Steel, R. P., & Ovalle, N. K. (1984). A review and meta-analysis of research on the relationship between behavioral intentions and employee turnover. *Journal of Applied Psychology, 69*, 673–686.

Steele, C. M. (1988). The psychology of self-affirmation: Sustaining the integrity of the self. In L. Berkowitz (Ed.), *Advances in experimental social psychology* (Vol. 21, pp. 261–302). New York: Academic Press.

Storms, M. D. (1973). Videotape and the attribution process: Reversing actors' and observers' points of view. *Journal of Personality and Social Psychology, 27*, 165–175.

Surowiecki, J. (2004). *The wisdom of crowds*. New York: Doubleday, Anchor.

Svenson, O. (1981). Are we all less risky and more skillful than our fellow drivers? *Acta Psychologica, 47, 143–148.*

Swann, W. B., Jr. (1983). Self-verification: Bringing social reality into harmony with the self. In J. Suls & A. G. Greenwald (Eds.), *Social psychological perspectives on the self* (Vol. 2, pp. 33–66). Hillsdale, NJ: Erlbaum.

Swann, W. B., Jr. (1999). *Resilient Identities: Self, relationships, and the construction of social reality*. New York: Basic Books.

Swann, W. B., Jr., & Pelham, B. W. (2002). Who wants out when the going gets good? Psychological investment and preference for self-verifying college roommates. *Journal of Self and Identity, 1*, 219–233.

Swann, W. B., Jr., & Read, S. J. (1981). Self-verification processes: How we sustain our self-conceptions. *Journal of Experimental Social Psychology, 17*, 351–372.

Swann, W. B., Jr., Wenzlaff, R. M., Krull, D. S., & Pelham, B. W. (1992). The allure of negative feedback: Self-verification strivings among depressed persons. *Journal of Abnormal Psychology, 101*, 293–306.

Tafarodi, R., & Swann, W. B., Jr. (2001). Two-dimensional self-esteem: Theory and measurement. *Personality and Individual Differences, 31*, 653–673.

Tangney, J. P., & Fischer, K. W. (1995). *Self-conscious emotions: The psychology of shame, guilt, embarrassment, and pride.* New York: Cambridge University Press.

Taylor, S. E., & Brown, J. D. (1988). Illusion and well-being: A social psychological perspective on mental health. *Psychological Bulletin, 103*, 193–210.

Tepper, B. J. (2001). Health consequences of organizational injustice: Tests of main and interactive effects. *Organizational Behavior and Human Decision Processes, 86*, 197–215.

Tesser, A., & Rosen, S. (1975). The reluctance to transmit bad news. In L. Berkowitz (Ed.), *Advances in experimental social psychology* (Vol. 8, pp. 193–232). New York: Academic Press.

Thibaut, J., & Walker, L. (1975). *Procedural justice: A psychological analysis.* Hillsdale, NJ: Erlbaum.

Thompson, C. A., Beauvais, L. L., & Lyness, K. S. (1999). When work–family benefits are not enough: The influence of work-family culture on benefit utilization, organizational attachment, and work-family conflict. *Journal of Vocational Behavior, 54*, 392–415.

Tice, D.M. (1991). Esteem protection or enhancement? Self-handicapping motives and attributions differ by trait self-esteem. *Journal of Personality and Social Psychology, 60*, 711–725.

Triandis, H. C. (1996). The psychological measurement of cultural syndromes. *American Psychologist, 51*, 407–415.

Tuckman, B. W. (1965). Developmental sequence in small groups. *Psychological Bulletin, 63*, 384–399.

Turner, J. C., Hogg, M. A., Oakes, P. J., Reicher, S. D., & Wetherell, M. S. (1987). *Rediscovering the social group: A self-categorization theory.* Oxford, UK: Blackwell.

Tyler, T. R., & Degoey, P. (1995). Collective restraint in a social dilemma situation: The influence of procedural justice and community identification on the empowerment and legitimacy of authority. *Journal of Personality and Social Psychology, 69*, 482–497.

Tyler, T. R., DeGoey, P., & Smith, H. (1996). Understanding why the justice of group procedures matters: A test of the psychological dynamics of the group value model. *Journal of Personality and Social Psychology, 70*, 913–930.

Tyler, T. R., & Lind, E. A. (1992). A relational model of authority in groups. In M. Zanna (Ed.), *Advances in experimental social psychology* (Vol. 25, pp. 115–191). San Diego, CA: Academic Press.

Tyler, T. R., & Sears, D. O. (1977). Coming to like obnoxious people when we must live with them. *Journal of Personality and Social Psychology, 35*, 200–211.

Vandello, J. A., & Cohen, D. (1999). Patterns of individualism and collectivism across the United States. *Journal of Personality and Social Psychology, 77*, 279–292.

Van den Bos, K. (1999). What are we talking about when we talk about no-voice procedures? On the psychology of the fair outcome effect. *Journal of Experimental Social Psychology, 35*, 560–577.

Van den Bos, K. (2001). Uncertainty management: The influence of uncertainty salience on reactions to perceived procedural fairness. *Journal of Personality and Social Psychology, 80,* 931–941.

Van den Bos, K., Brockner, J., Stein, J., H., Steiner, D. D., Van Yperen., N. W., & Dekker, D. M. (in press). The psychology of voice and performance capabilities in masculine and feminine cultures and contexts. *Journal of Personality and Social Psychology.*

Van den Bos, K., Bruins, J., Wilke, H. A. M., & Dronkert, E. (1999). Sometimes unfair procedures have nice aspects: On the psychology of the fair process effect. *Journal of Personality and Social Psychology, 77,* 324–336.

Van den Bos, K., Ham, J., Lind, E. A., Simonis, M., van Essen, W. J., & Rijpkema, M. (2008). Justice and the human alarm system: The impact of exclamation points and flashing lights on the justice judgment process. *Journal of Experimental Social Psychology, 44,* 201–219.

Van den Bos, K., & Lind, E.A. (2002). Uncertainty management by means of fairness judgments. In M. P. Zanna (Ed.), *Advances in experimental social psychology* (Vol. 34, pp. 1–60). San Diego, CA: Academic Press.

Van den Bos, K., & Lind, E. A. (in press). The social psychology of fairness and the regulation of personal uncertainty. In R. M. Arkin, K. C. Oleson, & P. J. Carroll (Eds.), *The uncertain self: A handbook of perspectives from social and personality psychology.* New York: Taylor & Francis.

Van den Bos, K., Wilke, H. A. M., & Lind, E. A. (1998). When do we need procedural fairness? The role of trust in authority. *Journal of Personality and Social Psychology, 75,* 1449–1458.

Van den Bos, K., Lind, E. A., Vermunt, R., & Wilke, H. A. M. (1997). How do I judge my outcome when I do not know the outcome of others?: The psychology of the fair process effect. *Journal of Personality and Social Psychology, 72,* 1034–1046.

Van den Bos, K., & Miedema, J. (2000). Toward understanding why fairness matters: The influence of mortality salience on reactions to procedural fairness. *Journal of Personality and Social Psychology, 79,* 355–366.

Van den Bos, K., Poortvliet, P. M., Maas, M., Miedema, J., & Van den Ham, E. J. (2005). An enquiry concerning the principles of cultural norms and values: The impact of uncertainty and mortality salience on reactions to violations and bolstering of cultural worldviews. *Journal of Experimental Social Psychology, 41,* 91–113.

Van den Bos, K., Vermunt, R., & Wilke, H. A. M. (1997). Procedural and distributive justice: What is fair depends more on what comes first than on what comes next. *Journal of Personality and Social Psychology, 72,* 95–104.

Van den Bos, K., Wilke, H. A. M., Lind, E. A., & Vermunt, R. (1998). Evaluating outcomes by means of the fair process effect: Evidence for different processes in fairness and satisfaction judgments. *Journal of Personality and Social Psychology, 74,* 1493–1503.

Van de Vliert, E., & Janssen, O. (2002). "Better than" performance motives as roots of satisfaction across more and less developed countries. *Journal of Cross-Cultural Psychology, 33,* 380–397.

Van Prooijen, J.-W., Karremans, J. C., & Van Beest, I. (2006). Procedural justice and the hedonic principle: How approach versus avoidance motivation influences the psychology of voice. *Journal of Personality and Social Psychology, 91*, 686–697.

Van Prooijen, J.-W., Van den Bos, K., & Wilke, H. A. M. (2002). Procedural justice and status: Status salience as antecedent of procedural fairness effects. *Journal of Personality and Social Psychology*, *83*, 1353–1361.

Vermunt, R., & Steensma, H. (2003). Physiological relaxation: Stress reduction through fair treatment. *Social Justice Research, 16*, 135–149.

Vermunt, R., van Knippenberg, D., van Knippenberg, B., & Blaauw, E. (2001). Self-esteem and outcome fairness: Differential importance of procedural and outcome considerations. *Journal of Applied Psychology*, 86, 621–628.

Verplanken, B., & Holland, R. (2002). Motivated decision-making: Effects of activation and self-centrality of values on choices and behavior. *Journal of Personality and Social Psychology, 82*, 434–447.

Vroom, V. H. (1964). *Work and motivation.* New York: Wiley.

Vunderink, M., & Hofstede, G. (1998). Femininity shock: American students in the Netherlands. In G. Hofstede (Ed.), *Masculinity and femininity: The taboo dimension of national cultures* (pp. 139–150). Thousand Oaks, CA: Sage.

Walker, L., LaTour, S., Lind, E. A., & Thibaut, J. (1974). Reactions of participants and observers to modes of adjudication. *Journal of Applied Social Psychology, 4*, 295–310.

Walster, E. (1966). Assignment of responsibility for an accident. *Journal of Personality and Social Psychology, 3*, 73–79.

Wanous, J. P. (1980). *Organizational entry: Recruitment, selection, and socialization of newcomers*. Reading, MA: Addison-Wesley.

Weary Bradley, G. (1978). Self-serving biases in the attribution process: A reexamination of the fact or fiction question. *Journal of Personality and Social Psychology*, *36*, 56–71.

Weigel, R. H., & Newman, L. S. (1976). Increasing attitude-behavior correspondence by broadening the scope of the behavioral measure. *Journal of Personality and Social Psychology*, *33*, 793–802.

Weigel, R. H., Vernon, D. T., & Tognacci, L. N. (1974). Specificity of the attitude as a determinant of attitude-behavior congruence. *Journal of Personality and Social Psychology*, *30*, 724–728.

Weiner, B. (1979). A theory of motivation for some classroom experiences. *Journal of Educational Psychology, 71*, 3–25.

Weiner, B. (1985). An attributional theory of achievement motivation and emotion. *Psychological Review, 92*, 548–573.

Weinstein, N. D. (1980). Unrealistic optimism about future life events. *Journal of Personality and Social Psychology, 39*, 806–820.

Weiss, H. M., & Cropanzano, R. (1996). Affective events theory: A theoretical discussion of the structure, causes and consequences of affective experiences at work. In B. M. Staw & L. L. Cummings (Eds.), *Research in organizational behavior* (Vol. 18, pp. 1–74). Greenwich, CT: JAI Press.

Weiss, H. M., Suckow, K., & Cropanzano, R. (1999). Effects of justice conditions on discrete emotions. *Journal of Applied Psychology, 84*, 786–794

Wicker, A. W. (1969). Attitudes versus actions: The relationship of verbal and overt behavioral responses to attitude objects. *Journal of Social Issues, 25*, 41–78.

Wiesenfeld, B., Swann, W., Brockner, J., & Bartel, C. (2007). Is more fairness always preferred?: Self-esteem moderates reactions to procedural justice. *Academy of Management Journal, 50*, 1235–1253.

Wong, P. T. P., & Weiner, B. (1981). When people ask "why" questions, and the heuristics of attributional search. *Journal of Personality and Social Psychology, 40*, 31–38.

Wortman, C. B., & Brehm, J. W. (1975). Responses to uncontrollable outcomes: An integration of reactance theory and the learned helplessness model. In L. Berkowitz (Ed.), *Advances in experimental social psychology* (Vol. 8, pp. 277–336). San Diego, CA: Academic Press.

Wrightsman, L. S. (1992). *Assumptions about human nature: Implications for researchers and practitioners.* London: Sage.

Zapata-Phelan, C., Colquitt, J., Scott, B. A., & Livingston, B. (2008). Procedural justice, interactional justice, and task performance: The mediating role of intrinsic motivation. *Organizational Behavior and Human Decision Processes, 108*, 93–105.

Zuckerman, M. (1979). Attribution of success and failure revisited, or the motivational bias is alive and well in attribution theory. *Journal of Personality, 47*, 245–287.

AUTHOR INDEX

G

H

I

J

K

L

M

T

V

W

Y

Z

SUBJECT INDEX

I

N

O

T

V

W